The Hermetic Deleuze

NEW SLANT: RELIGION, POLITICS, AND ONTOLOGY

*A series edited by Creston Davis, Philip Goodchild,
and Kenneth Surin*

Joshua Ramey

THE HERMETIC DELEUZE

Philosophy and Spiritual Ordeal

Duke University Press Durham and London 2012

© 2012 Duke University Press
All rights reserved
Printed in the United States of America
on acid-free paper ∞
Designed by C. H. Westmoreland
Typeset in Charis by Tseng Information Systems, Inc.
Library of Congress Cataloging-in-Publication Data
appear on the last printed page of this book.

*Cover art for the paperback book
by Paul du Coudray*

Ce qui fonde alors c'est l'épreuve

—GILLES DELEUZE, *What Is Grounding?*

Contents

List of Abbreviations ix
Acknowledgments xi
Introduction: Secrets of Immanence 1
1. Philosophical Modernity and Experimental Imperative 11
2. Dark Precursors: The Hermetic Tradition 32
3. The Force of Symbols: Deleuze and the Esoteric Sign 82
4. The Overturning of Platonism 112
5. Becoming Cosmic 148
6. The Politics of Sorcery 171
7. The Future of Belief 200
Coda: Experimental Faith 219
Notes 225
Bibliography 275
Index 283

List of Abbreviations

AO: *Anti-Oedipus*
ATP: *A Thousand Plateaus*
B: *Bergsonism*
C1: *Cinema I: The Movement-Image*
C2: *Cinema II: The Time-Image*
CC: *Essays Critical and Clinical*
D: *Dialogues*
D2: *Dialogues II*
DI: *Desert Islands and Other Texts (1953–1974)*
DR: *Difference and Repetition*
E: *Expressionism in Philosophy: Spinoza*
ES: *Empiricism and Subjectivity*
FB: *Francis Bacon and the Logic of Sensation*
LS: *Logic of Sense*
F: *The Fold: On Leibniz and the Baroque*
MSP: "Mathesis, Science, and Philosophy"
NP: *Nietzsche and Philosophy*
PI: *Pure Immanence: A Life*
PS: *Proust and Signs*
WG: *What Is Grounding?*
WIP: *What Is Philosophy?*

Acknowledgments

My sense of dependence upon a vast network of allies and cohorts is so strong that it seems almost impossible to know where to begin. Deleuze's advice was to begin in the middle, so I will start in the thick of it. Rocco Gangle's constant support and companionship, from the moment we met in 2003, has been an unfailing source of energy for the premonitions and intuitions this book attempts to put into form. Without Christian Kerslake's pioneering and peerlessly researched forays into the rhizome of Deleuze's philosophical and spiritual genealogy, and without his unfailing encouragement, this project would never have reached fruition. Paul Harris was an enormous ally, and his proposal that we coedit *SubStance* 39, no. 1, "Spiritual Politics after Deleuze," was absolutely crucial to the development of the ideas expressed here. I am deeply indebted to all the contributors to that volume for how they refined and deepened the aspects of Deleuze's thought this book attempts to elaborate. I also want to thank Patricia Pisters for inviting me to be an instructor at Deleuze Camp 2010 in Amsterdam, where key sections of the book were presented for the first time to Deleuze scholars. The enthusiasm of the students, and of instructors Gregg Lambert, Ian Buchanan, James Williams, Elena del Rio, and Eleanor Kauffman, were invaluable for the final stages of the work.

I owe Creston Davis an enormous debt for the enthusiasm he showed for the earliest version of this manuscript, and for presenting it as such to the New Slant series for consideration. I also want to thank the other series editors, Ken Surin and Philip Goodchild, as well as Reynolds Smith and Courtney Berger at the press, for affording me the time and space I needed to bring the book to completion. In particular I want to thank Philip for the dedicated attention he gave to reading the manuscript, and to Courtney for her astute advice on some of the final editing choices.

   The ideas I have attempted to work through here emerged in and through the intersection of multiple crossroads, in a rich nexus of pedagogical, artistic, philosophical, and spiritual friendships. From this perspective, I would like to thank Janet Leslie Blumberg, my undergraduate mentor, who first introduced me to the legacy of Renaissance humanism, and to the spiritual intensities of critical thought. I would also like to thank my graduate school advisors John Carvalho, Walter Brogan, Julie Klein, and James Wetzel, who allowed me so much room to wander and experiment. And finally, I have to thank the myriad friends and companions who, through thought, art, and life, have helped make my work what it is: John, Michelle, and Philip Ramey, Hugo Delpech-Ramey, Emmanuelle Delpech, Aron Dunlap, Paul and Anne du Coudray, Clark Roth, Rick Alton, Ed Kazarian, Lucio Angelo Privitello, Matthew Haar Ferris, Amir Vodka, Inna Semetsky, Cleo Kearns, Erik Davis, Jason Smick, Anthony Paul Smith, Dan Barber, Margaret Manzer, and the students of the Fall 2010 Deleuze and Guattari Seminar at Haverford College.

Introduction

Secrets of Immanence

In his eulogy for Gilles Deleuze in 1995, "I'll Have to Wander All Alone," Jacques Derrida suggested that there was still something secret in Deleuze's thought, something not yet understood. Derrida writes, "I will continue to begin again to read Gilles Deleuze in order to learn, and I'll have to wander all alone in this long conversation that we were supposed to have together. My first question, I think, would have concerned Artaud, his interpretation of the 'body without organs,' and the word 'immanence' on which he always insisted, in order to make him or let him say something that no doubt still remains secret to us."[1]

In his inspired madness, Antonin Artaud envisioned the organs of the human body as the "judgments of God," as pinions and philters engineered by a jealous and vindictive divinity to inhibit movement, energy, and lines of new life.[2] The decadence and debilitation of twentieth-century Western culture were, for Artaud, linked directly to such judgments, and to the technoscientific apparatus—military, industrial, nutritional, and hygienic—continuously marshaled in the name of God and order to stultify the human body. Artaud's theatre of cruelty was designed to disturb this docile creature, to shock and shatter its organs, and to force the body to react otherwise than in accordance with the habitual limits of sense and sensibility. As he wrote, "when you have made him a body without organs, / then you will have delivered him from all his automatic reactions / and restored to him his true freedom."[3] For Artaud, humanity possessed a "body without organs," a subtle body accessible at the extremes of experience—in suffering, delirium, synesthesia, and ecstatic states. What do such experiences have to do with philosophy, and with Deleuze's philosophy of immanence in particular, about which Derrida insisted something has continued to remain secret?

The term "immanence" has several interlinked meanings in Deleuze's work.[4] In one sense, immanence functions in his work as a kind of metaphilosophical axiom, an injunction to philosophize from a perspective according to which being is never to be conceived as transcendent, but as immanent to thought. What this prescription assumes is that, at least under certain conditions, thought can adequately express being; that is to say, the conditions of philosophy, for Deleuze, are those under which there is no longer any difference between thought and being. However, this does not mean, for Deleuze, that thought can adequately represent being.[5] For Deleuze, it is only under certain intense conditions that the real is conceivable; the realization of being in thought occurs within the mind, yet paradoxically beyond its representational capacities. Put laconically, the mark of the real in thought, for Deleuze, is when the unconceivable is conceived, the insensible sensed, and the immemorial remembered. Throughout his work, Deleuze links thought to a traversal of precisely that "Body without Organs" envisioned by Artaud.[6] Extending Artaud's vision of a renewed sensibility into his own unique vision of thought, Deleuze argues that immanent thought, at the limit of cognitive capacity, discovers as-yet-unrealized potentials of the mind, and the body. That is to say, what connects Deleuze to Artaud is the conviction that what matters for life, and for thought, is an encounter with imperceptible forces in sensations, affections, and conceptions, and that these forces truly generate the mind, challenging the coordination of the faculties by rending the self from its habits.[7]

It is the argument of this book that the power of thought, for Deleuze, consists in a kind of initiatory ordeal. Such ordeal transpires through an immersion of the self in uncanny moments when a surprising and alluring complicity of nature and psyche is revealed. In this sense, thought, for Deleuze, is a theatre of cruelty, an agon of peculiarly intensities, leading him to speak, in many places, of a kind of direct fusion between the most literal and most spiritual senses of life (*DR*, 25). But what exactly would a "spirituality" be that could be also the most literal sense of life? And how could the work of such a stridently naturalistic and, at least on some readings, strictly materialist philosopher such as Deleuze entail the necessity of spiritual ordeal?[8]

This issue has been a source of ambivalence for contemporary philosophers in Deleuze's wake, and increasing effort, of late, has been devoted to comprehending the sense of spiritual striving and esoteric reverie that profoundly animate Deleuze's thought. It remains unclear precisely how to interpret and evaluate the role of spirituality within Deleuze's system.[9] My contention is that references to spirituality in Deleuze are neither incidental nor merely heuristic, and that, when properly appreciated, Deleuze's unique and vital synthesis of natural and spiritual perspectives stands as a contemporary avatar of Western esoteric or "hermetic" thought, and must be understood as a contemporary, nonidentical repetition of this archaic tradition.

The hermetic tradition derives its name, and its legacy, from the figure of Hermes Trismegistus, a legendary Egyptian sage who taught that knowledge of the cosmos could be the engine of profound spiritual transformation, enlightenment, and liberation. The *Corpus Hermeticum*, a third-century collection of Alexandrian Greek texts purported to be a record of Hermes's teachings, offers a holistic vision in which the cognitive cannot be sundered from the affective any more than can the natural from the spiritual, and where any genuine increase in knowledge is tantamount to a transformation of the self. The most famous document of the *Corpus Hermeticum*, the *Tabula Smaradigna* (Emerald Tablet), teaches that materiality and spirituality are profoundly united, and that life itself is a process of theandric regeneration in which the nature of the divine is both discovered and produced in an unfolding of personal and cosmic, evolutionary and historical time: "As above, so below." In short, hermetic thought identifies the very process of natural life with a manifestation of encosmic divinity. In this tradition, there is no clear distinction between the rational and the spiritual; philosophical speculation is viewed as an attempt to explicate transcendental structures common to natural and spiritual realms.[10] For these reasons, and for others soon to be explored, Deleuze's insistence upon the nature of thought as spiritual ordeal, as a transformative encounter with nature, is clearly an avatar of the hermetic tradition.

4 Introduction

The principles of nearly all strands of Western esotericism can be traced back to the teachings of Hermes Trismegistus. As Christianity and Judaism began to coalesce unified sets of doctrines and practices, other currents of thought within the late Roman Empire—not only Jewish or Christian, but also Neoplatonic and pagan—developed syntheses of near-eastern and Egyptian wisdom traditions with classical Greek philosophy. Within this milieu an Alexandrian current produced a set of writings that become known as the *Corpus Hermeticum*. This collection of texts purports to be an ancient record of the teachings of a certain "Hermes" to his disciples (and of Hermes's protégés to other students). Although Hermes is presented as an archaic hierophant, Garth Fowden and others have shown that this figure, whom the Renaissance revered as "Thrice-Greatest Hermes," was a second-century conflation of the Greek Hermes and the Egyptian Thoth, the unique product of a distinctly Alexandrian spiritual imagination.[11] The *Corpus Hermeticum* contains parallels to both Jewish and Christian religious ideas, as well as to concepts in Gnostic and Neoplatonic philosophy. This is part of why the texts, when they were recovered from the Medici trove of Byzantine manuscripts and translated by Marsilio Ficino, were considered an exceedingly ancient record of "Aegiptian" wisdom. Hermes himself was seen by Renaissance thinkers as an important precursor to the wisdom of Moses, Plato, and Christianity. In 1614 Isaac Casaubon demonstrated that the vocabulary and style of the texts was too recent to be a product of Pharaonic Egypt, but Fowden and others have argued that there is more continuity in the texts with ancient Egypt than Casaubon realized.[12]

The distinctly Egyptian spirituality maintained in these texts, although they were written in Greek and presented as "reports" of conversations between Hermes and his adepts, indicates that Egyptians, rather than Alexandrian Greeks, wrote the texts. The texts seem to stand, Fowden contends, for a renegade and apocalyptic spirit in Egypt. At one point in the *Corpus*, there is even a bloodstained prophecy hinting that Rome will one day fall, and that Egypt's ancient religious and political prerogative will then be restored.[13] This restoration is presented as a renewal of an "enchanted" cosmos, in which humans will once again be able to commune freely and directly with the divine through intimate relations with nature. In the meantime, and in anticipation of this immanent eschaton, Hermes's own teachings are intended to combat the nihilism of the late antique age with instructions on how to escape the powers of fate, perform alchemical transformations, and renew the world and the self through theurgic ritual.

Because of the wide circulation of the texts, their anonymous authorship, and the correspondences between their teachings and those of Jewish, Gnostic, Neoplatonic, and early Christian sects, the *Corpus Hermeticum* became part of the fabric of syncretistic late antique thought. The texts were probably widely read by cultured Greeks as well as by the marginalized Alexandrian noncitizens whose spiritual and political desire they more clearly express (as evidenced especially in their valorization of "low" magic and sorcery, and instructions for alchemical operations). One of the most fascinating aspects of the story of hermeticism is that, although the Western esotericism that emerged from its inspiration became largely the prerogative and practice of cultured elites (such as Ficino, the Freemasons, and the Order of the Golden Dawn), the roots of Western esotericism itself lie in a kind of eclectic, bastard, and nomadic spirituality, one without pure origin or urtext, situated at the crossroads of competing civilizations and conflicting orthodoxies. This point will be particularly important in connection with Deleuze's own affirmation of the spiritual significance of lower, bastard, minor, and nomadic races, and the power they have to articulate the utopian and eschatological contours of immanent thought (*WIP*, 109).

Deleuze's work constantly recapitulates hermetic themes, and can be placed within a series of post-Kantian romantic thinkers critical of the sterility of Enlightenment reason who found inspiration in the Renaissance revival of hermetic tradition.[14] For both Deleuze and the hermetic tradition generally, certain intense, mantic, initiatory, ascetic, and transformative practices are necessary for thought as much as for meditational or visionary experience. Conversely, for both Deleuze and hermeticism, authentic thought is identified, beyond mere accumulation of cognitions, with an expansion of the mind's ability to endure the intense modes of perception and communication necessary for psychic reintegration and cosmic renewal. Thought in this way might be defined, for Deleuze as for the tradition, as a regenerative principle of natural and social development.

However, it should be said at the outset that situating Deleuze directly in the hermetic tradition is a somewhat complex affair. Deleuze is a post-Kantian thinker removed by time and cultural circumstance from the premodern ethos of hermeticism. Furthermore, Deleuze's interest in hermetic themes appears as a subtle motif whose implications need careful unfolding. Even more challenging is the fact that Deleuze's own contemporary take on hermeticism is a departure from, as much as an extension of, traditional patterns of spiritual ordeal. Perhaps most challenging of all is the general academic-philosophical prejudice against the threatening proximity of intuitive, mystical, or even simply more emotional modes of mind to the cold calculations of pure reason, especially when such calculations appear in principle to be open, democratic, and formally unimpeachable in contrast with the dark and esoteric yearnings expressed in the gnomic pronouncements of initiates. To read Deleuze in relation to the hermetic tradition, therefore, requires several stages of exegesis and argumentation.

I attempt to clarify Deleuze's peculiar take on the history of modern philosophy and his insistence that modern philosophy, despite its extreme sobriety and skepticism, represents a distinctly experimental usage of mind (chapter 1, "Philosophical Modernity and Experimental Imperative"). Once it is clear how and in what sense Deleuze reads modern thought as experimental, I then attempt to demonstrate how Deleuze's own experimental ethos echoes a premodern philosophical tradition that integrated spirituality into the practice of dialectic and critical reflection: Neoplatonism, from Plotinus to the Renaissance (chapter 2, "Dark Precursors: The Hermetic Tradition"). The particular strand of Neoplatonic thought that interests Deleuze is closely tied to the hermetic tradition, and it is out of this hermetic strand of Neoplatonic thought that Deleuze's conception of immanence in philosophy emerges. Once this groundwork is established, it becomes possible to trace the contours of hermeticism within Deleuze's systematic thought.

This tracing begins with Deleuze's lifelong interest in the power of symbols, highlighting the enduring importance, for his overall system, of approaches to knowledge (both theoretical and practical) that attempt to integrate body and mind, scientific research and spiritual insight (chapter 3, "The Force of Symbols: Deleuze and the Esoteric Sign"). From here it becomes possible to see how a hermetic impulse to unite thought with affective, corporeal, and spiritual transformation plays out across Deleuze's mature work. I then argue that Deleuze's systematic project of "overturning Platonism" should be read as a contemporary hermetic effort to resituate philosophical speculation within an experimental exploration of nature (chapter 4, "The Overturning of Platonism").

Deleuze's clearest model for this project, and for thought as a contemporary hermeticism, derives from the work of art. Chapter 5, "Becoming Cosmic," outlines how reflection on certain artistic procedures leads Deleuze to develop a unique vision of philosophical practice and its relations to both science and art. Chapter 6, "The Politics of Sorcery," examines Deleuze and Guattari's regard for specific ritual practices, in particular sorcery and therapeutic healing rituals. I argue that Deleuze and Guattari take such practices not as archaic vestiges, but as models of contemporary transformative practice. In chapter 7, "The Future of Belief," I address some of the major objections to Deleuzian and Deleuzo-Guattarian spirituality, and attempt to respond to a series of modern misgivings about the contamination of rationality by affective and perceptual intensities, and by spiritual ordeal. My intent here is to at least challenge presumptive suspicion against anything other than purely rational reflection—a suspicion that, despite the many critiques of pure reason since Kant, continues to block appreciation for affective and putatively spiritual modes of apprehension.

The stakes of this last contention, as I see them, go beyond debates over the corpus of Gilles Deleuze. Despite vast evidence that many Western philosophers—both ancient and modern—have been invested in some sort of spirituality (be it theurgical, thaumaturgical, mystical, alchemical, kabalistic, or theosophical), thinkers explicit about their hermetic or esoteric proclivities have always been positioned as bastard and nomadic outliers of philosophy, heretical outcasts of theology, or as reactionaries interfering with the full realization of reason, enlightenment, and progressive politics.

In making explicit the importance of hermeticism in Deleuze's thought, I am inviting the charge that Deleuze was embroiled in that morass of obscurantism and irrationalism Freud once called "the black mud tide of occultism."[15] As a systematic body of work, Deleuze's thought creatively repeats the interests of previous philosophers in the metaphysical and epistemological valence of phenomena that have been marginalized as uncanny, paranormal, occult, and even supernatural. Nested within esoteric insights, Deleuze's work trades on a foreign language within the language of modern philosophy, a language of intense, intuitive, and spiritual apprehensions that have, for the most part, been placed on the outside of reason and beyond the pale of enlightened, progressive, and reasonable discourse. It is perhaps this feature that continues to mark the work of this major twentieth-century thinker as minor.[16]

In the face of contemporary ambivalence over the validity and significance of esoteric, let alone "occult," apprehensions of nature and mind, the political risk of this reading should be immediately apparent. Reading Deleuze as hermetic in any sense may force a departure from received presuppositions—modern, secular, or merely academic—about what rightfully counts as thought. I take that risk in part because I am convinced that the marginalization of hermetic traditions, and the suspicion and contempt in which they are still held by much of contemporary thought, constitutes a symptomatic repression of the complexity of both the history of modern philosophy and the stakes of contemporary culture, which is, from the internet to the cinema, completely obsessed with magic and with the occult.

However, I can of course only speak for my own convictions that this spiritual material can and must be addressed, at least here, through the modest step of taking Deleuze's spiritual debts to the hermetic tradition seriously. I do this by arguing for three interlinked claims: that Deleuze's systematic thought is not fully comprehensible without situating it within the hermetic tradition; that Deleuze's writings make a subtle yet distinctive contribution to contemporary hermetic knowledge and practice; and that the experimental stakes of modern and contemporary philosophy, as Deleuze conceived them, call for a revision and extension of the perennial hermetic project: the proliferation, differentiation, and nonidentical repetition of cosmic processes of regeneration and renewal.

What is at stake for Deleuze in thought—and at stake in this book—is ultimately a political issue. Indicating the contours of a renewed spirituality of thought and a new vision of the mutual intercalation of material and spiritual forces is part of an attempt to fulfill the task of philosophy in late capitalism, a task Deleuze himself characterized as the renewal of "belief in the world" (*C2*, 188). My particular extension of this task, by pushing Deleuze further in the direction of his own hermeticism, is motivated by the conviction that to challenge the all-pervasive magic of that confluence of desire and power Isabelle Stengers once described as the great "capitalist sorcery," requires an exceedingly sober attempt to countenance the aspects of social and natural reality thus far confined to the gnomic dictates of inchoate spiritual gurus on the one hand, and to the black arts of the industrial-entertainment complex on the other. Thinking more stridently through the spiritual dimensions of Deleuze's work may enable us to forge new alternatives to the sinister perversions of belief in capital times, as well as to usher in a more concrete and complex sense of how to engender new relations between knowledge, power, and the spiritual forces of desire.

1

Philosophical Modernity and Experimental Imperative

Ordeals of the Mind

Early modern philosophy, whether rationalist or empiricist, tended to starkly oppose rationality to affective, imaginative, and spiritual modalities of mind. Despite this situation, Deleuze argues in several places in his books and lectures, modern philosophers such as Spinoza, Leibniz, and Hume were nevertheless inspired by enigmas that challenged the framework of propositional and syllogistic thinking. From Deleuze's perspective, modern thought was inspired by certain unthinkable notion of the infinite, of the absolute, and of God, and the analytical rigor of modern philosophy belies an inherently experimental character that should not so quickly be presumed separable from affective and even distinctly spiritual modes of apprehension. In a lecture course held on Spinoza in 1980, Deleuze associates this secular, atheist, or at least nontheological usage of the concept of God with the mannerist movement in the early Baroque period.

With its exaggerations, elongations, and distortions, mannerism might be understood, in very general terms, as the attempt within representational painting to present the unrepresentable, to make the invisible visible, and to render the infinite in the finitude of lines and color.[1] Deleuze notes that mannerism brings an extraordinary energy into painting, and that this energy has a striking parallel in modern philosophy.

> In a sense, atheism has never been external to religion: atheism is the artistic power at work on religion. With God, everything is permitted. I have the distinct feeling that for philosophy it's been exactly the same thing, and if philosophers have spoken to us so much of God . . . [it was from] a joy arising from the labor they were involved in. Just as I said that God and Christ offered an extraordinary opportunity for painting to free lines, colors and movements from the constraints of resemblance, so God and the theme of God offered the irreplaceable opportunity for philosophy to free the object of creation in philosophy (that is to say, concepts) from the constraints that had been imposed on them . . . the simple representation of things. The concept is freed at the level of God because it no longer has the task of representing something . . . It takes on lines, colors, movements that it would never have had without this detour through God.[2]

For Deleuze, the modern conceptions of God as nature in Spinoza, as necessary illusion in Hume, or as limit idea in Kant form the conditions within which reason immanently breaks with representation. For the early moderns it is not, as perhaps it was for the medievals, the reaching of the mind to God, but the paradoxical necessity of an idea of the infinite within the finite mind that demands creative assimilation. With post-Cartesian philosophy, the idea of the infinite came to signify not the abundance of divine plenitude, but the inability of the mind to reach rational closure, to think reality as a whole. In this sense the infinite, as a limit of sensation or cognition, is a force that disrupts the faculties, defies categories, and destroys the framework of representation. With its nontheological conception of God, modern thought approaches the infinite as an unthinkable thought.

However, this thought, for Deleuze, becomes the moment at which reason is challenged to construe that which cannot be comprehended. To put it in Deleuze's language, with the idea of God, the unthinkable becomes positively problematic, rather than an impasse or a prelude to skepticism. Deleuze argues that the idea of God is not a problem among others but is, in a certain way, the transcendent source of problems, a provocation within the modern mind that invites modernity not so much to doubt its ability, as to be provoked into conjecture, and to conceptually invent. As he puts it with Guattari in *What Is Philosophy?*, a profound shift in the parameters of thought emerged in the passage from the seventeenth century to the eighteenth:

> What manifests as the mutation of light from the "natural light" to the "Enlightened" is the substitution of *belief* for knowledge, that is, a new infinite movement implying another image of thought: it is no longer a matter of turning toward but rather one of following tracks, of inferring rather than grasping or being grasped. Under what conditions is inference legitimate? Under what conditions can belief be legitimate when it has become secular? This question will be answered only with the creation of the great empiricist concepts (association, relation, habit, probability, convention). But conversely, these concepts, including the concept of belief itself, presuppose diagrammatic features that make belief an infinite movement independent of religion and traversing the new plane of immanence (religious belief, on the other hand, will become a conceptualizable case, the legitimacy or illegitimacy of which can be measured in accordance with the order of the infinite). (*WIP*, 53)

When Deleuze and Guattari assert that the meaning of belief in the modern era is contingent on new diagrammatic features, what they mean is that even if modern belief names "God" as its object, the movement such beliefs inspire trace out unforeseeable directions of thought and practice, vectors of which religious practice would become only one among many. The problem is not how to distinguish the religious as opposed to the irreligious, the pious from the impious, but rather to discern the effects of different practices of belief. As Deleuze will put it in *Cinema II*, the criteria of belief in the modern era is not whether it is in the right object, but whether it produces the right effect—whether, that is to say, it renews our belief in the world by expanding our receptivity against the deadening effects of habit and the quest for control.

In short, with modernity's experimentalism, religious faith is no longer the paradigm of belief. The model, rather, becomes the ordeal—at once epistemic and ethical—of living in a world whose ultimate structure remains inaccessible to thought, and yet forces thought to conceive it, much after the fashion of how the mannerist painters addressed the infinite in the finitude of color. In *What Is Philosophy?*,

Deleuze and Guattari assert that the early modern mannerist impulse nevertheless reached its apex in two religious thinkers, Pascal and Kierkegaard. These men were "concerned no longer with the transcendent existence of God but only with infinite immanent possibilities brought by the one who believes God exists" (*WIP*, 74). Deleuze and Guattari note that Kierkegaard's knight of faith and Pascal's gambler are personae extracted from the Old Testament, brought forth in philosophy to rival Socrates's ironic stance with one that is humorous, even absurd (*WIP*, 74). If Socrates is ironic because, tragically, he knows something that in some sense cannot be said, Pascal and Kierkegaard face the *comic* necessity of saying something that cannot in fact be known, let alone understood.[3] In their break with pure reason, and in the way they marshal archaic, mythical personae against the complacencies of philosophical discourse, there is a kind of defiance to Pascal and Kierkegaard. Deleuze and Guattari assert that these Christian existentialist thinkers "recharge immanence." That is to say, they reenergize the gesture of exposing the mind to a series of essentially unsolvable problems: Who am I in the face of an unknown God? Where am I in a decentered world? What am I in the face of my obscure material potencies? With their vertiginous view of faith, and with their refusal to indulge metaphysical comforts, Pascal and Kierkegaard are paradigmatic for modernity (*WIP*, 74). Beyond their particular religious commitments, they exemplify the liberating power of thought when it has foregone reassurances of a systematic order, and submits itself more fully to the infringement of the infinite upon existence.

Deleuze and Guattari's remarks here hearken back to some of Deleuze's earliest ideas. As early as a 1956–57, in a lecture course titled *Qu'est-ce que fonder?* (What is grounding?), Deleuze describes the origin of thought as a creative repetition of the mythological founding of human societies (*WG*, 2).[4] As Deleuze points out, to found a city or establish a nation is to mark out and define a territory. But such marking necessarily involves a confrontation with powers and potencies that give the hero or heroine the right to a territory. Ulysses must undertake an odyssey to recover a household. To ascend the throne of Thebes, Oedipus must defeat the Sphinx, just as Cadmus had himself founded Thebes by destroying its autochthonous monster, the serpent. Moses, to establish the Hebrew people, must defeat the Egyptian magicians. Deleuze points out that even in the founding of kinships, the process of making a claim upon a bride, an ordeal is involved: "For example: in claiming the hand of the daughter . . . one takes as arbiter the father who is the third, the foundation. But the father can say: undergo an ordeal, kill the dragon. That which grounds is an ordeal. To confront the foundation is not without danger; the pretenders have neither Penelope nor power" (*WG*, 4).

In mythical founding ordeals, there is no guarantee. To fail is to die. As power of the Theban ground, the Sphinx poses a problem, a riddle Oedipus must solve or be destroyed. Responding to the question, What goes on four legs in the morning, two in the afternoon, and three at night?, Oedipus correctly answers, "human beings," and thereby undoes the enigma of the Sphinx (who, now answered, destroys herself). However—and this point is crucial for Deleuze—the successful founding act does not mean that the riddle of human existence is resolved, let alone that society is made completely secure. On the contrary, through his ordeal Oedipus riddles the state, and simultaneously becomes a problem to himself. In solving the riddle, Oedipus discovers the enigma of his own (in)humanity, discovering too late that he is the man destined to murder his father and commit incest with his mother (*DR*, 195). To found is thus to confront destiny, and to go to the limit of one's power in that confrontation. Thus Deleuze says that every ordeal of grounding is a "conciliation between the will and what ought to be," a conciliation that remains incomplete and whose enigmatic character becomes reflected in the anxiety of civilization about its own ungrounded nature. As Deleuze observes in *Difference and Repetition*, when Oedipus asks Tiresias why the city is cursed, the answer is too much for him; it is overwhelming. "The event and the act possess a secret coherence which excludes that of the self . . . they turn back against the self which has become their equal and smash it to pieces, as though the bearer of the new world were carried away and dispersed by the shock of the multiplicity to which it gives birth: what the self has become equal to is the unequal in itself" (*DR*, 90).[5]

In the "What Is Grounding" lectures, Deleuze goes on to argue that there is a repetition of the ambiguity inherent to the act of archaic founding in the problem of grounding in modern philosophy. Just as the city seems constantly threatened by the inchoate ground on which it is founded, so does modern reason seem threatened by the forces it is incapable of conceiving and yet is forced to think. In his mature work,

Deleuze attempts in some sense to obviate this often-repressed dimension of the unrepresentable in thought. As he puts it in *Difference and Repetition*, "It is not a question of acquiring thought, nor of exercising it as though it were innate, but of engendering the act of thinking within thought itself" (DR, 114). And it is clear in *Difference and Repetition* that the mythical ordeal of founding is germane to the intellectual act of grounding. Throughout *Difference and Repetition*, Deleuze argues that the birth of thought takes place within the uncanny and the unrecognizable, in the sensible and the affective, in the element of a transcendental indiscernibility. However, the unthinkable or indiscernible—that which *must* but *cannot* be thought—is not the contingently inchoate, but a properly transcendental opacity germane to reality itself. Thus, *ideas* for Deleuze are not simple unities but imbricated multiplicities, reflections in some sense of the density of the real itself.

What matters then, in an idea, is not its ability to represent reality, but the range of experimental possibility it opens onto. Deleuze argues that what marks an idea is a simultaneous distinctness and obscurity, since it is a distinct apprehension of as yet unrealized, inchoate potency. In some sense the *enigmatic* or the uncanny is the singular condition of each idea, a condition approached as such, according to Deleuze, only in moments when the mind is confronted with its own limits and sundered from itself. As Deleuze puts it, "Thought is determined in such a manner that it grasps its own *cogitandum* only at the extremity of a fuse of violence which, from one idea to another, first sets in motion sensibility and its *sentiendum*, and so on. Ideas, therefore, are related not to a Cogito that functions as ground or as a proposition of consciousness, but to the fractured I of a dissolved Cogito; in other words, to the universal ungrounding which characterizes thought as a faculty in its transcendental exercise" (DR, 194).[6]

At stake in this insistence upon a peculiar opacity at the heart of thought is what could be called Deleuze's *intensive naturalism*, his view that mind is a particularly "involuted" dimension of nature. Prior to the development of distinct concepts, there is a dramatic encounter with a region or domain of potential sense, which Deleuze calls a "plan(e) of immanence." These planes are multiple, and can be laid out within color, in painting, in sounds, even in scientific functions or philosophical concepts. In this way, art, science, and philosophy all have peculiar modes of thought. Each setting out of a plane or plan is experimental and hazardous, subject not only to historical contingency, and to the aleatory and stochastic dimensions of nature, but to the active risking or redoubling of chance that thought represents. In *What Is Philosophy?*, Deleuze and Guattari write of the necessarily hazardous and heretical dimension of thought, evoking the surly and twilit legacy of outlying realms of experience.

> Thinking provokes general indifference. It is a dangerous exercise nevertheless. Indeed, it is only when the dangers become obvious that indifference ceases, but they often remain hidden and barely perceptible, inherent in the enterprise. Precisely because the plane of immanence is prephilosophical and does not immediately take effect with concepts, it implies a sort of groping experimentation and its layout resorts to measures that are not very respectable, rational, or reasonable. These measures belong to the order of dreams, of pathological processes, esoteric experiences, drunkenness, and excess. We head for the horizon, on the plane of immanence, and we return with bloodshot eyes, yet they are the eyes of the mind. Even Descartes had his dream. To think is always to follow the witch's flight. (*WP*, 41)

A traditional and rationalistic perspective must be puzzled by this connection between thought and witchcraft, between the Dionysian excess of the moonlit hours, and the sober reflections of the day. In a key chapter of *Difference and Repetition*, "The Image of Thought," Deleuze argues that in the history of philosophy the ordinary parameters of perception—the relatively stable nature of quantities and qualities, the subject and predicate terms of opinion and habit—have always been implicitly taken as transcendent reference points for thought, as if it were self-evident that the world ultimately consisted in some kind of unity, regularity, and harmony, and as if thought consisted, after all, in being a mirror of that world (*DR*, 129). This "image of thought" as well-grounded (whether in stable ideas or consistent natural phenomena) implicitly presupposes that all thought, no matter how elaborate, will return us to a recognizable world, and restore the mind to a sense of being well placed. But Deleuze argues that thought has its genesis in problems and questions that are themselves manifestations of imperceptible intensities, forces, and dynamics unapparent to perception. Thinking in this sense is identical to learning. As Deleuze puts it, "learning evolves entirely within the comprehension of the problem, as such, in the apprehension and condensation of singularities and in the ideal composition of events and bodies. Learning to swim or learning a foreign language means composing the singular points of one's own body or one's own language with those of another shape or element, which tears us apart but also propels us into a hitherto unknown and unheard-of world of problems. To what are we dedicated if not to those problems which demand the very transformation of our body and our language?" (*DR*, 192).

On this view, ideas are not simply given, but must be learned, and learned repeatedly, in repeated acts of tracing or following. Learning is always transformative, since for Deleuze there is no genuine question that is not linked to an imperative, to a sense of being forced to ask a certain question, an ordeal to which one rises or against which one falls. Ideas are developed in response to particular demands, even *as* demands (*DR*, 197). Ultimately, thought occurs not in habitual usage but in the very genesis of the faculties themselves: we comprehend swimming only in the element of learning how to swim, of a singular differentiation of the idea of swimming across the iterations of a unique repetition of that idea (*DR*, 192). Thought is a "witches' flight" in the sense of carrying us to beyond the frontier of what the body and the mind have been presumed able to do.

Immanence, Theological and Modern

When Deleuze and Guattari argue that Pascal and Kierkegaard model an act of founding paradigmatic for all of modern philosophy, they contend that, after the collapse of scholasticism, all modern philosophy becomes involved in a peculiar ordeal, an ordeal otherwise known as the "justification of belief" (*WIP*, 53). This project is, most famously, an attempt to address skeptical arguments about the reliability of sense perception, but it is also an opening for a kind of philosophical spirituality different from that connected with medieval philosophy. To found the life of faith, Pascal's gambler stakes his life on the chance of God's existence. Kierkegaard's knight of faith, Abraham, founds the faith of Israel, but does so by enduring the trial of being commanded to sacrifice the very son through whom that people have been promised to emerge. But already in Hume and Kant, Deleuze argues, there is a sense of confronting existence as a challenge to the very possibility of thought itself.

In its search for a ground, for the justification of belief, Deleuze argues that modern philosophy discovers the problem of *immanence* (what Kant will take up as the immanent critique of reason): the paradoxical questioning by reason not by the world, but by reason's own ground. This critique, which Deleuze argues already began with Hume, consists in the attempt to legitimate judgments without reference to any term or entity outside the capacities of a finite mind (*ES*, 28).[7]

What Deleuze means by immanence, however, goes beyond both Hume's empiricism and Kant's critical program, and in a way that may strike some readers as pre-modern (or at least pre-critical), Deleuze is not a thinker of human finitude. Despite Deleuze's status as a post-Kantian, his conception of immanence is not linked to the theme of finitude but to the recuperation of mystical and heterodox notions of mind *as microcosmic*. In order to comprehend this deep root of Deleuze's conception of immanence, it is necessary to revisit the theological debates from which it springs.

In medieval philosophy, conceptions of immanence and transcendence outlined possible relations between God and creation. According to traditional perspectives in monotheism (including the Jewish, Christian, and Islamic), it is necessary to conceive of God as both immanent and transcendent to creation. In order to accord with scriptural and prophetic revelations, God must be conceived as a personality with whom it is possible to enter into real relations across a real distance. Therefore God must transcend God's creation. Yet if God is truly sovereign, nothing in creation can derive from a source other than God's own substance. God must be, in this sense, immanent to creation. However, despite its complete ontological dependency upon God, the perfect nature of God must be distinct from that of creation, since creation itself manifests imperfection, or at least certain limitations that can never be imputed to God. There is thus an obligation on orthodox thinkers to find ways to limit or contain the immanence of God, in keeping with the need to maintain a real sense of divine transcendence.

When Spinoza infamously identified God with nature, he collapsed the distinction between God and creation, and eliminated the idea of God as in any sense transcendent. Deleuze and Guattari call Spinoza the "Christ of Philosophy" for the radicalness of this notion of divine immanence (*WIP*, 60). The achievement of Spinoza was that, rather than eliminate perfection, infinite power, or even eternity from the philosophical lexicon, Spinoza presented these divine dimensions as aspects of nature understood as one infinite substance: *deus sive natura*. For Deleuze, Spinoza's inclusion or implication of divine perfections within (and as) the contours of the world constitutes a solution to the problem of modern philosophy: how to think the reality of the infinite as immanent to the perspective of a finite mind, and how to think finitude as an aspect of nature viewed as absolute substance.[8] For Deleuze, this is the peculiar immanence of modern philosophy, the problem of a thought that has lost all relation to transcendence — not because transcendence has evaporated, but because transcendence has been completely absorbed into immanence. The essential modern problem, for Deleuze, is not that there is no longer a God to believe in, but that the world has taken on the attributes of God and, *mutatis mutandis*, the world has become uncanny, vertiginous. In immanent thought, the spatial, temporal, historical, erotic, and volitional dimensions of finite existence have become more than contingent, more than accidental — these hazardous dimensions have become absolute. Perhaps this is why Deleuze and Guattari wrote, "Immanence can be said to be the burning issue of all philosophy ... It is not immediately clear why immanence is so dangerous, but it is. It engulfs sages and gods. What singles out the philosopher is the part played by immanence or fire. Immanence is immanent only to itself and consequently captures everything, absorbs All-One, and leaves nothing remaining to which it could be immanent" (*WIP*, 45).

Despite this fiery imperative, Deleuze contends that modern philosophy has capitulated, time and again, to the same temptation as theology, namely the temptation to make immanence immanent to something else. Immanence, in modernity, becomes immanent to a series of miniature transcendences: to humanity itself in early modern skepticism and humanism; to the cogito of Descartes; to the transcendental subject of Kant; and to phenomenological consciousness in Husserl (*WIP*, 46).[9] What would it be for modern philosophy to think an immanence not immanent "to" anything, whether God, humanity, or the transcendental ego?[10]

If immanence is in some sense thinkable only beneath or without the parameters of a transcendent God, a paradigmatic humanity, or transcendental categories of possible experience, then immanence might seem to be related to something diabolical, inhuman, chaotic. Deleuze himself occasionally entertains the language of "chaos" as a description of immanence. However, Deleuze qualifies this language by insisting that what matters for immanence is the singularity of events, rather than some conception of nature as random or unpredictable. Deleuze avers that thought is never an approach to sheer or total chaos, but to singularities that mark the border between at least two different orders. In his work on Foucault, Deleuze clarifies this point when he writes, "Chaos does not exist; it is an abstraction because it is inseparable from a screen that makes something—something rather than nothing— emerge from it. Chaos would be a pure Many, a purely disjunctive diversity, while the something is a One, not a pregiven unity, but instead the indefinite article that designates a certain singularity" (F, 76). Because of the anonymous and contingent nature of all singular configurations, immanent thought is subject to illusion and to distortions, even to delusion. This is partly due to the fact that there is no transcendent criteria for which singularities matter for thought, or for how, why, and when they matter. For this reason, Deleuze is clear that immanent thought can often fail to be creative, and can produce hallucinations, erroneous perceptions, and bad feelings.[11] However, Deleuze argues that if we are to think at all, there is no choice but to risk these dangers.

In his late work, Deleuze emphasizes repeatedly that the renewal of belief in this world is the very definition of thought: "It may be that believing in this world, in life, becomes our most difficult task, or the task of a mode of existence still to be discovered or our plane of immanence today" (WIP, 75). Deleuze and Guattari even argue that thought itself requires a kind of conversion. This *convertio* (turning) is not away from the world, but toward it. It is an "empiricist conversion," a kind of restored vision that rediscovers the world with its "possibilities of movements and intensities, so as once again to give birth to new modes of existence, closer to animals and rocks" (WIP, 75).

This passage, resonant with many others in Deleuze's work, suggests that to rediscover the grounds of belief is to discover a mode of existence that appears to be "less" than human, less than perfectly rational or enlightened—a kind of feral, even mineral, mode. Thus from his earliest essays to his last, Deleuze argues that the peculiarly experimental, immanent mode of grounding called for by modern philosophy, will have to be linked to a transformation of human life as much as human rationality.[12] He often determines the form of life in which we might once again believe in the world as some as-yet-unrealized mode of animal, mineral, even cosmic existence, one that breaks with preconceived notions of human capacities for thought, affect, and agency. But what could it possibly mean to ground philosophical thought—traditionally conceived of as the rational, discursive activity of a distinctly enlightened, definitively human individual, in the prerational, inhuman, impersonal, and preindividual? Deleuze means many things by this suggestion, but we cannot comprehend Deleuze's meanings without situating Deleuze in the hermetic tradition, an ancient spiritual paradigm linking thought to processes of transformation in which thought is always an ordeal of becoming-other, a radical transformation of the self that dislocates the center of consciousness and makes it susceptible of nonordinary states of affect and perception. This is the microsmic conception of mind upon which Deleuze's coneption of immanence ultimately depends and which Deleuze in his own way transforms.

Immanent Eschatologies

As we mentioned already, in *Difference and Repetition,* Deleuze compares thought to Artaud's theater of cruelty. "Recall Artaud's idea: cruelty is nothing but determination as such, that precise point at which the determined maintains its essential relation with the undetermined, that rigorous abstract line fed by *chiaroscuro*" (*DR*, 29). To think, for Deleuze, is to delve into an opaque and inchoate ground, to be saturated in the nearly unbearable intensity of events, until a concept erupts like an abstract line emerging suddenly from material and spiritual forces. Even in a rationalist like Spinoza, what we encounter in the *Ethics*, according to Deleuze, is not a system of demonstrations, but an ordeal in which the mind is given new eyes. In *Spinoza: Practical Philosophy*, Deleuze writes that "the purpose of demonstration functioning as the third eye is not to command or even to convince, but only to shape the glass or polish the lens for this inspired free vision" (*SPP*, 14). Deleuze then elaborates on Spinoza by way of Henry Miller, that great writer of life as adventure and ordeal, who wrote, "You see, to me it seems as though the artists, the scientists, the philosophers were grinding lenses. It's all a grand preparation for something that never comes off. Someday the lens is going to be perfect and then we're all going to see clearly, see what a staggering, wonderful, beautiful world it is" (*SPP*, 14).[13]

Deleuze relates artistic experimentation to esoteric knowledge and experience. Both on his own and in collaboration with Guattari, Deleuze is explicit about the fact that immanent thought is involved with an exploration of extremes, and with abyssal adventures of great risk and tremendous ordeal. The value of such ordeal generally goes unrecognized by academic and bureaucratic modes of evaluation, and is held in contempt by the social *doxa*. Deleuze and Guattari write,

> Take Michaux's plane of immanence, for example, with its infinite, wild movements and speeds. Usually these measures do not appear in the result, which must be grasped solely in itself and calmly. But then "danger" takes on another meaning: it becomes a case of obvious consequences when pure immanence provokes a strong, instinctive disapproval in public opinion, and the nature of the created concepts strengthens this disapproval. This is because one does not think without becoming something else, something that does not think—an animal, a molecule, a particle—and that comes back to thought and revives it. (*WIP*, 42)

Henri Michaux's writings record prolonged experiments with psychopharmacology in order to explore other possible mediations between the infinite and the finite, the absolute and the particular, the self and the world.[14] Deleuze and Guattari also refer later in this same chapter to Artaud's work on the peyote dance, which Artaud sought out in northern Mexico as a way of passing beyond the ego to the discovery of cosmic dimensions of the self. Deleuze and Guattari's constant references to artistic, personal, and spiritual experimentation as requisite for thought form a kind of mantra, a refrain, and suggest that there is much more at stake than mere metaphor in their description of thought as a "witch's flight."

The emphasis on experimentation here is a clue not only to the nature of immanence as the vocation of modern thought, but also to the connection of immanent thought to an esoteric or hermetic conception of mind. Deleuze and Guattari describe certain writers as having the ability to undergo intense ordeals, as able to sustain or incarnate terrible contradictions or extreme "differences in kind" in their works. Writers "use all the resources of their athleticism" to install themselves within difference as a kind of Dionysian space of undoing, animals torn apart in a perpetual show of strength. "Every writer dips into a chaos, into a movement that goes to the infinite" (*WIP*, 172).

However, Deleuze is also clear about the specific limitations and contingent possibilities of experimentation, recognizing, with Guattari in *A Thousand Plateaus* that "absolute deterritorialization" would be tantamount to a kind of heat-death (*ATP*, 145). Caricatures of Deleuze to the contrary, no simple mandate for proliferation or divertissement will suffice as the mantra of immanence. Which experiments matter, and when, and how? Although the rule of immanence entails a rejection of any specific tradition or traditional set of practices as preeminent, throughout Deleuze's work there is a tableau, a kind of index of experimentation, upon which not only a certain artistic modernism is inscribed, but, more elusively, a series of references to occult topics such as the hermaphroditic character of human sexuality, the idea of the world as a cosmic egg, messianic mathematical intuitions, divination practices, geomancy, sorcery, shamanism, and ritual-therapeutic processes.[15] Are the references to such practices mere metaphors for thought, simply pedagogical examples, or does the discovery of any plan(e) of immanence depend, in some sense, upon an esoteric apprehension of reality?

Deleuze and Guattari seem to wonder about this themselves, when they conclude *What Is Philosophy?* with the following extremely dense and cryptic passage.

> *Philosophy needs a nonphilosophy that comprehends it; it needs a nonphilosophical comprehension just as art needs nonart and science needs nonscience.* They do not need the *non* as beginning, or as the end in which they would be called upon to disappear by being realized, but at every moment of their becoming or their development. Now, if the three *nons* are still distinct in relation to the cerebral plane, they are no longer distinct in relation to the chaos into which the brain plunges. In this submersion it seems that there is extracted from chaos the shadow of the "people to come" in the form of art, but also philosophy and science, summon forth: mass-people, world-people, brain-people, chaos-people—non-thinking thought that lodges in the three, like Klee's nonconceptual concept or Kandinsky's internal silence. It is here that concepts, sensations, and functions become undecidable, at the same time as philosophy, art, and science become indiscernible, as if they shared the same shadow that extends itself across their different nature and constantly accompanies them. (*WIP*, 218)

These extraordinary words suggest that there is some kind of revolutionary, even utopian dimension to immanence, an apocalyptic, eschatological impulse leading through the chaos into which the brain plunges and upon which it draws its plan(e). But surely this eschatology is drenched in obscurity. What would it mean to ground art, science, and philosophy upon a common, animating, "non-philosophical" principle? How would the eschatological ethos of a transformed people be, *per impossible*, the "lived reality" of immanence?

This is a major question for Deleuze, since, as Christian Kerslake has pointed out, when Deleuze argues that thought needs a nonphilosophy, and a nonphilosophical comprehension of the creation of concepts, he seems to be violating the metaphilosophical injunction against transcendence, positing some kind of experience of immanence as transcendent to thought, and as that by which thought would be judged.[16] In other words, if it is not to philosophy per se that thought is immanent, then it seems that philosophy would have its origin and end not within itself, but in some kind of "transcendent" experience to which thought would bear witness.[17] If the vocation to immanence (also shared by art and science) is somehow linked to the instauration of a future life, a life to come, then in some sense philosophy would be ancilla to this as-yet-uncomprehended form of life. The anticipation of some as-yet-unrealized immanence would be necessary for philosophy, and would in some sense transcend philosophical practice while making it possible and necessary.

It was this elusive eschatological sense of immanence that Derrida, in his eulogy for Deleuze, suggested was still "secret" in Deleuze's conception of immanence, and had to do with Deleuze's connection to the work of Artaud. Artaud's experiments, and his search for a hidden experience of the self beyond the ego, were transactions taking place at a level of spiritual and physical ordeal. If for his conception of immanence Deleuze is drawing as deeply as Derrida suggests upon Artaud, and upon the experimental spiritualities of many other modern artists, in the last analysis the secret of immanence, and of Deleuze's philosophy, may not be hidden or obscure, but simply esoteric in the sense of being "within" a nonphilosophical experience of immanence as precisely that "inner light" that, according to many traditions of esoteric gnosis, animates all genuine knowledge. To take Deleuze's "esoteric" interests seriously would mean, in this case, to read Deleuze's philosophy with constant reference to how his concepts ramify experimental spiritual traditions, from ancient theurgy to modern aesthetic experimentation.

The World as Belief Experiment

To fully understand Deleuze's conception that thought is linked to transformative ordeal and preindividual modes of existence, it is necessary to situate Deleuze within a longstanding tradition of esoteric thought in Western culture. Western Esoteric thought identifies humanity itself with a supraindividual, impersonal, encosmic, and immanent divinity. Broadly speaking, this tradition views human life as a process of theandric redemption whereby the full nature of divinity is discovered and produced through the unfolding of human destiny over cosmic and historical epochs. The particular and predominant tradition in Western esoteric thought that concerns me here, and that is most central to Deleuze's own conception of philosophy, is the hermetic tradition. This tradition derives from the teachings of Hermes Trismegistus, the legendary Egyptian sage who taught that knowledge of the cosmos was at the source of all spiritual, personal, and collective transformation. Crucial to the hermetic tradition, and why Deleuze can be placed within it, is the connection Hermes makes of thought to spiritual ordeals: metaphysical insight is gained on the basis of mantic, transformative, and initiatory processes that develop the human capacity to sustain the modes of existence that correspond to otherwise hidden potentials for individual regeneration and cosmic renewal. If Deleuze's conception of the modern project as a renewal of belief in the extremis of immanence entails that thought must align itself with experimental modes of existence, then arguably Deleuze's own philosophy of immanence, and his radical take on philosophical modernity, is both an extension and transformation of the hermetic tradition.

This claim entails that, in a modality that identifies the philosophy of immanence as a distinctly modern repetition of mythical acts of founding, thought, as a renewed belief in the world, would be actualized in tandem with a discovery, affirmation, and the production of intensified forms of life. In keeping with the hermetic ambition to creatively renew the cosmos, Deleuzian philosophy can be read as an attempt to map or diagram those transformations or "conversions" that develop an immanently creative principle of knowledge and belief. This distinctly practical philosophy proceeds through intense ordeals. At its apex, thought, for Deleuze, manifests an intensity that expands and alters the limits of human subjectivity, bringing mental life closer to the life of animals and rocks, but also to imperceptible forces, and to the imbricated rhythms of affective dynamisms, the deep pulsations and vibrations of the cosmos itself. To diagram the flows of such cosmic intensities is the peculiar grounding or "founding" proper to the Deleuzian conception of immanence.

In opposition to certain scholars intent on making finer distinctions, I follow Antoine Faivre's *Access to Western Esotericism* in using "hermeticism" as interchangeable with "Western Esotericism."[18] Faivre includes a plethora of practices and traditions within Western esotericism, including theurgy, alchemy, kabbalah, astrology, divination, and Western appropriations of Asiatic traditions such as transcendental meditation, yoga, and tantra. In very general terms, Western esotericism or hermeticism is the search for gnosis, for the inner or secret truths of God, nature, or both, an empowering wisdom that is a force of personal, social, and cosmic regeneration. The basic teachings of the *Corpus Hermeticum* are found in *The Emerald Tablet*. This text explains that the cosmos was constructed on the principle "as above, so below," for the purposes of accomplishing the "mystery of the One Thing."[19] As Hermes explains to his adepts, this One, or All, extends itself through complex hierarchies of interdependence, from the stars down to the human soul. The microcosm is constituted by the same principles as the macrocosm, and the stars have an influence that is as much personal as it is physical. A human being's entire identity, body and soul, is a receptor and potential transformer of a long chain of sympathetic influences. To attain communion with divinity is the goal of life, and this goal is achieved through a process of learning that is simultaneously an embodying of the archetypal structure of cosmic reality. The personal is the cosmic: since the cosmos is a living body, all its participating members are unified; the fate of one is the fate of the All. By virtue of a spiritual power sometimes called *nous* (mind), or otherwise called *pneuma* (soul) or *dynamis* (potency), the cosmos is held in organic unity with itself. Liberation from the evil powers of fate takes place on the basis of a *theosis*, an identification of the soul with the creative influence of God. Such theosis or "theandry" culminates in the repetition of practical processes of accessing, activating, and elaborating various centers of material and spiritual renewal. This repeating (and nonidentical) renewal takes place through a kind of intellectual love manifested as the possibility not of escape from, but a transformation of, debased creation, a raising up of that which has been lost and a calling down of that which has been forgotten.[20]

Within Western philosophy, this kind of "optimist gnosis" was deeply appealing to Neoplatonic sensibilities, since it is precisely the attempt to "regrow" one's spiritual wings that inspired the Platonic philosopher (at least on the Plotinian model) to engage in dialectic. Although the Neoplatonists rarely cite the *Corpus Hermeticum*, this may have more to do with the text's popular, nontechnical character (and its anti-imperial polemic), than with any reticence to explicitly relate the teachings of Hermes to those of Pythagoras or other Greek masters (such as Plato himself).[21] Later, Renaissance Neoplatonists, especially Marsilio Ficino and his protégé Pico della Mirandola, would look to Hermes Trismegistus as a model and source of perennial wisdom fully compatible with Plato, Aristotle, and scriptural revelation. Ficino considered Hermes to stand within a *prisca theologia*, a pure or perennial theology, that included Moses, Plato, and Christ. For the Renaissance mind, Egyptian *magia*, the Chaldean Oracles, Judaic law, Greek philosophy, and monotheistic theology could all be construed as successive revelations of a unified truth. Frances Yates went so far as to argue, in her monumental studies of Renaissance thought, that Ficino, Pico, and even the heretic Giordano Bruno philosophized out of a hermetic core of philosophical conviction, rooted in the creative attempt to complete and ramify the prisca theologia.[22] Because it delved beyond any merely intellectual framework for wisdom, hermeticism helped to buttress the interest of Renaissance philosophers in astrology, divination, sorcery, and other forms of occult practice. For Yates, the validation of *magia naturalis* was part of an emergent experimental confidence that would later culminate in the founding of a secular culture grounded in modern science. Yates argued that the importance of hermeticism for the emergence of modern science lay in its teaching that mind actively transforms the cosmos (as much as the self) in accordance with the activation of a higher or magical will. In this way, for Yates, Renaissance hermeticism anticipates both modern experimental science and the Promethean voluntarism of modern subjectivity.[23]

During the Renaissance, however, the revival of hermeticism was an attempt to graft Christianity, with its myth of cosmic fall and redemption, to a more active vision of the presence of an encosmic God than traditional theology had to that point emphasized. In this way, hermeticism played a key role in the emergence of experimental immanence as a theme in modern philosophy, precisely in the sense in which Deleuze refers to immanence in his comparison between mannerist painting and modern philosophy. And Deleuze places himself—if somewhat subtly and obliquely—in this very tradition. In very general terms, Deleuze can be situated within hermetic tradition since in his philosophy all thought is immediately a process of transformation and metamorphosis. In *Difference and Repetition*, he argues, "Every body, every thing, thinks and is a thought to the extent that, reduced to its intensive reasons, it expresses an Idea the actualization of which it determines. However, the thinker himself makes his individual differences from all manner of things: it is in this sense that he is laden with stones and diamonds, 'and even animals.' The thinker, undoubtedly the thinker of eternal return, is the individual, the universal individual . . . We are made of all these depths and distances, of these intensive souls which develop and are re-enveloped" (DR, 254). For Deleuze, the process of individuation is an expression of cosmic, "intensive" depths and distances, as if ideas were a measure of, and measured by, their expression of the cosmos itself. For hermeticism, mind itself emerges through intensified apprehensions and experimental work (the alchemical magnum opus) within cosmic hierarchies and otherwise imperceptible mediators, in a process of theandry and theosis by which the initiate might traverse, and ultimately identify with, the divine life of the One-All. The traditional goal is the unity of humanity and divinity: redemption, deification, and empowerment. The alchemical dream of all hermetic science is to complete the task of the redemption of the soul without the sacrifice of the body, and without the sacrificial reduction of matter to form. In the modern, secularized thought of Deleuze, hermeticism takes on the guise of a "deterritorializing" of both spirit and organic matter, envisioning both as expressions of an "anorganic" and "machinic" play of forces. Yet despite his irreligiosity, Deleuze still conceives of the liberating potencies of deterritorialization as a matter of experimental theandric aspiration, an elaboration of the cosmos as a Bergsonian "machine for the making of gods."[24]

In other words, the posture of the ancient tradition may not be as far from Deleuze's own contemporary attitude as one might initially think. Despite occasional pretensions to a pristine or "perennial" tradition, Western esotericism, from alchemy to theosophy, has been engaged in a somewhat improvisatory, or at least seminomadic attempt to divine the number and kind of archons that govern access to greater or deeper insights into the whole and to one's place within it, and thereby to discover the cosmic self of a nonegoic or "higher" mind. Deleuze's own oblique version of esoteric gnosis involves a rupture with any static conception of types, symbols, or archons in favor of a mobile conception of the rudiments of transformation, one that affirms the machinic and schizoid potencies of a "dissolved Self" capable of starting from anywhere and affirming eternal return through its adventures (*DR*, 254). Despite his fascination with themes of imperceptibility, escape, and "absolute deterritorialization," Deleuze is clear that the full realization of such states is death itself, and for that reason continually traces the specific contours, conditions, and limits of experimental ordeals. Thus what I would call a certain "pragmatics of the intense" illumines the viable modes of contact (even *a contrario*, in the case of failures) with the profundities of immanence, and it is this careful attention to the details and difficulties of various experimental states that registers the impress of hermetic science in the background of Deleuzian philosophy. If, as Deleuze and Guattari insist, there is no deterritorialization without a reterritorializing, then the hermetic tradition is the final, if still ambiguous, reterritoriality of immanent thought itself. That, at any rate, is the working hypothesis of this book.

Deleuze's hermeticism is a distinct mode of practical philosophy: philosophy as spiritual ordeal. This reading takes the corpus of Deleuze as a contemporary quest for that subtle sense of interconnection and cooperation with nature that has been the perennial ambition of Western esotericism. Some version of hermeticism is the "nonconceptual concept" or "internal silence" that Deleuze and Guattari said, in their last work together, cast its "shadow" upon art, science, and philosophy (*WIP*, 218). In this way, Deleuze's thought is an attempt to radicalize Bergson's affirmation of creative emotion as a force to which philosophy itself is subordinate, since "everything happens as if that which remains indeterminate in philosophical intuition gained a new kind of determination in mystical intuition—as though the properly philosophical 'probability' extended itself into mystical certainty" (*B*, 112). Against the suspicions and reservations of a patently secular age, I evoke the hermetic tradition precisely to cultivate a clearer sense of how, for Deleuze, the mystical perspective activates a power to traverse the depths of time in a "cosmic Memory" that "actualizes all the levels at the same time, that liberates man from the plane or the level that is proper to him, in order to make him a creator, adequate to the whole movement of creation" (*B*, 111).[25] Deleuze's own thought reaches complete expression only insofar as immanence is realized not only in the creation of philosophical concepts, scientific functions, and artistic percepts, but within the lineaments of an open series of spiritual experiments to which Deleuze's work bears wry and canny witness.

2

Dark Precursors
The Hermetic Tradition

> Thunderbolts explode between different intensities, but they are preceded by an invisible, imperceptible *dark precursor,* which determines their path in advance but in reverse, as though intagliated. Likewise, every system contains its dark precursor which ensures the communication of peripheral series. —GILLES DELEUZE, *Difference and Repetition,* 119

In *What Is Philosophy?*, Deleuze and Guattari observe that immanence, in the monotheistic theological traditions, is generally understood as a presence of the divine essence in creation, an immanence tolerated only at "local" levels. In other words, theology treats creation as a kind of terraced fountain in which immanence, like water, is allowed to fill out each level only if it comes from a higher source and descends to a lower one (*WIP,* 45).[1] In the Christian theological tradition informed by Neoplatonist emanation schemes, creation is conceived as an interlocked hierarchy of levels of being transcending one another and leading to an ineffable source. That which is higher in the order of being is what it is through its aspiration to that which is above it; that which is below receives its being from participation in a higher source. That is to say, being is not univocally distributed, but comes in degrees.

In *Expressionism and Philosophy: Spinoza*, Deleuze argues that immanent thought has its origins in an idea of being as "expression," and in a general program of "expressionism" in philosophy. In expressionist thought, being is not essentially substance, but unfolding power and dynamic process. This tradition has its roots in Neoplatonic schemas of emanation and in orthodox accounts of creation. In theological terms, the idea of an ultimate reality that is fundamentally will rather than substance is strongly suggested by scriptural accounts of creation, but was in some ways held back by the influence of classical Greek metaphysics, which tended to obscure the question of cosmogenesis by presuming the eternity of the world, and reality as an eternally perduring substance rather than a singular act of manifestation. Expressionism began to gain traction, however, in later attempts to use Neoplatonic ideas of emanation to understand creation. In this medieval and mystical vision, the divine plenitude was conceived of as flowing down from or expressed through a transdescendence in the orders of being, from those essential created forms Augustine called *rationes seminales* (*logoi spermatikoi*) to the lowest orders of mineral and material substance.[2]

Medieval theologians such as Nicholas of Cusa and Meister Eckhart (following John Scotus Eriugena and Pseudo-Dionysius) emphasized that each being, in its emergence and its essence, was a singular and contingent manifestation of divine plenitude, a unique theophany, rather than a mere reiteration of a species. In this way, each being in creation could be construed as inherently divine and possessed of a hidden supernatural essence. This theory of creation diverges from Aristotelian emphasis on species, genera, and categorical distinctions based on observations and anatomy, and tends to develop in an apophatic conception of nature as ultimately unknowable. In the *Periphysion*, Eriugena goes so far as to identify the nature of each creature with the essence of an unknowable God.[3] Eriugena argues that if God is the source of all being, and yet in himself transcends every definition of being, then the ultimate essence of each creature, whose nature comes from God, must transcend itself. Eriugena writes, "Every visible and invisible creature can be called a theophany, that is, a divine apparition. For every order of nature from the highest to the lowest, that is, from the celestial essences to the last bodies of the visible world, the more secretly it is understood, the closer it is seen to approach the divine brilliance."[4] Nicholas of Cusa puts the point somewhat more cryptically when he writes that in the moon the universe is "contracted" into the particular and specific nature of the moon, while God in the moon remains absolutely indivisible or "maximum." God in the moon is "the moon . . . without plurality and difference."[5] Thus with the notion of theophanic expression, an immanent conception of divinity was introduced into the thought of the world as creation, yet without violating the stipulation that God's essence be ultimately transcendent to the created orders—ineffable, unknowable, and absolute.

With the emergence of nominalist trends, later medieval theology approached the limits of the Neoplatonic schema, which depended on a realism about universals. Nominalism, in very general terms, construed names not as a power to capture real being, but as merely conventional signs. The issue is much more complex than can be encompassed here, but this view gained prominence in part because Christian philosophy began to confront the possibility that human life on earth was not at the center of fixed cosmic hierarchies.[6] The encompassing or distributed view of essences, along with their expression in abstract or general terms, became less convincing in a physical cosmos whose appearances were set off against a background of infinity. With nominalism, the *form* of the universe loses its exemplary status, leading to Nicholas of Cusa's famous argument (attempting to stave off the corrosive effects of nominalism) that there can be no perfect shape within the universe, but only an approximation of God as absolute maximum, the being "whose center is everywhere and whose circumference is nowhere."[7]

Cusa's thought of divine presence within an infinite universe involved a series of paradoxes, including the ultimate paradox that God must be conceived of as in all things in a sense that all things are not in God. Otherwise, the heresy of pantheism lurked, and the nature of the world would be identified with that of God. While Cusa was determined to avoid the theological and political implications of pantheism, it was Spinoza who became the "Christ of Philosophers" when he extended the immanent vision to the absolute, ultimately identifying nature as a univocal expression of divine substance, and God with nature. Spinoza's vision of reality is of central significance to Deleuze. Spinoza argued that the singular modes of substance are not partial or analogical reflections of a more eminent reality, but immediate, "immanently caused" expressions. Thus Spinoza abolished any hierarchy in the absolute by which the divine being might be determined as more or less present at various levels or orders of being (a thought germane to traditional accounts of creation as diverse receptions of the divine as gift).[8] As opposed to Cusa and the creationist tradition (as well as to Jewish and Islamic orthodoxy), Spinoza understood God's being to be in no sense eminent, let alone donated as gift, but to exist in creation in exactly the same sense as it is in itself. God is directly the cause of all being, and is to be identified with every being. Thus God is univocally, immediately identical with nature, as such.

This pantheism, however, is better understood as a kind of naturalism rather than a mysticism, where the univocity of God and of nature—or both—is taken on the basis of faith alone. Be that as it may, it is a naturalism that breaks with the Aristotelian approach to understanding life. If the nature of life is approached in terms of differences between individuals, one arrives at a kind of compendium of genera and species, as in Aristotelian biology, but not at a sense of the immediate *identity* of the whole of nature as it is present in every part (or in every relation of which nature is composed and which nature composes). To arrive at this alternative conception of nature as immediately God, Spinoza proposed that the mind must be capable of ascertaining "common natures" or "common notions," principles of order or structures of relations (such as extension) that are found univocally in every entity or relational modality. As Deleuze puts it in *Expressionism in Philosophy*, "by inquiring how these relations vary from one body to another, we have a way of directly determining the resemblances between two bodies, however disparate they may be . . . in the limit Nature as a whole is a single animal [*un même Animal*] in which only the relations between the parts vary" (E 278).

Spinoza's basic move here, which will be crucial to much of Deleuze's work, is to shift from a perspective on nature wherein each individual is defined by the internal relations of parts that compose it (the potentials it actualizes), to a perspective according to which all relations are external to the terms involved. The one substance is, as it were, the infinite set of all possible relations, and each entity is a particular expression of organizations common to other organizations across an infinite plane of nature. The goal of thought here is not to discern how bodies differ, but to discover the relations common to them all.

But such common natures, or common notions, are not immediately apparent. To discern common notions, one has to arrive at a level of extreme generality, a use of reason *sub specie aeternitatis*. Natural languages and habits of perception tend to produce the illusion that given sets of particular individuals constitute unique, irreplaceable instances, and are not expressions of one infinite substance. (This perspective is also behind the illusion of teleology, the idea that each individual can be defined by a particular purpose for its existence.) Against such habits, a kind of philosophical practice is required that can provide insight beyond all misplaced concreteness.[9] An experimental usage of reason, one that elaborates relations occluded by the ordinary meanings of terms, is necessary. Such is the *more geometrico* of Spinoza, a method of explication whose very form is meant to lead the mind beyond ordinary intuitions.[10] Along these lines, Deleuze explicitly links the rise of a univocal conception of being—first with Duns Scotus, then with Spinoza, and culminating, according to Deleuze, in Nietzsche—to a will to experiment (*DR*, 41). In Deleuze's version of philosophical modernity, a univocal conception of being is an effect of an experimental affirmation of the world beyond what is sensibly observable and what is divinely revealed. However, such experimentation is not a matter of mere fantasy or delirious imagination, but emerges from an intense exposure of mind to the relations, events, and processes of which it is really composed. The question becomes, however, not how to distinguish true ideas from false, but how to discover more adequate or more comprehensive and "intense" levels of thought and being. The search for adequate "common notions" of nature, for the structures of the one Animal that is God or Nature, is immediately the quest for how to intensify thought itself.

In *What Is Philosophy?*, Deleuze and Guattari contrast the immanent protocols of art, science, and philosophy with the aspirations to transcendence that underwrite the production of religious figures. They argue that religion summons revelation, and establishes its icons and typologies, by drawing upon immanence only in order to foreclose upon it. Religions "invoke dynasties or gods, or the epiphany of a single god" in order to construct icons that fundamentally restrict and thus distort the infinite (*WIP*, 202). Religion in this way appears as a figure of ressentiment, as a reactionary will to glorify the status quo, or to "paint a firmament on the umbrella [of opinion]," rather than to do what art, science, and philosophy do when they open the delicate sieve through which a little pure chaos itself might enter (*WIP*, 202). In other words, religious pantheons do no more than crystallize the perennial character of the everyday, forming a kind of *urdoxa*: domestic relations as embodied by Hera as the eternal wife, or nature's destructive potentials as figured in Kali.

But Deleuze and Guattari also acknowledge a less conventional mode of religious thought, one that is not a sheltering of opinion or a restriction of infinity to finite figures. They detect a struggle or contestation on behalf of immanence within religious ideas, where "disturbing affinities" appear on a common plane of immanence between philosophical concepts and the "diagrammatic movements" of certain religious motifs, such as the "to-ing and fro-ing" of *I Ching* hexagrams (*WIP*, 91). Deleuze and Guattari mention that their contemporaries Christian Jambet, Henry Corbin, and Guy Lardreau were all involved in disinterring immanent movements in the mystical and esoteric systems of religious thought (*WIP*, 223). I will argue here that a series of premodern thinkers—John Scotus Eriugena, Nicholas of Cusa, Pico della Mirandola, and Giordano Bruno, were engaged in just such a struggle for immanence within Neoplatonism and Christianity, and that this struggle marks them as "dark precursors" to Deleuze's system. These thinkers, accused of heresy and subversive motives, could be said to have attempted (at great risk, in many cases) to institute a "plan(e) of immanence" within theological discourse, producing paradoxical and esoteric systems of knowledge.

In order to fully comprehend the nature of Deleuze's thought, and the strangely esoteric overtones of immanence, we must delve more deeply into this minor tradition, and into roots of immanence in medieval and Renaissance traditions of expressionism. Deleuze reengineers these resources in specific (and at times extremely abstruse) ways to produce his own peculiar post-Kantian version of immanence. Despite the fact that, following Spinoza, Deleuze will eliminate the hierarchical and analogical senses of being, it is demonstrable that Deleuze retains much of the pragmatic elements of pre-Spinozistic, late-Neoplatonic conceptions, particularly insofar as these views are influenced by hermetic conceptions of thought as coincipient with theurgy and *magia naturalis*—that is to say, with practices of transformation.[11] In a Neoplatonic legacy highly significant for Deleuze, thinkers such as Iamblichus, Pseudo-Dionysus, John Scotus Eriugena, Nicholas of Cusa, Pico della Mirandola, and Giordano Bruno all thematize a connection between thought and cosmic revitalization that situates philosophy within a more encompassing vision of human creativity as theandry, and of natural existence as a process of theurgical transmutation. Deleuze's systematic thought, in its own enigmatic yet persistent way, directs us through its reflections on art, science, and philosophy, toward a contemporary variation on perennial hermetic themes.[12]

Platonism and the Problem of Participation

In his study of the history of the concept of expression inherited and transformed by Spinoza, Deleuze begins in the depths of Platonic tradition. Deleuze begins by observing that Plotinus had perceived that Plato was ultimately unable to solve the problem of how the many and the one are unified in the forms (*E*, 169). In the *Parmenides*, Plato seems to have been undecided as to whether participation occurs through imitation, through a part-whole relationship, or through the influence of a *daimon*, a mediating spirit (*E*, 169). Deleuze notes that, in any case, participation of the real in the ideal, of existence in essence, appears to be something forced or imposed from the outside (*E*, 170). Plotinus's insight, according to Deleuze, was to realize that Plato had asked the wrong question. Plato had asked how it might be possible for the many to participate in the One, but should have asked how it might be possible for the One to give the many the ability to participate. For Plotinus, participation is a "giving" in the sense that the One gives of itself unilaterally to the many. The many, in this sense, are not imitators or parts but recipients: the many are brought into being by being themselves recipients, and what is received is particular, contingent being as an unforced donation from the One. This Plotinian notion was repeatedly cited in medieval philosophy, that each being in existence is what it is because it receives being "according to its capacity."[13]

However, since the One is beyond being, the one is "above its gifts, and it gives what does not belong to it" (*E*, 171). As Proclus later understood it, the principle of participation is not itself participable: to be one (of the many, among the many) is a gift of the One in the sense that both the receiver and received are donated from the One.[14] A being becomes what it is to the degree that it receives its being from a transcendent source. The cause of each being remains *eminent*, at a distance crossed only as each "turns toward" its source. The One as cause of all proceeds, but remains in itself. As Deleuze puts it in *Difference and Repetition*, "The Platonists used to say that the not-One distinguished itself from the One, but not the converse, since the One does not flee that which flees it; and at the other pole, form distinguishes itself from matter, or from the ground, but not the converse, since distinction itself is still a form" (*DR*, 28).[15] In causal terms, while an emanative cause remains in itself, the effect it produces is external to and does not remain within the cause. In the Neoplatonic schema, expression is always an expression of a higher or eminent nature in lower or lesser realities. The many express the one, but the one does not fully express itself in the many.

Christian theology appropriated Plotinian emanationism, as did Judaic and Islamic thought, in an attempt to reach an orthodox answer to the question of how, given the transcendence of the divine nature, creation could truly express the nature of the creator. In addition to having an absolute beginning in God, it is also clear that creation develops over time. To account for this, St. Augustine had posited that in the beginning God had created *rationes seminales* (or, in Greek, *logoi spermatikoi*), essential forms that continue to develop over time, on the model of emanative causation.[16] Later Christian philosophy began to realize a problem with standard emanationism: it tends to make the substance of the universe manifest something less than the perfect goodness of God. Creation itself might even seem to be an essentially tragic diminution, as envisaged by Gnosticism. To avoid this consequence, Christian theology increasingly turned to apophatic or paradoxical formulas in order to preserve the unity and interconnectedness of being while at the same time preserving the transcendence of God and the inherent goodness of created order. John Scotus Eriugena, for example, argued that the doctrine of creation implies that the ultimate nature of each entity, as donated from God, is unknowable in the same sense that the divine is itself inscrutable. And later, for Nicholas of Cusa, God's being is explicated only in itself (as unfathomable generosity) and is known only approximately or as *complicatio* in the world. This cryptic formula—God in creation is complicatio what God is *explicatio* in himself—protects divine transcendence, but also registers divine immanence as mandated by scripture. Since scripture asserts that creation manifests the nature of God (Psalms 19), creation requires something stronger than emanation, a paradoxically "immanent" uniqueness of each thing as a perfect expression, in its own way, of divine life. Thus Cusa asserted, "There is nothing in the universe that does not enjoy a certain singularity that cannot be found in any other thing."[17]

Although this notion of *singularitate* (uniqueness) might have been unthinkable for Plotinus or Porphyry, Iamblichus of Chalcis, the fourth-century Syriac Neoplatonist, had already anticipated Christian notions of the unique status of temporal and finite entities in his reflections on theurgy.[18] Deleuze does not mention Iamblichus in his account of the roots of expressionism, but Iamblichus's position, of all those in Neoplatonism, has perhaps the most proximity to Deleuze's own. For Iamblichus, the ritual practice of pagan theurgy, in which the material world is ordered so as to be rendered "fitting" for the divine, is not a constraining of the spiritual in the material, let alone a coercion of gods by humans. In fact, Iamblichus argues that theurgy is such a powerful form of cooperation and communion that it is not on the basis of contemplation (*nous*), but through theurgy itself that the soul returns to the One. Iamblichus develops this thought at length in his *On the Mysteries of the Egyptians*, a response to the view of Porphyry (Plotinus's successor) that religious practice could not constitute a path to unification with the One.

Porphyry held that the soul was not locally present in the body, but has only an occasional disposition toward or inclination to the body.[19] Iamblichus disagreed. What is at issue is the locus, the point of contact between the human and the divine, the one and the many. Is it material or immaterial? Where do the incorporeal and the corporeal convene? For Iamblichus, it is in theurgy that this union has its nexus. The effectiveness of religious ritual depends on the fact that the gods, as immaterial beings, are nevertheless met in a specific place, since sacrifices are not simply sent up, but also draw the gods down.[20] This entails, however, that there must be some aspect of materiality worthy of the gods, some eternal aspect or perfect dimension of the material cosmos itself. There must be a site of real contact between soul or spirit and materiality, and this site, Iamblichus argues, is constituted by the sympathies or inherent harmonies that are the rudiments of rightly constructed rituals.

The effectiveness of theurgic rites implies that certain material configurations are inherently "fitting" for the divine. But this can be only because theurgies activate harmonies, sympathies, and proportionalities that are truly redolent of the absolute, the ineffable One. The very existence of such *symbola*, however, would entail that matter is not the lowest emanation but is (at least potentially) perhaps even more resonant with the transcendent One than pure spirit. As Iamblichus puts it,

> In the highest level of beings, the abundance of power has this additional advantage over all the others, in being present to all equally in the same manner without hindrance; according to this principle, then, the primary beings illuminate even the lowest levels, and the immaterial are present immaterially to the material. And let there be no astonishment if in this connection we speak of a pure and divine form of matter; for matter also issues from the father and creator of all, and thus gains its perfection, which is suitable to the reception of gods. And, at the same time nothing hinders the superior beings from being able to illuminate their inferiors, nor yet, by consequence, is matter excluded from participation in its betters, so that such of it as is perfect and pure and of good type is not unfitted to receive the gods; for since it was proper not even for terrestrial things to be utterly deprived for participation in the divine, earth also has received from it a share in divinity, such as is sufficient for it so be able to receive the gods.[21]

In other words, if the gods are pleased to inhabit the scents, sounds, and gestures of hieratic and mantic practice, this would have to be on the basis of an ineffable common measure between material particularity and the absolute, the One itself. Somewhat scandalously for Neoplatonic tradition, Iamblichus concluded that noesis is only a penultimate stage in purification and ascent to the One, and that complete intuition requires the *ekstasis* of ritual practice, theurgic rite.[22] Ultimate unity with the One, if indeed the One is All, cannot be simply noetic without being immediately theurgic.

To a certain extent, as Gregory Shaw has pointed out, in Iamblichus the viability of theurgy is even a *critique* of the powers of human reason to attain union with the divine nous.[23] In some sense the gods appear through inanimate objects and irrational souls, rather than through reason. As Iamblichus puts it, "Just as God sometimes makes an innocent fool speak words of wisdom—by which it is clear to all that the speech is not human but divine—in this same way God reveals ideas (*noemata*) that transcend all [human] knowledge through [material] things deprived of knowledge."[24] Iamblichus's thought here, which anticipates later developments in creation theology and liturgical theory, is that the One in its unutterable singularity is somehow better attested by the ineffability of matter itself, because the very singularity of material forms is redolent of the absolute.[25] Of course, for Iamblichus, this is in no sense a *given* attribute of matter, since materiality participates in divinity only when hieratic, priestly, or divinatory rites order the elemental so as to reveal the divine. But due to the appropriateness of certain times and places—beyond human origin yet forming the basis of human actions—theurgy is not the control of divinity by humans, but an activity demonstrating the profound presence of the divine at every level of existence. In this sense, theurgy is not manipulation, but revelation. From this Iamblichian motif, a new Neoplatonist emerges, one who is neither a rationalist nor an isolated contemplative, but a divining, healing, and prophesying sage—a visionary or type of hierophant, as indeed Plotinus himself was regarded by the subsequent Platonic schools.

This theurgical strand of Neoplatonism becomes appropriated, in innovative ways—and with a certain amount of outright plagiarism—by Christian theology. In the mystical and apophatic tradition Iamblichus anticipates, God gives to each being everything that it can receive, including God's "supereminent unity" (as the *singularitate* of each existent). For theology to avoid any vestige of Gnostic, Manichean, or Docetist heresy, God's unity and being cannot be "held back" from creation without the world appearing to be an incomplete or hesitant donation on God's part. However, the attempt to radicalize divine immanence while preserving transcendence is a highly paradoxical enterprise. The dilemma is that either one preserves an analogical sense of divine presence to each singular being, a sense that can never be directly identified, or one embraces the univocity of being, in which everything, as an expression of the same divine will, exists in the same sense as it does in God.

Much of philosophical modernity manifests what Cyril O'Regan calls a "Gnostic return," as thinkers from Bruno, Boehme, Hegel, and Schelling, to the "death of God" theology of the 1960s, all situate the life of God within cosmic vicissitude, fully implicating the divine nature in chaotic or even evil processes of fall and redemption over cosmic time.[26] This claim of complete immanence is precisely the heterodox and pantheist perspective that the orthodox expressionist tradition attempted to avoid. On this issue Deleuze writes that, "One must however recognize that this expressionist tendency was never fully worked through. It was encouraged by Christianity, by its theory of the Word, and above all by the ontological requirement that the first principle be a Being [rather than the abstract One]. But Christianity also repressed it, through the still more powerful requirement that the transcendence of the divine being be maintained. Thus one sees philosophers constantly threatened by the accusation of immanentism and pantheism, and constantly taking care to avoid, above all else, such an accusation" (*E*, 177). Despite the fact that, to put it mildly, the defense of orthodoxy is not Deleuze's ambition, it is nevertheless in the struggles of orthodox and heterodox thinkers such as Cusa (who was accused of heresy) and Bruno (who was openly heretical), that certain logical and conceptual innovations are made that crucially inform Deleuze's own systematic work.

The cosmological and metaphysical problem for orthodox Christian thinkers was that, if in creation the same divine being both the expressor and expressed of a world, how it is possible to avoid the unwanted consequence that God's nature might be limited to the expression of intramundane or merely encosmic possibilities? Some kind of process theology seems to loom, whereby God's essence would be seen as restricted by time, or even that God might be forced to discover God's own essence through time.[27] This would entail a limitation of divine perfection as subordinate to temporal cosmic process. Partially to avoid the potentially heretical implications of divine immanence, mystical or apophatic theology came to treat any cognitive or rationalizing apprehension as ultimately indirect, symbolic contruals of God. Nicholas of Cusa is paradigmatic here, with his attempt to construe the infinite on the basis of a symbolic or enigmatic method.[28] But already Eriugena, as Deleuze notices, uses the "resources of symbolism" to maintain the inexpressible at the heart of expression (*E*, 178). And while Deleuze does not mention them, Marsilio Ficino and his student Pico della Mirandola used the resources of the symbol to establish sympathies and analogies that express a uniquely catholic, hermetic, and syncretist philosophy. Giordano Bruno will turn the resources of symbolism, in a stridently heretical key, closer to Deleuze's own tenor, toward a "natural theology" of explicitly pagan provenance.

Nicholas of Cusa

As developed through a long series of medieval reflections, "Christ the Word" is seen as the ultimate paradigm of creation as a whole. If the world has an essential nature, that nature is bound up with its contingency. According to orthodox teaching, Christ is the ultimate manifestation of a contingently realized essence: his singular personality and unique will perfectly synthesize freedom and nature, eternal intention and spontaneous response. The life and teachings of Jesus, as eternal exemplar, form a microcosmic and immanent paradigm of expression, since Christ is the perfection of creation.[29] Meditating on the paradoxical status of Christ, in *Of Learned Ignorance* Nicholas of Cusa attempts to map the difference between God and creation beyond the abstract dualisms of the many and the One, dualisms germane to traditional Neoplatonism. For Cusa, God is in the world, and the world in God. In a complex sense, "God, therefore, is the enfolding (*complicatio*) of all in the sense that all are in God, and God is the unfolding (*explicatio*) of all in the sense that God is in all."[30] Rather than being subordinate to one another in relations of derivation and supersession, worldly entities are seen to exist as a "complication" of God, and things explicate God by revealing that which is "implied" in their various singular trajectories. Deleuze glosses Cusa: "All things are present to God, who complicates them. God is present to all things, which explicate and implicate him" (*E*, 175). Cusa uses mathematical ideas to illustrate this thesis. At the infinite, the infinite line, triangle, and sphere are identical. They remain distinct in our minds only until they reach infinity, a point at which their shapes are no longer discernible. The nature of the triangle, at the infinite, is identical with the nature of the sphere and the line. This "inherence" or "implication" of the sphere and the triangle, at the infinite, is inaccessible to reason.[31] To put this in Kantian terms, it is an identity that can be thought, but not understood. At the limit of its capacity, reason is beholden to a symbolic apprehension of ultimate reality as a *coincidentia oppositorum* of the finite and the infinite.

Thus, for Cusa, the nature of God is expressed in creation, but knowledge of the absolute as manifest in creation remains approximate—symbolic at best. Rational thought amounts to a *docta ignorantia*, a "learned ignorance" cognizant of the rift between local apprehension and ultimate dimension. What emerges from Cusa is thus a view of reason as beholden to certain symbolic ciphers. Deleuze, for somewhat different (but related) reasons, will develop a view of thought as contingent upon certain symbolic or "intensive" apprehensions, ideas that are never inherently clear, since the infinite speeds and imbricated densities of the sense of the world can never be fully clarified, but only continuously traversed (*D2*, 150). As is clear in both *Difference and Repetition* and *Proust and Signs*, Deleuze derives his theory of ideas from Cusan insights, according to which the world can never be fully revelatory of God, even though God is the real content of every idea.

Unlike for Deleuze, there is for Cusa an ultimate point of orientation for the mind, a meeting point in the maximum inherence of humanity in God: the full implication of God in humanity in the incarnation of the Second Person of the Trinity. And it is the ontological and epistemological centrality of Christ the Word that makes Cusa's system a departure from traditional Neoplatonic understandings of emanation. Deleuze describes Cusa's as a vision in which being and unity are "a co-presence of two correlative movements" that come "to be substituted for a series of successive subordinate emanations. For things remain in God no less than God remains in himself, in complicating them" (*E*, 175). There is in Cusa no transcendence of unity (the One) over being. Deleuze argues that it was precisely such a turn that led to the discovery of what are, in his system, the categories of immanence: complication, explication, inherence, and implication. These terms dominate Deleuze's own work in *Difference and Repetition*. Elaborating on Cusa, Deleuze writes,

> The presence of things to God constitutes an inherence, just as the presence of God to things constitutes an implication. An equality of being is substituted for a hierarchy of hypostases; for things are present to the same Being, which is itself present in things. Immanence corresponds to the unity of complication and explication, of inherence and implication. Things remain inherent in God who complicates them, and God remains implicated in things which explicate him. It is a complicative God who is explicated through all things: "God is the universal complication, in

the sense that everything is in him; and the universal explication, in the sense that he is in everything."[32] (E, 175)

As we will examine closely in chapter 4, Deleuze's own vision is a kind of naturalized version of Cusa's theological metaphysics. For Deleuze, thought and being find their reality in intensive magnitudes that implicate quantities and qualities (but are not reducible to their explication, as such). That is to say, following Spinoza, Deleuze will substitute a set of encosmic dynamisms (imbricated, virtual intensities) for a transcendent God.[33] We will see that Giordano Bruno, after Cusa, already makes a similar move. And like Bruno, Deleuze preserves Cusa's basic schema of expression as an absolute complicated in all things. For Deleuze, intensities (whether of color, sound, or affect) are implicated in quantities and qualities, while quantities and qualities inhere in intensities without making them completely explicit (DR, 232–34).

Prefiguring Deleuze himself as well as Spinoza, Bruno will ultimately embrace the naturalistic-cum-pantheistic possibilities of divine immanence. But for Cusa and his theological predecessors, pantheism had to be avoided. Cusa sought to avoid pantheism through his notion of God as absolute maximum. To call God absolute maximum is to attribute to God a completeness of which there is only a vestige within the universe. But this vestige is real: the universe truly reveals the nature of God, if only in a contracted sense. To avoid pantheism, Cusa argues that a real, substantial (countable) infinite cannot be "in" the universe, but can be approached only as a limit-idea: the maximum or minimum of any idea—whether a moral idea of justice, an aesthetic idea of beauty, a physical idea of center or circumference—is never found in nature, and thus there is always an asymmetry between explicated and contracted being. Cusa's famous mystical formula, God is a circle whose center is everywhere and whose circumference is nowhere, means that no matter the scale, God's being, as absolute maximum, cannot be identical with that of the universe. Physically speaking, infinite dimensions or attributes of any kind would be inherently impossible to locate, and thus while the universe really expresses God's nature, it cannot express it fully or completely.[34] Nevertheless, from reflections on the limits of our understanding, we gain a sense of God, and a sense of absolute reality. We are invited by the universe itself to conceive the inconceivable when our concepts point to a ground or coherence that is found only in the limits of applying those concepts to the universe itself. And yet this implies a quite radical immanence of God in nature: nature must truly speak of God. Thus, as Deleuze notes, in Cusa "God must be defined as identical to Nature *complicative* and Nature identical to God as *explicative*" (*E*, 176).

In this vision, what orients knowledge of the absolute, and unites the series of divine complication and cosmic explication, is the mediation of Christ as Word, the eternal wisdom of God expressed as creation. Deleuze notes that for Cusa, as for Meister Eckhart, God first expresses himself in the Word and then the Word expresses itself as creation (*E*, 176). This "trinity" constitutes expression: complication, explication, implication, where implication or inherence is modeled by the paradoxical instance of the absolute maximum in the relative maximum, the second person of the trinity in the God-Man Jesus Christ. Implication or inherence is thus the middle term between complication and explication—reality has the structure of an "implication" of the absolute in the relative term, and that of an "inherence" of the relative in the absolute. This basic logic will dominate Deleuze's systematic expositions of immanence, from *Difference and Repetition* to his late work on Leibniz, *The Fold*.

Hermeticism in the Renaissance

What was at stake in Cusa's logic of the absolute, for the subsequent history of modern philosophy? In *The Legitimacy of the Modern Age*, Hans Blumenberg argues that the real crisis that produced the modern era's obsession with epistemology was not so much the rise of experimental science in the late sixteenth century and the seventeenth, but the theological crises of the late fifteenth century through the sixteenth century, crises caused by the demise of Aristotelian cosmology and the rise of nominalism in theology. This crisis was registered forcefully in Cusa's writings, since Cusa fully admitted that there were no good grounds for viewing the earth or its inhabitants as a physical or metaphysical center of divine attention. As Blumenberg puts it,

> The indicative function of a cosmic position comes to nothing in a world in which man has become a being who regulates and centers himself in the world, or has begun to see himself as such. The question of *where*

man may find himself in a pregiven world of natural things has lost its relevance for his self-consciousness. In this context the concept of freedom as man's special independence from the determination of nature gains a new aspect. Not only is man's moral quality seen as the epitome of his capacity for self-determination, but also his self-consciousness is freed from its orientation to nature and nature's "framework of positions." . . . If the Cusan can be regarded as a forerunner of Copernicus in any respect at all, then it is surely in the fact that, for him, man's cosmological placement gives no information as to what he can credit himself with and regard as his worth.[35]

In *On Learned Ignorance,* Cusa essentially argues that since the absolute cannot be *placed* relative to the cosmos, but is "One in All," a phrase Cusa explicitly attributes to Hermes Trismegistus, "we are also unable to understand how God can manifest Himself to us through visible creation."[36] For Cusa, the visible order of cause and effect and the apparent regularities of physical systems cannot be part of any argument for God's existence, let alone an indication of his purposes, as they were in Aquinas's cosmological proofs. Cusa writes, in a passage worth quoting at length for its presentation of a problematic that dominates the thought of this era,

> [God] is not like our intellect, which is only known to Him and us; which, before coming to think, had no form, but proceeds, when thinking, to take the form of color, sound, or something else from the images in the memory; then, after taking on another form of signs, words or letters, it manifests itself to others. God does not manifest Himself in that way. Whether his purpose in creating the world was to manifest His goodness, as pious people believe, or whether, as the Infinite Necessity, He created it to do His Will and have creatures who would be obliged to obey Him, who would fear Him and who would be judged by Him, it is clear whatever His purpose may have been, that He does not assume another form, since He is the form of all forms; and it is likewise clear that He does not manifest Himself in positive signs, for these signs, if they existed, would naturally in their turn demand others in which to exist, and so on to infinity.[37]

Blumenberg argues that modern anxiety is born here, with the indiscernibility of divine purpose. That is to say, modern skepticism is born in the inscrutability of God before it emerges through Cartesian doubt about the reliability of the senses. Cusa himself avoids the issue of whether the world is to be taken as a manifestation of God's goodness or simply his power (this task would fall to Leibnizian theodicy). However, Cusa insists that, either way, there will be no basis in cosmology or in natural theology to argue for either position. Strangely enough, however, Cusa takes the fact of our inability to construe the divine purpose from the nature of nature not as a cause for despair but for a renewed appreciation for finite natures taken as enigmatic symbols:

> Every creature is, as it were, "God-created" or "finite-infinity," with the result that no creature's existence could be better than it is. It is as if the Creator had said "Let it be produced" and, because God, who is eternity itself, could not be brought into being, that was made which could most resemble God. The inference from this is that every creature, as such, is perfect, though by comparison with others it may seem imperfect. God in His infinite goodness gives being to all in the way in which each can receive it. With him there is no jealousy; He communicates being without distinction; and, since all receive being in accord with the demands of their contingent nature, every creature rests content in its own perfection, which God has freely bestowed upon it. None desires the greater perfection of any other; each loves by preference that perfection which God has given it and strives to develop and preserve it intact.[38]

Cusa's move here, Blumenberg notes, flies in the face of the traditional notion that in creating the world God did not create all that he could have and prescinded from complete self-expression.[39] The world for Cusa is a perfect divine expression, albeit a divine nature manifest *complicatio* (or in condensed fashion, in nature). The human mind, however, can conjecture its way toward ever-greater understandings of the divine as implicated in the natural, universal *complicatio*. To "learn ignorance" is to learn one's limitations. But this also implies that to learn the limits of oneself is to be all that one can be, an expression of the "implication" of divinity. Cusa writes,

> A creature is not God, nor is it nothing; it is, as it were, posterior to God and prior to nothing, or it stands between God and nothing, according to one of the sages: God is the opposite of nothing with being as the intermediary. And yet it cannot be a compound of being and non-being. It

seems, therefore, that it is neither being, for it is derived from being, nor non-being, for it is prior to nothing, nor a compound of these; and in considering these separately or conjointly, our intellect, which is unable to reconcile contradictories, does not comprehend the being of a creature, though it knows that every creature has its being from the maximum. As being *ab alio*, it is unintelligible, since the being from whom it comes is incomprehensible—just as the being of an accident is not intelligible, as long as its subject of inhesion is not understood. This creature, qua creature, therefore, cannot be called one, since it is derived from unity; it cannot be said to be more than one, since it owes its being to unity; nor can it be at once one and more than one. In virtue of its nature its unity lies in a plurality. What we have said here ought equally to be applied, it seems, to simplicity and composition and to the other contradictories.

Since the creature is created by the being of the maximum, and since in the maximum there is no difference between being, doing, and creating, then it seems that it is one and the same thing to say that God creates as to say that God is all things. If, then, creation means that God is all things, how can the creature be conceived as other than eternal, when the being of God is eternal, or better, eternity itself? No one doubts its eternity in-so-far as the creature itself is the being of God; in-so-far, therefore, as it is temporal it is not from God, for He is eternal. How reconcile a creature's being at once temporal and eternal? Necessarily the creature's existence was possible from eternity in the Being; yet it was not possible for it to exist prior to time, for before time there was no 'before'; consequently it has always been when it was possible for it to be.[40]

This vertiginous thought on the eternal coexistence of creatures with the creative will led to the accusation of pantheism, which Cusa took great pains to avoid. Whether he succeeded or not (and whether or not pantheism matters), the resonance here between Cusan anthropology and hermetic theandry is profound: in each case, to realize or activate what has always been possible for one to be is the theosis into which we are enjoined.[41] In Cusa, this amounts to an affirmation of each living creature as a singular implication of the maximum. Apprehending the divinity of all things without the framework of fixed and visible cosmic places is the new horizon Cusa opens within Renaissance philosophy. Cusa's is an hermetic horizon in the sense that a new, esoteric cartography will take over for the older Aristotelian mapping of the cosmos according to visible and stable places. This new mapping must be nomadic, in keeping with the idea that human freedom and self-consciousness are now part of a "self-fashioning" that takes over for any clear sense of being well placed among hierarchical orders of being.[42]

However, there are essentially two related but competing hermetic paths departing from the standpoint of Cusan anthropology: the eclectic Christian esotericism of Pico della Mirandola and the heretical pagan *magia* of Giordano Bruno. The new conception of human prerogative that Cusa's work proved was necessary in an infinite or unbounded cosmos is palpable in all of Pico's writing. While Pico retains Cusa's Christology, which orients human conjecture towards its primordial archetype in that *Verbum* which is the divine exemplar, Bruno asserts that a cosmos that is inherently divine has no need for a central point of reference, and that it is in the infinity of its vicissitudes that the cosmos can be known as divine. These two very different paths are both hermetic, since both view knowledge as essentially theurgic: for both Pico and for Bruno the essential nature of the cosmos is revealed in a transforming identification with the divine through intensifying our relations to cosmic dynamics. However, for Pico such creative intensification—moral, intellectual, and magical—is ultimately grounded by Christology, by the mediating exemplar of the redeeming God-Man as the prototype of homo creator.[43] By contrast, Bruno explicitly rejects Christology as in fact an inhibition to *magia naturalis* and to science.

The difference between Pico's and Bruno's appropriation of hermeticism as a mode of completing the project of Cusan expressionism is instructive in approaching Deleuze's view of thought. Deleuze situates thought between the affirmation of an unqualified intensification of immanence (which leads him close to Bruno) and a typology of specific modes of affirmation according to a selective principle, analogous to Nietzsche's ordering of types (but also leading to a relatively hierarchical thought closer to Pico's).[44] Somewhere between these two impulses, we will find in Deleuze a certain recapitulation of the Renaissance affirmation of humanity as both *homo creator* and *homo magus*, and lurking in Deleuze's thought a kind of apocalyptic humanism that, in the form of "the people to come," aspires to realize the ambitions of hermeticism by developing new modes of cooperation between humanity and cosmos, mind and matter.

Before explicating such a speculative hermeticism in Deleuze, we must first undertake a brief recapitulation of hermeticism, and linger for a moment longer on the contrast between Pico and Bruno. The major role of the *Corpus Hermeticum* in the Hellenistic era, as Garth Fowden has shown, was as a practical guide to how one might escape fate.[45] In one of the most famous and typical of his "sermons," Hermes describes to his student Asclepius how it is possible to liberate one from the powers of the fates by purification and prayers to a God, or "Father," outside the cosmic wheels. Even though Iamblichus refers deferentially to Hermes Trismegistus, the specifically philosophical significance of the *Corpus Hermeticum* only came to the fore during the Renaissance, before going underground into the various alchemical, theosophical, and kabbalistic schools. This clandestine legacy, though clearly present in Newton, Leibniz, and Hegel, was largely left to be explored by the societies of Rosicrucians, Freemasons, and later by nineteenth-century occultism, theosophy, and anthroposophy (from Martinism to the Order of the Golden Dawn). During the Renaissance, however, Hermeticism had a brief moment of public and academic respectability, and a place in official Western philosophical discourse. This was due largely to Marsilio Ficino's argument for the centrality of Hermes Trismegistus for establishing a *prisca theologia*, or "pristine theology," within which all past and present wisdom figures could be circumscribed. The establishment of this genealogy was taken to be so important that in the process of translating Plato, Ficino was ordered by the Medicis to translate the *Corpus Hermeticum* first, since the text was thought to be able to establish the universal and perennial roots of Christian doctrine. If the prisca theologia could be traced to Hermes Trismegistus, a universal wisdom tradition could be established that would derive from ancient pagan theology originating in Egypt, spreading through Persia and Chaldea to Greek philosophy and Near-Eastern wisdom traditions, and culminating in that ultimate magus, Jesus Christ.[46]

From Ficino's perspective, Hermes Trismegistus was "thrice great" because he was the greatest philosopher, priest, and king.[47] Such a claim effectively made Hermes the ideal precursor to the Renaissance ideal of humanity, and a precursor of Christ himself.[48] Because of the basic similarity between hermetic cosmology and the biblical account of creation, Ficino was led to argue that catholic theology should be consonant with the prisca theologia he believed was manifested in the *Corpus Hermeticum*. While presenting God as a transcendent creator, the *Corpus Hermeticum* also affirms the world as a true divinity, and man as a "great wonder" who can, through rites of purification, be liberated from encosmic powers (the "thirty decans" of astrological influence), and from fate.[49] This process of theandry occurs through the construction and correct usage of images and talismans, and is consummated in, among other things, effective alchemy and magic.[50] As Ficino and his student Pico embrace hermeticism, the result is a sort of Christianization of the man-as-microcosm thesis.

This was something of a break with the conception of natural knowledge of divinity as articulated in the context of medieval theology. Here, humanity belongs to a specific place in the chain of being, and the mind comprehends God primarily through reflection on the wonders of creation, the orders of reality.[51] But in the emergent post-Copernican cosmology, whose influence is already felt in Cusa, the earth and humanity are no longer at the center of concentric circles of a well-placed natural order. It was necessary, then, for the Renaissance to re-conceive knowledge of God (and of the absolute) within an acentric cosmos. If the centrality of humanity could no longer be physically grounded, connections between morality and metaphysics were no longer self-evident. But as Foucault argued in *The Order of Things*, the Renaissance view of language as a symbolic transcription of the hidden fecundity of nature (expressed in conceptual, historical, and physical "sympathies") promised to compensate for the deteriorization of Ptolemaic cosmology. As many critics have observed, Renaissance confidence in humanity is in fact a confidence in language, as such, to endlessly renew the possibility of meaning. Such confidence is not placed in the correspondence of any one proposition with one fact, but in a holistic view of meaning as situated within a total system of signs that unfold in continuity with the book of nature itself. What emerges here is what has been called an "emblematic" worldview, a perspective that takes images of nature—from mathematical diagrams to animal forms to poetic tropes—as ciphers by which to explore the as-yet-unknown.

At the end of the first chapter of *The Order of Things*, Foucault reminds us that during the Renaissance, language was viewed as capable of activating nature's inherent powers, even if signs pointed toward an inexhaustible plenitude of meaning that could never be captured in a single, finite expression. This view of language is grounded, as William B. Ashworth puts it, in an "emblematic world view," where relations between each and every entity can at least potentially come to symbolize an indefinite number of other relations in a kind of "fractal" vision of reality.[52] Language is here considered an elaboration of the fabric of nature rather than a simple representation of it.[53] Thus, the Renaissance could accept the indefinite expansion of linguistic meaning, as such, as a kind of revelation. Foucault observes that this view justified the quest for esoteric knowledge that could be found in the occult resonances of language. But this "kabbalistic" view of language also affected the character of natural history, creating the possibility of an inner or secret knowledge of nature on the basis of natural signs. As Foucault puts it,

> For [the Renaissance mind] it was very possible that before Babel, before the Flood, there had already existed a form of writing composed of the marks of nature itself, with the result that its characters would have the power to act upon things directly, to attract them or repel them, to represent their properties, their virtues, and their secrets. A primitively natural writing, of which certain forms of esoteric knowledge, and the cabala first and foremost, may perhaps have preserved the scattered memory and were now attempting to retrieve its long-dormant powers ... it was all *legenda*—things to be read. But it was not for this reason that they preferred the authority of legend to the precision of an unprejudiced eye, but that *nature*, in itself, is an unbroken tissue of words and signs, of accounts and characters, of discourse and forms.[54]

The knowledge of a peacock, for instance, would have included not only anatomical or otherwise ethological observations, but the legends, myths, historical mentions, names in all languages, associated astrological signs, and any other desiderata to which the peacock may be connected. Foucault continues,

> To know an animal or a plant, or any terrestrial thing whatever, is to gather together the whole dense layer of signs with which it may have been covered; it is to rediscover also the constellations of forms from which they derive their value as heraldic signs. Aldrovandi was neither a better nor a worse observer than Buffon; he was neither more credu-

lous than he, nor less attached to the faithfulness of the observing eye or the to the rationality of things. His observation was simply not linked to things in accordance with the same system or by the same arrangement of the *episteme*. For Aldrovandi was meticulously contemplating a nature which was, from top to bottom, written.[55]

The possibility of a unified "prose of the world" lay, for the Renaissance, in a divine (but to some extent hidden) donation of sense that manifests equally as nature and as language (as referent and as sense). Through Kabbalah and other combinatorial magics, through astrology, the redolent wisdom of ancient texts, and through the construction of symbols, talismans, and emblems, Renaissance thinkers believed in the possibility of indexing the universal sympathies uniting the world with itself. This indexical enterprise was a practice of continuous interpretation. But skepticism had as yet no place: even if accessing an infinity of meaning and implication the nature of discourse itself posed no inherent problem—meaning was being. As Foucault puts it,

> Perhaps for the first time in Western culture, we find revealed [in the Renaissance] the absolutely open dimension of a language no longer able to halt itself, because, never being enclosed in a definitive statement, it can express its truth only in some future discourse and is wholly intent on what it will have said; but even this future discourse itself does not have the power to halt the progression, and what it says is enclosed within it like a promise, a bequest to yet another discourse . . . The task of commentary can never, by definition, be completed. And yet commentary is directed entirely towards the enigmatic, murmured element of the language being commented upon: it calls into being, below the existing discourse, another discourse that is more fundamental and, as it were, "more primal," which it sets itself the task of restoring.[56]

The comprehension of this more primal sense of being, which for Foucault returns to Western culture only in the modern era with the rise of experimental usages of language in poetry and the modern novel, is directly linked, in the Renaissance, to the task of "Natural Magic," since here the "fundamental configuration of knowledge consisted of the reciprocal cross-reference of signs and similitudes. The form of magic was inherent in this way of knowing."[57] Deleuze's aesthetics in some sense unites the modern impulse toward experimentation with the Renaissance dream of magia naturalis, since Deleuze will affirm over and over that the peculiar renewal of "belief in the world" effected by some contemporary artists is a renewal and transformation of life itself. In this way Deleuze offered the twentieth century not so much an antihumanism as an eschatological vision of humanity beyond any simple divide between nature and culture, being and meaning, bodies and sense. Two Renaissance precursors, Pico della Mirandola and Giordano Bruno, anticipate in outline Deleuze's own vision.

The Magic Christian: Pico della Mirandola

According to esoteric Jewish teachings, the body of the godhead, *shekinah*, is fragmented, lost among the evils of a fallen world. But the development of human knowledge and creativity is, in this view, the redemptive work of humanity and the restoration of the godhead itself.[58] Pico della Mirandola (1463–1494) had the privilege of access both to the Medici trove of manuscripts and to the teaching of Spanish kabbalists exiled in Italy. Inspired by both Hermeticism and Kabbalah, Pico defined *magia* as the attempt to "marry the worlds," to rejoin heaven to earth.[59] The brilliant protégé of Marsilio Ficino, Pico worked in multiple languages and is said to have assimilated every document the Florentine Academy could expose to him, from philosophy and theology to the *Corpus Hermeticum*. Pico was also able to study esoteric Judaism with Spanish exiles, which led to a life-long devotion to Kabbalah. Pico once argued that, along with the miracles recorded in the Gospels, Kabbalah constituted the greatest confirmation of the divinity of Christ.[60] Pico was so extraordinarily ambitious that he proposed to defend, before the assembled theologians of the world, a synthetic philosophy of 900 points integrating Christianity, Judaism, Islam, and the pagan traditions in one vast synoptic vision. At the time, he was twenty-five years old.

Pope Innocent's censors condemned 13 of the 900 points as potential heresies, and Pico's defense never took place. Mortified, Pico fled Italy and spent the rest of his life in a series of despondent attempts to rework his original vision. In his mistitled *Oration on the Dignity of Man*, which was to be the opening speech at the debate (one of Pico's letters indicates it should have been called "Oration in Praise of Philosophy"), Pico imagines a humanity created without place, "superfluous" to the cosmic orders. Recapitulating the style in which Hermes addresses his adept in the *Asclepius* sermons, Pico imagines God to have said,

> "We have given to thee, Adam, no fixed seat, no form of thy very own, no gift peculiarly thine, that thou mayest feel as thine own, have as thine own, possess as thine own the seat, the form, the gifts which thou thyself shalt desire. A limited nature in other creatures is confined within the laws written down by Us. In conformity with thy free judgment, in whose hands I have placed thee, thou art confined by no bounds; and thou wilt fix limits of nature for thyself. I have placed thee at the center of the world, that from there thou mayest more conveniently look around and see whatsoever is in the world. Neither heavenly nor earthly, neither mortal nor immortal have We made thee. Thou like a judge appointed for being honorable, art the molder and maker of thyself; thou mayest sculpt thyself into whatever shape thou dost prefer. Thou canst grow downward into the lower natures which are brutes. Thou canst again grow upwards from thy soul's reason in the higher natures which are divine."[61]

For Pico, because humanity has no eternal exemplar, no substantial form, and no fixed essence, traditional attempts to account for the uniqueness of the human person and the prerogative of human freedom were insufficient. Paradoxically, for Pico, although human action cannot go beyond the range of cosmic potentials (from angelic to mineral), neither can humanity be identified with any discrete set or subset of these potentials—it is not enough to say, for example, that humans are rational animals. Humanity has a capacity to transform and transmute its very essence. However, Pico's thought is not yet that modern voluntarism that will connect the liberation of the will to the celebration of the arbitrary fiat. Rather, in Pico there is a paradoxical identification of the human will with a motility internal to the range of cosmic dynamics, in keeping with Augustinian conceptions of the will as more or less active or realized relative to its objects.[62] The divine prerogative to remake oneself is also a mandate to "marry the world" though good works, especially through authentic theurgy and magic. Pico writes, at a later stage of the *Oration*,

> I have also proposed certain theses concerning magic, in which I have indicated that magic has two forms. One consists wholly in the opera-

tions and powers of demons, and consequently this appears to me, as God is my witness, an execrable and monstrous thing. The other proves, when thoroughly investigated, to be nothing else but the highest realization of natural philosophy. The Greeks noted both these forms. However, because they considered the first form wholly undeserving the name magic they called it *goeteia*, reserving the term *mageia*, to the second, and understanding by it the highest and most perfect wisdom. The term "magus" in the Persian tongue, according to Porphyry, means the same as "interpreter" and "worshipper of the divine" in our language. Moreover, Fathers, the disparity and dissimilarity between these arts is the greatest that can be imagined. Not the Christian religion alone, but all legal codes and every well-governed commonwealth execrates and condemns the first; the second, by contrast, is approved and embraced by all wise men and by all peoples solicitous of heavenly and divine things. The first is the most deceitful of arts; the second, a higher and holier philosophy. The former is vain and disappointing; the later, firm, solid and satisfying. The practitioner of the first always tries to conceal his addiction, because it always rebounds to shame and reproach, while the cultivation of the second, both in antiquity and at almost all periods, has been the source of the highest renown and glory in the field of learning . . . his beneficent magic, in calling forth, as it were, from their hiding places into the light the powers which the largess of God has sown and planted in the world, does not itself work miracles, so much as sedulously serve nature as she works her wonders. Scrutinizing, with greater penetration, that harmony of the universe which the Greeks with greater aptness of terms called *sympatheia* and grasping the mutual affinity of things, she applies to each thing those inducements (called the *iugges* of the magicians), most suited to its nature. Thus it draws forth into public notice the miracles which lie hidden in the recesses of the world, in the womb of nature, in the storehouses and secret vaults of God, as though she herself were their artificer. As the farmer weds his elms to the vines, so the "magus" unites earth to heaven, that is, the lower orders to the endowments and powers of the higher.[63]

For Pico, the created world, though fallen, can be restored through knowledge of its true forms. This secret knowledge is available through processes first espied by the Egyptian sorcerers and the Chaldean oracles, transmitted to the West through Plato and the *Corpus Her-*

meticum, preserved in Jewish Kabbalah, experimented upon in Arabic and medieval alchemy, and sanctified in the Christianized taxonomy of spirits undertaken by Pseudo-Dionysius in *The Divine Names*.[64] Pico himself used gematria (kabbalist number magic) in his *Heptaplus* to recombine the letters of the first words of Hebrew scriptures so as to reveal the presence of an encosmic, theandric Christ. Corresponding Hebrew to Latin letters and recombining them, "In the beginning God created the heavens and the earth" reveals its true sense: "the Father, in the Son and through the Son, the beginning and end or rest, created the head, the fire, and the foundation of the great man with a good pact."[65] What Pico sees in Genesis is not only trinitarian and christological, but a revelation of the world as Adam Kadmon, the universe as "the great man," or a single body of which all the parts of the universe form its members, a notion connected to Indian theosophy as well as Jewish mysticism.[66]

Hans Blumenberg contends that Pico's sentiment, emergent in Cusa and taken to heretical extremes in Bruno, is in some ways more traumatic for Christian civilization and more defining for modernity than the rise of empirical science.[67] A concept of freedom emerges in Pico that is not yet the Prometheanism it would become for later moderns, but an injunction to humanity to cooperate with the divine. Contrary to what one might expect, this is not exactly a humanism. For Pico, *homo magus* is both more and less than human(ist): if *magia naturalis* is the paradigmatic human activity, this is because humanity is not a fixed essence but a mediator, a liminal space between the animal and the angelic, the elemental and the astral, earth and heaven. The human essence is constituted not by fixed proportions or through clear analogies, but by an open series of sympathies and affinities that must be continuously reconstructed through a creative elaboration of signs and similitudes.

Although Pico, in his later works, denied any causal power to astrological omens, he maintained a mystical and esoteric use of Kabbalah as a divinatory technique of interpretation.[68] But there was already evidence in both the Christian Pseudo-Dionysius and in the *Corpus Hermeticum* that some forms of practical and ritual magic (especially theurgy) could be reconciled with Christian dogma.[69] Such is the reconciliation between Christology and *magia* that inspired Pico, as well as Ficino.

Pico added to Ficino's rather staid Orphism a practical Kabbalah, which gave the magus a more active relationship with the angelic world (Ficino's was ultimately a system of contemplation, not of magical action or transformation, although he seems to have experimented with, and not only theorized, a system of musical magic).[70] Pico defined (and was prepared to defend) natural magic (beyond that used purely for contemplative ascent) in the following ways:

> Given any practical object, the operation that acts on it (*quae eum practicat*) is nobler than that which contemplates it [thesis 3:46].
> No power exists in heaven or earth seminally and separated that the magician cannot actuate and unite [thesis 9:5].
> The form of all magical power comes from the soul of man standing, and not falling [thesis 9:12].
> If there is any nature immediate to us that is either simply rational, or at least exists for the most part rationally, it has magic in its summit, and through its participation in men can be more perfect [thesis 9:14].
> To operate magic is nothing other than to marry the world [thesis 9:13].[71]

Pico's philosophical goal in defending magic was to create a more meaningful connection between theology and natural philosophy than could be conceived by mere scholasticism. He in fact thought that this connection was the key to reconciling various wisdom traditions with Christianity, and that certain healing and divining magics would be the logical and glorious outcome of the synthesis of all philosophies in one system. Pico thus went far beyond Ficino in reviving the hermetic figure of *homo magus*, the idea of a human "operator" who is able, through moral purity and mental acumen, to ascend through levels of natural, mathematical, and finally divine orders, before reaching parity with divine *mens* and becoming a cocreator with God.

For Pico, inherent natural sympathies—the "knowledge things have of each other"—are effective within a divine economy of exchange wherein the lower (i.e., animal) is disposed to receive what the higher (i.e., human) gives, just as the higher in turn receives from the lower, on which the higher depends. Central here was the notion of Christ as incarnate Word, but with the added twist that *Christos Redemptor* is now *Christos Magus*. Just as for Cusa, the Word incarnate forms the axial or nodal point of the intracosmic and extracosmic Maximum. For Pico, Christ fully realizes the possibilities of magia in his own miraculous life, now nonidentically repeated in the faithful lives of his followers. The practice of magic is thus a process of spiritual ascent and descent "on" the hierarchies, and this analogical, hierarchical order legitimates the link between natural philosophy and theology, making possible a marrying of earth and heaven. But Pico's vision of concord did not succeed, and in a certain way the church's subsequent rejection of Giordano Bruno's more radical, divisive, and renegade hermeticism can be read as an effect of Pico's own inability to marry the church and the prisca theologia.

Magis Laboratae Theologiae Doctor: Giordano Bruno

In a move that anticipates Deleuze's own perspective, Giordano Bruno (1548–1600) breaks completely with the Christology of Cusa and Pico, and substitutes the vicissitudes of the "infinite universe and worlds" for the *pleroma* of the Second Person.[72] Bruno was burned as a heretic in 1600. In the record of his trial, *The Expulsion of the Triumphant Beast* was the only text mentioned by name. A diatribe against the moral and political corruption of his day, the *Expulsion* is a satirical allegory in which Jove calls together the pagan pantheon in order to make some long-overdue reforms. What Jove orders is a cleansing or "expulsion" of unseemly, indecorous, or otherwise immoral aspects of the gods' past and present lives.[73] One by one, Jove examines the natures of the constellations—Orion, the Pleiades, Scorpio, Cancer, and so on—and asks the assembled company of the gods to either conserve the positive or expunge the negative attributes associated with the constellations' mythical and legendary past.

The treatment of two constellations, Orion and the centaur Chiron, contain thinly veiled references to Christ, and the manner in which these are treated demonstrates the essence of Bruno's disdain for orthodox Christianity, particularly for orthodox theologies of God's incarnation in Christ. The *Expulsion* is also a measure of Bruno's distance from the piety of Pico della Mirandola. To deal with Orion, the trickster Momus proposes a gesture that wise Minerva ironically agrees to. The gods decide to send Orion to the human race as a teacher. Orion can perform miracles such as walking "over the waves of the sea without sinking, without wetting his feet," and his impressive talents will reveal to humans everything Jove intends them to know.[74] Tongue only partially in cheek, Minerva announces Orion's display of power will effectively show that "the human intellect, through which [human beings] seem to see best, is blindness, and that that which according to reason seems excellent, good, and very good, is vile, criminal, and extremely bad." Minerva continues, "I want them to understand that Nature is a whorish prostitute, that natural law is ribaldry, that Nature and Divinity cannot concur in one and the same good end, and that the justice of the one is not subordinate to the justice of the other, but that they [Nature and Divinity] are contraries, as are shadows and light."[75] This is Bruno's thinly veiled objection to Christianity's veneration of the miracles of Christ, which leads to contempt for Nature. Since God can suspend natural law at any moment, what is the use of the study of nature for a person of faith?

Most devastatingly, Orion's miracles will convince the world that "philosophy, all contemplation, and all magic that could make them similar [the gods] are nothing but follies, that every heroic act is only cowardice, and that ignorance is the best science in the world because it is acquired without labor and does not cause the mind to be affected by melancholy."[76] Momus insinuates that the cultivation of the Cusan "learned ignorance" will cause, among other things, the devaluation of any philosophy other than the scholastic Judeo-Hellenic synthesis of Christian theology. Finally, the effect of Christ's miracles will be that the gods themselves will be dismissed as "chimeras and fantasies," as indeed they were by St. Augustine and the early fathers.[77]

Bruno's attack on Christology is deep and pointed. In the *Expulsion*, Chiron the centaur is rejected as a parody of the hypostasis of two natures, human and divine. Speaking of the horse-man, Momus claims not to be able to appreciate such a combination of human and beast as anything more than a degraded beast or a debased human:

> And Momus said: "Now what do we wish to do with this man inserted into a beast, or this beast inserted into a man, in which one person is made of two natures and two substances concur in one hypostatic union? Here two things come into union to make a third entity; and of this there is no doubt whatsoever. But the difficulty lies, namely, in deciding whether such a third entity produces something better than the one and the other, or better than one of the two parts, or truly something baser. I mean, if the human being has been joined to equine being, is

there produced a divinity worthy of the celestial seat, or rather a beast worthy of being put into a flock and a stall? Finally (no matter how many times Isis, Jove, and others may have remarked on the excellence of being a beast and said that for man to be divine it is fitting that he have of the beast, and that when he yearns to show himself deeply divine, he makes up his mind to let himself be seen in such measure as a beast), I can never believe that where there is not a whole and perfect man or a perfect and whole beast, but a piece of beast with a piece of man, there could be anything better than where there is a piece of breeches with a piece of coat, whence there is derived a garment better than a coat or breeches, or even one as good as the latter or the former."[78]

If the treatment of Orion expresses Bruno's indignation at the way traditional orthodoxy's elevation of Christ's uniqueness led to the degradation of wisdom, philosophy, and magic, then the gods' treatment of the centaur expresses Bruno's profound distaste for the notion of Christ as the hypostasis of two natures. Bruno here deliberately distorts the orthodox statement of the nature of Christ: two natures in one hypostasis, without confusion. But Bruno's specious presentation of the doctrine is no simple rejection of theology. The reasoning behind Bruno's objection to the notion of a God incarnate in the man Jesus is not that it overly elevates the position of the human, but that it arbitrarily degrades the entirety of the rest of the cosmos, including the beasts. Bruno's naturalistic ambition is to be able to affirm the world itself as the object of an affirmation theology reserves for Christ. For Bruno the world itself is divine. This is why, parenthetically, Momus mentions that Isis, Jove, and other gods have all affirmed that it is fitting that when a man wants to show himself deeply divine, he appears as a beast.

Bruno's objection to the incarnation is that the moral and ontological exemplarity of Christ militates against the imagination of a genuine infinity of divine apparitions. For Bruno, Christo-centrism distorts the nature of the world by restricting the range of what can be potentially valuable, powerful, or true to a particular image of mediation. Bruno's alternative, his "more difficult theology," is a kind of hermetic naturalism, in which nature itself is conceived as a fully immanent divinity, *mater materia*.[79] This view is not so much against incarnationalism as it is for a kind of radically plural "animist" incarnationalism, a panoply of natural spirits rather than a central human figure. Bruno's is a faith in something we might call a feral Christ, a Christ that is a cosmic Christ and not the storied Christ of the Gospels.[80]

The notion that, when it comes to transformative practice, it is more spiritually profound and philosophically decisive to look to the animals, or to look to an immanence luring us toward animality, has a long history, and has been profoundly disturbing to any orthodoxy that posits the dignity of the human essence as a primary manifestation of, or at least central analogy with, the divine essence. Giorgio Agamben, however, has recently discovered that in a certain thirteenth-century Hebrew bible kept in the Ambrosian Library in Milan, there is an illustration of the elect in glory feasting on the bodies of the Leviathan and the Behemoth, but with a strange detail. The saints in glory have the heads of animals.[81] From an orthodox perspective, this illumination is a picture of the eschaton, in which the reconciliation of creation with itself is promised—beast with beast and beast with human essence. At the end of time can we safely envisage ourselves as fully "contaminated" by our animality. But the challenge of Bruno, like that of Bataille, Nietzsche, and Deleuze, is the challenge of conceptualizing an *immanent* sense of such a theriomorphic eschaton. It is a challenge to think divine animality as a dimension not of the hereafter but of the here and now. What exactly is this ferality that for so many rogues and heretics corresponds to belief in this world?

In *A Thousand Plateaus*, Deleuze and Guattari envisage animal faith as a form of *sorcery*, an operative capacity attendant on the powers of the psychic mutation and physical rarefaction of which sorcerers are known to be capable.[82] Deleuze and Guattari's argument, in line with Bruno's affirmation of magia, is that sorcery is not an outlying phenomenon, but a model of what all human life might be, beyond the entrapments of the traditional human essence. For Deleuze, sorcerers are able to disorganize the body creatively to avoid the confines of the human organism, confines Deleuze explicitly equates, following Antonin Artaud, to the "judgments of God" (*ATP*, 150).[83] Like Deleuze, Bruno holds that genuine thought and action involve a decisive break with the human condition. It is ultimately the antiexperimental character of Christology that Bruno disdains, insofar as it has been used by ecclesiastical authority to keep humanity enchained to sterile tradition and rote repetition.

Bruno was apparently so disturbed by the consequences of faith in Christ (as he understood it) that, in the *Expulsion*, he insinuates that the inability of modern civilization to firmly establish itself against barbarism was an effect of the doctrine of incarnation, with its elevation of "holy asininity" or "learned ignorance" to the epistemological throne of grace. Perhaps from our perspective, 400 years of colonialism, imperialism, and "nation building" later, we can only view Minerva's alternative to "the folly of the cross," which she calls "Industry, Military Training, and Military Art," with grim irony. The secular age has not lived up to Bruno's expectations. Indeed, the substitution of nation-state for church has not been the improvement Bruno hoped it would be, as evidenced by current attempts to rethink secularism without its complicity in the debacles of colonialism and capitalism.[84] But the fracture that would divorce modern political economy, founded on abstract reason, from anything resembling the wisdom of natural philosophy, contemplation, and magic was not yet, in Bruno's era, a clear fault line. Bruno, like Pico before him and Tommaso Campanella after him, maintained a utopian hope in the possibility of political and religious authority structures that would be grounded in a complex vision of rationality encompassing the best of both an informed faith and a magical reason—a more difficult but profoundly utopian theological politics.

In opposition to Pico, Bruno developed a view of magical sympathies that set the possibility of personal, social, and cosmic transformation neither in the intermediate status of humanity nor in the central mediating role of Christ, but in the fecundity of matter itself: "Forms do not exist without matter, in which they are generated and corrupted, and out of whose bosom they spring and into which they are taken back. Hence, matter, which always remains fecund and the same, must have as the fundamental prerogative of being the only substantial principle; as that which is, and forever remains, and the forms together are to be taken merely as varied dispositions of matter, which come and go, cease and renew themselves, so that none have value as principle."[85] In essence Bruno is claiming here that form, as a principle of the actual, is insubstantial by contrast with the fecundity of matter. Bruno here anticipates Deleuze's own teaching, according to which actual quantities and qualities merely explicate what is implicit in intensive quantities. Extensions and qualities are subordinate to the intensive series of singularities whose existence they incarnate (*DR*, 247). In one passage (among many) that seem to be an elaboration of a vision Bruno only partially realized, Deleuze writes that "qualities and extensities, forms and matters, species and parts are not primary; they are imprisoned in individuals as though in a crystal. Moreover, the entire world may be read, as though in a crystal ball, in the moving depths of individuating differences or differences in intensity" (*DR*, 247). For Deleuze, as for Bruno, there is an intensive continuum that, while subject to the contingencies of physical, chemical, geological, and historical change, forms the "differentials," or ideal relations, to which all such change attests.

Deleuze sees the alternations, bifurcations, and imbrications of material transformation in terms of series of virtual or ideal relations that are incarnate in such changes, effected by them, but irreducible to spatiotemporal locations. It often seems as if Bruno is attempting, with his theory of the superiority of matter to form, to conceive of what Deleuze will theorize in terms of the explication of intensive quantities in the extensive.[86] Bruno continues,

> This is why we find philosophers who, having pondered thoroughly the essence of natural forms, such as one may see in Aristotle and his kind, have finally concluded that they are only accidents and peculiarities of matter, so that, according to them, it is to matter that we must accord the privilege of being act and perfection, and not to the things of which we can truly say that they are neither substance nor nature, but relative to the substance and nature—that is to say, in their opinion, matter, which for them is a necessary, eternal and divine principle, as it is to Avicebron, the Moor, who calls it "God who is in everything."[87]

Bruno's claim here, which is in some respects an anticipation of Deleuze's thought, is that discrete, actual composites of matter and form should not be conceived of as real individuals. It is matter itself that is "act and perfection." For Bruno, individuation takes place within an infinite universe and on the basis of an infinitely fecund matter, one that functions as what Deleuze will call an intensive *spatium* or virtual depth (*DR*, 246).[88]

Bruno's view is an attempt to revise the Aristotelian doctrine of substance. In Aristotle's theory of individuation, what makes up a corporeal (sublunary) individual is a particular unity of matter and form. Form is that by virtue of which an individual (primary substance) is known as the individual it is, and is known to belong to a species (secondary substance). Individual horses are members of the species by virtue of the presence of the form of horse in particular matter. Yet for Aristotle, matter does not in any unproblematic sense exist without form. Every discernible individual is always already a matter-form composite. This is so much so that matter by itself is an almost-nothing, *prope nihil*. Yet Aristotle also claims that matter is a principle of individuation, or that in virtue of which one horse is different from another.[89] How can this be, since for Aristotle matter is passive, the receiver of form, and all knowledge is knowledge of form? Matter cannot be comprehended except through a kind of extreme abstraction. The specific difference matter makes can only be dimly espied through the interstices of analogical relations that distinguish proximate individuals (matter-form composites). The differences the material cause makes can only be discovered by comparison, and never known in themselves.

But Bruno contends that Aristotle's doctrine of form is incoherent. Individual substances are subject to decay, destruction, and death. To this extent, individual substances are not self-subsistent entities. Individuals pass into and out of existence. Recognizing this problem, Aristotle had distinguished between primary substances, such as individual horses or oak trees, and secondary substances, the class or species to which horses and trees belong. Aristotle did this in order to account for the fact that particular entities appear and disappear while the form individuals take continues to exist. Bruno argues that Aristotle cannot coherently call primary substances "substances," because according to the *Categories* substance is the opposite of accident, and all particular individuals have accidental properties (location in space, skin color, hitches in their gaits).[90] Insofar as matter represents the accidental aspects of an individual, individual substance is likewise accidental. If a form is "impugned" by accidental properties, then in some sense the forms (of species) cannot be eternal. What is the warrant for thinking of forms as essences of eternal species, given that all substantial individuals perish?

Aristotle argued that to account for knowledge it is necessary to suppose the existence of forms that can be abstracted from matter. It is precisely this idea of knowledge as abstraction that Bruno sought to overcome. Early in his career, Bruno had abandoned Aristotle's doctrine of substance for a Democritean or Epicurean atomism that held that form is a mere effluence or accidental disposition of matter. But Bruno rejected this line of thought in *Cause, Principle, and Unity*, when he concluded that matter could not individuate itself, which in his earlier view it would have to do.[91] Bruno's mature view of individuation is of a "double contraction," involving two types of substance: form, which is the power to make, and matter, which is the power to be made. For Bruno both of these principles represent eternal potentials. By form Bruno means the "world soul" in its primary manifestation as "mind." The world soul is the universal principle, immanent to the universe itself, by virtue of which individuals are endowed with form. Yet the world soul itself is not limited by the entities that are individuated on the basis of its principle. Bruno thus has a conception of primary substances that involves no accident, since the forms of individuals are a perpetual donation from a world soul that, while fully immanent to and animating individuals, nevertheless remains unaffected by their generation and destruction. Whether or not it is ultimately coherent (or more coherent than Aristotle's view), this notion of world soul has much in common with Deleuze's conception of virtual intensive quantities that govern individuation by implicative and serial complication, and are irreducible to actual transformations.

For Bruno, individual entities are generated, transformed, and perish within the world soul, but the world soul is not itself generated, transformed, or in danger of extinction. In this way, the world soul in Bruno might seem to be a disguised return to Aristotle's notion of secondary substances. But secondary substances (such as the species horse) exist for Aristotle only in an analogical sense as compared with the primary substance, the actual matter-form composite that is an individual horse. For Bruno, the world soul does not contract into a finite individual, but is an infinite principle contracted "in infinite matter." The world soul manifests as perishing individuals, but does not perish. In this way the Aristotelian secondary substance, whose eternal or stable nature derives from an abstract character is reconceived by Bruno as the real expressive power of a world soul identified with a perpetual process of individuation.

In this sense, Bruno thinks of the world soul as the immanent cause of the existence of the universe, the formal principle of universal substance, a cause fully immanent to its effects. As Leo Catana points out, for Bruno, as for Spinoza, "God" should not be conceived as the first cause or the transcendent principle of the universe, but as the infinite, animate universe itself.[92] "God" is simply the name of the one infinite reality composed of world soul and matter (what Deleuze, following Bergson, refers to as the Open Whole or One-All).[93] In this view, it is no longer necessary to conceive of God as incorporeal. For Bruno, the infinite universe itself is the sole substantial individual, a material and infinitely reshaping power. Matter in this view is not nonbeing, but is in form the way a point is in a line, not as cause but as "beginning" or "principle." In this way Bruno calls matter "divine." Matter gives being to form as an eternal principle of composition.[94]

However, Bruno also imputes individuating power to the world soul. This view might seem inconsistent, since Bruno calls matter the power to be formed and the World Soul the power to form, such that one must be active and the other passive.[95] Yet Bruno insists that both powers are active and contribute equally to individuation: the World Soul as first cause, and matter as perpetual beginning or immanent principle of form, like the way matter and form always emerge as coimplicated in the composition of music. The World Soul contains an indefinite variety of possible forms, but it is due to the power of matter that certain forms attain a determined existence. That is to say, a temporary individual "unity" is due to the infinite power of *mater materia* to unify or hold form in existence.

Thus Bruno describes individuals in the universe as "contractions" of matter and the World Soul. As Dicsono, the pedant character in *Cause, Principle, and Unity* puts it, "this form [World Soul] is defined and determined by matter, since, on the one hand, possessing in itself the faculty of constituting the particulars of innumerable species, it happens to restrict itself in order to constitute an individual, and, on the other hand, the potency of indeterminate matter, which can receive any form whatsoever, finds itself limited to a single species. Thus, one is the cause of the definition and determination of the other."[96]

It might seem that despite the acknowledgment of the world soul's drive toward manifestation, matter nevertheless takes all the initiative. This is a controversial issue in interpretation. Graham Harman, for instance, argues that effectively the principle of form plays no significant role in Bruno's theory of individuation.[97] A more generous view is voiced by Leo Catana. As Catana understands it, in Bruno there is a dialectical relationship between matter and the world soul. The world soul actively restricts or contracts indeterminate matter to a species, but matter likewise defines and determines the world soul. Matter and the world soul are thus codetermining principles. The world soul contains an infinite number of possible species (rather than the finite and limited set figured in Aristotelian secondary substances), but matter makes those species forms emerge through its powers of differentiation. This is why Bruno determines that individuation involves a *duplex contractio* (double contraction) of matter and the world soul. Matter accounts for the concrete differences of various individuals, because its *conditione* (complexion) is a principle of determination. The world soul, which is the formal principle, can be contracted in matter to the extent that certain materials have the capacity to receive certain forms. Thus, in contrast to Aristotle, Bruno does not believe matter receives its life from form. Form is not the only principle of the individual; soul is not the only life of the body. Rather, an individual is alive because a form of the world soul has been contracted by matter. Matter is thus alive, and the entire universe is animated. All things are living in a univocal sense, and there is no longer a hierarchy of rational, animal, sensate, and insensate forms of being. Humans are not distinguished by their rational capacities but by the particular kinds of bodies they have—the particular matter which has attracted and contracted the World Soul.

Mater Materia and the Frenzy of Immanence

Part of what distinguishes Bruno as an especially important "dark precursor" to Deleuze is the real connection Bruno establishes between the mind's ability to apprehend the cosmos, and the necessity for that apprehension of certain intensely contracted states of affect. For Bruno, a kind of affective vertigo is inseparable from knowledge of nature, in a way that is similar to Deleuze's affirmation of the artist as a "cosmic artisan" in touch with profound cosmic dynamics through an extraordinary sensitivity to the unknown in nature and affect (*ATP*, 342). In *The Heroic Frenzies*, Bruno appropriates the tradition of Petrarchan love poetry to outline the contours of how, through forms of intense mental contraction, a thinker can become deeply enfolded in matter itself.[98] His argument is that the poetic motion repeats that "contraction" in which matter and the World Soul intensely conjoin to form those atomistic "minima" that constitute the infinite worlds. In this sense, as Catana argues, Bruno's is a traditionally Neoplatonic view of mind as participant. However, for Bruno the consummation of mind (nous) is not a contemplative elevation to the One but a descent or diving into a kind of archetypal, inner world.[99] Bruno held that a certain movement of "contraction" was common both to the ontological process by which the One becomes many in the sensible world, and to the noetic process by which mind moves from the many to the One of truth itself. Contraction is thus movement along the esoteric "Golden Chain" of being, an idea that has its origins in Homer, but that in Neoplatonism represents the hierarchically intercalated bonds along which the higher levels are understood as the causes of the lower levels (the highest activity of one order epitomized in the lowest activity of the order directly above it).

According to Plotinus, it is possible to ascend to the Ideas (the Platonic Forms) by moving up the chain. Bruno seems to ignore, if not to outright reject, traditional notions of how to move on the chain, including the contemplative prayer advocated by Pseudo-Dionysus, Aquinas, Cusa, and Ficino. Bruno in fact uses the Golden Chain as a memory system that might indicate how to link items of knowledge horizontally (providing a kind of Renaissance precursor to the internet). The ambiguity between natural and supernatural usages of mind in Bruno is a constant point of tension in the scholarly literature. Rita Sturlese attempts to refute Frances Yates's theory that mnemonic images were taken by Bruno to correspond to occult astrological powers, since Bruno himself calls the signs conventional.[100] But others have argued that the notion of "convention" in Bruno nevertheless has an operative potential to transform self and world that cannot be called natural in any reductive sense. As Leo Catana puts it, this is because Bruno has a Neoplatonic, noninstrumental conception of memory as a recollection of unconscious sense experience. For Bruno, Catana argues, "Memory does not depend solely on sense data, but also entails that the structure of reality is somehow present in human memory, albeit not necessarily contemplated actively . . . Memory's experimentation, even with 'arbitrary signs,' as Sturlese calls them, may open up contemplation of an ontological structure which, although subjectively discovered, has an independent and objective existence. Such an interpretation would make Bruno's claim of a unified nature of descent and noetic ascent comprehensible."[101]

For Bruno, as much as for Deleuze, there is an objectively problematic aspect of memory, one we become aware of, at least initially, in emotionally intense "contractions" that form the seeds of superior insight. We could say with Deleuze that for Bruno certain intensities, whether of memory or sensation, lure us further and further into the depths of nature, until the maker becomes unmade and remade, the hunter, the hunted, the knower, the known. Bruno writes of such ecstatic and deeply vertiginous states:

> I say very few are the Acteons to whom destiny gives the power to contemplate Diana naked, and the power to become so enamored of the beautiful harmony of the body of nature, so fallen beneath the gaze of those two lights of the dual splendor of goodness and beauty, that they are transformed into deer, inasmuch as they are no longer the hunters but the hunted. For the ultimate and last end of this chase is the capture of a fugitive and wild prey, through which the hunter becomes the hunted, the pillager becomes the pillaged. Because in all the other species of the chase undertaken for particular things, it is the hunter who seeks to capture those things for himself, absorbing them through the mouth of this particular intelligence; but in that divine and universal chase he comes to apprehend that it is himself who necessarily remains captured, absorbed, and united.[102]

Bruno's search for a kind of mannerist connection between mind and world, a link between subject and object through sensible and memorial intensities, is a profound precursor to Deleuze's philosophy of immanence. In Deleuzian terms, the inchoate depths of Bruno's atoms become the imperceptible intensive spatium, the proliferating virtual field of problems explicated in actual extensions, quantities, and qualities.

But how exactly, according to Bruno, does matter contract form? Bruno develops his notion of matter from Plotinus. Plotinus had distinguished between two kinds of matter: corporeal and intelligible.[103] Corporeal matter for Plotinus is privation and a kind of nonbeing, a source of weakness and vice in the soul that must be avoided so as to make the soul virtuous and perfect. Intelligible matter, however, can be shaped by higher entities and the One. It is a principle of indeterminacy, but it is not condemned as evil because it is that which receives the influence of the One. Following Avicebron and David of Dinant, Bruno deliberately elides Plotinus's two senses of matter, calling matter itself a potency to contract into either corporeal or incorporeal entities.[104] For Bruno, incorporeal entities are the actualization of a single potentiality and therefore do not change; corporeal entities change over time, in a process of individuation involving the world soul. But both actualizations are in the same infinite matter. Matter as such thus takes on the aspect Plotinus reserved for intelligible matter alone: many forms in an undifferentiated unity.[105] Because Bruno denies Aristotle's division of the sublunary and superlunary spheres, he assigns corporeality to everything in the infinity of universes and worlds. The individuating power of matter thus operates at every level; individuation is the power of corporeal matter to contract form.

This position has obvious theological ramifications. Contraction is a concept Bruno inherits in part from Cusa's notion that the universe is a *complicatio* of God's infinite essence. Cusa thinks the divine essence, *explicatio*, would be an actual infinity and a coincidence of contraries. For Cusa, only in God could all potentials be actualized simultaneously. If God is unlimited, then God's essence must combine predicates that limited or finite beings cannot manifest (i.e., God would be like a woman both old and young at the same time). But Bruno ascribes this attribute to matter itself. Matter has the power to contract form since matter has the attributes Cusa reserved for God.[106] For Bruno the *mysterium conjunctionis* is the (divine) universe itself in its dual aspect of world soul and matter. Matter is divine, or like God in the sense that matter combines Plotinus's corporeal and intelligible matters into one power of being-in-act. Contractions of matter exist unfolded in successive individuals, but matter also exists as the substrate of all contractions in a *complicatio* or "enfolding." Matter is simultaneously a "virtual" substrate of all actualities and the power of entities to exist. Matter as pure actuality is the existence of all that which simultaneously is and is not contracted in a universe of perpetual transformation.

In this view, all development occurs through a process of bonding that Bruno names "love," but which is, for him, a kind of Leibnizian communication of each to all. As Bruno puts it in his *General Account of Bonding*:

> For indeed, anything which is considered in the chaos and in brute matter, and is also said to be love, is simultaneously said to be a perfection. And whatever is said to be imperfect, disordered and not to be, is

understood not to be love. Thus, it is established that love is everywhere a perfection, and this bond of love gives witness everywhere to perfection. When an imperfect thing desires to be perfected this, indeed takes place in something which is imperfect, but not because it is imperfect. Rather, this happens because of a participation in a perfection and in a divine light and in an object having a more eminent nature, which it desires more strongly inasmuch as the object is more vivacious. That which is more perfect burns with greater love for the highest good than that which is imperfect. *Therefore, that principle is most perfect which wishes to become all things, and which is not oriented to any particular form but to a universal form and universal perfection. And this is universal matter, without which there is no form, in whose power, desire, and disposition all forms are located*, and which receives all forms in the development of its parts, even though it cannot receive two forms at the same time. Hence matter is in a sense divine, just as form, which is either a form of matter or nothing, is also in a sense divine. There is nothing outside of matter or without matter, otherwise the power to make and to be made would be one and the same thing, and would be grounded in one undivided principle, because the power to make anything and the power of anything to be made would be either present or absent together. There is only one potency taken absolutely and in itself . . . it is not a foolish opinion which was defended by David of Dinant and by Avicebron in his *Fons vitae*, who cited the Arabs who also ventured to assert that God is matter.[107]

As absolute potency to be otherwise, matter is divine. By contrast, it is precisely the immutable or static character of form that renders form unproductive, on its own. For Bruno, the ultimate power of matter is its energetic role, and the vicissitudes of this energy cannot be determined in advance according to a schema of a fixed set of shapes or types, even if these are mathematical. Despite his enthusiasm for the Copernican move beyond Ptolemaic geocentrism, Bruno famously reproached Copernicus for having "studied mathematics more than nature," just as he criticized Aristotle for never tiring of dividing in reason that which is unified in nature.[108] For Bruno, Copernicus's system, if it is worth anything at all, must be more than a mathematical device, because no mathematical apprehension can do more than abstract from the process of the world.

Bruno does not reject the relevance of mathematics for describing patterns, but its usage is limited. Fernand Hallyn formulates Bruno's perspective in *The Poetic Structure of the World* in the following way:

> Ultimately, it is the dissociation between form and image of the universe that Bruno radicalized, and in the very name of the *decorum* of the infinite: if, by its form, the universe represents the divine being, it can only do so by presenting the unrepresentable as such. It is therefore necessary for its form to be such that no "image" can contain it, and so to be infinite. God, moreover, cannot "appear" except in unrepresentable form; organistic *decorum* cannot reside in the finite perfection of mathematical relationships. Bruno situates it in inexhaustible energy, with respect to which all things, including distance and time, are equal.[109]

This characterization of Bruno's "baroque" approach to the infinite resonates with the mannerism Deleuze affirmations with his description of thought as a "creation of concepts" on a plane of immanence or energetic vector (*WIP*, 41). In Bruno's view, if the worlds are infinite, and infinity is unrepresentable without distortion (even in mathematics), then to think the infinite requires either a break with representation entirely or a usage of representation against its ordinary deployment. Since like Deleuze, Bruno chooses the latter option, the arcana, symbols, and emblems of magical and esoteric discourse have extreme relevance for philosophy. Deleuze is also drawn to the possibility of certain types of image formation and symbolism when they are taken not as imaginative constructions but as diagrams of real relations between the known and the unknown. Bruno's usage of the history of symbolism in the *On the Composition of Images, Signs, and Ideas* is a mannerist one: a speculative quest for an image of that which is beyond all image.[110] This is the paradoxical situation in which Bruno's complex memory system comes to play both a rational and an esoteric, symbolic role. The signs of the memory system are conventional, but they correspond to reality only in an oblique or "occult" fashion, since what the signs ultimately refer to are the infinitesimals (differentials) of a cosmic becoming that is unlimited.

However, the admission of the conventional nature of language does not lead Bruno to the abandonment of truth, but to an affirmative multiplication, of sign systems. Bruno's difference from Cusa here, who centered the "measurement" of the infinite on the paradoxical nature of Christ, is well marked by Christopher I. Lehrich, who illustrates

Bruno's thought in terms of a distance from both Copernicus and from traditional hermeticism that depends upon a geocentric model of the cosmos. For Bruno, these models have artificially limited the unlimited by positing the earth, in the former case, and the sun in the latter, as cosmic centers. Lehrich writes,

> Bruno's point, I suggest, is that when he reads either Copernicus or Hermes, he encounters a brilliant mind attempting to formulate an analogy to the universe as it really is. Both analogies are entirely legitimate, yet they disagree utterly . . . both cosmologies are centered and finite: Hermes' is geocentric, Copernicus' heliocentric, but in either case beyond the ultimate distance there is always an end or limit. This Bruno could not accept as anything other than a convenience of the finite mind. For him, then Hermes was a prophet in the same sense as Copernicus—or vice versa.
>
> Bruno attempts to reconcile an uneasy blend of several types of cosmological analogies—mathematics, classical mythological imagery, the art of memory, atomism, Copernicanism—into a single nearly infinite analogy. Such a model would not accurately describe the universe as it really is, but it would be much more adequate. It would be utterly unlimited, not susceptible to reification or fixing. Its very nature would reflect the radical otherness of the cosmic infinity.[111]

Scholars debate how these different analogies were actually linked, and whether they actually cohered in Bruno's mind in any systematic way. It suffices to remark, for our purposes here, that Bruno is situated on the fraying edge of the world Foucault defined in *The Order of Things*, as the Renaissance world of similitude, a world where things and words resonate, connect, and mark their identities through relations of convenience, empathy, analogy, and sympathy. In the magia naturalis of the Renaissance (that was both paradigmatic and completely "rational" for this period), plants, animals, minerals, and even human beings were "ruled" by different celestial powers that governed different aspects of physical and psychological reality. It was possible to construct images—of, say, Saturn as an old man with camel's feet and a sickle—in order to work magic on objects under Saturn's purview. Thus, Agrippa writes, "Mercurius [i.e., Hermes] Trismegistus writes that a demon immediately animates a figure or statue well composed of certain things which suit that demon; Augustine also mentions this in the eighth book of his *City of God*. For such is the concordance of the world that celestial things draw super-celestial things, and natural things, supernatural things, through the virtue running through all and the participation in it of all species."[112] This passage is a clue to understanding the epistemological significance Bruno accords to images. As Agrippa argues, images are indispensable for magic. Images, when correctly constructed, are not illustrations or examples but talismans and emblems, ensigns of reality. Magical action, whether taking the form of divination, augury, or healing, requires images, since magic depends on seeing the world itself as shadow or simulacrum of Nature's absolute infinity. As Hilary Gatti notes, Bruno's atomism implies that all visible actuality is a simulacrum of atomic forces that are themselves unrepresentably intelligent and animated, willful and unpredictable, yet somehow responsive to the evocative and invocative powers of certain images and signs.[113]

This means that Bruno's theory of the power of the image, as Nuccio Ordine has described it, has to do with how an image becomes operative and "veridical" not by virtue of its verisimilitude but by its ability to serve as a node or transfer point in an infinite network of energetic relays, exchanges, and transitions. Bruno's poetics, essential to his understanding of magic (which works constantly with images to direct energy and to evoke the otherwise invisible), is thus a mannerist poetics, in the sense that the rules of decorum incumbent upon the superior fabulist (or magus), is not a matter of the imitation of generic conventions or repetition of codified natural resemblances, but of using images as projective or conjectural, as access to imperceptible forces. Bruno himself used images not only to remember (by constructing Lullian memory theaters) but also to attempt to access that which cannot be seen. Thus the image in Bruno is both where knowledge is housed and also where it reaches its own limits, a limit that only the heroic will can cross. As Agrippa put it, in his usual bombastic tone,

> You must know that these kind of figures are nothing unless they are vivified so that there is in them . . . a natural virtue, or a celestial virtue, or a heroic, animistic, demonic, or angelic virtue. But who can give soul to an image, life to stone, metal, wood, or wax? And who can make children of Abraham come out of stones? Truly this secret is not known to the thick-witted worker . . . and no one has such powers but he who has cohabited with the elements, vanquished nature, mounted higher than

the heavens, elevating himself above the angels to the archetype itself, with whom he then becomes co-operator and can do all things.

Agrippa's infamous arrogance is tempered by the more sophisticated approach of Bruno, who like Pico before him upholds strict requirements of intense moral purification and self-reflection, in short great humility, for the approach to the absolute.[114] Bruno would agree with Agrippa that only certain quickened minds can "vivify" magical images.

This is what Bruno argues by analogy in *The Heroic Frenzies*, when he affirms the ecstatic state or "frenzy" proper to intellectual ascent and genuine magical action by contrasting conventional, imitative poetry and genuine invention. Imitative poets are incapable of genuine invention, and restricted by conforming to rules of generic convention. Such is Bruno's critique of the Petrarchan love tradition, which for Bruno is a soulless parody of the genuine erotic and heroic passion for truth Plato had described in the *Phaedrus* and the *Symposium*. *The Heroic Frenzies* attempts to show the process in which images pass from imitation to invention.[115] Not unlike in Deleuze's aesthetics, this happens through a subtraction of the image from cliché: Bruno does not abandon or parody the conventions of the love tradition, but he intensifies them by putting them to a baroque usage. The deep interpreter of nature is both like and unlike the Petrarchan lover—like him in his passion, but unlike him his object, which is no mere woman but mater materia herself.

But how exactly does this passion of the image, the passionate, forced, almost desperate struggle to invent a fitting figure become the essence of knowledge? This is a question to be put to Deleuze as much as to Bruno, insofar as Deleuze attempts to develop an account of thought centered on passionate rapport with the unthinkable. Deleuze is able to use the resources of the Kantian theory of ideas to elaborate a transcendental account of symbols that makes good on Bruno's ambition. Meanwhile, for Bruno, what ultimately distinguishes a true image of nature from a false one is not that it correctly imitates nature, but that it suggests what nature *may* be. As Ordine puts it, the genuine image forges a passage beyond the "shadows" of nature, diving across the Neoplatonic *vestigium*, nature conceived as the "threshold" of ideas.[116] In contrast to the stale Petrarchan conventionality to which the *The Heroic Frenzies* is vehemently opposed, for Bruno it is philosophy as a truly inventive poetry that makes the rules of its own art.[117] The effectiveness of an image lies precisely in the affect that it continues, in the sense that we speak of certain artworks as *moving*.[118] Bruno's view of mind is that it is immanent to the fecundity of the *infiniti universi i mondi*, and he believed consort with nature's infinity forced him to become other than himself, to undergo the greatest destructions and undoings, the hunter becomes the hunted.

Bruno's criticism of generic conventions and imitative poetry is not anomalous, but part of a larger crisis, in Renaissance aesthetics. Robert Klein explains that Bruno's philosophical interpretation of art in terms of *magia* indicates a growing consciousness that, just as experimental science operates in advance of its metaphysical grounding, so also in painting the *maniera* or style could take on an autonomy—especially in the great works of Caravaggio—that defied Aristotelian conventions for how various subjects should be portrayed, how form should properly inhabit meaning. Klein observes,

> The ruin of a certain theory of art gave birth in these years to a renewed general aesthetic. Humanism had posed the problem of the relations between idea and form which expresses it in rhetoric, logic, poetry, and the visual arts; it endeavored to join the "what" to the "how," to find for formal beauty a justification more profound than the need for decoration. But, as far as it went, it never denied that in all these fields "what is expressed" must be present prior to its expression. That is why, speaking simplistically, humanism came to an end in the sciences just as the method of investigation became fruitful by itself, and in art just as the execution—the *maniera*—became an autonomous value. When artistic consciousness reached such a stage, around 1600, it found no art theory that could account for it. There was only the ancient natural magic—that is to say, a general aesthetic unaware of itself, which Bruno hastily developed in the magnificent essay he entitled *De vinculis in genere*.[119]

What Bruno attempts to do in *On Bonding* is not to deduce the possibility of bonds from the attributes of material substances, but to describe the various conditions under which certain bonds (especially love) appeared to be active. Thus *On Bonding* offers something like a "mannerist" approach to ontology, in the sense that relations are there seen as prior to terms, and substances subordinate to accidental configurations of contiguity, proportion, or symmetry, causing love or power to flow to greater or lesser degrees.[120] Bruno derived his conception of the variety of bonds from alchemical and natural magical principles. Thus the theory of natural magic came to form the basis for a new aesthetic in the face of the demise of classicism, with its rules of convention, proportion, and proper generic mediation of subject matter and form. What mannerism seems to discover is a kind of magical power of form to bring into being. Just as there is a plurality of bonds or chains through which the souls of all things are moved, there must be a variety of beauties whose charm is not merely reflective but generative. As Klein puts it, for Bruno "the artist who wishes to move himself must be moved."[121]

In his commentary on love in Plato's *Symposium*, Ficino had already argued that this love is not only emotional but physical, and as "magnetism" love is the essence of magical power. Ficino writes, "Why is Love called a Magus? Because all the force of Magic consists in Love. The work of Magic is a certain drawing of one thing to another by natural similitude. The parts of this world, like members of one animal, depend all on one Love, and are connected together by natural communion."[122] This is the theme Bruno takes up in *On Bonding*. In this work Bruno analyzes the variety and types of possible bonds, where physical and psychic bonds are considered from an operational perspective with no clear division between "subjective" and "objective" components. In keeping with the Platonist tradition Ficino inherited, Bruno asserts that "all bonds are either reduced to the bond of love or are based on the bond of love."[123] This notion of cosmic energy as fundamentally erotic can be traced to the *Asclepius*, one of the central texts of the *Corpus Hermeticum*, where Hermes teaches that the creator is drawn down to earth from above because of passionate love (eros) for it.[124]

Deleuze's complex ontology locates desire as an essential moment of every concrete assemblage. And In *Anti-Oedipus*, Deleuze and Guattari will use the same materialist language as did Bruno when they identify God with self-regenerating matter, and when they affirm their own belief not in a transcendent creator but a God "defined as *Omnitudo realitas*, from which all secondary realities are derived by a process of division" (*AO*, 13). For Deleuze and Guattari, the life of "God" is identical with an anorganic life, a series of resonant disjunctive syntheses. This vision is consonant with the hermetic traditions of alchemy and magia naturalis that already attempted to map the syzygies that were nodal points of spiritual and material reality. The problem for thought, in this view, becomes how to think a selective principle of organization or "harmony" within a cosmic process of unlimited becoming that has no center or endpoint outside its multiple immanent circuits. Deleuze will attempt to find such a criteria in his unique interpretation of Nietzsche's notion of eternal return, and will in fact characterize the "affirmation" of the eternal return as a kind of esoteric insight, a wisdom that renders the mind adequate to the act of creation (*DR*, 296). In fact, Deleuze is more explicit than many readers have perhaps realized in aligning the powers of eternal return with specifically esoteric apprehensions of nature, such as have populated the hermetic tradition from antique eras to the present.

3

The Force of Symbols
Deleuze and the Esoteric Sign

At exactly what point do Bruno, Cusa, and the Renaissance revival of hermeticism have their most profound influence on Deleuze? Although there are multiple points of contact, it is Deleuze's conception of signs and his theory of semiosis that are most beholden to Cusa, Bruno, and the Renaissance milieu generally. Despite the fact that Spinoza's advance on Neoplatonism is decisive for Deleuze, and that Deleuze derives his paradigm of immanent thought from Spinoza, the "plane" drawn by Spinoza's *more geometrico* is nevertheless not the one drawn by Deleuze. What Deleuze does do—both explicitly and implicitly—is develop "baroque" usages of signs such as those envisioned by Cusa and Bruno, where confidence in the adequacy of language can in turn be related back to the confidence of the hermetic tradition in the powers of emblems, symbols, and sigils to activate the deep, if always hidden character of nature. As we saw apropos Foucault, in the Renaissance, signs and symbols, although limited, could surpass the restrictions of ordinary perception and rationality by activating otherwise imperceptible sympathies, analogies, and connections. Deleuze's conception of the possible adequacy of signs is a recapitulation and contemporary elaboration of the Renaissance view. The enigmatic yet distinct presence of being in signs forms the crux of immanence in Deleuze's thought—the point at which immanence emerges and is most strongly effective in the mind.

Being in Signs: The Crux of Immanence

In the Renaissance and Neoplatonic precursors to Deleuze's philosophy of immanence, the nature of the world is envisioned as a contingent manifestation and partial disclosure of an ineffable yet fundamental reality. Any entity or event constitutes only a finite, temporary revelation of the ultimate nature of that reality. This logic of expression, whether keyed to orthodox or heretical theologies, posits that the ultimate sense of expression can never be derived from the manifest nature of the objects expressed. Rather, the nature of expressed being must somehow be inferred from the structure of expression itself, from some sense of disclosure immanent to the disclosing process and only partially realized in any given entity or event.

In short, the form of the world is in no sense given in advance of its singular and irreversible advent (in both a temporal and ontological sense). The ontological cannot be extricated from the temporal, the historical, and the perspectival; the ontological cannot be extricated from the volitional. From an expressionist perspective, the ultimate metaphysical question is what kind of will is expressed in the world, and whether that will is ultimately immanent or transcendent, personal or impersonal, benevolent or malevolent, conscious or unconscious, complete or incomplete, beautiful or sublime, self-exhausting or self-donating. It is within the debate over the ultimate character of any "will-to-expression" that Deleuze situates his own position.

Deleuze explicitly defines his own metaphysical point of departure as that of "certain Neoplatonists" (*PS*, 45). In *Proust and Signs*, Deleuze writes,

> Certain Neoplatonists used a profound word to designate the original state that proceeds any development, any "explication": *complication*, which envelops the many in the One and affirms the unity of the multiple. Eternity did not seem to them the absence of change, nor even

the extension of a limitless existence, but the complicated state of time itself (*uno ictu mutationes tuas complectitur*). The Word, *omnia complicans*, and containing all essences, was defined as the supreme complication, the complication of contraries, the unstable opposition. From this they derived the notion of an essentially expressive universe, organized according to degrees of immanent complications and following an order of descending explications. (PS, 45)

Paradigmatically in the philosophy of Nicholas of Cusa, the doctrine of Christ the Word provided an ingenious metaphysical device by means of which to bind a logic of sense to a logic of reality: just as Christ incarnate unifies the disparate orders of being, Christ the Word unites the ultimate, eternal sense of things to contingent, concrete expressions, both in language and in action. Like Bruno before him, Deleuze evacuates this Christological center, but preserves something essential from Christology. Rather than rejecting the notion of a semiotic and ontological center, Deleuze attempts to account for an indefinite multiplicity of sense that is always excessive to the conditions of its emergence, a theory of both sense and existence as embedded in overlapping series of imbrications. One could say that for Deleuze, the *verbum* is, strictly speaking, virtually everything and everywhere. Deleuze thus subtracts from Neoplatonism a purely immanent notion of expression, one that does not follow an order of descending explications, but ramifies itself in a nomadic and anarchic distribution.

But Deleuze's thought about immanence harbors an interesting tension. On the one hand, immanence is as a kind of methodological or metaphilosophical imperative, an imperative perhaps realized most perfectly by Spinoza's *more geometrico*. This is the imperative that thought be or become (is or should be) fully immanent. According to this imperative, thought should not have recourse to any entity, axiom, or presupposition that cannot be evaluated on the basis of principles immanent to finite thought by right (WG, 4). With this aspect of immanence, Deleuze extends the Kantian project of outlining the conditions of a finite mind's experience of the world into an account of the genesis of mind itself, rather than a simple elucidation of its proper function.

There is another, somewhat more cryptic sense of immanence in Deleuze's work. This is the sense that, quite apart from thought, immanence is the character of a singular flow of impersonal consciousness, *une vie* (a life). This is a sense of immanence Deleuze tends to develop more fully in his later work. Immanence as "a life" is not a reference to an organism, but an "anorganic," prereflective consciousness that implicates everything in itself, leaving nothing outside—not even thought itself—to which a life could be considered immanent.[1] In his last published essay, Deleuze writes, "The indefinite aspects in a life lose all indetermination to the degree that they fill out a plane of immanence or, what amounts to the same thing, to the degree that they constitute the elements of a transcendental field . . . the One is not the transcendent that might contain immanence but the immanent contained within a transcendental field. One is always the index of a multiplicity: an event, a singularity, a life" (*PI*, 30). In this perspective on immanence, reference to the intensive conditions of thought are displaced by references to "virtualities, events, singularities . . . the immanent event is actualized in a state of things and of the lived that make it happen" (*PI*, 31). How are these two dimensions of immanence—thought and life—to be understood in tandem? How can immanence be both the hallmark of philosophy, as a practice of thought, and of life as the singularity of *une vie*?

Deleuze's attempt to answer this problem (or unfold its dimensions) over the course of his career takes him into the same disputed territory as that claimed by Cusa and Bruno with their attempts to situate the finite mind in relation to the infinite. Both Cusa and Bruno had conceived of reason as dependent upon signs or symbols that were reliable yet ultimately inadequate mediations. While Cusa's confidence in the sign is grounded in the ultimate dependence of all sense on the paradoxically immanent and transcendent exemplar, Christ the Word, Bruno's construction of images, signs, and ideas places confidence only in the ability of heroic minds to contract and thus contact the profound dynamics of an immanent and univocal cosmic vicissitude. In the somewhat underacknowledged wake of Bruno (as much as in the avowed wake of Scotus, Spinoza, and Nietzsche), when Deleuze affirms the univocity of being, he does so not at the level of substance, but at the level of expression itself. For Deleuze, univocity is not a given, but a generated and generative power, productive only as a "power of thinking which is in itself equal to the power of producing or acting" (*E*, 181). Apropos Spinoza, Deleuze writes,

Things in general are modes of divine being, that is, they implicate the same attributes that constitute the nature of this being. Thus all likeness is univocal, defined by the presence in both cause and effect of a common property. The things that are produced are not imitations any more than their ideas are models. There is nothing exemplary even in the idea of God, since this is itself, in its formal being, also produced. Nor conversely do ideas imitate things. In their formal being they follow from the attribute of thought; and if they are representative, they are so only to the extent that they participate in an absolute power of thinking which is in itself equal to the absolute power of producing or acting. Thus all imitative or exemplary likeness is excluded from the relation of expression. God expresses himself in the forms that constitute his essence, as in the ideas that reflect it. Expression characterizes both being and knowing. But only univocal being, *only univocal consciousness*, are expressive. Substance and modes, cause and effects, only have being *and are only known through* common forms that actually constitute the essence of the one, and actually contain the essence of the others. (*E*, 181)

For Spinoza, to be or become expressive, at the level of thought, is not to imitate an exemplar, nor is it to adumbrate or approximate an ideal. Rather, to express (to think and to act) is to produce more of the orders and connections that are immanent and constitutive for thought and being. However, in Spinoza's philosophy, adequate knowledge, knowledge *sub specie aeternitatis*, is distinct from knowledge in and through signs. To know in signs is to know inadequately, through apophasis or by analogy, since all signs bear historical and cultural codings that interfere with apprehension of the immanent, univocal inherence of substance in modes. Yet philosophy itself must transpire in signs. How, then, does philosophy hope to be adequate to the movements of infinite substance? How can philosophy think univocity? For Deleuze, the solution lies in the discovery of imperceptible, intensive forms that lurk beneath representation. If being is univocal, then "substance and modes, cause and effects, only have being and are only known through common forms that actually constitute the essence of the one, and actually contain the essence of the others" (*E*, 181).

But signs—natural, linguistic, or otherwise—cannot be direct transcriptions of common forms, since such forms are not individual substances but types of relations. As Spinoza put it, there are different kinds of signs, but none of these are adequate to express clearly and distinctly the differential forms common to causes and effects, bodies and affects, substances and modes in their infinity.[2] The finitude of the sign is inadequate to the infinity of relations expressed in the actual confluence of modes.[3] Deleuze notes that "through univocity, Spinoza gives the idea of expression a positive content, opposing it to the three sorts of sign. The opposition of expression and signs is one of the fundamental principles of Spinozism" (E, 182). It is possible to express something that is nevertheless impossible to directly signify. Spinoza's geometrical method, for this reason, attempts to move the mind beyond or through linguistic signs to a "metasemiotic" mode of apprehension or superior insight beyond the limits of a thought bound to signification.

It is arguable, however, that on this point Deleuze diverges to a certain degree from Spinoza, since Deleuze, throughout his work, entertains the possibility that signs might be adequate to expression in a way not countenanced by Spinoza. Indeed, Deleuze suggests in *Difference and Repetition* that the sense of the virtual, redolent with multiple potentials, is "symbolic without being fictional" (DR, 208). Deleuze also argues that the meaning of univocal being itself, as the eternal return of difference, is realized in a peculiarly complex instance of symbolism: the simulacrum. He writes,

> When eternal return is the power of (formless) Being, the simulacrum is its true character or form—the "being"—of that which is. When the identity of things dissolves, being escapes to attain univocity, and begins to revolve around the different. That which is or returns has no prior constituted identity: things are reduced to the difference which fragments them, and to all the differences which are implicated in it and through which they pass. In this sense, the simulacrum and the symbol are one; in other words, the simulacrum is the sign *in so far as the sign interiorizes the conditions of its own repetition*. (DR, 67, emphasis added)

That which can return, and yet be the same, is a simulacrum, a sign that is its own substance. But what would it mean for a sign to "interiorize the conditions of its own repetition"? With Guattari, Deleuze will eventually develop a nonlinguistic theory of semiosis, according to which signs function not as terms of reference but as systems of relay, harbingers of movement and indexes of expressive relations between forces.

This lends an entirely novel meaning to "interpretation," far from the linguistic turn that dominated the philosophy in Deleuze's milieu. He writes,

> Interpretation establishes the "meaning" of a phenomenon, which is always fragmentary and incomplete; evaluation determines the hierarchical "value" of meanings and totalizes the fragments without diminishing or eliminating their plurality. Indeed aphorism is both the art of interpreting and what must be interpreted; poetry, both the art of evaluating and what must be evaluated. The interpreter is the physiologist or doctor, the one who sees phenomena as symptoms and speaks through aphorisms. The evaluator is the artist who considers and creates "perspectives" and speaks through poetry. The philosopher of the future is both artist and doctor—in one word, legislator. (*PI*, 66)

This confluence of art and medicine, aesthetics and pragmatics, echoes across Deleuze's constant regard for artists and thinkers whose work seeks to activate the transformative potentials of certain intense vectors of sensation, affects, and concepts. As early as his adolescent writings, Deleuze was inspired by the idea of a "medicinal thought" embodied in symbolic and esoteric apprehensions of nature, and this interest is continuous with Deleuze's dedication to the aesthetic project of the symbolist moderns. To fully understand the proximity, in Deleuze's mind, of conceptual creation to aesthetic and "medicinal" symbolic activity (therapeutic, theurgical, and thaumaturgical), it is necessary to carefully regard Deleuze's abiding interest in symbolic modes of discourse.

At early and late stages in his career, Deleuze sought to excavate a mode of symbolic knowledge that would manage, beyond the limitations of signs noted by Spinoza, to be adequate to expression. This effort can be described as the search for a symbol that might diagram the real contours of an unrepresentable nature. My contention here, in the course of disinterring a "hermetic" core of Deleuzian philosophy, is that such knowledge, if realized, would embody that "prephilosophical" or "nonphilosophical" sense of immanence Deleuze and Guattari saw as casting its "shadow" upon art, science, and philosophy. In *Difference and Repetition*, Deleuze explicitly avers that his theory of ideas is related to the project of *mathesis universalis* (*DR*, 190). This early avowal can be productively connected to his later search for a "world people" or "brain people" who would, at an eschatological limit, have passed beyond the segmentation of knowledge in art, science, and philosophy in some as-yet-unrealized integral life of knowledge, such as that long dreamt of in the esoteric tradition of mathesis universalis. In Deleuze's early and latest works, a certain kind of symbolic knowledge seems to constitute the possibility of a vital transcription of immanence as an open set of enigmatic yet adequate signs.

Mathesis Universalis

"Mathesis, Science, and Philosophy" was one of Deleuze's earliest publications. The piece appeared in 1946 as the preface to a reissue of the French translation of Johann Malfatti de Montereggio's *Mathesis, or Studies on the Anarchy and Hierarchy of Knowledge*.[4] Malfatti, a truly fascinating figure in his own right, was a nineteenth-century Italian doctor who practiced medicine in the tradition of Schellingian *Naturphilosophie*. Among his patients were members of the Bonaparte family, as well as Ludwig van Beethoven. In addition to being a doctor, Malfatti was also one of the most influential esotericists of the nineteenth century. His writings profoundly influenced the philosophies of French Martinists such as Gérard Encausse (Papus). René Guénon, the leading French esotericist of the early twentieth century, reviewed the edition of Malfatti's *Mathesis* that included Deleuze's preface, and Guénon acknowledged its historical significance for the history of occult philosophy.

Deleuze was twenty-one years old when he was invited by the editors of the small press "Griffon d'Or" to compose his preface. Deleuze asked to have this work, along with five other early essays, suppressed from his official bibliography. We may speculate as to the exact reasons Deleuze made this request, but the recent translation and publication of "Mathesis, Science, and Philosophy," (and the scholarly discussions it has provoked) indicate that Deleuze's consistent (if often oblique) references to esoteric discourses throughout his oeuvre had deep roots.[5] François Dosse, Deleuze's biographer, suggests that Deleuze may have been asked to write the preface by Marie-Madeleine Davy. This extraordinary person, a scholar of medieval philosophy and passionate spiritualist, organized salons at her estate outside Paris as a cover for resistance activities (which included harboring Jews, as well as British and American soldiers). The salons were the site of encounters between many leading French intellectuals, such as Sartre and Bataille, as well as a very young Gilles Deleuze.[6]

The company also included a number of French esotericists and devotees of occult philosophy, such as Marcel Moré. Deleuze's work from this period reflects a profound fascination with esoteric themes, inspired perhaps by Davy's own conviction that a secret and subversive medieval tradition of Neoplatonic thought contained a revolutionary gnosis waiting to be rediscovered and redeployed in Europe. Malfatti's work may even have been a subject of some discussion at Davy's salons. A vast and arcane synthesis of Western and Eastern (specifically Indian and tantric) natural philosophies within a unified symbolic framework, Malfatti's work envisages a medicine that would be effective not simply through technical proficiency, but as a lived embodiment of knowledge, a practical path to healing through the elaboration of sympathies, symbioses, and vibrational patterns. Such a science would be feasible on the basis of maps of the body taken as a microcosmic field of intensities (on the model of the Indian chakras).

Malfatti's work can be placed within a romantic tradition of mathesis universalis, the dream of a "science of sciences" that would, if realized, constitute the unity of life and knowledge. But the romantic conception, culminating perhaps most forcefully in Schelling's *Naturphilosophie*, draws deeply upon Renaissance inspiration. As Frances Yates has argued, part of what led to Giordano Bruno's burning at the stake was his advocacy of a "new religion" that would be centered on "Love, Art, Magic, and Mathesis." Bruno's version of mathesis was inspired by the work of Raymond Lull, a thirteenth-century Catalan. Lull's *ars generalis ultima* devised a mechanical means for elaborating possible combinations of a number of fixed propositional elements. Lull's system, designed to demonstrate philosophical and theological truths, was inspired by Arab astrologers who had developed a technique of combination, the *zairja*, which was used to calculate ideas by mechanical means. Ironically, Lull's purpose in developing his *ars magna* was to convert Arabian Muslims. Supposing that the Arabs would accept the same basic theological premises as Christians, Lull thought the infidels would necessarily be led to truth simply by working through a complete range of possible combinations of basic ideas. Bruno used Lull's principles to elaborate his subversive and antitheological philosophy of nature, applying the method of combining images, signs, and ideas in order to explore the infinite universe and worlds.

In mainstream Western philosophy, mathesis universalis is generally associated with Leibniz. Inspired by Lull, Leibniz had envisaged an *arithmetica universalis* or *scientia generalis* that would allow a kind of internal elaboration of all possible relations between all concepts in all disciplines. Mathesis would be a kind of universal formal grammar whose permutations would enable exhaustive knowledge. Regarding this, Allison Coudert has argued that Leibniz was almost certainly influenced by Jewish Kabbalah, with its own esoteric use of combinatorial procedures for exploring the mysteries of the Godhead through gematria and other arithmosophical theurgies.[7] Despite the arcane sources of his inspiration, however, Leibniz was not alone among mainstream early modern philosophers in the quest for a "science of sciences," nor was he alone among moderns in his quest for secret knowledge, as evidenced, for example, by Newton's vast writings on alchemy. Even Descartes, who argued for a rigid distinction between mind and matter, had insisted on their practical unity at the level of "the living." As Deleuze puts it in his preface to Malfatti's work, "Beyond a psychology disincarnated in thought, and a physiology mineralized in matter," even Descartes believed in the possibility of a unified field "where life is defined as knowledge of life, and knowledge as life of knowledge" (*MSP*, 143). This is the unity, Deleuze asserts, to which Malfatti's account of mathesis as a "true medicine" aspires.

Deleuze explicitly refers to mathesis universalis at several key points in *Difference and Repetition*, particularly in connection with what he calls the "esoteric" history of the calculus (*DR*, 170). As Christian Kerslake has argued, Deleuze's reference here is not merely to obscure or unusual interpretations of mathematics, but to the decisive significance of Josef Hoëné-Wronski, a Polish French émigré who had elaborated a "messianism" of esoteric knowledge based on the idea that the calculus represented access to the total range of cosmic periodicities and rhythmic imbrications.[8] The full implications of Deleuze's connection to Wronski are beyond my scope here, but Deleuze himself claims in *Difference and Repetition* that there is a "mathesis universalis" that corresponds to his theory of ideas and that this mathesis has its roots in the "esoteric history of differential philosophy" (*DR*, 181, 190).[9] Deleuze suggests that his own theory of ideas has strong ties to a calculus of relations among ideal events that now and then "explode into the actual" (*DR*, 190). It is therefore crucial, in understanding his work as a whole, to gain a sense of the deep impression earlier esoteric approaches to ideas through symbolism made on Deleuze's mind.

Deleuze presents Malfatti unfolding his version of mathesis through a complex symbolism derived from esoteric Hindu iconography. Using a series of hermaphroditic representations of the esoteric nature of the decade (1–10), Malfatti elaborates an arithmosophy that purports to be a symbolic map of the body in connection with its cosmic dimensions. Despite the exoticism this method involves, in his preface Deleuze systematically rejects the idea that mathesis is an inexact science, let alone an obscurantist mystification. He writes, "To believe that mathesis is merely a mystical lore, inaccessible and superhuman, would be a complete mistake. This is the first misunderstanding to be avoided. For mathesis deploys itself at the level of life, of living man: it is first and foremost a thinking of incarnation and of individuality. Essentially, mathesis would be the exact description of human nature" (*MSP*, 143). For the young Deleuze, mathesis would be the most concrete sense of life, rather than a cache of secret knowledge. As such, it is an activation of individuating forces. After observing that the approaches of both science and philosophy produce false dualisms between mind and matter, thought and sensation, Deleuze invites us to consider mathesis as an attempt to develop a form of knowledge that would be impossible for either the scientific or philosophical method, but that might nevertheless be essential to them both. The catch, and what makes the basic project of mathesis an enduring point of reference for Deleuze's later theory of ideas, is that the esoteric tertium quid would not stand as knowledge without standing immediately as an experience of the intensive and imbricated structure of natural rhythms, durations, and periodicities structuring life itself.

The question that animates Deleuze's reading of Malfatti is quite precise: What is the nature of a symbolic knowledge that can express life as such? Deleuze already seems to be looking for a usage of signs and symbols that would overcome Spinoza's critique of signification as inadequate. But as nearly any account of symbolism must admit, symbols are both distinct and obscure, since symbols develop only when a particular object or image stands for or "incarnates" several events, objects, or images. Yet Deleuze argues that the obscurity or density in symbols is not due to the vagaries of the imagination, and that symbols are constructed in accordance with highly precise patterns in natural dynamics. In fact Deleuze argues that ordinary perceptual states are incipient symbols. In the "Mathesis" essay, Deleuze points out that when a cube, which has six sides, can only display at most three at a time, the cube does not distort but rather implies the real (vectorial) nature of space. If a cube showed all six of its faces at once—if it fully "clarified" its nature—it would violate the law of spatial appearances, as such. Does the fact that we only see three sides of a six-sided figure imply that sight, or sensation generally, is inadequate to reality, or inherently distortional? It might seem so, but Deleuze asks us to consider the fact that if the entire cube were completely manifest or transparent to one perspective, it would be complete at the cost of having no dimensionality at all. It would not be what it is, as a cube, but some impossible object that could manifest all of its dimensions at once. Yet the constraints of appearance are immediately the dimensions of the real: the cube in its own unique way reveals or "symbolizes" space. As Deleuze puts it, "Why are the 6 faces given as 3? It is simply because everyday space is 3-dimensional. In taking a moment to reflect, it will be seen that the 6 faces as such only make sense in reference to a plane. The only way for 6 to exist *en bloc* in a space of 3 dimensions is to exhibit 3 of them" (*MSP*, 149).

What Deleuze is claiming here, essentially, is that a cube's three-sided appearance is a symbolic presentation of the truth of space.[10] The cube's "enfolding" of space for our perception (the six-sided object in a three-sided appearance), can be read as a kind of symbolism proper to the nature of perception itself. Deleuze also notes that numerology, which is the basis for much esoteric science, operates according to this same principle of imbrication. The question of the symbolic power of seven—and the answer to the question "How is the world revealed as 7" or "What is the 'sevenness' of the world?"—can be read as the same kind of question as "why does a cube, which has 6 sides, appear as 3-sided?" What seven reveals as the seven-ness of the world is implied in what it is to be 7, just as a cube reveals the nature of space as inherently vectorial, torsional, and planar.

Malfatti's esoteric numerology is elaborated by way of a treatment of Hindu iconography.[11] Malfatti preferred the Hindu imagery to Pythagorean mysticism, according to Deleuze, because of the tendency of the Greeks to reduce the meaning of the numbers to static geometrical forms (*MSP*, 154). The superior gesture, made by the Hindu icons, is to create symbols that embody the peculiar movements or "energies" particular to each number. From the Hindu perspective, Malfatti proceeds to explain the symbolic or esoteric dimension of seven. Seven is the number of Saturn, "father of time," the number of abstract perfection prior to incarnation. Eight, or the double four, the number of Jupiter, Household, or Kingdom, would be seven as unfolded, as incarnate in the "undulating images of appearance" (*MSP*, 149). As Deleuze puts it, "7 is concept": it does not yet represent the individual become real but is "the multiple development of the universal in innumerable individualities" (*MSP*, 149). It is also the principle (rather than the phenomenality) of appearance. Represented in straight lines, seven represents the extension of the surface operating in three dimensions (length, breadth, depth). Deleuze notes here that symbolism performs a "reduction" that is the inverse of the scientific reduction of quality to quantity (*MSP*, 150). Symbols condense qualitative aspects of the real that are effective differently across different kinds of objects or events; this condensation incarnates, as it were, the abstract in the concrete, rather than subordinating individual idiosyncrasies to experimental constants.

Following this meditation on numerology, Deleuze moves to a reading of *Éventail*, a poem by Mallarmé. Deleuze argues that the poem is the essential symbolic procedure (and throughout the rest of his career it will be largely in the context of artistic practice that Deleuze will continue to appreciate symbolic knowledge in connection with the possibility of an esoteric science of life). In *Évantail* (Fan), a fan closed, not open, distills the essence of movement. Its stillness is a pure potential, a kind of involuted or "complicated" infinity, "*Dont le coup prisonnier recule / L'horizon delicatement* [Whose imprisoned stroke thrusts back / The horizon delicately]." Drenched in voluptuousness, these lines symbolize movement in a particularly concise way (*MSP*, 158). The fan's stillness is imbued with an unlimited density of potential movement, and in such potentiality lies the entire mystique of what will have occurred with any movement, any gesture.

The effect of the poem is not so much to explain as to motivate, or even energize. Energetically speaking, the meaning of a symbol in some sense is the ramifying series of actions whose potentials a symbol condenses. To comprehend a symbol is to be able, or even in some sense to be compelled, to perform the action it inscribes, or at least to find oneself drawn into the event it ramifies. In this sense, to comprehend a symbol is to respond to it. With this accent on action, Deleuze links mathesis, with its symbolic vocabulary, directly to a creativity that is equally spiritual and material. He writes,

> According to Malfatti, the mysterious character of mathesis is not directed against the profane in an exclusive, mystical sense, but simply indicates the necessity of grasping the concept in a minimum of time, and that physical incarnations take place in the smallest possible space—unity within diversity, general life within particular life. At the limit, we could even say that the notion of the initiate is rationalized to the extreme. If *vocation* defines itself through the creation of a sensible object as the result of a knowledge, then mathesis qua living art of medicine is the vocation *par excellence*, the vocation of vocations, since it transforms knowledge itself into a sensible object. Thus we shall see mathesis insist upon the correspondences between material and spiritual creation. (MSP 151)

This passage anticipates much of Deleuze's later efforts to conceive of modes of cognition and awareness that, while nonrepresentational, are nevertheless adequate and effective apprehensions. Here Deleuze suggests that what the initiate attempts to divine quickly and microscopically in symbolism are the fundamental dynamics or "incarnations" of general life within particular life. As his work unfolds, Deleuze will develop an "anorganic" vision of life as consisting in fundamentally abstract relations of spatial and temporal lines. These lines not only do not fully crystallize in individuals, but also produce individuations that cross distinctions between species, between the natural and the artificial, and between organic and inorganic realms.

Life for Deleuze is an open set of relations that are continuously composed, decomposed, and recomposed on a "plane of consistency" or abstract "body without organs" (*ATP*, 270). That is to say, for Deleuze, the real character of life is manifest not in the functions and organization of actual organisms, with their structural and metabolic properties, but in how organic forms express a virtual energetic field—a plan(e) of consistency—subtending the living and dying of particular organisms (*ATP*, 270). Deleuze will think of this plane as a set of singular traits—speeds and slownesses, from one perspective, and a manifold of affects, from another—that the actual nature of organisms, species, subjects, and objects only partially realizes at any one moment, in any given individual. Even though such extremely abstract relations are ultimately unrepresentable, Deleuze develops a notion of a *nonrepresentational thought* that links ideas to an intuition of just such fundamental "dramatizations" of life.[12] And such a vision, elaborated in his maturity, is what he already interpreted from very early on as the archaic ambition of any mathesis universalis. In some sense, all of Deleuze's later theory of ideas grows from an early and abiding fascination with esoteric symbols as a potential index of the nondiscursive and intensive levels of life.

What symbolic knowledge seems to make possible, to the young Deleuze, is a kind of cognition that can, through a sort of intuitive leap, develop an image capable of effectively altering reality in conformity with itself. The desire to discover such images of "deep" nature will continue to haunt Deleuze's thinking. Deleuze's later conceptions of great speeds that are nevertheless not motions, and of spaces that are nevertheless without extension, are two key examples. Deleuze's *Logic of Sense* argues that to ramify the potential significance of events, what matters is the speed at which one is able to creatively replay, or "counter-actualize" what happens to us, as we instantaneously divine possible meanings. This concept is clearly rooted in Deleuze's notion, expressed in the "Mathesis" preface, that to be effective, symbols must grasp the dynamics that inspire them in a minimum of time (*LS*, 178). And the notion that mathesis attempts to conceive physical incarnations in the smallest possible space also anticipates Deleuze's theory, later developed in *Difference and Repetition*, that singularities (such as those involved in the surface tension at the boiling point of water) occupy a particular form of compressed space, an intensive *spatium*. In this indivisible or virtual space "there is in general no quality which does not refer to a space defined by the singularities corresponding to the differential relations incarnated in that quality" (*DR*, 210). It is to think such relations, and the transformative power they might have for those able to operate them, that Deleuze's philosophy is dedicated. And it is an eminently practical philosophy that carries out such a thought.

Life Collective and Singular

The question guiding Malfatti's approach to mathesis universalis, is how such imperceptible forces of transformation might be captured so as to reveal a pragmatic or operable pattern.[13] When we consider what it is to live, we are confronted with a variety, a diversity.[14] But it is also evident that life manifests recurrent and imbricated patterns of symbiosis, ubiquitous intercalations. Symbiosis comes to play an important role in Deleuze's thought in *A Thousand Plateaus*, but this late theme is yet another echo of Deleuze's early, mathesis-inspired attempt to think a knowledge of life that would be the life of knowledge. In his preface to Malfatti's *Mathesis*, Deleuze formulates the basic character of life as a paradox: it is only when and to the extent that each entity or individual incarnates the powers of life in itself that resonance and symbiosis can be fully established between every one. He writes,

> Prefiguring the relation between man and the infinite, the natural relation unites the living being with life. Life, in the first instance, seems to exist only through and within the living being, within the individual organism that puts it in action. Life exists only through these fragmentary and closed assumptions, each of which realizes it in its own account and nothing more, in solitude. That is to say that universality, the community of life, denies itself, gives itself to each being as a simple outside, an exteriority that remains foreign to it, an Other: there is a plurality of men yet, precisely, each one must in the same way assume his life for himself, without common measure with others, on his own account; the universal is immediately recuperated. And in this sense life will be defined as complicity, as opposed to a crew. (*MSP*, 144)

It is significant, for all of his work to come, that Deleuze's reflections on the knowledge of life move directly from the metaphysical to the social and political. Deleuze's mature overtures toward a philosophy of nature are set in the explicitly political context of the *Capitalism and Schizophrenia* project. Although he will eventually discard any emphasis on the existentialist theme of solitude, Deleuze will continue to argue that the basis for symbiosis and solidarity is an endlessly renewed series of disjunctive syntheses: relations in which entities resonate and exchange not in spite of but through their differences, forming unforeseeable hybrids, novel assemblages. Deleuze seems to already be searching for such a perspective in his early affirmations of mathesis. As envisaged by Malfatti, life's individuating tendency—and the capacity of the whole to "symbolize" itself in each individual—is a clue to the nature of life as an "open whole." The absolute character of life is not that of a totality in which parts are absorbed (a crew), but a paradoxically open whole unified by a distributive mode of expression.

In this view, what is common to each part is also what radically individuates them. That is to say, the experiences that define collective existence are also those that distinguish separate individuals: birth, love, the acquisition of language, and death, divide as much as they unite. Deleuze writes,

> In complicity . . . there is indeed a common world, but one whose community comes into effect, once more, through each member realizing it for himself without common measure with others, on his own account, and with no possibility of substitution. Clearly, the principal human realities of birth, love, language, and death describe this same profile: Under the sign of death, everyone exists as non-substitutable and cannot have himself replaced. And this, precisely, is the universality of death. In the same way, life is that reality wherein the universal and its proper negation are one." (*MSP*, 145)

There are clear echoes here of both Heidegger's and Sartre's existentialism. But if existentialism takes the priority of existence over essence as indicating the solitary nature of authentic consciousness, the early Deleuze's position is a departure from its existentialist milieu. For Deleuze, the precedence of existence over essence signifies not that life comes to self-consciousness in the anguish of solitary beings, but that life is, by definition, inherently multiple: "To say that in man in general, essence and existence are dissociated, is to say that there are several men (extension)" (*MSP*, 151). On this view, to note that existence does not follow from essence, in a particular individual life, is simply to notice the fundamentally ecstatic and collective character of life. Birth, love, language, and death do not separate life into singular conscious beings without joining them in unconscious or at least imperceptible modes of connection, in profound sharings of that very same reality that distinguishes us as separate beings.

This insight—that it is that which separates that unites, that which divides which binds—arrives by way of a "hermaphroditic" account of how the cosmos as a whole is repeated in human sexual relations, and explored by esoteric sciences such as tantrism.[15] Following Malfatti, Deleuze envisages the power of sexuality as a cosmic passage from a static circle (closed individuality) to a dynamic ellipse (a dual-centered syzygy).[16] Here Deleuze makes another significant departure from his existentialist milieu, within which sexual union seemed to represent an always-ambiguous possibility for a betrayal of one's autonomy and authenticity. For Deleuze, it is relationality, and thus sexuality, that takes ontological priority over any isolate existence. It is as if the movements of eros form the truly expressive substance of life, with the birth and death of individuals forming only temporary foci in a larger, hermaphroditic circuit of energy. Sexuality is thus both an image and experience of the opening of two closed spheres onto an elliptical, asymmetrical whole. Sexuality thus forms a concrete syzygy, a coincidence of contraries. Here difference is not the subject of a dialectical mediation, but sustained through the establishment of an intensive distance.

The young Deleuze even speculates that this "torsional" dynamic symbolizes the transcendental genesis of space and time. That is to say, the drama of sexual communion incarnates the oblong, "out of joint," inherently vectorial nature of spatiotemporal experience. Deleuze writes, "What will be the human concept *par excellence*, then? God, unity of essence and existence, is conceptualized by the circle: equivalence and rest, indifference of the interfocal zone, and pregenesthetic life. With the ellipse, however (or rather the ellipsoid, always in movement), we will rediscover separation, duality, the sexual antithesis of foci. Space is the passage from the unlimited circle to the limited ellipse, and time the passage from the unity of the center to the dualism of foci: the three dimensions are born" (*MSP*, 152). In many traditions of esoteric knowledge and practice, ritualized sexuality symbolizes and incarnates the "realization" of God.[17] Deleuze's elegy to the transcendental role of sexuality resonates across esoteric traditions of thought about the "metaphysics" of sex, from Tantrism to Sufism. Such traditions of spiritual sex attempt to harness the deeply cosmic nature of sexuality, its potential to activate and energize centers of consciousness within the body (such as the chakras in tantric thought).

In a way that anticipates his later work with Guattari, with whom Deleuze would argue for the necessity of revolution at the level of desire, or "desiring-production," his early ruminations on the erotic dovetail with a political vision. Deleuze writes,

> What characterizes complicity is precisely that it can be ignored, denied, betrayed. The term "everyone" denies the universal so effectively, at the very moment it affirms it, that it is easy to notice only this negative aspect. This consists in passing from a state of latent, ignorant complicity to a complicity that knows and affirms itself as such. Not, certainly, the point where each loves as everyone, but where everyone loves in their singular manner. It is at the very moment when the living being persists stubbornly in its individuality that it affirms itself as universal. At the moment when the living being closed in upon itself, defining the universality of life as an outside, it did not see that it had, in fact, interiorized that universal: realized the universal on its own account, and defined itself as a microcosm. The first goal of mathesis is to assure this awareness of the living in relation to life and thus to ground the possibility of knowledge of individual destiny. (*MSP*, 145)[18]

What Deleuze means here by the singularity of each as the "interiorization of the universal," is not the truism that each individual destiny is unique, but that life, as the repetition of a process that is universally recursive, is a singular repetition, in each organism, of all previous civilizations and the history of organic life. Beyond a passive repetition of metabolism, habit, and memory, there is also the necessity that each individual life consciously reenact or nonidentically repeat the entire drama of *cosmic* destiny. In very broad strokes, we already have the contours of Deleuze's notion that an open series of disjunctive syntheses is in fact the very life of the absolute, a multiplicity engendering further multiplicities. We also have the emergence, here, of the paradoxical thought (expressed in *Difference and Repetition*) that it is precisely that which differentiates that most profoundly connects or resonates the disparate (*DR*, 69). In this way, the young Deleuze affirms a peculiar version of the hermetic "man the microcosm" thesis. He writes, "Beginning with a purely natural and unconscious complicity where each individual only posits himself in opposition to others, and more generally to the universal, it is a question of passage to a complicity that knows itself, where each grasps himself as '*pars totalis*' within a universe that he already constitutes. In other words, federation" (*MSP*, 145).[19]

Here symbolic knowledge is not only a force energizing individual decision and action, but is linked to a power of social cohesion, to "federation." In the vision under consideration here, a fully realized mathesis universalis would form the most intimate knowledge of the real grounds of social life.[20] Since such knowledge would symbolize the rhythms and periodicities, essential bifurcations and hidden lines of force both individuating and uniting life, it could ground a utopian politics of solidarity, complicity, and federation. More profound than the represented identities that form the objects of science and philosophy, mathesis would deal with the deep interrelationaities of existence, revealing patterns for the appreciation of difference at subdiscursive and subrepresentational levels. The young Deleuze is not reticent to identify the initiatory powers of mathesis with a power to conduct individual lives into the fundamental rubrics of the infinite, into the life of God. His prose on this point becomes rhapsodic. He writes,

> Thus we see that unity comes about at the level of conscious man; very far from transcending the human condition, it is its exact description. It must simply be remarked that such a description must position man in relation to the infinite, the universal. Each individual exists only by denying the universal; but insofar as man's existence refers to plurality, the negation is carried out universally under the exhaustive form of each and every one—so that it is but the human way of affirming what it denies. We have called this mode of affirmation conscious complicity. *And initiation is nothing other than this.* Initiation does not have a mystical sense: it is thought of life and the only possible way of thinking life. Initiation is mysterious only in the sense that the knowledge that it represents must be acquired by each person on their own account. The initiate is living man in his relationship with the infinite. And the key notion of mathesis—not at all mystical—is that individuality never separates itself from the universal, that between the living and life one finds the same relation as between life as species, and divinity. Thus the multiplicity of living beings which knows itself as such refers itself back to unity, which it describes in inverse relief, the circle as the simplest case of the ellipse. This is why we need to take Malfatti's words seriously when he reminds us that the circle, the wheel, represents God: "Mathesis would be for man in his relations with the infinite, what locomotion is to space."
>
> Mathesis is therefore neither a science of life, nor a philosophy. It is something else: a knowledge of life. It is neither the study of being,

nor the analysis of thought. Furthermore, the opposition of thought and being, of philosophy and science, have no meaning for it, seeming illusory, a false alternative. Mathesis situates itself on a plane where the life of knowledge is identical with the knowledge of life; it is simply awareness of life. Malfatti announces its *cogito* thus: *sum, ergo cogito; sum ergo genero*. That is to say that its method will be neither scientific nor philosophical. To its object, which is quite particular, must respond a particular method. (MSP, 147)

What is at issue for Malfatti (and for Deleuze's mature speculations on nature) is the excavation of (ordinarily) imperceptible relations that can be activated and transformed under intense, rituo-therapeutic conditions, engendering healing, creativity, and the generation of novel forms of life.[21] But my entire presentation here, and Deleuze's presentation of Malfatti, begs a serious question. In what sense is mathesis universalis a genuine possibility? *Is* there a mediating set of symbols expressive of the individuating powers of the whole? Part of why Deleuze does not answer this question, but simply indicates that mathesis is a potential knowledge of life, is because it is not a question that can be answered a priori. The question cannot be decided in the abstract, but only by reference to the productive capacities of concrete experiments in symbolism, insofar as they have been developed and tested.

Deleuze remained haunted by the possibility of an ecstatic and therapeutic approach to knowledge his entire career. Part of what is so extraordinary about this early essay, despite the somewhat obscure nature of its intimations, is the way Deleuze is already attempting to think in terms of a "plane" on which a certain projection of life, a lived experience of knowledge, can figure as a dynamic act of transformation or even of creation: *sum ergo genero*. Deleuze's early thoughts on mathesis thus anticipate many of the features he will later ascribe to the plan(e) of immanence or composition. He will even eventually claim, with Guattari, that the plane of composition is composed by "sorcerer's drawings," a clear harkening back to the symbolic language of Malfatti's ecstatic mathesis: "The plane of consistency is the intersection of all concrete forms. Therefore all becomings are written like sorcerer's drawings on this plane of consistency, which is the ultimate Door providing a way out for them . . . The only question is: Does a given becoming reach that point?" (ATP, 251). One cannot help wondering, given passages like this in his later writings, whether or not there is throughout Deleuze's work a kind of secret priority or silent prerogative given to esoteric knowledge and practice as a clue to the multiple meanings of immanence, such that to completely comprehend the significance of Deleuze's philosophy one would have to delve more deeply into previous esoteric traditions. My hypothesis is that we should continue to see, on the horizon of Deleuze's work, the persistence of his adolescent vision of an ecstatic, erotic, and unfinished project of mathesis universalis as that "prephilosophical" or "nonphilosophical" apprehension of immanence alluded to on the final pages of *What Is Philosophy?* Although in his adolescent work Deleuze distinguishes mathesis from both science and philosophy, this separation is ultimately superseded by Deleuze's attempt to articulate the nature of immanent thought that subtends art, science, and philosophy. *What Is Philosophy?* attempts to articulate an immanence common to art, science, and philosophy. Would not contact with the plan(e) of immanence involve something like a process of constructing a symbolic network, a "brain people," that would be the peculiar genius of an as-yet-unrealized mathesis universalis? (*WIP*, 218). The utopian aspects of immanence emphasized in *What Is Philosophy?* strongly connect with the simultaneously medicinal and apocalyptic tenor of Deleuze's early view of mathesis. What remains to be understood is how the ordeals necessary for such symbolic mapping become integrated into Deleuze's systematic philosophy. Deleuze never completely collapses the philosophical concept and the esoteric symbol. Yet Deleuze seems to be arguing, over the course of this work, that in some sense art, science, and philosophy are all informed by an apprehension of immanence whose immediate, if enigmatic, expression would be the symbolic language of a mathesis universalis yet to be realized, wherein, as Malfatti himself claimed, "mathesis would be for man in his relations with the infinite, what locomotion is to space" (*MSP*, 146).

The Force of Symbols

The persistence of interest in symbolic discourse for Deleuze's philosophy is remarkable for what one might call Deleuze's "materialism" of the symbol, the strangely physical force Deleuze imputes to symbols. Deleuze's theory, as he emphasizes in a late interview, is a departure from any theory that relegates symbols to reverie, to the ephemera of dreams or the lures of inchoate fantasies (*N*, 66). In two of Deleuze's last essays, "To Have Done with Judgment" and "Nietzsche and St. Paul, Lawrence and John of Patmos," Deleuze approaches in profound ways his early interest in mathesis. And here again is a crucial reference to Antonin Artaud. Artaud had envisioned a kind of theater that would wrest audiences from torpor and habit by means of extreme visual and sonic intensity. Such a theater was designed to force a reorganization of the body and sensibility, and thus to have done with "the judgments of God" that limit and encumber the body, restricting flows of energy and desire (*CC*, 131). In a similar vein, D. H. Lawrence argued that literature must enact a retrieval of the chthonic, quasidivine powers of nature as the basis for overcoming the spiritual sterility of the modern world. This project, like Artaud's, was linked directly to a renewal of the body. For Lawrence (as for Nietzsche, Artaud, Miller, and Burroughs), the West's ethos, its core symbolic cache, had become decadent, decrepit. What Lawrence found it urgent to envision was a new civilizational dynamic that could be dimly espied in the symbolic networks of archaic pagan religion. Lawrence perhaps most extensively tested the limits and conditions, the impasses and agonies, of such a project of retrieval in *The Plumed Serpent*.[22]

Lawrence's last published work was a long essay on the apocalypse.[23] Here Lawrence seeks to disinter an authentic, pagan core of Christian revelation, a genuinely universal religion of the earth. But this requires hearing an obscured voice within the overt tone of the book. As opposed to the sedate, mystical, and "aristocratic" perspective governing the love-message of the Gospels (in particular the Gospel of John), John of Patmos's is an angry voice, the voice of the resentful masses calling for the destruction of the world. But Lawrence notices, beneath the calls for universal destruction, "flashes throughout the first part of the Apocalypse of true cosmic worship."[24] Behind the figure of the judging, avenging Christ, with the keys to the gates of hell and the Seven Stars of Orion in his hands, is a *Kosmokrator*, a cosmic lord, "Lord of the Underworld," and "Hermes, the guide of souls through the death-world, over the hellish stream."[25] Lawrence sees in this Christ "some of the old pagan splendor, that delighted in might and the magnificence of the cosmos, and man who was a star in the cosmos."[26]

Lawrence believed it was the task of his literature to renew the possibility of a lived relationship to the *natural* divinities of life. "We and the cosmos are one," Lawrence writes, and evokes the hermetic tradition when he argues that "the cosmos is a vast living body, of which we are still parts. The sun is a great heart whose tremors run through our smallest veins. The moon is a great gleaming nerve-center from which we quiver forever . . . it is a vital power, rippling exquisitely through us *all the time* . . . Now all this is *literally* true, as men knew in the great past, and as they will know again."[27] As Kerslake has pointed out, Lawrence was inspired by certain esoteric readings of the apocalypse as a kind of tantric "map" of the body's energies, a plan whose comprehension might enable mystical transmutations.[28] In *Essays Critical and Clinical*, Deleuze follows up on Lawrence's approach by connecting Lawrence's thought to his own conception of a "body without organs" that "is an affective, intensive, anarchist body that consists solely of poles, zones, thresholds, and gradients . . . [Lawrence] paints a picture of such a body, with the sun and moon as its poles, with its planes, its sections, and its plexuses" (CC, 131). To access this level of the body is to move beyond its discrete parts, and to map its energy flows with reference to larger cosmic patterns and dynamics (as has long been the approach to the body in terms of chakras activated by hatha yoga, or in terms of the meridians used in traditional Chinese medicine).

For Deleuze, Lawrence teaches us to read the imagery in the *Apocalypse* against the grain, to discover the hidden power of its symbols. Deleuze notes that Lawrence contrasts the power of the symbol, as a "force of decision," with the power of allegorical interpretation (CC, 39). Deleuze argues that allegory is always a mode of judgment, a desire to bring the interplay of images and associations to a discrete, "final" point, as in the final point of the last judgment in which power over life and death is subordinated once and for all to the Divine Will. In contrast to allegory, with its punctual, segmented nature, the symbol is not a terminus but a relay of powers, a node in a series of decisions. Response to a symbol motivates a decision not for this or that, but a decision to decide.

In a recursion to the thought of his early *What Is Grounding?* lectures, in this late essay Deleuze once again considers the symbolic power of the Sphinx's riddle: What goes on four legs in the morning, two in the afternoon, and three at night? The answer, of course, is "man," but Deleuze here argues that it is inappropriate to read the riddle as simply an allegory of humanity, as if the "point" of each stage were always the same, or as if each phase of life were an aliquod part of an organic totality. Deleuze insists, rather, that life is symbolized in the riddle "only if one feels the three groups of images in the process of whirling around the most mysterious point of man: images of the animal-child; then those of the creature on two paws, a monkey, bird, or frog; and then those of the unknown beast on three paws, from beyond the seas and deserts" (*CC*, 48). What one becomes, over time, in the distinct durations of childhood, maturity, and old age, is each time the effect of a singular vector, with its unique and unforeseeable drama.

Deleuze's thought hearkens back, here, to the hermetic vision of Pico della Mirandola, who had described a humanity created not in keeping with a particular form, but as superadded to the cosmic orders. This parataxic position of humanity renders it capable of undergoing extreme ordeals, of traversing the entire chain of being, from mineral to angelic.[29] The realization of human perfection, in this view, is possible only because there is no human essence, God having given Adam "no form, no fixed seat." Being created *imago dei*, for Pico, is not to be a well-placed "rational animal" at the center of stable hierarchies. The human prerogative is to be capable, for good or ill, of identification with any level of existence. The medieval chain of being that had an "allegorical" power in late scholastic cosmology, assigning to each individual a place, is reenvisioned by Pico as symbolic in precisely the Deleuzian sense of forming a milieu of transformation, an imbricated series of powers of becoming.

Lawrence's vision clearly recapitulates such Renaissance visions of humanity as microcosmic. For Lawrence, the mind reaches its full capacity not in a rationalizing or analytical vein, but in a *sommeil*, a somnambulance where, freed from the binds of self-consciousness, the self can explore the virtual range of its instinctual proclivities, its as-yet-unknown affects. Deleuze describes this self-involuting process not as stupor but as enlightenment, a genuine "awakening." He writes,

> One by one Lawrence sketches out certain characteristic features of the symbol. It is a dynamic process that enlarges, deepens, and expands sensible consciousness; it is an ever-increasing becoming-conscious, as opposed to the closing of the moral consciousness upon a fixed allegorical idea. It is a method of the Affect, intensive, a cumulative intensity, which merely marks the threshold of sensation, the awakening of a state

of consciousness: the symbol means nothing, and has neither to be explained nor interpreted, as opposed to the intellectual consciousness of allegory. It is *rotative thought*, in which a group of images turn ever more quickly around a mysterious point, as opposed to the linear allegorical chain. (CC, 48)

The emphasis on the immediacy of the symbol here recalls Deleuze's early argument that mathesis turns upon the possibility of a knowledge of life that occurs in the shortest possible interval, at maximum speed. It is the symbol that incarnates a minimum interval of force whose effect occurs at a maximum of velocity, imperceptibly fast. Symbolic knowledge is thus an awakening of consciousness, rather than an abstract subsumption of an object under a concept. To evaluate a symbol is not to explain but to decide, *to decide to decide*, in a movement that connects possible lines of action directly to unexplored levels of sensibility.[30]

Such symbolic procedure has a profound place in philosophy: when Deleuze follows Nietzsche in ascribing the title of "legislator" to philosophy, it is on the basis of an instituting power proper to symbolic discourse that the philosopher becomes legislator, laying down new laws of sensation, affect, and creation (*NP*, 92). Deleuze even goes so far as to say that in enlarging sensibility, the symbol performs an oracular function, literally "divining" those affects of which the mind and body may be capable. The will and the force of action and decision are linked not to rational deliberation but to symbolic intensity. Deleuze writes,

> This is precisely what the rotative symbol is. It has neither beginning nor end, it does not lead us anywhere, and above all it has no final point, nor even stages. It is always in the middle, in the midst of things, between things. It has only a milieu, milieus that are ever more profound. The symbol is a maelstrom, it makes us whirl about until it produces that intense state out of which the solution, the decision, emerges. The symbol is *process of action and decision*; in this sense, it is linked to the oracle that furnished it with these whirling images. For this is how we make a true decision: we turn into ourselves, upon ourselves, ever more rapidly, until a center is formed and we know what to do. (CC, 49)

Allegorical thought aims to specify in advance what is possible or impossible in a given milieu, from the point of view of a predetermined set of ends and aims. Symbolic thought provokes a decision to decide, to leap, whirl, or rotate, and thus to change the level or perspective of organization. To symbolize is to act within the middle of things. In his late interviews, collected as *Negotiations*, Deleuze laments that the symbolic dimension is missing from much of contemporary philosophy, obsessed as it is with a search for first principles, rather than thinking through the immanent forces of a milieu (*N*, 121). The centers formed in symbols are not separable from the intensities symbols incarnate; yet the inspiration or "enthusiasm" symbols inspire is not a totalizing fantasy or imaginary whole, but a physical-affective tracing of real virtual potencies.[31]

Deleuze's "physics" of the symbol has a strange consequence: the more symbols are understood as transcriptions of "cosmic" dynamics, the more their spiritual aspect—the aspect of symbols that relates to spiritual transformation—becomes clear. On this point, Deleuze's approach to the symbol (and more generally his conception of the transcendental imagination) is deeply resonant with that of Henry Corbin, who identified an "imaginal" mode of mysticism where aspects of humanity and divinity enter into a creative zone of indiscernibility. Although his own work focuses on Sufi mysticism, Corbin asserts that the idea of the imagination as a real intermediary was central to the Renaissance and reemerged with romanticism. And for Corbin, as for Deleuze, it is crucial to distinguish the imagination from mere fantasy. Corbin writes,

> We wish to stress on the one hand the *Imagination* as the *magical* production of an *image*, the very type and model of magical action, or of all action as such, but especially of creative action; and, on the other hand, the notion of the image as a body (a *magical* body, a *mental* body), in which are incarnate the thought and will of the soul. The Imagination as a creative magical potency which, giving birth to the sensible world, produces the Spirit in forms and colors; the world as *Magia divina* "imagined" by the Godhead, that is the ancient doctrine, typified in the juxtaposition of the words *Imago* and *Magia*, which Novalis rediscovered through Fichte. But a warning is necessary at the very outset: this *Imaginatio* must not be confused with *fantasy*. As Paracelsus already observed, fantasy, unlike Imagination, is an exercise of thought without foundation in nature, it is the "madman's cornerstone."
>
> This warning is essential.[32]

Not only is Deleuze's notion of symbolic power directly indebted to Novalis's idea of a "magical idealism," and his late thought of the transcendental field indebted to Fichte, but the kind of warning Corbin issues here resonates across Deleuze's work with Guattari, when Deleuze attempts more explicitly to develop a taxonomy of various "practical" avenues into the absolute, from psychedelia to the aesthetics of free indirect discourse.[33]

In his mature thought, Deleuze grounds this "poetic physics" in the specifically temporal nature of the imagination, in the productions of crystals of time, of what he will call "time-images" in his books on cinema. In *Negotiations*, Deleuze elaborates:

> That is why I don't attach much importance to the notion of the imaginary. It depends, in the first place, on a crystallization, physical, chemical, or psychical; it defines nothing, but is defined by the crystal-image as a circuit of exchanges; to imagine is to construct crystal-images, to make the image behave like a crystal. It's not the imaginary but the crystal that has a heuristic role, with its triple circuit: actual-virtual, clear-opaque, seed-environment. And in the second place, all that matters about the crystal itself is what we see in it, so the imaginary drops out of the equation. What we see in the crystal is a time that's become autonomous, independent of motion, temporal relations constantly inducing false moves. I don't believe the imaginary has any power, in dreams, fantasies . . . and so on. The imaginary is a rather indeterminate notion. It makes sense in strict conditions: its precondition is the crystal, and the unconditioned we eventually reach is time. (*N*, 66)

The form that a particular image takes is the expression of a virtual seed that manifests an actual form. Through the imagination, one construes, or "actualizes," a particular temporal shape, an arrangement of the potencies of time. Yet here it is as if Descartes's certainty that even in dreams squares have four sides were grounded not in the reason that recognizes such forms, but in the imagination that invents in accordance with shapes it haptically (rather than optically) traces. The imagination is a way of feeling our way through the world in which we must try out an idea before we even know (or "see") what it is. And yet the lines along which we grope (in obscurity) remain distinct, differential lines of potential. Deleuze's theory of the unfolding of the crystal is in part an attempt to deal with this paradox of obscurity and distinctness proper to the imagination generally, and to symbols in particular.

Deleuze's contention throughout his work is that symbols function in an oracular manner, incarnating lines of force along which as yet unforeseen actions may occur. But what is prophesied has, somehow, a specifically physical meaning. Why? For Deleuze, the physical world is not constituted simply by extensive quantities and qualities, but by intensive or imbricated (vibratory, rhythmic) attributes. The empirical for Deleuze includes the virtual, whose nature only becomes apparent serially, differentially, and in resonance across disparate instances. Only in certain extreme instances of perception, such as somnambulance or vertigo, do we have the potential to directly access the virtual, intensive, and immanent being of the sensible. Insofar as symbols transmit such differential spectra, symbols are in some sense diagrams of immanence, of difference and repetition at the most abstract level. But such symbolic power can be real only if the imagination is acknowledged as something other than fantasy or projection. Only if the imagination is a "willing of what is" do symbols function as some kind of practical schema of absolute life, of immanence.

The "symbolic force" of immanence had something to do, at least in the mind of the early Deleuze, with the unfinished project of mathesis universalis. If symbolic power captures the powers of immanence, it does so through acts of imagination that are properly transcendental, that develop ideas whose role, while not available to ordinary states of conscious perception, are nevertheless essential and imperative for thought and action and transformation. But the prospect of the reality of such ideas raises a real problem for philosophy, since philosophy is distinct from, although related to, the development and deployment of symbols. If the symbols of any ersatz attempt at mathesis universalis were to express a practical unity of life (and such unity is also what Deleuze seems to be aiming at with his notion of the plan(e) of immanence subtending science, art, and philosophy), it is arguable that even for the late Deleuze, the "unthought in thought," the "non-philosophy" or "pre-philosophical" essential to conceptual creation would itself be a kind of intuitive symbolic gnosis, a mathesis universalis (*WIP*, 59). However, as Deleuze himself points out in his preface to Malfatti's work, mathesis is itself neither scientific nor philosophical, neither hypothetical nor conceptual. Yet Deleuze's major works continue to show his experimenting with discursive strategies and theoretical frameworks that feature philosophy itself as beholden to and attempting to embody some kind of transformative knowledge. In short, Deleuze continues to be haunted by the connection of philosophy to symbolic iterations—artistic, scientific, and esoteric—that would be adequate for the expression of immanence and indispensible for philosophy as an act of creation.

4

The Overturning of Platonism

> You have to present concepts in philosophy as though you were writing a good detective novel: they must have a zone of presence, resolve a local situation, be in contact with the "dramas," and bring a certain cruelty with them. They must exhibit a certain coherence but get if from somewhere else. —GILLES DELEUZE, *Desert Islands and Other Texts (1953–1974)*, 141

Despite the fact that Deleuze does not explicitly write as an esotericist, his major works nevertheless proceed in a rather gnomic mode of philosophical discourse, a discourse inspired by the paradoxical, the problematic, and the uncanny. In this way, Deleuze's texts enact what they often claim: genuine thought unfolds through a discourse that runs counter to prevailing images of rationality, enlightenment, and truth. Philosophical discourse, for Deleuze, does not emerge without provocation, elicitation, and a certain forcing. Thought for him is a kind of passion, an excess manifest as creation as much as critique. Thought is a critique of cliché and habitual forms of thought, and a creation of modes of life, even evoking an entirely transformed sensibility (*NP*, 101).

The Image of Thought

For Deleuze it was Plato who discovered, but also restricted, the true nature of philosophy as spiritual ordeal. Socrates leads his interlocutors into the dizzying perplexity of a seemingly interminable dialectic. But there is an implicit presumption in Plato's dialogues that in any genuine act of thought, however arduous, productivity can be guaranteed in advance by the inherent connection between the good and the true: a truly good will to thought will always move us closer to the truth, and unworthy suitors to the hand of the good and true will be sifted, like chaff from wheat.

The deep connection in Plato's mind between philosophical inquiry and moral purification bequeathed to Western philosophy what Deleuze calls, in *Difference and Repetition*, an implicit "image of thought." This image determines the philosopher as, above all, a person of good will, inherently possessed of a "good will to truth." But from Plato to Hegel, Deleuze contends, the good will of philosophy functions ultimately in the service of established values and of the state. The will of philosophy, with its quest for truth, is to establish (or reestablish) identity, order, and continuity against the forces of difference, chaos, and discontinuity. However subversive Platonism might have been to its Greek milieu, under the auspices of the Platonic image, thinking in the West became a conservative affair: a will to buttress the mind and the status quo against challenges to order, discipline, and control.

Despite modern philosophy's critical ambition, the conservative tendencies in the Platonic image of thought are repeated in the idea of a *cogitatio natura universalis* (natural universal reason) Descartes asserted was common to all humanity. For Deleuze, the persuasive force of Descartes's grounding of being in the subject, cogito ergo sum, is less radical than it may appear to be, since it depends on the implicit presupposition that it is in the nature of thought itself, in its innate nature, to seek the truth with a good nature and a good will. Deleuze points out that the coherence of an idea of naturally donated "good sense" depends not on an explicit philosophical justification, but on the implicit idea that "everyone knows" what it means to think (*DR*, 129). A thinking thing cannot want to be deceived: any deceiver must be external to thought, outside the circuit of consciousness. Self-consciousness is presumed by nature to be constituted by a desire to avoid deception, betrayal, violence to itself. But this distinction of the subject from its potential vicissitudes, in Deleuze's view, is inimical to thought. In *Difference and Repetition*, he asserts just the contrary:

> Thought is primarily trespass and violence, the enemy, and nothing presupposes philosophy: everything begins with misosophy. Do not count on thought to ensure the relative necessity of what it thinks. Rather, count upon the contingency of an encounter with that which forces thought to rise up and educate the absolute necessity of an act of thought or a passion to think. The conditions of a true critique and a true creation are one and the same: the destruction of the image of thought which presupposes itself and the genesis of the act of thinking in thought itself. (*DR*, 139)

Under the auspices of the image of thought, what remains unasked are the truly critical questions: Why the need for order? Who requires continuity? When and under what conditions is truth to be preferred to illusion? For Deleuze, the postulates of common sense legislate that the productions of thought must be inherently recognizable, even if the object of thought is difficult, paradoxical, or even unthinkable. It is the image of thought that prevents philosophy from completing the project of Platonism, since under this aegis thought can never truly break with opinion (*doxa*). Wedded to a representational model of concepts, philosophy continues to fashion its ideas according to the implicit parameters of common sense. Beyond the postulates of the image of thought lies a great risk, a confrontation with allies other than those of good and common sense in the quest of truth.[1] Such a "thought beyond the image of thought" would, Deleuze asserts, "find its difference or its true beginning, not in an agreement with the *pre-philosophical* Image but in a rigorous struggle against this Image, which it would denounce as *non-philosophical*. As a result, it would discover its authentic repetition in a thought without Image, even at the cost of the greatest destructions and demoralizations, and a philosophical obstinacy with no ally but paradox, one which would have to renounce both the form of representation and the element of common sense" (*DR*, 132). Across numerous traditions, paradox is one of the classic literary modes of spiritual ordeal, always aimed at unsettling the mind and enabling it to apprehend levels of interconnection, relationality, and interdependence that are not rationally accessible.[2] It is within such an "overturned Platonism" that we again discern the lineaments of the hermetic Deleuze, a Deleuze whose philosophy is geared as much to spiritual transformation as to conceptual creation.

Platonic Ordeal

Despite Plato's moralism, Deleuze argues that it is nevertheless within the Platonic corpus that a subversive and profound notion of thought lies in wait. Even though, following Nietzsche, Deleuze asserts that "the task of modern philosophy has been defined: to overturn Platonism," he insists that much should be retained from Plato: "That this overturning should conserve many Platonic characteristics is not only inevitable but desirable" (*DR*, 59). What is it that Deleuze—the hermetic Deleuze, that is—would have us retain?

In *Difference and Repetition*, Deleuze observes that Plato's confidence in the ordeal of the dialectic is grounded in a mythical conception of the dialectic as an odyssey, a return to lost origins. That is to say, the difficulties of dialectical ordeal recapitulate a cosmic process of metempsychosis: the procession and return of souls to their true autochthony in the invisible, changeless realm of the idea. Plato presents Socratic dialectic as a kind of exercise, a training that is productive for thought despite the failure of the participants to produce satisfactory definitions or complete concepts. Going beyond what Plato might have averred, Deleuze asserts that the failed or incomplete nature of dialectic is in fact *necessary*. Plato himself would have admitted that since the immutable and eternal ideas cannot be discursively represented, they must form the object of some kind of access other than what ordinary linguistic and conceptual expression allows, and it is for just such intuition that dialectic prepares.

But the questions remains open: if not by discursive mediation, by what power are the ideas apprehended? Some kind of mediation is necessary. But how is it to be construed? Deleuze writes, "With Plato, the issue is still in doubt: mediation has not yet found its ready-made movement. The Idea is not yet the concept of an object which submits the world to the requirements of representation, but rather a brute presence which can be invoked in the world only in function of that which is not 'representable' in things. The Idea has therefore not yet chosen to relate difference to the identity of a concept in general: it has not given up hope of finding a pure concept of difference in itself" (*DR*, 59).[3]

In what sense is Plato's theory of ideas linked to the development of a pure concept of "difference in itself"? On this issue, Deleuze contrasts Plato with Aristotle. For Aristotle, individuals are particular combinations of matter and form. Individuals differ insofar as they manifest differently actualized potentials. Individuals (primary substances) are the substances they are in relation to a discernable essence (substance in a secondary sense) whose potential they more or less actualize. Conceptual activity, for Aristotle, is the mind's ability to abstract form from matter. All knowledge, as knowledge of form, is an abstraction from a series, and is in this sense a generalization. A concept of justice, for example, is developed from reflections on how the potentials of justice have been more or less actualized in various individuals. Species of justice, or beauty, as much as of trees or horses, can likewise be determined based on abstraction from individuals.[4]

For Aristotle, what makes a thing knowable, whether this is a natural or an artificial kind, is that it can be classified into species and genera that are prior, at least in the order of knowledge, to individual differences. (It is somewhat unclear in Aristotle in what sense primary substances, such as individual horses, are dependent upon secondary substances, such as species essence of horseness.) Indeed, Aristotle claims there is no science of the singular, and by implication no science of difference, as such. That is to say, intelligible differences, for Aristotle, are always differences known by and through comparisons of sameness or similarity. But comprehensible differences are, as Deleuze puts it, always relatively large differences, ones that can be clearly perceived or represented, and that can delineate individuals, genera, and species. This means that ultimately difference has no concept of its own, in Aristotle's thought. Difference is meaningful only within a process of comparison, such as in the construction of an analogy by which it is judged that a horse is both like and unlike a mule. For Aristotle, a difference that cannot be articulated by comparison between two identities is essentially meaningless, and may as well be considered, like prime matter, as inconsequential for thought.

In Plato, however, difference is not conceived of in terms of comparison or opposition. Difference, in Plato, seems to be approached "in itself," and this is part of what inspires Deleuze. Socrates's search for definitions (of love, justice, excellence, and so on) is a search for the presence of a stable form within a shifting world of appearances, for true being in the realm of becoming. But the definition of a form is not a generality discovered through processes of abstraction from empirical aggregates or collections of experience. In the *Statesman*, for example, Socrates is not looking for the list of attributes that will distinguish the set of all authentic rulers from those who lack such attributes, but seeking to apply a test whose result will make the difference between a leader and a charlatan.[5] As Deleuze puts it, this is because each individual relates to its archetype (an idea) as a copy to its model. What matters, for Plato, are not external affinities between various copies, but internal relations between copies and ideal models. Plato seeks to distinguish, Deleuze argues, authentic from inauthentic copies, and above all to eliminate simulacra, those particularly malicious appearances that are neither originals nor imitations, neither models nor copies.[6] "It is clear that Plato distinguishes, and even opposes, models and copies only in order to obtain a selective criterion with which to separate copies and simulacra, the former founded upon their relation to the model while the latter are disqualified because they fail both the test of the copy and the requirements of the model. While there is indeed appearance, it is rather a matter of distinguishing the splendid, well-grounded Apollonian appearances from the other, insinuative, malign and maleficent appearances which respect the ground no more than the grounded" (*DR*, 265). As Deleuze puts it, the "brute presence" of the idea is a kind of trial that singles out a "line of authentic descent" from within an indifferent mixture, a materiality that has no specifiable relation to form, but that persists as a kind of inchoate medium, an "indefinite representing multiplicity" (*DR*, 60). Unlike in Aristotle, in Plato identity is not realized as a reciprocal relation between mater and form, potentiality and actuality. If anything, in Plato materiality must be eliminated, or at least refined, in order for a distinct individual manifestation to be distinguished from its simulacra. It is as if matter constitutes a set of inchoate elements to be sifted: "The search for gold provides the model for this division" (*DR*, 60). For Plato, the faculty that recognizes the forms—the basis of all identity, both semantically and ontologically—is not a faculty that represents, but one that intuits a movement of descent. As Deleuze puts it, "Difference is not between species, between two determinations of a genus, but entirely on one side, within the chosen line of descent: there are no longer contraries within a single genus, but pure and impure, good and bad, authentic and inauthentic, in a mixture which gives rise to a large species. Pure difference, the pure concept of difference, not the concept in general, in the genus and species" (*DR*, 60). Deleuze suggests that when Socrates attempts to distinguish the true leader from the charlatan in the *Statesman*, or true erotic ecstasy from delirium in the *Phaedrus*, there is no question of attempting to establish species and genera. For Plato it is a matter, rather, of divining a singularity, a "dialectic of the immediate" that divides the true from the false claimant, the worthy suitor from the impostor. Deleuze characterizes this as a "question not of identifying but authenticating" (*DR*, 60). That is to say, Plato's project is not to organize being into species and genera, but to divide the world of appearances into true and false imitations, images that are genuine inheritors of the idea, on the one hand, and on the other hand images that are impostors, simulacra. As Deleuze puts it, "This problem of distinguishing between *things and their simulacra* within a pseudo-genus or a large species presides over [Plato's] classification of the arts and sciences. It is a question of making the difference, thus of operating in the depths of the immediate, of a dialectic of the immediate. It is a dangerous trial without thread and without net, for according to the ancient customs of myth and epic, false claimants must die" (*DR*, 60).

Plato distinguishes the false claimants from the true by referring their claims to what Deleuze calls a "mythical" ground: participation. The claim to participation is not simply the claim to be identified as a member of a class or token of a type. It is a claim to have passed a test or to have a basis for one's claim. The difference between the just and the unjust, pretenders to justice and authentic stewards of justice, is not a difference between any two, but an internal and constitutive difference. It is the difference an "immediate fact" of participation makes. Unlike the Aristotelian development of form in matter, the participation of becoming in being is not the development of a material substrate. It is the selection of an icon from within a prodigious field of idols, false images. The interplay of epistemic and ontological registers here is deliberate, and is why Deleuze can claim that Platonic dialectic, as much as the Platonic cosmology, is in the last instance, a moral vision. That a false suitor such as the unscrupulous Meno contradicts himself when asked to define excellence means not that he has not yet found the answer to the question "What is excellence?" but that he is not (yet) the kind of person who could understand the question. Meno contradicts himself in laying claim to virtue—not because he lacks the ability to correctly define a genera, a generic category, but because he illegitimately claims to participate in the idea of excellence. Socrates's question is not simply *what* is excellence, but are *you* excellent?

What is important about this picture for Deleuze's own theory of ideas is that, as Plato presents him, Socrates does not show himself to be a worthy suitor of the ideas because he produces definitions, but because he understands the nature of the problems—the tests, the ordeals—demanded by a life defined by the hypothesis of the ideas. The problem is that knowledge is not a matter of generalization but of participation, and participation, at the level of dialectic, is a movement of purification begun in self-examination. In the *Apology*, when Socrates learns that the Delphic oracle has declared him the wisest of the Athenians, he responds with a life lived in the attempt to refute the oracle. This attempt is an ordeal by means of which Socrates attempts to determine his own worth, the coherence of his own beliefs. Socrates lives his life through a question: What is it to be wise? The irony of Socrates's life is that his own answer is embedded in the structure of his life lived as a question, a life that demonstrates that to be conscious of ignorance is wisdom.

Problematic Ideas

What can be preserved in Platonism, for Deleuze, is the notion that philosophy is a specific form of education, an apprenticeship activated by the discovery of that which is truly different: the idea. In Plato, the ideas (or forms) do not appear in a perceptible diversity, but constitute a supreme and nonsensible power of iteration. But as Deleuze points out, because the forms do not appear directly in the empirical, they introduce a regime of obscure signs into the sensible world, traces of the ideal in the real. These traces can only be perceived as problematic, as moments where the continuum of time and circumstance is at odds with itself. The idea is never given in a complete *pleroma*, and can only be grasped as sign.

When determining, for example, who counts as a sophist, as opposed to a philosopher, or what counts as a merely "acquisitive" as opposed to a "productive" art, or even what counts as a winged as opposed to nonwinged animal, Plato does not present individuating differences in terms of generalizable criteria. Plato's divisions thus "lack sufficient reason," as Aristotle claimed (*DR*, 59).[7] A capricious or itinerant form of differentiation that "jumps from one singularity to another" is precisely what is so curious and compelling for Deleuze about the Platonic method of thought (*DR*, 59). In Plato, "the Idea is not yet the concept of an object which submits the world to the requirements of representation, but rather of a brute presence which can be invoked in the world only in function of that which is not 'representable' in things" (*DR*, 59). Thus, in Platonic dialectics the relation between an idea and a participant or *icône* of that idea is in some sense occult, inexplicable. The idea institutes a relation that cannot be represented, yet is there. The relation between the ideal and the real, in Plato, constitutes an enigmatic presence of sense.

Deleuze's thought is a kind of spiritual exercise. It is not accidental that Socrates refers to himself as a midwife, claimed to have learned about the forms from a sorceress, and was constantly accused of bewitching or spell-binding his interlocutors. According to Plato, it was the accusation of religious innovation that led to Socrates's execution. This accusation must have been linked, in part, to the challenging redistribution of sense and sensibility that would have been inspired by the hypothesis of the forms: this belief would have led one to live one's life differently, in view of different realities, as Socrates's young admirers often remark. There is already in Socrates a sense that to apprehend ideas is to be changed and transformed. It is this transformative dimension of ideas that inspires Deleuze's own conception of thought.

Socrates's capriciousness, his lack of systematic exposition, demonstrates that, in a certain way, he does not subordinate difference to representable divergence, or to what will amount in later philosophy to subordination of difference to the powers of the One, the analogous, the similar, and the negative—ways difference fails to be thought "in itself," but is conceived in relation to something else (*DR*, 59). Faced with a host of "suitors" or "claimants" to the right to define and thus to participate, Socrates "tests" to see if the claim holds. But this test is an enigma, a problem posed to the claimant: Do you know the nature of the question to which you are giving an answer, the essence of the problem to which you are giving a solution? False claimants contradict themselves performatively, because their character is not fit for the truth of the idea in which they claim to participate. Deleuze argues that even if Plato ultimately believes that philosophical inquiry returns us to a state in which what is problematic in embodied existence is fully resolved, restored to the idea, the dialectic is nevertheless always tinged with irony, and "irony consists in treating things and beings as so many responses to hidden questions, so many cases for problems yet to be resolved" (DR, 62, 63). Even if the Platonic philosopher is assured of the ultimately unproblematic nature of the ideas to which he or she belongs by right, the idea is a source of irony, never a means of identifying but a way of problematizing, a manner of posing questions.[8]

Since being is other than becoming, and discourse is within becoming, discourse is always less than full speech about being. The philosopher's questions never lead directly to truth, but only to other questions. But for this inconclusive dimension can be read as a positive aspect of learning, since learning the difference between the ideal and the actual worlds is an initiation into the significance of signs. In Platonic terms, in learning difference one learns how to distinguish between two kinds of images or appearances: true icons and false imitations. As Deleuze puts it, "Neither the problem nor the question is a subjective determination marking a moment of insufficiency in knowledge. Problematic structure is part of objects themselves, allowing them to be grasped as signs, just as the questioning or problematizing instance is a part of knowledge allowing its positivity and its specificity to be grasped in an act of *learning*. More profoundly still, Being (what Plato calls the Idea) 'corresponds' to the essence of the problem or the question as such" (DR, 64).

To call Platonic "Being" the essence of a problem or question is a kind of doublespeak on Deleuze's part. It is here that Deleuze begins to interpolate his own views with Plato's. For Deleuze, questions or problems, "problematic structure," is a transcendental dimension, in the sense that the true forces and elements involved in any material, social, or historical configuration must be understood in terms of ideal problems whose complete contours are not fully given. Such dynamics, for Deleuze, should be considered ideal because they can, under a variety of conditions, account for why any actual configuration becomes unstable or enters into unpredicted relations and unforeseen modes of communication with other entities. In fact, for Deleuze, such a multiplicity of sense is virtually present at every moment, even if our awareness of these potentials is limited to our ability to decipher them in signs. Signs have a more intimate relation with ideas, for Deleuze, than they do for Plato, since for Deleuze the multiple and mutable character of the sign extends to ideas themselves.

In a certain way, one can read Deleuze's theory of ideas as the exploitation of a possibility that is foreclosed by Plato in the *Theaetetus*. At the end of that dialogue, Socrates explicitly considers the possibility that genuine knowledge may be knowledge not of identity but of difference. In the final attempt to define knowledge after the failed attempts to define knowledge as perception, and then as true opinion, Socrates proposes that knowledge might be "the ability to tell some characteristic by which the object in question differs from all others" (208c).

> Theaetetus. As an example of the method, what explanation can you give me, and of what thing?
> Socrates. As an example, if you like, take the sun: I think it is enough for you to be told that it is the brightest of the heavenly bodies that revolve about the earth.
> Theat. Certainly.
> Soc. Understand why I say this. It is because, as we were just saying, if you get hold of the distinguishing characteristic by which a given thing differs from the rest, you will, as some say, get hold of the definition or explanation of it; but so long as you cling to some common quality, your explanation will pertain to all those objects to which the common quality belongs.
> Theat. I understand; and it seems to me that it is quite right to call that kind a rational explanation or definition.
> Soc. Then he who possesses right opinion about anything and adds thereto a comprehension of the difference which distinguishes it from other things will have acquired knowledge of that thing of which he previously only had opinion.

Although this possibility initially looks promising, Socrates goes on to refute it by asking whether true opinion is not, by itself, already knowledge of difference, of "distinguishing characteristics"? If I have a true opinion that the person I see in front of me is Socrates, because I see someone snub-nosed and otherwise like Socrates, what else makes it a true belief other than the true opinion that Socrates is a snub-nosed person? True opinion seems already to be a recognition of significant difference. But to have a true opinion of difference is to perceive such difference, and if perception is nothing but perception of difference, then knowledge would amount to exactly what Protagoras claimed it was—a "measure" relative to each perceiver's apprehension of difference. If Protagoras is right, what is the sense in saying that some are wiser than others? Why defer to some opinions and reject others? If all knowledge is perception, then all perception is knowledge: different claims to knowledge devolve into differences in perception, a bland relativism.

Deleuze, however, argues that thought is somehow an apprehension of difference, as such.[9] In Heraclitean fashion, Deleuze grasps the nettle and avers that indeed all is becoming: there is neither perceiver nor perceived apart from events of becomings-perceived. However, Deleuze simultaneously affirms that what is in becoming is not simply the empirical understood as the flux of appearances, but a virtual and differential "being of the sensible," a transcendental consistency within the play of appearances. In *Nietzsche and Philosophy* Deleuze admits the "pre-Socratic" character of his affirmation of thought as an affirmation of forces, but insists that the meaning of thought as a relation to force is post-Kantian in the sense that it is an element of critique. The affirmation of difference is no longer simply metaphysical, an issue of the submission of thought to the true, but of legislation or judgment: thought is creation on behalf of or in view of forces, such that different forces constitute a variety of mental elements, whose truth is measured by the nobility or baseness of the life they manifest (*NP*, 92).

Plato had rejected Heracliteanism on grounds of incoherence. It is important to linger over Plato's argument here, in order to comprehend the radicality of Deleuze's own view. What does it mean to be "small" or "large," per se? No sense experience will tell us.[10] When we hold up our first three fingers for inspection, the index finger looks smaller than the middle finger, but the ring finger, smaller than the middle finger, looks larger than the index finger. The index finger can only be said to be large by one comparison and small by another. The conclusion is that it is always equally appropriate to attribute contrary predicates to the same subject, and that rather than produce knowledge, the sensible world produces only an incoherent "qualitative contrariety." If smallness or largeness, per se, is in any sense "in" the sensible world, the mind makes contact with this idea not as a quantity or quality, but as an unlocalized instance that organizes or is somehow deployed within sensation. But every idea is also distorted by the particularities of the sensible because objects of perception always combine logically incommensurable predicates.

What this means, for Plato, is that the sensible world is inherently deceptive; it does not provide the conditions for knowledge, since in his view knowledge is of universals or it is no knowledge at all, but mere imagination or belief. Yet such knowledge is extremely elusive. Largeness and smallness cannot be "in" perception, but can only be manifest in how they are compromised by, even betrayed by, appearances. It is the instability of perception, its vertiginous or slipshod character, that calls for the necessity of stable forms. Thus Plato took sensible becoming—indeed, took life itself—only as so many occasions to recollect the forms, to discover the necessity of a return to incorporeal, imperceptible, and intransitive reality.

Deleuze himself aims to affirm an equally incorporeal, imperceptible and intransitive reality, but a reality of difference: a reality of the idea that is not self-unified but inherently multiple. Ideas, for Deleuze, are a kind of transcendental multiplicity of which the diversity of spatiotemporal experience is a partial revelation. Deleuze thus seeks to "naturalize" the Platonic ideas by conceiving them not as static beings but as pure "Becomings": pure dynamics of nature from which all forms emerge and into which they perpetually devolve, only to emerge again in ever new forms. An idea is a unique, repeating node within this process, an abstract capture of temporal processes and spatial organization.

Deleuze thus follows Plato in conceiving of the sensible as a kind of manifold or manifesting apparatus for the otherwise imperceptible. He further follows Plato in the notion that it is something immeasurable that provokes the mind—qualitative contrariety, is also for Deleuze that which arouses thought. But Deleuze gives a positive significance to qualitative contrariety by relating it back to a phenomenon of imperceptible intensity at the heart of the empirical:

> Qualitative contrariety is only the reflection of the intense, a reflection which betrays it by explicating it in extensity. It is intensity or difference in intensity which betrays it by explicating it in extensity. It is intensity or difference in intensity which constitutes the peculiar limit of sensi-

bility. As such, it has the paradoxical character of the limit: it is the imperceptible, that which cannot be sensed because it is always covered by a quality which alienates or contradicts it, always distributed within an extensity which inverts or cancels it. In another sense, it is that which can only be sensed or that which defines the transcendent exercise of sensibility, because it gives to be sensed, thereby awakening memory and forcing thought. (DR, 237)

Deleuze's move, then, is to take what for Plato were interruptions in the circuit of ideal communication between the soul and the forms as the genetic elements of reality itself. Rather than situate mind at an ultimate remove from sensation, or contrast the instability of sensation with the stability of the idea, Deleuze posits the genesis of mind in direct encounters with imperceptible forces of perception, moments when the subtle and elusive patterns of difference and repetition animating life force the mind to interpret and even to create.

Intensive Difference and Eternal Return

At the center of Deleuze's theory of ideas is the notion of intensity. Deleuze is attempting to account for how and why it is that when certain affective states reach given thresholds of intensity, the mind is invited to fuse its faculties in acts of conjecture that connect otherwise independent circuits of sensation, habit, memory, and understanding. Natural disasters, important political events, certain moments in a love affair, sequences in a film, passages in a piece of music, and many other intensities can force sensation, memory, and thought to overstep their ordinary bounds. Even in something as simple as the colors in certain paintings—Van Gogh's yellow, for instance—one sees in color more than mere sensation. Van Gogh's yellow invites one to construe something like a force animating that color, as if that yellow were a sign of something that is not color, although manifest in and as color. For Deleuze, instances such as Van Gogh's yellow are windows into an immanent set—open and unbounded—of differential elements. The singular and the intense to which ideas bear witness replace the Platonic idea as the real genetic element of sense. The sense of ideas, for Deleuze, in no way transcends natural or empirical experience, but forms an intransitive, untensed aspect of the sensible itself, the uncanny aspect of sensation that potentially interrupts habit, provoking experimentation and creation. Put laconically, the intense is sensation become sign, and thought is the discovery of potentials indicated by such signs.

In this sense, there is for Deleuze another possible meaning of Platonic recollection. For Deleuze there is a form of recollection, rather than being an attempt to attain eternal truth, that would not so much produce a logos aspiring to eternity as grasp a kind of hieroglyphics of time itself. Deleuze invokes the hieroglyph in his study *Proust and Signs*, since in some sense a hieroglyph is a sign whose meaning remains immanent to an image (*PS*, 101). Unlike an alphabetic character, whose appearance is merely an index, the hieroglyph's particular appearance is essential to its meaning. In some sense hieroglyphs *present* the meaning to which they refer. They distinctly yet obscurely embody sense. As Deleuze explores this notion in the context of Proust, if a certain glance is a sign of love, this sign is hieroglyphic in the sense that its meaning cannot be abstracted from that glance. To think not on the basis of the logos but of the hieroglyph is to be forced to interpret, to generate sense in the face of an uncanny and latent realm of significance.

To invert Platonism is to discover a thought that remains within signs, rather than reaching beyond them. Overturning Platonism involves a kind of cognitive vertigo: disconnected from ideal reference points, signs are destined to remain obscure. As Deleuze puts it apropos Proust, the jealous lover would be lost if the search for truth were for an ultimate guarantee against betrayal—in fact it is to a certain mode of betrayal that thought must remain vulnerable, to be thought at all, since identity and truth are not guaranteed by authentic relations of appearance to essence. On the contrary, "things are simulacra themselves, simulacra are the superior forms, and the difficulty facing everything is to become its own simulacrum, to attain the status of a sign in the coherence of eternal return" (*DR*, 67).

Here we must enter one of the most elusive dimensions of Deleuze's thought. How does something become its own simulacrum? And why think of such a passage or process as constitutive of identity? The basic way Deleuze reasons here is that, at a transcendental level, identity is a function of imperceptible interplays of force. Since a simulacrum is neither an original nor a copy, only a simulacrum can "present" differential forces. A simulacrum can present the obscurity proper to the real, its unlimited depth, and does so "symbolically" by activating a number of possible relations between ongoing processes of transformation in the shifting and variable relations at the real, the intensive depths of space and time. In this sense, the simulacrum is not so much an appearance as a power to disconnect appearance from any a priori model or paradigm. A simulacrum sends a potentially unlimited number of resonances into effect. With the attribution of reality to simulacra, the eminence of Plato's forms becomes the radical and uncanny immanence of nature in hieroglyphic signs.

And the coherence of the world, for Deleuze, is not an intuition of that eternally self-same reality to which all signs ultimately point, but is grounded on the periodicity of cosmic repetitions—an ultimate "cosmic" form of repetition Deleuze conceives on the model of Nietzsche's doctrine of eternal return. Following Pierre Klossowski, Deleuze interprets eternal return not as the notion that the same events recur endlessly, but that "the same" is itself a kind of consistency emerging only through the return of difference (DR, 67).[11] As Deleuze puts it, "That is why the eternal return is called 'parodic' [by Klossowski]: it qualifies as simulacrum that which it causes to be (and to return). When eternal return is the power of (formless) Being, the simulacrum is the true character—the 'being'—of that which is" (DR, 67). On this interpretation, eternal return entails that (one, same) differing repetition is ultimate nature, and only difference—only the differential processes of individuation unencumbered by their temporary species or social forms—truly returns.

If reality is a simulacrum, then the "truth" of reality cannot be discovered by distinguishing the authentic from the inauthentic, the accidental from the essential, the artificial from the real. The authenticity of the real is discovered, in Deleuze's view, in certain kinds of betrayal. True vitality is found only in certain obsessions, knowledge in a kind of intimacy with the obscure, the true nature of time in discontinuity, and genuine health only in extremes. If the "upright" Platonist proceeds out of the cave, out of the world of appearances, the overturned Platonist is a diver who plunges into the depths of the cave itself, into the uncanny world of difference and repetition. Here,

> every thing, animal, or being assumes the status of simulacrum; so that
> the thinker of eternal return—who indeed refuses to be drawn out of the

cave, finding instead another cave beyond, always another in which to hide—can rightly say that he is himself burdened with the superior form of everything that is, like the poet "burdened with humanity, even that of the animals." These words themselves have their echo in the superposed caves. Moreover, that cruelty which at the outset seemed to us monstrous, demanding expiation, and could be alleviated only by representative mediation, now seems to us to constitute the pure concept or Idea of difference within overturned Platonism: the most innocent difference, the state of innocence and its echo. (DR, 67)

If simulacra are images that defy description as either model or copy and manifest an indefinite relation to the depths of forces that converge within them, then the "superior forms" are simulacra: manifestations of differential forces of nature, hidden in the imbricated complexities of human emotion and in the legends of our obscure and feral depths. Knowledge is thus for Deleuze not of the order of reflection, but based on a complicity, an intense implication of mind in simulacra, and in the lines drawn by the differential tendencies simulacra symbolize.

What is especially significant for the lineaments of the hermetic Deleuze is the way this thought hearkens back to previous hermetic thinkers in Neoplatonism. Deleuze will come to think of the absolute as a plane of immanence or composition, one that contains all potential series, folds, or "complications" (in the sense in which Nicholas of Cusa originally used the term to describe the material universe as God in a "complicated" state). Deleuze explicitly cites Cusa in order to explain his theory of essence in *Proust and Signs* (PS, 45). For Cusa, in the mind of God, the world exists explicitly as a universal "coincidence of contraries," and not as a set of logically compatible ideas.[12] As did Bruno, Deleuze takes Cusa's *coincidentia oppositorum* as a description not of God but of the world, of the multiplying and multiple series of becomings. In being forced to think, the mind confronts not the terrors of brute existence, but the strange ecstasy of being burdened with all that with which one must but cannot fully identify: the alterity of other human beings, the murmurings of animal flesh, the vibratory patterns in mineral or microscopic levels. The conscious, reflective mind is only ever dimly aware of strange echoes among discontinuous yet resonating differences, yet these are the paths leading through the caves of an inverted Platonism. This path is one of initiation, of an alchemical reduction to core elements and a recreation possible only on the basis of a process of immolation.

For Deleuze, the ability to hear the cavernous echoes connecting simulacra in Plato's cave as "originary" is itself a kind of second innocence. This innocence is not the naiveté of Meno's slave, who must be led, step by step by Socrates, to understand the Pythagorean theorem, and not the seeming innocence of Socrates himself, who with his plain speech hides the teeming *sileni*, the grotesques that constitute that strange collection of virtues that so fascinated Socrates's lovers. Rather, the second birth Deleuze conceives is something like the birth of superior from inferior matter in alchemy, a *refusal* of flight to the ideas for the sake of the redolence of inchoate potential. This is the refusal to identify the inherently problematic with falsehood, and a decision to affirm the open and inconclusive nature of becoming. This will creates a new kind of thought, a thought riven by fascination with unknown nature, a passionate thought, a new and uncanny vocation—a vocation to difference and repetition.

Repetition for Itself, Difference in Itself

> We must believe in a sense of life renewed by the theatre, a sense of life in which man fearlessly makes himself master of what does not yet exist, and brings it into being. And everything that has not been born can still be brought to life if we are not satisfied to remain mere recording organisms.—ANTONIN ARTAUD, *The Theatre and Its Double*, 13

Despite their profound differences, Deleuze observes that both Kierkegaard and Nietzsche were united in their quest to determine the conditions of genuine repetition.[13] For Deleuze, Kierkegaardian irony and Nietzschean humor are philosophical attempts to convey the contours of a "theatre of repetition" in which thought attempts to "become equal" to the inhuman events that befall it, and to will something in nature and create something in culture that is unrepeatable, even if this creation is almost unbearable. The difference between them, of course, is that Nietzsche's heroic and Dionysian immolation, the *amor fati* of metamorphosis, is opposed to Kierkegaard's patient and melancholic meditation. Yet Deleuze opposes the work of both these antisystematic thinkers to that "theatre of representation" in which modern thought had hitherto taken refuge.

> The theatre of repetition is opposed to the theatre of representation, just as movement is opposed to the concept and to representation which refers it back to the concept. In the theatre of repetition, we experience pure forces, dynamic lines in space which act without intermediary upon the spirit, and link it directly with nature and history, with a language which speaks before words, with gestures that develop before organized bodies, with masks before faces, with specters and phantoms before characters—the whole apparatus of repetition as a "terrible power." (*DR*, 10)

Both Nietzsche and Kierkegaard bring forces into philosophy, forces that pass above or below conceptualization, concealing ideas within animals, pseudonyms, fables, and myths. Repetition is always linked, for Deleuze, to a power to hide or conceal. As Deleuze puts it, "Repetition is truly that which disguises itself in constituting itself, that which constitutes itself only by disguising itself . . . there is therefore nothing repeated which may be isolated or abstracted from the repetition in which it was formed, but in which it is also hidden" (*DR*, 17).[14]

In *Difference and Repetition*, Deleuze argues that nature does not truly repeat itself, at least not as "nature" is understood to be the subject of observational science and the incarnation of physical laws (*DR*, 3). What is constructed in a laboratory is merely a situation that resembles nature in its free state, and the results of experiment represent generalities about factors that are equivalent only from the point of view of general laws. Not only do experiments leave out a number of variables in any given situation, they select elements to which phenomena are to be reduced: "Experimentation is thus a matter of substituting one order of generality for another: an order of equality for an order of resemblance" (*DR*, 3). A bird in flight and a bee in flight, a diving whale and a diving penguin, the camouflage of a spider and that of a chameleon may resemble one another, and there may be abstract equivalents involved. But what would it mean to say that two flights repeat one another, or that two dives, two disguises, or two performances are repetitions?

It does not suffice to say that events resemble one another (*DR*, 1). To say that there is resemblance, even to an extreme degree, is not to say that there is repetition. As long as we consider particulars, repetition is conceived as taking place in terms of general laws governing what can be substituted or changed within a domain while its principle remains the same. But similarity is not identity; recurrence is not repetition. What can be repeated, if repetition is truly possible, would have to be something other than mere reiteration or duplication. The paradox is that for an event to repeat itself exactly, there would have to be something irreplaceable in it, something singular. This singularity, as repeated, would have to be something other than a particularity or set of particularities. As Deleuze puts it, "Repetition as a conduct and a point of view concerns non-exchangeable and non-substitutable singularities . . . if repetition is possible it is due to miracle rather than to law" (*DR*, 1–2). What truly repeats is irreplaceable, irreducibly different. If the whale and the penguin both dive, in what sense are they repeating the act of diving? Even if the penguin repeats his own dive 1+n number of times, this is because, paradoxically, there is something about diving that is made distinct only as iterated. The essence of diving is, as it were, a singularity manifest only across the passage from one dive to another. Only a series of dives can reveal what is singular in diving, which is why Deleuze argues for a "differential" view of the singular as that which *makes* change.[15]

Deleuze argues that repetition is "hidden" in regularity in the way that rhythm is hidden in cadence (*ATP*, 313). In any musical phrase, a given cadence or meter hides a singular "rhythmic character," a kind of persona or unique intensive quantity. Rhythmic inflection is manifest only in the repeating phrases of a cadence, but is nevertheless never reducible to the recurring beats. What defines a rhythm is not subject to measurement. Rhythm is an intensive quantity, as opposed to an extensive or measurable value. Intensity is a physical phenomenon, since it exists only as heard or felt, but it is also irreducible to the qualities of an instance or iteration. In fact, across different performances of the same cadence, it becomes clear that rhythm is inherently unequal. The "feel" or groove of a rhythm is constituted by an intensive series that is perceived without being measurable. Rhythm involves an awareness more subtle than perception can capture, yet neither the sense of rhythm nor its performance can exist except as an aspect of a sensation (sounds and silences) to which it is nevertheless irreducible.

What Deleuze means when he argues that the "unequal is the most positive element" in repetition is that, in the case of rhythm, there would be no compelling, listenable, repetition, and thus no groove (lift, flow, or swing) unless every cadence contained a sort of imperceptible hitch or glitch, an inequality between beats (*DR*, 21). This irregularity could be called the specific difference peculiar to rhythm. For Deleuze every repetition is rhythmic in the sense that repetition is always a set of "rhythmic events that are more profound than the reproduction of ordinary homogeneous elements" (*DR*, 21).[16] To discover the essence of repetition, thought must broach an order operative beneath generality, such as an order embodied in cadence or habits or metabolic cycles. Any unity of repetition would consist in serial coherence that holds beyond the opposition between events that happen once and those that happen several times.

Where is the model of such an order and coherence found? Deleuze argues that the work of art exemplifies pure repetition. "The repetition of a work of art is like a singularity without a concept," Deleuze writes (*DR*, 1). We must look to art, Deleuze suggests, because art does what morality and science cannot. Artworks paradoxically repeat the unrepeatable, yet without establishing any regime of generality, any "concept" that would reinscribe difference as a variant of the same. Deleuze writes, "If repetition exists, it expresses at once a singularity opposed to the general, a universality opposed to the particular, a distinctive opposed to the ordinary, an instantaneity opposed to variation, and an eternity opposed to permanence. In every respect, repetition is a transgression. It puts law into question, it denounces its nominal or general character in favor of a more profound and more artistic reality" (*DR*, 2–3). Art is transgressive because it indicates a coherence that is viable without the forms of generality, resemblance, and recognition upon which commonsense accounts depend. Because it more easily moves in an element that is insubordinate to common sense, art has a capacity to succeed where philosophy generally does not. Art discovers and ramifies characters, events, and affects that are not mere imaginings—not merely the way an artist wishes or fantasizes things might be—but count as explorations of real, if as-yet-unlived forms of life.

In its approach to the subrepresentational, for Deleuze the work of art harbors a capacity for a thought largely inaccessible for Western philosophy: a thought of difference in itself. Beginning with Aristotle, difference in philosophy is conceived as secondary to identity. In Aristotle, difference is not conceived on its own terms, but as dependent upon the form of judgments that discern relations of analogy and proportion between identities.[17] Deleuze argues that difference in Aristotle is a "synthetic and attributive predicate," and that difference is always subordinated to continuity within genera and within being itself (*DR*, 31). In Aristotle, different species within a genera are not defined by a difference "made" by genera, but by a difference contained within genera, in the sense that the genera of mammals contain all its different species. For Aristotle, there must be a set of common features before there can be a difference between members of a collection. Deleuze observes that, for Aristotle, relatively "large" differences between species represent the most important or most significant differences. Observable contrasts stand in for difference in itself. Deleuze argues that while in Plato difference divides and distributes essence in uncanny and imperceptible ways, in Aristotle a "middling" contrast secretly governs difference per se. Even the difference between genera is thought in terms of the sameness of the being they share, obscure as this analogy may be (*DR*, 33).

For Deleuze, analogical thought inhibits the emergence of a genuine concept of difference.[18] Analogical thinking derives from a philosophical will to unify generic and specific difference in a single coherent, "organic," representable whole of being.[19] Under conditions of analogy, each time a particular being is discerned or discriminated, a general form of difference is presumed to govern that case. Any judgment analogically attributing predicates to subjects, subordinating particularity to generality, "retains in the particular only that which conforms to the general (matter and form), and seeks the principle of individuation in this or that element of the fully constituted individuals" (*DR*, 38). What Deleuze is looking for are subindividual forces, "embryonic" or intensive and differential features that govern individuation at an imperceptible level. For Aristotle, fully constituted individuals realize their essence to a maximal degree, and it is the constituted essence that accounts for the distinction of an individual. Analogical reasoning is acceptable because of the presumed sameness of substance across its differentiations, regardless of the material complexity that might be afoot at the level of actual individuation.

The coherence of analogical thinking is underwritten by a traditional conception of essence, one with which Deleuze sharply breaks. In the traditional view, it is the essence of a substance, that which is the same over time, that individuates; difference, by contrast, is accidental, contingent, arbitrary. To think difference as productive, and as an individuating factor, Deleuze was convinced that being must be approached not in terms of analogy but of univocity. Being must be understood as said in a single sense of all that exists. But Deleuze conceives of the single sense in which everything can be said as difference—difference not as diversity, but as the irreducibility of a multiplicity of individuating process occurring in a nomadic and anarchic mode of distribution, under the auspices of eternal return. Insofar as it "appears," difference appears at the level of expressive, individuating powers by which individuals are constituted and which all individuals ramify. He writes, "When we say that univocal being is related immediately and essentially to individuating factors, we certainly do not mean by the latter individuals constituted in experience, but that which acts in them as a transcendental principle: as a plastic, anarchic and nomadic principle, contemporaneous with the process of individuation, no less capable of dissolving and destroying individuals than of constituting them temporarily; intrinsic modalities of being, passing from one 'individual' to another, circulating and communicating matters and forms" (*DR*, 38).

It was in certain gestures of art that Deleuze found his paradigm for a plastic, anarchic, and nomadic organizing principle. Although he takes inspiration from a series of artists across periods and genres, Deleuze was particularly fascinated with the high-modernist and post-romantic gesture of destroying any illusion of completeness or organic totality in the work of art. The modern work is composed from shards, fragments, and simulacra. Deleuze reiterates throughout *Difference and Repetition* that he was searching for a mode of thought connected to this sort of gesture, and that he took a modernist mode of selective affirmation as his primary discursive model. Part of why Deleuze can insist upon this connection between art and thought is that he never writes about art as a critic, but from the point of view of the intersection between artistic procedures and forms of life (*NP*, 102).

From this vantage, the key dimension of modernism, for Deleuze, is that it attempts to extract the singular from the cliché.[20] For Deleuze, what is explored in Joyce, in Francis Bacon's paintings, or in the work of filmmakers like Antonioni or Goddard, is the reality not of the self or the world as it appears to be given, but the singularities that exist or "insist" among the fragments of the world. As he puts it, the imperative of such modernism is such that "each term of a series (of images, words, sounds, gestures) being already a difference, must be put into a variable relation with other terms, thereby constituting other series devoid of center and convergence . . . Difference must be shown *differing*. We know that modern art tends to realize these conditions: in this sense it becomes a veritable theatre of metamorphoses and permutations" (DR, 56).

Somewhat as a doctor sees the body exhibiting certain signs—of life, of death, of sickness, of health, of power, of weakness, of sadness, of joy—the artist sees the world in terms of symptoms.[21] Art does not reject but confronts the illusions and mystifications of the present age: in creating, the artist is also a clinician. In an early essay Deleuze observes,

> The artist is a symptomologist . . . the world can be treated as a symptom and searched for signs of disease, signs of life, signs of a cure, signs of health . . . Nietzsche thought of the philosopher as the physician of civilization. Henry Miller was an extraordinary diagnostician. The artist in general must treat the world like a symptom, and build his work not like a therapeutic, but in every case like a clinic. The artist is not outside the symptoms, but makes a work of art from them, which sometimes serves to precipitate them, and sometimes to transform them. (DI, 140)

Francis Bacon's paintings of distended bodies, the nonsense words in Joyce's *Finnegan's Wake*, the nonsense of events in Lewis Carroll's Alice stories, and the inconclusive signs in Pynchon's *The Crying of Lot 49* all "permit several stories to be told at once" (LS, 260). Through unexpected conjunctive, connective, and disjunctive series, these works elicit resonance where there would otherwise be only static, noise. Arguably such modern styles establish *occult* communication between otherwise incompossible affects, percepts, and events.[22] It is crucial for Deleuze that such experimentation, however, is no mere "rhapsody of sensation" or arbitrary elective affinity at the subjective level. For Deleuze the truly "modern" work activates neither the fancy nor the imagination, but the viscera and the brain, which are themselves *folds* of cosmic becoming. If art succeeds, it invokes real if hidden modes of existence. It will affirm other possible modes of life beyond the clichés of what generally passes for life, and will discover life within uncanny imbrications of past and future, and at particularly tense conjunctions of affect, in order to explore an elusive multiplicity of sense. In the modern work, it is not at all a question of different points of view on one story supposedly the same, for points of view would still be submitted to a rule of convergence. It is rather a question of different and divergent stories, as if an absolutely distinct landscape corresponded to each point of view. There is indeed a unity of divergent series insofar as they are divergent, but it is always a chaos perpetually thrown off center which becomes one only in the Great Work. This unformed chaos, the great letter of *Finnegan's Wake*, is not just any chaos: it is the power of affirmation, the power to affirm all the heterogeneous series—it "complicates" within itself all the series (hence the interest of Joyce in Bruno as the theoretician of the *complicatio*). (DR, 123)

For Joyce, as for Bruno, the world is a coexistence of contraries, a *complicatio* of vicissitudes.[23] Bruno's vision of an infinite universe and worlds entailed that the coherence of the world was not given, but produced through intense contractions, through conjecture, apostrophe, and synecdoche. Artistic vision on this view is the power to render sustainable the intensities that would otherwise overwhelm the mind and debilitate life.[24] As Deleuze puts it in *Difference and Repetition*, "Difference must be shown differing. We know that modern art tends to realize these conditions: in this sense it becomes a veritable *theatre* of metamorphoses and permutations. A theatre where nothing is fixed, a labyrinth without a thread (Ariadne has hung herself). The work of art leaves the domain of representation in order to become 'experience,' transcendental empiricism or science of the sensible" (DR, 56).

Art becomes an exercise in transcendental empiricism insofar as it maps not the given coordinates of space and time, but the singular points of an intensive field, a space mapped not by fixed coordinates but by informal diagrams. Art's knowledge is therefore never a simple reflection of reality, but an exploration of potential lines of development, interrelation, and interdependence. The peculiar thinking of art takes place at a level of preindividual singularities and impersonal affects. At this level, alone, for Deleuze, does empiricism—the science of relations—become "transcendental": an exploration of the genetic conditions of real rather than merely possible experience. As he puts it in *Difference and Repetition*, "Empiricism truly becomes transcendental, and aesthetics an apodictic discipline, only when we apprehend directly in the sensible that which can only be sensed, the very being *of* the sensible: difference, potential difference and difference in intensity as the reason behind qualitative diversity. It is in difference that movement is produced as an 'effect,' that phenomena flash their meaning like signs. The intense world of differences, in which we find the reason behind qualities and the being of the sensible, is precisely the object of a superior empiricism" (DR, 57).

The object of superior empiricism is the world of simulacra, and the modern work indicates the conditions for the overturning of Platonism on the basis of its rapport with simulacra. Plato condemned simulacra for the state of "free, oceanic differences, of nomadic distributions and crowned anarchy, along with all that malice which challenges both the notion of the model and that of the copy" (DR, 265).[25] But for Deleuze, overturning Platonism has less to do with the negative notion of the ruin of the divine archetypes—the loss of essential forms—than with the displacement of such archetypes into powers in the sensible that subsist beneath harmonious forms. What is at stake in thought, for Deleuze as much as for Plato, is an apprenticeship or initiation into what is unsensed in the sensible. But unlike for Plato, for whom that apprenticeship in the unsensed is a flight from contingency and vicissitude—from "becoming"—and an approach to the immutable light of the forms, for Deleuze the truth of the as-yet-unsensed is an approach to creative forces discovered at the limits of life itself.[26] The modern work explores this exhilarating horizon, and in this way forms a new paradigm for philosophy. Modern art delineates a vocation that is not to clear and distinct ideas but to the depths of a nature and the vicissitudes of a time only obscurely betrayed in signs. Deleuze's own philosophy is especially indebted to the work of Marcel Proust.

Learning in Proust

> We learn nothing from those who say, "do as I do." Our only teachers are those who tell us to "do with me," and are able to emit signs to be developed in heterogeneity rather than propose gestures for us to reproduce. —GILLES DELEUZE, *Difference and Repetition*, 23

In the preface to the English edition of *Difference and Repetition*, written in 1994, Deleuze asserts that the project of that book had already begun in the earlier *Proust and Signs*.[27] In this book Deleuze develops a concept of apprenticeship, a new conception of what it means to learn that breaks decisively with the image of thought. In the classical image of thought, a thinker's "good will" leads her to truth. This model presupposes a natural alliance between the goodwill of the thinker and truth itself, between common sense and the "good sense" identities that are representable. But in the *recherches* of Proust, truth cannot be sought with goodwill. Truth in Proust is rather that which *befalls* us, as a kind of blow. As Deleuze puts it, "Philosophy, with all its method and goodwill, is nothing compared to the secret pressures of the work of art" (*PS*, 98). It is to Proust that Deleuze looks for a paradigm of what philosophy might become beyond its attachment to elements common sense can recognize, and beyond the presumption of a "friendship with concepts," by means of which it might preordain a natural affiliation of mind for truth. By placing philosophy in a subordinate position with respect to an apprehension of the "secret pressures" of the work of art, Deleuze reiterates that a hermetic mind—germane to art but redolent of the same therapeutic and transformative aspirations inherent in the enterprise of a number of spiritual practices—forms a paradigm for his own philosophical practice. And in keeping with the hermetic tradition's linkage of knowledge to spiritual ordeal, Proust's method involves a passage through involuntary memory that culminates in a "spiritualization" of signs that is simultaneously a subjective and cosmic act of alchemical transformation, a passage from the dross of time to a subtle vision of its real, spiritual contour.

In Proust's sprawling, hallucinatory vision, the truth of his experience is discovered through the becoming-art of his own disillusionment, disappointment, and loss.[28] For Deleuze, this vision is a quest for truth, for the only kind of truth that matters: not a generality, but a singular expression. Proust teaches that, against Plato's vision of the philosopher's internal affiliation with truth, the truth is never that which befriends us. Rather, truth for Deleuze is that which disguises itself, and reveals the essence of our lives to us in signs. The thinker is not the friend of the concept, but the jealous lover of the essence, an essence enigmatically sheathed in signs (*PS*, 15). It is the menagerie of signs that is the territory of genuine thought. As Deleuze puts it, "Creation, like the genesis of the act of thinking, always starts from signs. The work of art is born from signs as much as it generates them; the creator is like the jealous man, interpreter of the god, who scrutinizes the signs in which the truth betrays itself" (PS, 17).

Proust gives Deleuze a model of thought as a perpetual confrontation with signs. The Proustian articulation of thought in and as a shifting and problematic array of signs, a process of deciphering and reiteration, leads to Deleuze's own conceptual pragmatics, what he calls, with Guattari, a "laying out of a plane of immanence" (WIP, 43). Deleuze argues in *Difference and Repetition* that learning is not simply a matter of carrying into action a representation. It is, on the contrary, a matter of linking signs and actions, such as the multiple points of a body with the multiple signs emitted by an ocean wave (DR, 23). In learning to swim, we do not so much imitate the possible actions represented by a teacher as repeat her actual response to the waves we individually face. As Deleuze puts it,

> The movement of the swimmer does not resemble that of the wave, in particular, the movements of the swimming instructor which we reproduce on the sand bear no relation to the movements of the wave, which we learn to deal with only by grasping the former in practice as signs. . . . When a body combines some of its own distinctive points with those of a wave, it espouses the principle of a repetition which is no longer that of the Same but involves the Other—involves difference, from one wave and one gesture to another, and carries that difference through the repetitive space thereby constituted. To learn is indeed to constitute this space of an encounter with signs, in which distinctive points renew themselves in each other, and repetition takes shape while disguising itself. (DR, 23)

This is to say, it is in the singularity constituted by the encounter of a body with a wave that the "essence" of swimming exists. For Deleuze there is no merely discursive or simply representational content of the concept of swimming from which anything could be learned. On the contrary, the idea of swimming is indexed to events (and a series of events) in which the distinctive points of a body might combine with those of various waves. A teacher does not so much represent swimming to us as she transmits a differential relation between bodies and waves, a relation that must be repeated differently in the body of each student in order to take effect, in order to count as knowledge. Swimming is thus not a static notion but a dynamic form of becoming modulated across the body of a teacher through the body of a student.

In this sense, learning centers on problems, not on solutions. The essence of swimming is never a permanent solution to a problem. Rather, swimming introduces a "problematic field," enabling nonidentical repetition within a milieu. The real question is not "What is swimming?" but "*Where* can I swim?" "*When* can I swim?" or "*How long* and *how fast* can I swim?" These are questions determined by the essence of swimming as a virtual, differential power latent in signs. As Deleuze explains it,

> To learn to swim is to conjugate the distinctive points of our bodies with the singular points of the objective Idea in order to form a problematic field. This conjugation determines for us a threshold of consciousness at which our real acts are adjusted to our perceptions of the real relations, thereby providing a solution to the problem. Moreover, problematic Ideas are precisely the ultimate elements of nature and the subliminal objects of little perceptions. As a result, "learning" always takes place in and through the unconscious, thereby establishing the bond of a profound complicity between nature and mind. (*DR*, 165)

What is the character of this dark, unconscious complicity? For Deleuze it is the syntheses of a body that passively and continuously engender the context of new actions. These syntheses are produced not at the level of clearly identifiable objects, stable objectivities consciously apprehended, but with problematic, subperceptual forces that appear only as subliminal or unconscious elements (*DR*, 108–10). In a certain sense, for Deleuze, every perception is a new creation, and learning happens when a new mode of existence comes into being.[29] This is because every mode of life is a form of becoming that actualizes virtual potencies, creating new assemblages of bodies and sense. Learning takes place in this context, and happens through a kind of participation in the unknown, a projection of activity toward a virtual whole (i.e., swimming itself) that is never completely or directly lived, but manifest or ramified over multiple series of iterations (*DR*, 109).

The virtual character of ideas accounts for variations across processes of becoming. The possibility of continuing to swim is the possibility of continuing to swim otherwise, differently. What makes the idea of swimming in and of itself virtual is not because the virtual is vague or inexact, but because its potencies are replete without being hierarchically arranged—every iteration matters equally. Deleuze writes, "Far from being undetermined, the virtual is completely determined. When it is claimed that works of art are immersed in a virtuality, what is being invoked is not some confused determination but the completely determined structure formed by its genetic differential elements, its 'virtual' or 'embryonic' elements. The elements, varieties of relations and singular points coexist in the work or the object, in the virtual part of the work or object, without it being possible to designate a point of view privileged over others, a center which would unify the other centers" (*DR*, 209).

Despite manifesting a definite genetic structure, the virtual is not static but problematic, in the sense that it enables or in some sense provokes a question: How is this actuality related to its intensive, germinal, and embryonic conditions? If it is the vocation of thought to discover the genetic elements of reality, then it is incumbent upon thought to conceive ideas without governing hierarchy. But this is an activity that is much more familiar to the artist than to the philosopher. Every genuine work of art has an "embryonic" aspect in the sense that the realization of the work, its actualization, draws from the "complicated" structure of differential relations from which other versions of the same work and visions might have transpired (*DR*, 209). In a sense, for Deleuze, there is something radically uncanny about every actuality. Actuality is uncanny because it is open or inconclusive: its virtual dimension, ever present, does not constitute a totality or whole, but multiplies the sense of the actual. What is complete, replete, or resonant, in Proust's language, is "the ideal part of the object, which participates with other parts of objects in the Idea (other relations, other singular points), but never constitutes an integral Whole as such" (*DR*, 208, 209). Its embrace of the actual as uncanny is also part of what makes Deleuze's ontology resonate so strongly with the hieroglyphic worldview of the Renaissance and the Neoplatonic adepts of *magia naturalis*, for whom nature was a surface of sense manifesting infinite depths of possible transformative and regenerative possibilities.

Such a hieroglyphic sense of reality arguably inspires not only Deleuze's theory of ideas, but also the Proustian quest for hidden meanings. This apprenticeship is of the order of a hermetic initiation. At first Proust believes the signs coincide with the objects or persons who emit them. As Proust himself puts it, "I told myself that this was indeed the woman whom the name Duchess de Guermantes *designated* for everyone; the inconceivable life this name signified was actually contained by this body."[30] Eventually, however, Proust will realize that the true designations of signs, their "finality," are the qualities of worlds that cannot be directly lived, but that can only be revealed in the work of art itself. The parallel here with ritual or theurgic experience, in which the ordinary materials of nature are thought to take on their true form, could not be more precise.

Deleuze's own theory of ideas follows a pattern of initiation and hieratic experience. Deleuze argues that it is only from the problematic in experience, including the great "unanswerable" Kantian questions (What are the limits of the self? What would God be like? Where would the limits of the universe reside?), that we can actually learn. God, the Self, and the World introduce an infinite task into thinking, one that allows intimations of divinity, selfhood, and cosmic realty to be grasped as a signs. "Neither the problem nor the question is a subjective determination marking a moment of insufficiency of knowledge. Problematic structure is part of objects themselves, allowing them to be grasped as signs, just as the questioning or problematizing instance is a part of knowledge allowing its objectivity and its specificity to be grasped in the act of *learning*" (*DR*, 64). What makes swimming a multiplicity and not a static unity is that its iterations are not divergences from an essence, but differences genuine repetitions of Swimming will have ramified. Swimming, like all essences for Deleuze, is not static, immutable, and unchanging. Rather, essences are located within an imperceptible persistence proper to the singular character of multiplicities. In the case of God, as much as of swimming, we are dealing with a structure that is productive of difference—of forms of experience, and of time, as distinctive durations that renew the possibilities of sense.

This reflection on ideas returns us to learning in Proust, since Proust's literature, for Deleuze, explores the virtual component of learning in a paradigmatic way. When certain sensory experiences force Proust to reminisce, what he recalls is never simply another past experience. Rather, the reminiscence discovers an object (the city of Combray, the taste of a Madeline) that exists only in signs of what it *may* be, an essence discovered only afterwards, in recollection. From this perspective, the city of Combray "is" only its distribution across two series: that of a present, lived experience, and that of a later encounter, in a sensation given substance only through the reminiscence it inspires. The essences Proust discovers through involuntary memory are problematic, fraught with an ambiguity proper to their intransitive nature, a nature fully countenanced only in and as that open whole that constitutes his work. He does not know what these sensations portend, and must invent a new sense, a work of art, in order to think through the ramifications of such intense affects. Proust's ideas are neither in the taste of the Madeline in the present nor in the past which that taste evokes, but in a pure passage of time, always already past and always yet to come, a time that does not pass outside of literary diegesis.

The essence of Combray is unstable. It is sustained by or "inheres" in the virtual conjunction of two series, that of a past which is immemorial outside of the recherche itself, and that of a present experience, which forces sensation to confront an uncanny sign (*DR*, 122). In this sense, Proust's worlds are constituted by an obverse of the Platonic ideas, and it is Proust who truly succeeds in overturning Platonism. In Proust, it is not *we* who recall the essence of things from a mythical past. Rather, an artistically rendered past develops *us* as one of its points-of-view. Deleuze's way of conceiving this difference is along the lines of a contrast between logos and hieroglyph, between a discourse that seeks to overcome obscurity, and one that houses, protects, and shelters a distinct yet obscure multiplicity. In Proust, signs become hieroglyphic. Signs in Proust betray no ultimate meaning, but are reiterated to form hieroglyphs of multiple possible senses (*PS*, 101).

Deleuze generalizes this point: if artists are able to "recall" the truth of a given world—whether the countryside of Provence, the seas of the nineteenth century, or the ravaged countryside of post-war Italy—this is not because an artist has created a world "analogous" to the actual world, but because the subtle, even imperceptible singularities of experience provoked artistic repetition.[31] If Platonic essences have always already been present (if occluded, in time and embodiment) Proustian essences are never pregiven, and are not found apart from a creative act. In Proust the duplicity of sensation, the confusion in experience that provokes the need for recollection, does not need subordination to thought. It is not for Proust, as for Plato, that sensation requires an ideal standard or measure that will divide truth from mere appearance, reality from illusion. Proustian recollection is oriented not by anamnesis but by repetition, a repetition that will determine essence only under the conditions of repetition, when signs are creatively repeated. As Deleuze puts it, "The Search is oriented toward the future, not to the past" (*PS*, 4). That is to say, Proust is searching for a future that is available only on the basis of a repetition that will release something from the past that never belonged to it—something that was improper or *unheimlich* there, something that can live only in art, only in a style. Deleuze writes, "It is style which substitutes for experience the manner in which we speak about it or the formula that expresses it, which substitutes for the individual in the world the viewpoint toward the world, and which transforms reminiscence into realized creation" (*PS*, 111).

What is crucial for Deleuze about Proust's method is that here the mind is "adequate" to essence; the adequate thought of essence does not come before but *after* the advent of the signs that provoke thought and creation. In *The Search for Lost Time*, all that was given to Proust in childhood, adolescence, and love has become shard or trace, and experiences formerly lived but too intense to be thought now persist as signs from which style can remake a world. The essence of things is not beyond sensation, but is that which in sensation differs and repeats, or that which signals what it is only as relayed by another sensation (or by that which in memory cannot be remembered except as something forced or provoked by another memory). Proust's hieroglyphic discourse, where signs embody an elusive and complex density of sense, evokes essence without every fully clarifying or identifying them once and for all.

Proust's experience of time regained is simultaneously a virtualization of the inconsistencies or violent breaks in experience (anxiety, loss, pain, and dispossession become ideal problems or singularities), and an actualization of an aesthetic consistency. This singular consistency or assemblage literally constitutes a world. Rather than seeking a narrative that will reunite what is broken in experience, part of what makes modern art paradigmatic for thought, for Deleuze, is that its fragments and aberrant lines develop points of view that do not so much encompass as differently repeat experience in a way that produces new resonances and connections. It is this conception of an open whole of sense that distinguishes Proustian (and modernist) from Platonic reminiscence. As Deleuze puts it, "There is no Platonic reminiscence here, precisely because there is no sympathy as a reuniting into a whole; rather the messenger is itself an incongruous part that does not correspond to its message nor to the recipient of that message . . . one would look in vain in Proust for platitudes about the work of art as organic totality in which each part predetermines the whole and in which the whole determines the part (a dialectic conception of the work of art)" (*PS*, 114). Proust does not proceed, as Socrates does, along the lines of a dialectic—he does not set out, on the basis of any intuition of forms, to divide legitimate from illegitimate signs, reality from illusion, sophistry from wisdom. Nor does he search, after Hegel, for an encompassing dialectical totality mediated by contradictions. Proust discovers the essence of a world only in the singularity of creation.[32]

In both *Proust and Signs* and in *Difference and Repetition*, Deleuze invokes Nicholas of Cusa's notion of *complicatio* to explain how the "eternity" of sense, traditionally called "essence," is not a static existence but "the birth of Time itself" (*PS*, 45). For Cusa, Christ the Word was the supreme example of hidden nature as sign, since Christ's existence at the confluence of the Absolute Maximum (*explicatio*, as complete divinity) and Relative Maximum (*contractio*, as perfect humanity) is itself an enigmatic symbol, a coincidence of contraries. As should by now be somewhat more clear, Deleuze's own conception of expression still owes much to the Cusan idea of *complicatio*, which espies a universe in which the divine is obscurely enfolded yet fully present, if only "explicated" in actual states that can never completely reveal the "perplicated" fecundity of the virtual (*DR*, 280). As did Bruno, Deleuze rejects the possibility of a logos that could render any paradigmatic or central sense to complication. For Deleuze, as for Bruno, sense can have no single paradigm in actuality, and can come to be only as an infinitely enfolded set of glyphs, an infinity of uncanny avatars. This infinity—the unceasingly problematic nature of the virtual—gives the mind its vocation in signs. For Proust, "one must be endowed for signs," in order to think as much as to create (*PS*, 101). This endowment is also "hermetic" in the sense that it implies a simultaneous transformation of the self along with the discovery and reenactment of the singular genetic elements of experience, and the creative reimbrication of the world.[33]

It seems that, in a certain way, Deleuze points to art as a kind of eclipse of philosophy, at least insofar as philosophy has been tied to the Socratic image of truth as recollection. Deleuze writes, "The fact remains that the revelation of essence (beyond the object, beyond the subject himself) belongs only to the realm of art. If it is to occur, it will occur there. This is why art is the finality of the world, and the apprentice's unconscious destination" (*PS*, 50). What can art do that philosophy cannot? As Proust himself put it, "Thanks to art instead of seeing a single world, our own, we see it multiply, and as many original artists as there are, so many worlds will we have at our disposal, more different from each other than those that circle in the void" (*PS*, 42). Art takes as its material not the actual, but "unconscious themes and involuntary archetypes" (*PS*, 47). Deleuze even identifies the elements of the recherche with the "partial objects" of psychoanalysis, what Melanie Klein defined as those rags, toys, or even body parts children use as imaginary substitutes for objects or persons they fear are missing or incomplete or dangerous in some way. But Deleuze inverts the sign of partial objects, envisioning partiality not as lack but as excess of differential being. As Deleuze puts it, "The essential point is that the parts of the search remain partitioned, fragmented, *without anything lacking*: eternally partial parts, open boxes and sealed vessels, swept on by time without forming a whole or presupposing one, without lacking anything in this quartering, and denouncing in advance every organic unity we might seek to introduce into it" (*PS*, 161). Deleuze argues that when Proust compares his work to a gown or a cathedral, it is not in order to insist on a sublime form of unity, or even an obscure form of logos (the most basic meaning of "logos" in Greek is "coherent account" or "cohesive tale"). On the contrary, it is Proust's artistic prerogative to "emphasize his right to incompletion, to seams and patches" (*PS*, 161). The artist asserts her right against any metaphysical and organicist temptation. She finds the power of her work in her ability not to unite what is sundered from itself, but in her ability to evoke a resonance and a world of signs that resonates only because the essence the resonance evokes comes into being alongside the elements we might mistakenly think are "unified" or "gathered" in the work. As Deleuze puts it, "This seems a good definition of essence: an individuating viewpoint superior to the individuals themselves, breaking with their chains of associations; essence appears *alongside* these chains, incarnated in closed fragments, *adjacent* to what it overwhelms, *contiguous* to what it reveals. Even the Church, a viewpoint superior to the landscape, has the effect of partitioning this landscape and rises up itself, at the turn of the road, like the ultimate partitioned fragment adjacent to the series that is defined by it" (*PS*, 162). If "knowledge" refers to a generality of concepts, and to the stability of a rule for solutions (measuring techniques, approximation of particulars to a general standard, etc.), art does not result in what we have traditionally thought of as knowledge. Rather, it results in something stranger and more profound, something Deleuze is not embarrassed to call a "profound complicity between nature and mind" (*DR*, 165). Despite the reticence of modern skepticism (and the transcendentalism that accepts skeptical premises) about cognitive access to such profundity, it is nevertheless here, within such forbidden zones of mind that Deleuze situates the stakes of thought, as a transformative and healing practice. In order to confront the ethical and political stakes of such a reconception of thought, it is first necessary to expand the conception of the cosmic artisan to its full scope, and to elaborate the possible resonances between art, science, and philosophy from an immanent and hermetic point of view.

5

Becoming Cosmic

Deleuze's meditations on Proust's work form a template for how he approaches art, in general. For Deleuze, the artist is not one who represents the world or even one who expresses her soul, but a "cosmic artisan" who extends or *continues* intensive cosmic events through an extreme sensitivity to levels of experience that the habits of sensation and perception tend to occlude (*ATP*, 342). But what exactly does Deleuze mean by "cosmic artisan"? For Deleuze, the artist is comparable to an artisan in the sense that she does not so much fabulate as fabricate, developing intensive techniques to explore unforeseen dimensions of sound, color, and even of time itself. Deleuze thought this description was germane to a wide range of musicians, painters, poets, and novelists. But in particular, Deleuze was drawn to the music of Olivier Messiaen, Edgar Varèse, and Karlheinz Stockhausen, the literature of Woolf, Kafka, and Henry Miller, and the paintings of Cézanne, Klee, and Kandinsky. For Deleuze, what unites these artists is how they "drew lines" that distilled affects and percepts into molecular and cosmic "blocs," rendering palpable the imbricated rhythmic or intense vibrational states of matter itself (*ATP*, 343). What interested Deleuze in these artists was patently hermetic, insofar as these works attempted, explicitly and implicitly, to convoke cosmic potencies in ways that closely paralleled ritual, theurgic, and alchemical patterns of transformation, healing, and gnosis.

From Proust to the Cosmic Artisan

At times Deleuze is explicit about the spiritual potencies of art. In *Cinema II: The Time-Image*, he describes the work of certain filmmakers as restoring belief in the world by descrying as-yet-unlived possibilities lurking within the clichés of habitual actions and reactions (*C2*, 172). In particular, for Deleuze, it was the Italian neorealists and French New Wave *auteurs* who used discontinuities and displacements of spatiotemporal experience to form something like a cinematic variation on the Proustian *recherche*. "Proust indeed speaks of cinema, time mounting its magic lantern on bodies and making the shots coexist in depth. It is this build-up, this emancipation of time, which ensures the rule of impossible continuity and aberrant movement" (*C2*, 39). Continuities that cannot be lived, movements that cannot be *lived* but must be *thought*—these are the key elements of the avant-garde cinema of midcentury Europe. While disorienting, for Deleuze, this cinema is not destructive but salutary. Aberration and discontinuity may be therapeutic to the extent that they can condition the brain and the body to endure and even enjoy a more profound existence, one that is closer to the multiplicity of discontinuous durations of which "anorganic" life is composed.

At work here is a deeply ethical program, in the Spinozistic sense of ethics as an expansion of what a body can do. Stereotypical plots, predictable patterns of emotional tension and release, and the limits of ordinary perception in some sense interfere with a discernment of coexistent pasts and futures, or of a comprehension of the way affects are conditioned by unconscious responses to imperceptible forces. Cinema at its best, for Deleuze, reveals how our actions are haunted by glitches and passivities signaling that our bodies and minds are tied to and extended through discontinuous durations. We live not only the time of the diurnal, but also through tectonic, geophysical, animal, and even world-historical modes of duration that overlap but are discontinuous with our conscious experience of time.[1] Cinematic work has the potential to activate our attention to hidden aspects of temporal experience, since the cinema can "impossibly" show the past and the present in their discontinuity. This renewed perspective, Deleuze argues, can effect a restoration of "belief in the world," a faith that the traumatic and fateful character of events and their effects upon our lives are not irreversible and may be subject to intervention.

As we have seen already, Proust engages in the project of restoring faith in a world by displacing the problem of "the whole" of experience. His enterprise is to move away from a problem of recalling the past as it was given and reorient toward what can be created. For Deleuze, this is a task peculiar to the artistic moderns: not to explore the inner realm of subjective feeling, but to renew a sense of there being a world that can be re-made. Deleuze writes,

> The entire problem of objectivity, like that of unity, is displaced in what we must call a "modern" fashion, essential to modern literature. Order has collapsed, as much in the states of the world that were supposed to reproduce it as in the essences or Ideas that were supposed to inspire it. The world has become crumbs and chaos. Precisely because reminiscence proceeds from subjective associations to an originating viewpoint, objectivity can no longer exist except in the work of art; it no longer exists in signification as stable essence, but solely in the signifying formal structure of the work, in its style. It is no longer a matter of saying: to create is to remember—but rather, to remember is to create, is *to reach that point where the associative chain breaks, leaps over the constituted individual, is transferred to the birth of an individuating world.* (PS, 111)

This notion of an art that reveals fundamental complicities between nature and mind, is one that Deleuze takes not only from Proust, but from a broader reading of the history of art. It is in some of his later, more general comments on art that Deleuze (alone and with Felix Guattari) becomes more and more candid about the hermetic capacity of art to renew the world, and belief in the world, through the production of visionary experience. Filmmakers such as Godard and Fellini, for Deleuze, follow Proust in offering a new sense of the world, a belief in a world ravaged by war and haunted by the Kafkaesque specter of "total administration." In the wake of the catastrophe of the actions of the Second World War, the films of Italian neorealism and the French New Wave construct images that break with what Deleuze calls the "sensory-motor link," the direct link between perception and action. Deleuze calls such images "time-images" (*C2*, 22–23). These images, while disorienting, are also therapeutic to the extent that they enable *thought* where one can no longer *react*. The time-image suggests a subtle revisioning of human capability. The task of avant-garde film, for Deleuze, is to create in the spectator a kind of "spiritual automaton" a kind of golem that can transmit the spiritual sense of the world directly to the brain, bypassing ordinary physical and psychic capacity. The passivity of the automaton would be transformed by film into a creative receptivity that Deleuze says restores our faith in the world (*C2*, 170, 172). The images of the world that film extracts from our situation can render a glorious or astral body, a subtle body. As Deleuze puts it,

> Our belief can have no other object than "the flesh," we need very special reasons to make us believe in the body ("the Angels do not know, for all true knowledge is obscure . . ."). We must believe in the body, but as in the germ of life, the seed which splits open the paving-stones, which has been preserved and lives on in the holy shroud or the mummy's bandages, and which bears witness to life, in this world as it is. We need an ethic or a faith, which makes fools laugh; it is not a need to believe in something else, but a need to believe in this world, of which fools are a part. (*C2* 173)

For Deleuze, the auteurs who renew belief in the world do so by working with affects and percepts that are impersonal and preindividual, untied to the sensory-motor links of a body with a world. Films like *Last Year at Marienbad*, or even Godard's *Breathless* present the way lives are cross-cut by other lives and times never directly present to them, and demonstrate the way the lived coherence of time is riven with faulty memory, and how identity is haunted by the various personae we play out along our life lines. The effect of being confronted with these other dimensions in film is, according to Deleuze, a kind of second birth, the birth of a "spiritual automaton" more plastic than the lived body, capable of more profound links between affects and their milieus than habit and memory ordinarily allow.[2] In a world that challenges all hope, all belief, we film the world in order to rediscover our links with it: "The less human the world is, the more it is the artist's duty to believe and produce belief in a relation between man and the world, because the world is made by men" (*C2*, 171).

From a hermetic perspective, it is possible to see that the restorative gesture of the avant-garde has deep roots. Anticipating Italian neorealism by hundreds of years, Giordano Bruno wrote in *De la magia* that the creation of new worlds always involves disintegration or vicissitude. Bruno writes, "This is the most important and most fundamental and of all the principles which provide an explanation of the marvels found in nature; namely, that because of an active principle and universal soul, nothing is so incomplete, defective or imperfect, or, according to common opinion, so completely insignificant that it could not become the source of great events. Indeed, on the contrary, a very large disintegration into such components must occur for an almost completely new world to be generated from them" (*CPU*, 111). "Magical" knowledge, like the magic of a cinema able to access the crystals of time, is an intuitive knowledge of how seemingly meager or defective elements—disjointed times, disparate spaces, emaciated bodies—can in fact be the genetic elements of new worlds.[3]

The project of renewing belief in such a world goes beyond cinema, and in his work with Guattari, Deleuze is explicit about the hermetic and cosmic aspects of much of modern art. Apropos Proust, Deleuze and Guattari assert that art, despite its dependence upon transitory materials, preserves and is the only thing that is preserved (*WIP*, 163). For Deleuze, the quest of modern art is precisely to reveal genetic elements: the elements that, as virtual, are not directly experienced in sensation, yet constitute the "being" of the sensible in the precise sense that imperceptible vibrations constitute the being of every color. "Sensations, percepts, and affects are *beings* whose validity lies in themselves and exceeds any lived" (*WIP*, 164).[4] Artworks, in this view, stand as evidence of another "anorganic" life within life, and "affects are these nonhuman becomings of man" (*WIP*, 169). Clearly such "becomings" are salutary, and have a restorative and liberating potency. Deleuze and Guattari cite the French anthropologist J. M. G. Le Clézio on this point, who wrote that perhaps one day we will realize that there has never been art, "but only medicine" (*WIP*, 173). The aesthetic as medicinal, for Deleuze, has clear resonance with initiatory experiences aimed at the production of a body capable of the eternal repetitions of cosmic dynamics. Art from this perspective operates in a "zone of indiscernibility" where something transpires between nature and culture, at "that [embryonic, intensive] point that immediately precedes . . . natural differentiation" (*WIP*, 173).[5]

Proximity to embryonic states gives the modern work its aura of terror, "pure and simple terror" (*WIP*, 175). The modern work, in particular, renders the world strangely animated, uncanny. On this point, Deleuze and Guattari cite the painter Odelon Redon, who claimed that a certain flower "stares into my room all day" (*WIP*, 175). Part of what is disturbing about such a "cosmic" dimension of affects and percepts is that they seem to insinuate a recursion of our sensibility to what Freud called the "animist phase" of human development.[6] Many early twentieth-century artists were obsessed with "primitive" artifacts—masks, weapons, ceremonial objects—from animist and shamanic cultures. Yet if there is a kind of "spiritualism" of forces of line and color in painting, music, theater, and visual art, for Deleuze this is not so much a reflection of the reality of the supernatural as an intimation of forces that haunt nature from within.[7]

Deleuze and Guattari submit that this is why great painters approach color with "respect, almost dread," and take "great care" when "they join together sections or planes on which the type of depth [they are seeing] depends" (*WIP*, 179). The hermeticism of Deleuze's take on the arts is reflected in how he sees artists as visionaries, as *seers* who develop the rites and conditions under which the arcane forces of matter itself can be revealed. This is particularly clear in monochromes, where "the area of plain, uniform color vibrates, clinches, or cracks open because it is the bearer of glimpsed forces" (*WIP*, 181). Deleuze also sees something similar happening in film, when film develops a time image that shatters the frame and the montage, exposing a non-sequential order of connection that transforms possibilities of action into vectors of thought. But also, and perhaps most strikingly, some kind of deep apprehension of the vibratory state of matter seems to be occurring in music, when an artist like Stockhausen is exploring the interior life of tonality, breaking sound out of cliché, neutralizing timbre through electronic instruments, through the production of uncanny, cosmic mantras.[8]

In both *A Thousand Plateaus* and *What Is Philosophy?*, Deleuze and Guattari seem to be continuously ruminating over the subtle relations between artist practice and esoteric spiritual experience. And in the writings of Henri Michaux, Artaud, Lawrence, Henry Miller, and Stockhausen, aesthetic discipline in quest of an intensified spirituality is an explicit goal. It is in part Deleuze and Guattari's profound regard for these artists that place their own work in proximity to the hermetic, philosophical impulse—present in Cusa, Bruno, Spinoza, and others—to cultivate vision, even to establish, through philosophical syntax, the ritualistic, pragmatic contexts under which psychic and somatic transformation is made actual. With their affirmation of a "plane of immanence" that must be laid out and traversed, Deleuze and Guattari develop a thought that both invites and relies on participants whose exact natures are not known in advance, but appear in uncanny acts of mediation.[9]

Transvervals

In addition to their conception of art, a large part of what connects Deleuze and Guattari to the hermetic tradition is a speculative philosophy of nature. Artists can be called cosmic artisans to the extent that they operate upon "transversal" lines that cross, and thus unite different structures of materiality, desire, and affect. In their wide-ranging coauthored work, Deleuze and Guattari develop concepts that outline how a plane of immanence or consistency can be discerned that might account for a broad array of phenomena from the point of view of the complex motions or "becomings" of which they are composed, at extremely abstract levels. The development of a "transversal ontology" of forces that cross worlds is an attempt to conceptualize such forces in ways that allow them to be creatively ramified. That is to say, this metaphysics is immediately an ethics. As should by now go without saying, such an ambition is in keeping not only with Spinozism, but with hermeticism as well.

Throughout *A Thousand Plateaus*, Deleuze and Guattari argue that immanent thought—whether in the form of art, science, or philosophy—must be willing to follow its material, in the way that a metallurgist follows flows of ore. They aver that this thought can be neither migratory nor entirely sedentary, but must be nomadic, an ambulant or itinerant work, like that, at least historically speaking, of the itinerant metallurgist.[10] As itinerant, the metallurgist differs from both the migrant and the sedentary farmer. Mines must be near mountains or deserts, on frontiers far from the rich alluvial valleys of imperial, sedentary farming. Yet metallurgists require a consistent and stable food supply from those same farms, and so must remain near settlements. Between the sedentary and migrant types, the metallurgist is defined by the peculiarities of a nomadic space, a peculiar space Deleuze and Guattari call "holey space." This space is neither the empty, "smooth" space of the migrant, nor the fully "striated" space of the sedentary farms. The space of the mines and of metallurgy is connected with migratory space and conjoined with sedentary space—metallurgists are not of the land or of the soil but of the subsoil, the underground (*ATP*, 415).[11]

Rather than imposing forms on the earth, and rather than subjecting themselves entirely to the ebb and flow of capital, metallurgists follow the flow of a specific material, an ore. Deleuze and Guattari say that the smith "ambulates" with the ore, as do the nomads of the steppe with their packs of wild horses. Smiths do not wholly escape the agrarian and sedentary formations, but create "lines of flight" or "rhizomes," networks of relations that place the smiths in ambiguous positions: Are they slaves? Demigods? Heroes? Demons? And how do they manage to live so close to the forest, from which they get the charcoal needed for refinement processes—do they speak the language of beasts? Of trees? Of spirits?

For Deleuze and Guattari, the anomalous status of the smith cannot be explained in terms of its negative relationship with others. They argue that "their relation to others results from their internal itinerancy, from their own vague essences, and not the reverse" (*ATP*, 415). Deleuze and Guattari note that Husserl had some notion of an identity formed from "ambulant coupling[s]" with his notion of anexact essence (*ATP*, 408). Anexact essence, for Husserl, is neither prime matter, nor a sensible object. It is something between those two, what Deleuze and Guattari refer to as an "affect-event": a transformation taking place in matter that is not yet the imposition of a form, and yet is inseparable from expressive or intensive quantities.

Anexact essences are singularities extended over ordinary points, identities irreducible to the limits of natural species or cultural forms (*ATP*, 407). Such essences are grouped in a "machinic" (as opposed to organic or synergistic) manner. Deleuze and Guattari even speak of a "machinic phylum" defined as "*a constellation of singularities prolongable by certain operations, which converge, and make the operations con-*

verge, upon one or several assignable traits of expression" (*ATP*, 406). Connections that are "machinic" are neither organic nor mechanical, but can be traced in the operations of both organisms and in machines. In some sense, the way a horse relates to a plow in a field is related to the hands of a writer on a keyboard—not simply because of the fact that they are both working, but because of shared affects—contentment or fatigue, discouragement or satisfaction. The ultimate purport of such affects cannot be reduced to those individuals who express them. They are ultimately abstract quantities of motion and rest, speed and slowness, that are univocally expressed.

There are many different sympathies or symbioses between natural, social, and artificial forms of life, but the unity of these forms is in no sense a matter of arbitrary or even of merely elective affinity. The supposition of a machinic phylum is meant to explain how seemingly unconnected objects and events can nevertheless manifest uncannily similar attributes or aims. The machinic phylum would in effect be constituted by a variable set of traits put to service by both human and nonhuman agents. As Deleuze and Guattari put it in *A Thousand Plateaus*, "This operative and expressive flow is as much artificial as it is natural: it is like the unity of human beings and Nature" (*ATP*, 406). In the case of the metallurgist, specific operations allow the flow of ore to come to the fore as a flow, but never as a form separable from matter.[12] The smith, somewhat like an itinerant carpenter, follows the flow not only of the ore with which he or she is working, but the vicissitudes of market, social, and political forces.[13]

Although all artisans exist in this manner, the smith perhaps most clearly crystallizes what is only latent in other crafts. For it is in metals more than any other elemental sphere that it is unclear where a potency ends and a form begins. As Deleuze and Guattari put it, "An energetic materiality overspills the prepared matter, and a qualitative deformation or transformation overspills the form" (*ATP*, 410). Quenching, which finishes the forging, takes place after the form has been fixed. The existence of ingots, which are prepared potentials, cannot be reduced to mere potentials or stocks. Even though it seems like the distinction between form and matter is clearer nowhere else than metallurgy, what actually happens is a continuous development of form and a continuous variation of matter, comparable to that which takes place in music. Deleuze and Guattari write,

> If metallurgy has an essential relationship with music, it is by virtue not only of the sounds of the forge but also of the tendency within both arts to bring into its own, beyond separate forms, a continuous development of form, and beyond variable matters, a continuous variation of matter: a widened chromaticism sustains both music and metallurgy; the musical smith was the first "transformer." In short, what metal and metallurgy bring to light is a life proper to matter, a vital state of matter as such, a material vitalism that doubtless exists everywhere but is ordinarily hidden or covered, rendered unrecognizable, dissociated by the hylomorphic model. (*ATP*, 411)

The music of the smith is not just the sound of his hammer, but a transformational relation with the ore: the smith plays through the malleability of the ore; the musician forges through a continuous variation of notes. Smiths as much as musicians do not impose forms but transform materials: forms appear only as transitions. Metallurgy and music thus reveal "a life proper to matter."[14] Only here, "at the limit," do we perceive what Deleuze calls

> a single phylogenetic lineage, a single machinic phylum, ideally continuous: the flow of matter-movement, the flow of matter in continuous variation, conveying singularities and traits of expression. This operative and expressive flow is as much artificial as natural: it is like the unity of human beings and Nature. But at the same time, it is not realized in the here and now without dividing, differentiating. We will call an assemblage every constellation of singularities and traits deducted from the flow—selected, organized, stratified—in such a way as to converge (consistency) artificially and naturally; an assemblage, in this sense, is a veritable invention. (*ATP*, 406)

Deleuze and Guattari define an "assemblage" as any set of related elements that establish a territory in such a way as to alter the sense of the occupied territory, and indeed to internalize that territory so as to draw it into relations—both concrete and abstract—with other assemblages (*ATP*, 505). Here they speak of every assemblage, natural or cultural, as an "invention" in the sense that assemblages exist as transformations of *sense*, of translations or transitions between (and permutations of) forms of content and matters of expression. Because of their nomadic and transmutative aspect, assemblages must be discerned through a kind of *tracing* activity Deleuze and Guattari call "minor science." State science, with its methodism, reproduces but does not truly make: "the State is perpetually producing and reproducing ideal circles, but a war machine is necessary to make something round" (*ATP*, 367).[15]

Minor science approaches nature not in terms of genera or phylogenetic lineages, but in terms of a machinic phylum, an itinerant distribution that links traits in novel series. In making music, composers attempt to follow an esprit de corps of the notes themselves, as if the movement of sound was itself only an index of a greater movement, a becoming the music entertains by provoking it. From the perspective of the machinic phylum, certain swords are more like certain knives than other swords, just as certain pieces of chamber music, such as Steve Reich's *Music for 18 Musicians*, have more in common with electronic dance music than with classical music. The machinic phylum arranges forms of content and matters of expression in ways that are mobile and fluid, in constant states of flux; major or "state" science is blind to the intensive, potentially anarchic map of energetic flows.[16]

In *A Thousand Plateaus*, Deleuze and Guattari speak of certain passages of music becoming-horse or becoming-cosmic. But this is not because music represents emotions or characters, but because it mobilizes forces moving across various forms of life.[17] As they put it, "Music (in this case, Mozart's) takes as its content a becoming-animal; but in that becoming-animal the horse, for example, takes as its expression soft kettledrum beats, winged like hooves from heaven or hell; and the birds find expression in *gruppeti*, appogiaturs, staccato notes that transform them into so many souls" (*ATP*, 304). Here we see more distinctly the structure of an "animism" haunting Deleuze's ontology: under the spellbound conditions of composition, notes become birds that become souls. Notes do not represent but *become* horse steps, bird flight, or lovemaking. But this transmutation only occurs because in this process horses, birds, and love enter into new assemblages, and on that basis become something new, as yet unknown. The horse is "deterritorialized," transfigured into something else yet again: in music the horse becomes enigma, symbol, *arcana*. This "translation" of the cosmic occurs in music not because of any imitative power, but because of a potential for transmutation that cuts across all artistic activity like an abstract, nomadic line. As Deleuze puts it, "The painter and the musician do not imitate the animal, they become-animal at the same time as the animal becomes what they willed, at the deepest level of their concord with Nature" (*ATP*, 305).

However—and this is perhaps the most subtle and esoteric aspect of Deleuze and Guattari's view—it is not the sensible qualities of music itself (or of painting, or film) that constitute the intensities and singularities assemblages embody. If this were the case, every assemblage would simply be a kind of "rhapsody of sensations," a delirium tremens of unregulated sense experience such as the one Plato warns us against in the *Philebus*, a "becoming without measure." Deleuze and Guattari write,

> We are not at all arguing for an aesthetics of qualities, as if the pure quality (color, sound, etc.) held the secret of a becoming without measure, as in *Philebus*. Pure qualities still seem to us to be punctual systems: They are reminiscences, they are either transcendent or floating memories or seeds of phantasy. A functionalist conception, on the other hand, only considers the function a quality fulfills in a specific assemblage, or in passing from one assemblage to another. The quality must be considered from the standpoint of the becoming that grasps it, instead of becoming being considered form the standpoint of intrinsic qualities having the value of archetypes or phylogenetic memories. For example, whiteness, color, is gripped in a becoming-animal that can be that of the animal itself. Moby-Dick's whiteness is the special index of his becoming-solitary . . . a quality functions only as a line of deterritorialization of an assemblage, or in going from one assemblage to another. (*ATP* 306)

Assemblages are not punctual systems, but express functions or becomings whose organizing "points" are subperceptual intensities (despite the fact that these imperceptible intensities, such as the peculiar whiteness of Moby-Dick, exist only within percepts and affects). In the Melville assemblage, Moby-Dick's whiteness becomes an idea: the "whiteout" of Captain Ahab's obsession, carrying all the characters toward the white wall of death. Proust's reminiscences are somewhat more like a sensuous delirium, but they nevertheless act not as pure fantasies or simple reveries, but as a "becoming-child, a becoming-woman, as components of a deterritorialization passing from one assemblage to another" (*ATP*, 306).

From the perspective of a transversal ontology, music does not simply imitate life or merely suggest figures. Music captures and releases affects cutting across organic and inorganic life.[18] The relations between music and dance help to illustrate this point. Techno and jungle beats, for instance, are as much the affect of electricity through silicone chips as they are the untamed rampage of buffaloes and the eerie longing of hyenas. We dance these beasts not to comprehend something, to understand the "spirit of our times," but to connect the digital and the animal in an obscure affiliation, out of step with the times, untimely with respect to the slaughter of the animals and police-statist use of technological onslaught. Many forms of contemporary club, street, and trance dancing establish affects that express the becoming-digital of the herd even as they transform silicone silence into the noise of bodies reterritorializing the 1s and 2s: electronic astral travel.[19] Such a singular set of affects, crossing human, animal, and machine, do not reflect the times. Rather, the sonic bloc extracts something singular in the times: an anarchic longing for simultaneously primitive and advanced forms of interconnection and exchange.[20]

Another dance, that of the tarantella, has been known to cure victims of tarantula bites. For Deleuze and Guattari, this dance is effective not because the dancer imitates a spider, but because there are spider affects that cross with the dance or traverse it in an exchange that connects human and spider. One does not mimic the spider, one dances the spider's color, mood, or timbre. As Deleuze puts it, "The victim, the patient, the person who is sick, becomes a dancing spider only to the extent that the spider itself is supposed to become a pure silhouette, pure color and pure sound to which the person dances" (*ATP*, 305).

Because it looks for the interaction of real forces between the interstices of "major" or dominant modes of organization—that is, among species, historical periods, nation-states, social groups, and fully constituted human individuals—a transversal thought must be called "minor." Minor science maps forces of becoming-animal, becoming-molecular, and becoming-imperceptible, a knowledge that is also required for acts of sorcery. All genuine writers are in fact sorcerers, Deleuze and Guattari aver, because "they experience the animal as the only population before which they are responsible in principle" (*ATP*, 240). Animals territorialize through sound and line; writers territorialize by becoming-animal. This animal artistry has nothing to do with imitation, resemblance, or representation, but with the continuation of affect along aberrant lines.

But inasmuch as the author becomes animal, many animals express themselves by writing with their territories. Deleuze and Guattari note that the camouflage of chameleons and of certain fish does not imitate anything. The effort is not to resemble any other organism in particular, but to capture flows, movements, and trajectories proper to a given milieu.[21] In this sense a tropical fish symbolizes the enigma of the coral reef itself, as its "behavior" (if that term captures anything significant) recapitulates and condenses the evolutionary forces that have created the reef as milieu. Deleuze and Guattari see such a process of "involution" as inherently creative. A fish makes an abstract line or develops a unique variation on the themes of his world—a world that is, in itself, already an abstract line of life of which the fish itself is a part. Writers are sorcerers in the sense that they, too, deterritorialize and reterritorialize on their milieus, and become swept up by the impersonal affects that traverse them. The peculiar trait here (and perhaps a kind of minimal difference between the writer and the animal) is that, unlike the fish or the bird, the writer wills to deterritorialize to the infinite, to become everything and everybody, to become all the names of history, "to be present at the dawn of a world" (*ATP*, 280).[22]

Transversal ontology thus maps possibilities for theandric, cosmogonic activity, from the work of art to sorcery itself, that cross human and animal, organic and inorganic, natural and cultural domains. In this view the transversal of the world is not towards an integrational organicism, but through a differential field Deleuze calls a *synthesizer* (*ATP*, 342–43).[23] The characters, figures, or phrases, of an artist, are not so many parts seeking integration into a whole, but machines for extracting, distilling, and continuing impersonal affects, just as oscillators divide and recombine sound waves in a synthesizer. And just as synthetic sounds, at their most interesting, do not attempt to resemble the sounds of other instruments, but draw abstract diagrams of timbres, it is a principle of the successful cosmic artisan, generally, to first eliminate clichéd figures and stereotyped narratives in order to capture the imperceptible and the indiscernible, and to make new worlds from them. It is never a question of imitation, but of an approach to the unknown. Deleuze and Guattari write, "Suppose a painter 'represents' a bird; this is in fact a becoming-bird that can occur only to the extent that the bird itself is in the process of becoming something else, a pure line and pure color. Thus imitation self-destructs since the imitator unknowingly enters into a becoming that conjugates with the unknowing becoming of that which he or she imitates. One imitates only if one fails, when one fails" (*ATP*, 305).

Diagrams

Any attempt to use known materials to discern the as yet unknown is an activity Deleuze and Guattari call *diagrammatic* (*ATP*, 510).[24] A diagram, in this view, is a not a representation of knowledge, but a mark that potentially relates the known to the unknown. With a diagrammatic line, we pass from a limited milieu to an unlimited territory along a "cutting edge of deterritorialization" (*ATP*, 510). In this sense, Francis Bacon's paintings are diagrammatic. Through the incorporation of aleatory traces, the canvas is emptied of cliché, and that which is presented enters into polyvalent, unstable relations to otherwise imperceptible forces. The distortion of the human body in Bacon's work is not so much a terrifying violence as it is a glimpse of as yet unseen powers, forces that impinge upon the body or draw it into hybrid states, relations with an overwhelming yet constitutive Outside.[25]

Bacon begins his paintings with an aleatory or chaotic mark, a trait around which or through which he is then constrained to paint. Deleuze argues that when such a chaotic mark is incorporated into the painting, the entire work becomes "diagrammatic." When the composition is completed, it culminates in a "pictorial fact" that has nothing to do with verisimilitude or even with the merely formal fact generated by abstraction. The diagrammatic composition is a new being, an assemblage. What is realized here is a power that comes from beyond or before the conscious will, from a nature or an affect that is impersonal, preindividual, and complicit with chance.

From the chaotic trait there emerges not a depiction of the world but a new and anorganic figure. This figure is neither illustrative nor abstract, but "machinic." In his book on Bacon, Deleuze explains the process in the following way:

> The diagram was only a possibility of fact, whereas the painting exists by making present a very particular fact, which we will call *the pictorial fact* . . . what we will call a "fact" is first of all the fact that several forms may be included in one and the same Figure, indissolubly, caught up in a

kind of serpentine, like so many necessary accidents continually mounting on top of one another . . . But the fact itself, this pictorial fact that has come from the hand, is the formation of a third eye, a haptic eye, a haptic vision of the eye, this new clarity. It is as if the duality of the tactile and the optical were surpassed visually in this haptic function born of the diagram. (*FB*, 128–29).

In other words, the diagram is not the aleatory mark, but is a transcendental function that allows a new pictorial fact to emerge from the trait. Contact with chaos is never the goal, but only the beginning of an adventure that the emergent "third eye" of the painting will have espied. Such a haptic vision emerges between chaos and cliché, and results in an assemblage emergent through the aleatory mark it incarnates.

For Deleuze and Guattari, both Bacon's painting and Proust's literature share a common quest for a figure that is neither an abstract type nor an individual portrait. "Figures have nothing to do with resemblance or rhetoric but are the conditions under which the arts produce affects of stone and metal, of strings and wind, of line and color, on a plane of composition of a universe" (*WIP*, 66). To cultivate a figure is to develop a particular affect to such an extent that it begins to coalesce with as yet unknown entities. Bacon paints "portraits" of humans that are organized by a chaotic or random trait through which body parts (eyes, mouths), places (butcheries and living rooms), and states (being meat, being the Crucified) are related in ways they could not be otherwise (elongated, truncated, distended). Proust does not give us an "impression" of Combray through descriptive flourish, nor a "day in the life" of a person living there, but Combray in a tea-cup, Albertine in a bedroom, a nervous breakdown and a mystical epiphany in a sonata. As Deleuze puts it, "This [connection] is perhaps because Bacon, when he refuses the double way of a figurative painting and an abstract painting, is put in a situation analogous to that of Proust in literature. Proust did not want an abstract literature that was too voluntary (philosophy), any more than he wanted a figurative, illustrative, or narrative literature that merely told a story. What he was striving for, what he wanted to bring to light, was a kind of Figure, torn away from figuration and stripped of every figurative function: a Figure-in-itself, for example, the figure-in-itself of Combray" (*FB*, 56).

Bacon's paintings diagram intensive spaces, regions that cannot be approached through optic or manual terms alone. As Deleuze and Guattari describe it, diagrammatic transformations are those which start with a formalized regime of signs (in this case, the clichés of painting), and proceed to extract from them—or make a "machine" capable of extracting from them—a new set of potential traits or "particles-signs" (*ATP*, 145).[26] Once the diagrammatic moment has occurred, an abstract machine can be established that organizes or partially actualizes a new regime of sensation. In *Three Studies for Figures on Bends* (1972), for example, the trait becomes a hip socket that joins all three bodies in an impossible new human animality. The mark with which Bacon begins is not the final "matter of fact" or "brute fact" painted. Rather, the chaotic trait enables the painting to render a brutality or a "cruelty" (in Artaud's sense) of fact that it would not be able to do without that *trait* (meaning, in French, a line, but also a characteristic). The goal is always to create a new assemblage. As Deleuze puts it in his study of Bacon's paintings,

> Save the contour—nothing is more important for Bacon than this. A line that delimits nothing still has a contour or outline itself. Blake at least understood this. The diagram must not eat away at the entire painting; it must remain limited in space and time. It must remain operative and controlled. The violent methods must not be given free reign, and the necessary catastrophe must not submerge the whole. The diagram is a possibility of fact—it is not the Fact itself. Not all the figurative givens have to disappear; and above all, a new figuration, that of the Figure, should emerge from the diagram and make the sensation clear and precise. To emerge from the catastrophe . . . (FB 89)

In this sense, figures have an esoteric, symbolic function, serving as symbols and sigils in a ritual intended to map lines of force of cosmic rhythms and periodicities, ramifying the potential for new forms of life. Deleuze and Guattari even assert that such figures are like spirits or local divinities, governing the "conditions under which the arts produce affects of stone and metal, of strings and wind, of line and color, on a plane of composition of a universe" (*WIP*, 66). In some sense, the conditions of artistic production of new affects are the conditions of the most ancient method of divination: geomancy, which begins with aleatory marks on the ground. In this sense all genuine diagrams "divine" in the sense that they *prophesy* worlds by presenting a synecdoche of the imperceptible forces animating percepts and affects. Figures do not mimic, but express the otherwise inexpressible in the world.

There is thus a demiurgic and theandric quality of every artistic activity engaged in cosmic artisanship, in the laying out of every diagram. This is why Deleuze describes the diagrammatic power of figures as a beginning, an opening or disclosure, "like a beam of light that draws a hidden universe out of the shadows" (*WIP*, 66). Melville's Ahab and Bartleby are not merely "interesting characters," they are molecular forces, archetypal energies animating entire populations or fields (everyone in *Moby-Dick* as a dimension of Ahab). Deleuze and Guattari argue that Melville no more invents than reveals Ahab, just as in *The Plumed Serpent* Lawrence reveals in Quetzalcoatl a god more familiar to us than we might like to admit: Lawrence's Kate flees back to England not because the god is too strange but rather all too familiar, as the returned repressed of the European mind, a power that gives the lie to Kate's emaciated, decadent idea of love.

Conceptual Personae

Deleuze and Guattari call writers like Melville or Lawrence (as much as Kafka) "half" philosophers, and they assert that art thinks as much as philosophy, albeit on a plane of composition of a universe instead of a plane of immanence of thought. "Art and philosophy crosscut the chaos and confront it, but it is not the same sectional plane; it is not populated in the same way. In the one there is the constellation of a universe or affects and percepts; and in the other, constitutions of immanence or concepts. Art thinks no less than philosophy, but it thinks through affects and percepts" (*WIP*, 66). But how exactly does *philosophy* "crosscut the chaos and confront it" (*WIP*, 66)? Diagrammaticization in philosophy—the establishment of conditions for conceptual creation in the sense that Bacon and Proust prepare for the work of art—passes by way of mediating spirits Deleuze and Guattari call "conceptual personae" (*WIP*, 62). That is to say, Deleuze and Guattari assert that philosophical thought does not emerge directly from the self-consciousness of an author, but through the mediation of personae she elicits in thought. For example, the Idiot is a persona taken up in various ways by Cusa, Descartes, and Dostoyevsky. This persona is a "private thinker" who refuses established knowledge because she wants to know for herself, by the "natural light" (*WIP*, 62). Cusa's Idiot is a soul who has embraced "learned ignorance" in the face of a transcendent source of being, the Absolute Maximum, all measure of which is but a dim approximation, and of whose true nature every sign is enigmatic (*WIP*, 61). Descartes's Idiot discovers the cogito only after doubting everything, through the perhaps feigned or at least mimed idiocy that opens the *Meditations* (*WIP*, 62). Dostoyevsky's Idiot is not seeking the truth, but is idiotic precisely in rejecting the legitimacy of truth and reason, embracing the absurd as a way of embracing the wretched of the earth (*WIP*, 63). This final Idiot, perhaps the most extreme, commits himself to the ordeal of comprehending through madness and suffering "all the victims of history" and is "closer to Job than to Socrates" (*WIP*, 63).

Despite the inherently abstract character of philosophical thought, Deleuze and Guattari assert that conceptual activity remains immanent to certain mediators, to characters such as the Idiot who subvert opinion and the certainties of expertise in order to prepare for higher insight, for uncanny visions. "The philosopher is the envelope of his principal conceptual persona and of all the other personae who are the intercessors, the real subjects of his philosophy" (*WIP*, 64). The persona of the Idiot mediates a certain mode of life in thought, from Nicholas of Cusa's learned ignorance in the face of a God unthinkably infinite to the advent of the modern Idiot, the cogito, with Descartes. And by incarnating the stultification of thought in the face of the suffering body, the Idiot mediates to the mind the full impact of the irrational, as in the case of Dostoyevsky.

It would not be an overextension to call conceptual personae the peculiar diagrammatic functives of philosophy. That is to say, conceptual personae establish relations between concepts and the nonconceptual spirits with which thought is intimately bound up. In somewhat less mystifying terms, an aesthetic, ethical figure is one of the genetic elements of any conceptual outlay. Just as Socrates was the invention of Plato, conceptual personae are neither mere imitations, nor the simple internalization of psychosocial types. They are internal dramas, replays of historical and archetypal potentials whose repetition enables forces to play a role in concepts. Through conceptual personae, history and myth become productive as parameters of a specifically philosophical becoming.

Some mode of invocational or mantic discourse is at stake here. It is yet another indication of Deleuze's fundamentally hermetic stance that, as with the aleatory traits of Bacon's paintings, conceptual personae introduce an idiosyncratic, impersonal element into thought, and that somehow this "cosmic" element is the true subject of enunciation, the enigmatic voice of the real. When it comes to specifically philosophical thought, we might ordinarily consider the mind to be at its most conscious, willful, and deliberate. Deleuze and Guattari challenge this model by drawing out a peculiar passivity to thought, and the way in which thought is bound up with a passive synthesis of unconscious elements nevertheless essential to even the most active exercise of mind. Conceptual personae do not emerge through calculated deliberation; they befall the thinker in ordeals of becoming. Deleuze and Guattari are emphatic on this point: in philosophy it is not the "I" who speaks. "Conceptual personae are the true agents of enunciation. 'Who is "I"?' It is always a third person" (*WIP*, 65).

Traditionally, philosophy has been heavily invested in maintaining personal idiosyncrasies and physical peculiarities that are external to thought—to say nothing of the racial, class, and economic situation of various individuals. Without reducing the differences in systems of thought to sheer historical contingency, Deleuze and Guattari nevertheless insist that physical abnormalities, neuroses, moods, and even body types become dynamisms internal to thought, characteristics of a living thought. Through a kind of transcendental involution, pathic features such as madness, relational features such as being a friend or a lover, dynamic features such as leaping or dancing, juridical features such as being a claimant (Socrates), a lawyer (Leibniz), or a judge (Kant), all become dimensions of concepts. "The face and body of a philosopher shelters these conceptual personae who often give them strange appearance, especially in the glance, as if someone else was looking through their eyes" (*WIP*, 73). Philosophy itself is described here as a mode of mediumship, and thought is seen to involve a kind of séance where the mind channels mercurial avatars and confronts its atavisms. Just as the aleatoric trait is not yet the diagram, conceptual personae are not substitutes for concepts. And yet the daimonic power of conceptual personae seems essential to thought itself.

Deleuze and Guattari emphasize, in particular, the role of personae in Plato and Nietzsche—arguably the two most powerful writers and most artistic philosophers in the Western tradition. Plato and Nietzsche were especially devoted to mythical and archetypal patterns external to pure conceptual reason, and they wrote texts (Nietzsche's *Zarathustra*, and most of the dialogues of Plato) that were intended to function as initiatory rites. As Deleuze and Guattari put it, "Nietzsche's Dionysus is no more mythical Dionysus than Plato's Socrates is the historical Socrates. Becoming is not being, and Dionysus becomes philosopher at the same time that Nietzsche becomes Dionysus. Here, again, it is Plato who begins: he becomes Socrates at the same time that he makes Socrates become philosopher" (*WIP*, 65).

If conceptual personae were simply the historical figures or archaic myths to which philosophical concepts might be reduced—that is to say, if theory were simply the rationalization of perspective—then the distinction between concepts and conceptual personae would collapse. But in philosophical discourse, mythical, historical, personal, and political idiosyncrasy is transformed or transducted. In the texts of Plato, Socrates becomes something he never (historically) was at the same time that Plato discovers his own thinking, in the name or persona of Socrates.[27] And what does such a specifically philosophical becoming consist in, if not an initiation into the ways of certain transitive spirits, uncanny *daimonion* no less summoned as invented? Dionysus comes for Nietzsche, in the dead of night, as much as Nietzsche reinvents himself as Dionysus the crucified. The other who thinks in me, is always another, or a crowd of others, a pack, a band, a multiplicity (*ATP*, 249).

Deleuze reads the experiments of certain artists as attempts to access and render viable the inaccessible memories, unapproachable velocities, and overwhelming intensities—both affective and perceptual—of life itself. For Deleuze, certain styles, especially the Proustian recherche and the Baconian diagram, can be read as an attempt to liberate signs, sounds, and images from the interpretive closures caused by personal and historical trauma, or somewhat less dramatically, from the perspective of deeply embedded habits, and from all that is clichéd in culture. But Deleuze does not evaluate the success or failure of such artistic projects from the position of a traditional critic. For Deleuze, to evaluate a style or modus operandi is to evaluate a form of life, a modus vivendi. This mode does not crystallize the life of a subject or even an organism, but a cosmic life of as yet unknown parameters. From this perspective, the significance of the work of art lies not in the delight it provides, nor in the way it develops formal possibilities relative to the history of a medium, nor even in how it reveals historical or psychological truths, but in the extent to which it ramifies an undiscovered potency of life. For Deleuze, all genuine artistic experimentation must be understood as a local activation of otherwise imperceptible cosmic forces that move through natures, cultures, and psyches. When it is successful, the work of art suggests new modes of sensible and affective engagement within the world as multiplicity, clueing us in to the potencies of our existence in and as a massive, open-ended machinic phylum on which new possible assemblages can be constructed.

While artworks can truly become an exploration of such multiplicity, the work of a truly "cosmic" artisan, it is incumbent upon philosophy to think in a way that accounts for the immanent contours of the real. The transversal ontologies of *A Thousand Plateaus* attempt to develop a complex speculative metaphysics that can encompass structures germane to animal and human, civil and geophysical, natural and artificial modes of organization. The development of such a metaphysics is in part motivated by a desire to connect the potentials of aesthetic experimentation to utopian and revolutionary ethical and political projects. It is a metaphysics geared to uncovering new possibilities for ethical and political intervention. In this sense, Deleuze and Guattari work squarely in the hermetic tradition, not only in terms of their refusal of binary oppositions between the elemental and the cosmic, the human and the animal, the affective and the effective, but also because they are explicit about the ethical, political, cosmic, and spiritual stakes of contact with "unknown nature."

These stakes are nothing less than the ultimate prospects of cosmic and psychic reintegration. They are also, at least in the hermetic tradition, the spiritual stakes of philosophy itself, which explains why Deleuze incorporates a certain cosmic dimension into his account of philosophy as "the creation of concepts." Due to its immanent unfolding of "conceptual personae," the philosophical assemblage, in resonance with musical, nomadic, and minor scientific configurations, also reveals a constitutive cosmic "outside." Conceptual creation takes place on the basis of conceptual personae to the degree that philosophy precipitates forces of affect and percept into thought. Contact with cosmic forces becomes the basis on which thought thinks an always incomplete incorporation of historical, mythic, and biopsychic dimensions. Encompassing art, science, and philosophy, Deleuze's vision thus constitutes a distinctly contemporary hermeticism. What remains to be explored is the degree to which Deleuze's ethics and politics of experimental practice not only resonates with classical hermetic ambitions, but also provides a set of categories for rethinking contemporary ethical and political problems under the aegis of what Deleuze and Guattari call in *A Thousand Plateaus* a "politics of sorcery."

6

The Politics of Sorcery

Antoine Faivre, the eminent scholar of hermeticism, asserts that esoteric gnosis is a distinctly ethical activity in which metaphysical reflection is immediately a process of psychic and spiritual transformation. That is to say, the purpose of the hermetic vision is to cultivate a simultaneously spiritual and scientific perspective, one that is both the "elaboration of a *Naturphilosophie* and an ongoing resumption of the alchemical work of the self."[1] Likewise, Deleuze characterizes thought as a spiritual ordeal. And in a way that bears striking similarity to Deleuze, Faivre characterizes gnosis as a process of becoming, a transformation that involves the condensation, immolation, and reemergence germane to the alchemical magnum opus. That work, understood spiritually, rather than as the search for physical gold, is to forge a living and evolving renewal of "hermetic" traces—traces, that is, of wisdom about the operations of nature manifest in the symbolic discourse.[2]

Amor Fati

But what rapport, exactly, does Deleuze's ethical and political thought have, if any, with this antique, alchemical ethos? For Deleuze's is clearly *not* a thought attempting to return us to a lost Edenic state, or even to produce a new golden dawn of civilization. Deleuze never explicitly affirms the "reenchantment of nature" as a goal of art or thought, and never acknowledges any explicitly "religious" thinker as being capable of truly immanent thought. Such affirmations would perhaps carry Deleuze too close to the dangers of the transcendent reference points he attempts at all costs to avoid. (Although even for Faivre, it should be noted, the work of Hermes does not aim at an Eden to be simply recollected, but toward an eschaton it would be "incumbent upon the esoteric project to rediscover, to explore, and then to bring back to emergence.")[3]

Deleuze's own ethical perspective is deeply conditioned by his account of time.[4] In *The Logic of Sense,* his most sustained ethical reflection, Deleuze indexes human flourishing to the possibility of accessing alternative experiences of the events, conceptions that depend, in some sense, on extracting events from chronological time. This extraction involves a process of creative replay or "counter-actualization," a possibility that rests on a temporality that is neither linear nor irreversible, a "pure and empty form of time." Following the Stoics' theory of the "incorporeal" nature of events, Deleuze assigns the possibility of ethical transformation to an intransitive or "untensed" time in which the incorporeal sense of events (the sense not fully determined by bodily actions and reactions) persists and can be creatively varied. For example, when a person dies, the event is the result of physical causes, but the meanings of a death are multiple and thus both precede and exceed the physics of the event itself. The mental or ideal time in which the meanings of a death are played and replayed is not linear and sequential, but aberrant and discontinuous, the effect of life's being embedded in a relativity and an intensity proper to different experiences and different overlapping series of sense.

This is what Deleuze calls the time of Aiôn, as opposed to that of Chronos, the time of physical movements. Aiôn contrasts with Chronos in that it cannot be limited to the succession of presents. Aiôn's characteristic is always to elude the present (*LS,* 77). Aiôn infinitely subdivides itself into past and future at once, and so can be identified with neither (*LS,* 164). Since Aiôn's characteristic is to elude the continuity of experience, it is the time of non-sense. Yet, Deleuze argues, Aiôn's non-sense deeply and powerfully haunts the good sense of Chronos: Aiôn insists in the interstice of the instant, dividing the present from itself. This interstice is not the "passing" of the present as we live it, but a point that marks the present as present without itself passing. As Deleuze puts it, "Plato rightly said that the instant is *atopon*, without place. It is the paradoxical instance or the aleatory point, the nonsense of the surface and the quasi-cause. It is the pure movement of abstraction whose role is, primarily, to divide and subdivide every present in both directions at once, into past-future, upon the line of Aiôn" (*LS*, 166).

Deleuze illustrates his theory by way of Lewis Carroll. The proposition "Alice becomes larger," denotes an event taking place in time. But from the point of view of Chronos, the point of view of the actual growth of Alice in the present, the proposition is missing half its sense, namely that intransitive sense of "to grow" that signifies heading in (at least) two directions simultaneously: in the instant, Alice is simultaneously smaller than she is becoming, and larger than she is now. If there were only a chrono-logical time, there would be no coherent general or multiple sense of "to grow" or "growing," but only an abyssal, measureless present. Without the dimension of Aiôn, the multiple and overlapping senses of "to grow" would be inconceivable. Only the measureless instant of Aiôn makes possible the abstraction necessary for a truly multiple sense of becoming, a true continuum of sense distinct from the particular, local concatenations of bodies in linear temporal and causal sequences. Death happens in a specific passage of time (Chronos), but also in an instant that eludes time by being subject to future reinterpretation or replay. It is to Aiôn that we owe this possibility.

For Deleuze, ethics is intimately tied to the possibility of transforming sense in a way that expands the parameters of what is normally understood as personal identity. Because personal identity is not a static entity, but a persona one inhabits in accordance with the requirements of the continuous present—the role one plays that relates to other players and other roles—there is, for Deleuze, a possibility that one can abstract oneself, as a mime would, from the role one currently plays, while remaining within that role. From the "instantaneous" perspective of Aiôn, the self is, on one level, fully enmeshed through its bodily relations in the chronological present but can also see that body as a "metaphysical surface" on which to "counter-actualize" the events that take place. Redoubling the present, the subject taken as mime accesses an intransitive and incorporeal sense of events that can subvert and transform the ordinary contours of sense. The subject as *mimeur* would reanimate the life it mimes.

The ethical wisdom of such an actor-dancer is not the knowledge of how to escape from the traumas of embodied experience, but an ability to "redouble the role," to play with sense or "duplicate the lining" of sense, to selectively activate a nonsense that frees sense from its restriction to Chronos and the demands of ordinary time. This is a matter, as in *Alice's Adventures in Wonderland* and *Through the Looking-Glass, and What Alice Found There*, not of reacting to events but of extending their implications to unusual or unforeseeable conclusions, carrying lines of sense farther than they are intended to reach. To counteractualize is to replay, and in some sense outplay, the drama of events themselves.

While this characterization of ethics is rather abstract, it has profoundly concrete implications. Deleuze believes that what we have to learn from Alice is how to grasp ourselves as events, events with multiple senses flowing through imbricated singular forces below the surface of identity. Deleuze's view of ethics is conditioned by his confidence that the subject can contravene or redeploy the sense of events, drawing energy for an expanded sense of self that situates events in a widened, even cosmic field of interplay. The very "physics" of Alice's strange adventures—her ability to bend, shift, grow, adapt, and play along with nonsense, announce an unexpected set of ethical possibilities. Deleuze writes,

> The problem is . . . one of knowing how the individual would be able to transcend his form and his syntactical link with a world, in order to attain to the universal communication of events, that is, to the affirmation of a disjunctive synthesis beyond logical contradictions, and even beyond alogical compatibilities. It would be necessary for the individual to grasp herself as an event; and that she grasp the event actualized within her as another individual grafted onto her. In this case, she would not understand, want, or represent this event without also understanding and wanting all other events as individuals, and without representing all other individuals as events. Each individual would be like a mirror for the condensation of singularities and each world a distance in the mirror. This is the ultimate sense of counter-actualization. (*LS*, 178)

Deleuze's relation to historical hermetic perspectives is quite clear here: his affirmation of an ethical perspective from which wanting and understanding all events and all individuals as dimensions of oneself is precisely the affirmation embodied in theurgic, alchemical, and initiatory practices geared to unite the hierophant, the magus, or the shaman in fraternal and communal sympathy with many other forms of life. Deleuze himself, in *The Logic of Sense*, presents the Zen master—master of paradoxes, silences, and uncanny modes of power—as a model of ethical life (*LS*, 136). Becoming capable of "grasping ourselves as events" is precisely Deleuze's version of the hermetic view of time's unfolding "as above, so below." To view ourselves as "mirrors for the condensation of singularities" is to embrace the inherence of each event in every other event. It is to see each in all and all in each—which is, as in Renaissance philosophy, and in Bruno's writings in particular, one of the first principles of *magia naturalis*.

The invocation of *magia* in the context of ethics may seem somewhat strained, if not simply unusual, so it is worth dwelling on momentarily. As the monumental work of Marcel Mauss demonstrated, far from being linked to an automatic effect of wish fulfillment, magic is almost universally undertaken as a tentative, ambulant, and experimental enterprise.[5] The counteractualization of sense is a kind of magic in the sense that it is an effect dependent upon delicate mixtures that can and do fail to transmute the forces coursing through them. Surfaces that are not plastic, not flexible enough, or are expected to bear more than they can, fall apart. Words then become alienated from things, meaning fails, and the psyche fragments. At the extreme, this failure becomes the nightmare of psychosis, where the body and language are at war: "When this production collapses, or when the surface is rent by explosions and by snags, bodies fall back again into their depth; everything falls back again into the anonymous pulsation wherein words are no longer anything but affections of the body—everything falls back into the primary order which grumbles beneath the secondary organization of sense" (*LS*, 125).

What are the techniques that make our bodies capable of the adventure of sense? How do we become the avatars, and not merely the passive victims, of events? As usual, there is a clue, for Deleuze, in the affirmation and ramification of chance represented by the work of art. The peculiar way art manages to reproduce worlds without being restricted by the ends and purposes of ordinary time forges a "metaphysical" surface of sense where creative replay is possible. Above all, artworks manage to ramify series of potential actions or possible worlds, and to explore multiple or imbricating series of sense (both bodily and ideal) without fixation or attachment to any result in particular. Thus artistic experimentation models an anorganic vitality, one that can affirm not just one possibility, but chance as a whole, all chance for all times, in that intransitive temporality peculiar to thought. As Deleuze puts it,

> Only thought finds it possible *to affirm all chance and to make chance into an object of affirmation*. If one tries to play this game other than in thought, nothing happens; and if one tries to produce a result other than the work of art, nothing is produced. This game is reserved then for thought and art. In it there is nothing but victories for those who know how to play, that is, how to affirm and ramify chance, instead of dividing it *in order to* dominate it, *nor in order to* wager, *in order to* win. This game, which can only exist in thought and which has no other result than the work of art, is also that in which thought and art are real and disturbing reality, morality and the economy of the world. (*LS*, 60)

Deleuze believes that if philosophy is to continue to have any importance, after the critique of the image of thought and in view of the superiority of the work of art, it must find a way to ally itself with this project of a new relation to the aleatory. Deleuze's key ethical imperative is that the human subject must make herself worthy of both the singularity of events and the indefinite (and in principle infinite) connections between this event and all others. What is crucial, as James Williams puts it in his brilliant commentary on *The Logic of Sense*, is that Deleuze "constructs a system where the singular and the connected are in contact with one another but call for different responses—a difficult balance of what can only belong to individuals and what connects to all things."[6]

For Deleuze, the whole of ethics consists, in a way, of a refusal of revenge.[7] Ethics, for Deleuze, is affirmation, a becoming-worthy of the peculiar adventures that befall us. The ethical imperative is *amor fati*, the cultivation of a joyful, loving, and humorous relation to the events that wound us and make us (*LS*, 149). But this ethics is difficult and rare, and the act of turning our attention to how events can be so transformed or "replayed" is an extraordinary achievement of artistically and spiritually experimental thought. But even if a poetic (and hermetic) approach to ethics is more difficult, it also may be more liberating and empowering, and more rich, than any attempt to plumb the depths of the human personality (as in ego therapy) or to scale the heights of the divine attributes in search of an ultimate, absolute, and universal ground (as in religious consolations). Deleuze reserves some of his most passionate writing for this point.

> And how could we not feel that our freedom and strength reside, not in the divine universality nor in the human personality, but in these singularities which are more us than we ourselves are, more divine than the gods, as they animate concretely poem and aphorism, permanent revolution and partial action? What is bureaucratic in these fantastic machines which are peoples and poems? It suffices that we dissipate ourselves a little, that we be able to be at the surface, that we stretch our skin like a drum, in order that the "great politics" begin. An empty square for neither man nor God; singularities which are neither general nor individual, neither personal nor universal. All of this is traversed by circulations, echoes, events which produce more sense, more freedom, and more strength than man has ever dreamed of, or God ever conceived. Today's task is to make the empty square circulate and to make pre-individual and nonpersonal singularities speak—in short, to produce sense. (LS, 72–73)

This ethics would continually seek a maximum of creative reiterations or novel abstract potentials for each event, to be replayed in a way that closely parallels the work of art's singular intensity and breadth of interconnections.[8] Such a becoming-art and becoming-spiritual of life is the ultimate ethical goal outlined in *The Logic of Sense*.

The Limits of Experimental Life

The grounding of ethics in a kind of aesthetics of existence may give one reason to hesitate, however, to aver as I do that the "spirituality" of a creative uptake of events is more than mere metaphor. Perhaps Deleuze's interest in the possibility of an integral *mathesis universalis*, and his affirmations of symbolic modes of apprehension can be reduced to his affirmation of the aesthetic. It might be argued that Deleuze's esoteric interests, and his hermeticism, should be translated into, if not reduced to, a generalized affirmation of the becoming-art of life, conceived of simply as an ethics of self-cultivation. Esoteric tradition would then appear to function, in Deleuze's thought, simply as a kind of precursor to the aesthetic procedures, and esoteric trends in this view would persist in Deleuze's thought simply as a kind of prolepsis or extended metaphor. In this case, there would be little real connection, beyond a certain exemplary status, between hermeticism and the ultimate Deleuzian ethos.

However, as I have tried to demonstrate already, things are not quite so simple. Deleuze's interest in esoteric and hermetic themes of divination, transmutation, and the interconnection between personal and cosmic events is consistent across his work. And over the course of his work with Guattari, Deleuze begins to explicitly interpret the work of art itself as "medicine," and as a "cosmic" mode of activity such as that envisaged in his early utopian view of the symbolic promise of mathesis universalis. In this way, Deleuze's pragmatic work with Guattari connects to an encompassing vision of philosophy as an ordeal of self-grounding that has distinct ethical consequences, leading to normative conclusions. Deleuze's vision becomes, over time, a more and more explicit endeavor to justify those beliefs capable of activating a more intensely creative existence, and I have argued that this vision could not be a more authentic extension of perennial hermetic ambitions.

We can begin now to see, beyond the ontological and metaphilosophical issues, the complex ethical and political stakes of reading the philosophy of immanence as a thought of spiritual ordeal. In the works of the experimental modernists favored by Deleuze—among them Woolf, Lawrence, Kerouac, Michaux, Artaud, Miller, Pessoa, Joyce, and Proust (as well as a broader series of philosophers, composers, painters, and filmmakers), Deleuze seeks to map and affirm immanent practices that result in the renewal of vision and of belief in the world. Because of the way they break with the status quo and with established values, these heroes and heroines of immanence are more often than not scapegoats, nomads, outliers, or otherwise socially subversive.[9]

But the characters that fascinate Deleuze, such as those that populate the writings of Carlos Castaneda, Lawrence, Michel Tournier, Dickens, and Pessoa, tend to reach a limit, a wall beyond which their experiments cannot take them, a point at which their experimental flow dries out or cracks up.[10] Castaneda has a fatal flaw that prevents him from finishing his apprenticeship in sorcery. In *The Plumed Serpent*, Lawrence's Irish émigré Kate breaks off her marriage with a Mexican hierophant and "reterritorializes" to England. Charles Dickens's Riderhood, in "Our Mutual Friend," only momentarily experiences profound sympathies with those who otherwise despise him. Here we hit upon the key problem of how to connect Deleuze's immanent view of ethics and politics to the utopian visions of hermetic tradition. What are the limits of any experiment, and of life as experimentation? Is it possible to render viable the potentials immanent to creative life and thought, or does a people that can endure a full arrival of immanence always remain, in some sense, a transcendental idea, impossible to realize in practice?

Deleuze is somewhat elusive on this point. Alone and with Guattari, Deleuze attempts at all costs to be a thinker of the unrepresentable, and his effort, above all, is to descry in thought that which is beyond thought—that which forces us to think, but cannot itself be thought. This is part of why Deleuze has no pretension to directly, let alone completely, identify immanence with the lives of particular renegades, even if he admires them for being "capable of leaving."[11] The "different" or "extraordinary" individual, who experiences herself as multiple, who intensely becomes, is affirmed by Deleuze not in her actual or final state, but only in her movement, in the movement of "a life" that is impersonal, intransitive, and enigmatically present in constituted individuals. In *Difference and Repetition*, Deleuze aligns his thought on this point to Kierkegaard, who said that, when looking for the man of faith, he studied "only the movements."[12] In this way, Deleuze's affirmation of experimentation is never reducible to the successes or failures of a particular experiment, a single living being, but to virtual aspects incarnate in a life.

Yet what is at stake for Deleuze and Guattari in their meditations on art is the search for signs of a medicine, of some kind of reparative or at least ramifying power that can unite the subject to creative forces beyond life and death. Whether art can ultimately matter for politics is in some sense an issue of whether art can ramify the quest of the hermetic tradition for a healing knowledge of nature at one with a process of cosmic, psychic, and spiritual regeneration. Deleuze's lifelong dedication to the paradigm of modernist avant-garde experimentationalism, from this perspective, must be grounded in the spiritual ordeals modern artists undertook in the context of a disenchanted, industrialized, and fully administered world. Without emphasis on this archaic connection between modern art and archaic spiritual practice, Deleuze's own affirmations of the work of art fall prey to an ethical and political vagueness: the purpose of experimentation remains unclear unless it is tied to a normative spiritual affirmation. By insisting more decisively on the connection of creation to spiritual ordeal, we can close the circuit between the utopian ambitions Deleuze saw in his modernist champions, and the archaic visions of renewal traced to the legend of Hermes Trismegistus. From this perspective we might be able to rewrite, in contemporary key, Hermes's own instructions for how to anticipate an ecological and political eschaton centered on a renewed rapport between humanity and its cosmic milieu.

First we must approach what is the most difficult affirmation in Deleuze's perspective on life and time: "Doubtless, anything is possible" (*ATP*, 166). Deleuze demands that modern philosophy, taken as the project of radicalizing immanence and renewing belief in the world, must invent a set of immanent criteria that can be neither formulated without nor expressed in advance of its experiments. In this way immanent thought harbors a kind of blanket affirmation of expanded experimentation. But Deleuze also speaks as if the totality of experiments harbored some more secret teleology, a sense in which eternal recurrence tends to select affirmative, life-giving forces. At one point in *Anti-Oedipus* Deleuze and Guattari insist that "the plane is the totality of the full BwO's [Bodies without Organs] that have been selected (there is no positive totality including the cancerous or empty bodies)" (*ATP*, 165). This is an extraordinary and patently optimistic claim about a kind of finality or purposiveness germane to the logic of all expression. Yet here is a paradox that thinking immanence produces: it is impossible to judge in advance whether the elements of different assemblages, or the planes on which they insist, will be healthy or cancerous, salutary or deleterious to life. We cannot clarify the obscurity of cosmic potencies, linked as they are to a differential open series that includes the unconscious life of our own desire. The nature of the elements of an assemblage cannot clarify our particular desires to actualize them in the specific ways we do, since desire itself does not come before, but is defined by immanence within an assemblage.

Deleuze's turn to a more "vitalistic" notion of immanence late in his career—a notion as attentive to the intensities of affective life as it is to those inspiriting thought, per se—may have prompted Deleuze to recognize the limitations of a sheer affirmation of intensity or novelty, per se. If, as critics such as Girard and Rancière have pointed out, Deleuze's favored exemplars of modernist experimentalism present us with a series of doomed attempts to escape the strictures of self and society, it is necessary to discover a set of metapragmatic criteria on which to cultivate nonfatal immersions of immanence, and to discover a teleology proper to immanent vocations.[13] Perhaps Deleuze's tendency late in his career to read art as medicine (rather than modernism as a literary denouement of the esoteric tradition) was an effort to cultivate the criteria of a truly "practical" philosophy of the absolute, beyond any simple affirmation of divergent becomings.[14] To follow up on this possibility, it is necessary to delve more deeply into the esoteric practices that interested Deleuze, and to articulate the ethical and political stakes of his philosophical thought as a ramification of the hermetic aspiration to renew the earth as much as the soul through the creative travails of spiritual ordeal.

Mystic or Sorcerer?

There is an entire politics of becomings-animal, as well as a politics of sorcery, which is elaborated in assemblages that are neither those of the family nor of religion nor of the State. Instead, they express minoritarian groups, or groups that are oppressed, prohibited, in revolt, or always on the fringe of recognized institutions, groups all the more secret for being extrinsic, in other words, anomic. If becoming-animal takes the form of a Temptation, and of monsters aroused in the imagination by the demon, it is because it is accompanied, at its origin as in its undertaking, by a rupture with the central institutions that have established themselves or seek to become established.—GILLES DELEUZE, *A Thousand Plateaus*, 247

As early as the *What Is Grounding?* lecture course in 1955–56, Deleuze had defined the philosopher as one who "proposes infinite tasks as something which must be realized in this world" (*WG*, 4). In a reversal that is typical of his relation to modern philosophy generally, Deleuze argues that the "enlightenment" offered by philosophical knowledge is a repetition and intensification of mythic ordeals. As he puts it in that early lecture course, "*c'est qui fond alors c'est l'epreuve*": that which grounds is the ordeal (WG, 4). Although philosophical concepts for Deleuze are indeed abstractions, abstraction as a mode of immanent grounding, preserves the nature and intensity of those spiritual ordeals by means of which mythical discourse represents the founding acts of social life. That is to say, for Deleuze, philosophical grounding occurs through a transcendental repetition of the physical and emotional test of strength that earns one a right to found a city or a culture. "Claiming is claiming to something by virtue of a right" (WG, 6).

In Deleuze's writings, and in many of the writers and artists implicated in his work, the right to confront the inchoate ground has a certain affinity with mysticism. But Deleuze himself never identifies thought with mysticism, even though he evokes practices of divination, conversion, and renewed vision as conditions of thought itself.

Deleuze is especially frank about spiritual practice in his many references to Bergson, particularly in connection with Bergson's social thought in *The Two Sources of Morality and Religion*. As Christian Kerslake puts it in *Deleuze and the Unconscious*, a work that goes to great lengths to explain Deleuze's connection to Bergson's metaphysical view of religion, one of the primary points of connection between Deleuze and Bergson is their shared position that "the condition of any hierarchically ordered society is . . . the management or distribution of frenzy."[15] Bergson argues that it is not paradigmatically the objective, rational, scientific type, but the mystic who is the true model of psychic health, and of truly enlightened awareness. Rather than experiencing the world through observation and calculation, mystical intuition establishes a "superior equilibrium" between instinct and reason. This equilibrium, unlike that established by reason alone, is an intricately attenuated mode of alternation between instinctual feeling and reflective deliberation. For Bergson, the mystic's ability to "creatively vary" her awareness of the present in relation to the unknown depths of an immemorial past of cosmic events, and in relation to nonhuman modes of consciousness (in the *élan vital* taken as the life of God), is the very paradigm of humanity and health.[16]

Insofar as the mystic has a profound sense of connection to the whole of the universe, through a mysterious sympathy to many imbricated sets of memories and perceptual states, the mystic has a capacity for empathetic, symbiotic awareness that exceeds the calculating rationality capable only of acknowledging the stimuli in an immediate environment. As Deleuze puts it, for Bergson the mystic is far-seeing enough that she even has the capacity to re-create or "prepare" matter. However—and this is the crucial point for Deleuze—what the mystic represents is not a humanity in which the intellect is repudiated, but one in whom instinct and intelligence have become symbiotically united.

> And what is this creative emotion, if not precisely a cosmic Memory, that actualizes all the levels at the same time, that liberates man from plane or the level that is proper to him, in order to make him a creator adequate to the whole movement of creation? This liberation, this embodiment of cosmic memory in creative emotions, undoubtedly only takes place in privileged souls. It leaps from one soul to another, "every now and then," crossing closed deserts. But to each member of a closed society, if he opens himself to it, it communicates a kind of reminiscence, an excitement that allows him to follow. (B, 111)

Crucial here is the role of the mystic as legislator, a leader who enables the life of the society to grow into a more vital expression. In Bergsonian terms, the mystic's intense spirituality is in fact a kind of "innate science of matter," a deep connection between unconscious mind and material depth that enables an extreme degree of freedom, even up to the capacity to re-create the instincts. (Pico della Mirandola's vision of humanity as free because excessive, displaced, and neither finite nor infinite anticipates this dimension of Bergsonism.)[17] Mysticism is thus, for Bergson—and one might add, retrospectively, for Renaissance hermeticism—not so much an ability to distance oneself from time and circumstance through identification with God, but an intensification of cosmic memory, an involution in the past of a universe become a "machine for the making of gods."[18] What is important for Deleuze is that the mystic is not an exception to but rather an ideal type of human life. Deleuze describes this extraordinary feature of Bergsonism:

> It could be said that in man, and only in man, the actual becomes adequate to the virtual. It could be said that man is capable of rediscovering all the levels, all the degrees of expansion and contraction that coexist in the virtual Whole. As if he were capable of all the frenzies and brought

about in himself successively everything that, elsewhere, can only be embodied in different species. Even in his dreams he rediscovers or prepares matter. And durations that are inferior to him are still internal to him. Man therefore creates a differentiation that is valid for the Whole, and he alone traces out an open direction that is able to express a whole that is itself open. Whereas the other directions are closed and go round in circles . . . man is capable of scrambling the planes, of going beyond his own plane as his own condition, in order finally to express naturing Nature. (*B*, 106)

For Deleuze, as for Bruno before him, the image of a humanity profoundly united to cosmic dynamisms is not that of the mystical contemplative, but that of the magus or sorcerer. In the official annals of Western philosophy, positively invoking such occult personae, or even evoking them indirectly in connection with philosophical rationality, has always been a delicate issue, if not one fraught outright with implications as disturbing to modern, secular, and liberal culture as they were to cultures of scholastic and religious orthodoxy. Frances Yates suggests Bruno was burned at the stake for being a revivalist of a form of natural religion that would democratize the power of thought.[19] Even Bergson, despite his admiration for the mystic, expresses dereliction toward the magician as a mere technician, a charlatan. But against Bergson's contempt for magic as charlatanism, Deleuze avers the sorcerer's ability to "scramble the planes" of nature and fully embody the essence of creative evolution.

As a global and historical phenomena, sorcery is extremely complex, and Deleuze's references to sorcery focus on a rather narrow range of considerations. In *A Thousand Plateaus*, Deleuze and Guattari take an interest in a sorcery indexed to a series of becomings: becoming-woman, becoming-animal, becoming-molecular, and becoming-imperceptible. Techniques of sorcery, such as mantras, tantric states, hypnosis, entheogenic trance, and spirit possession, all implicate the human in what Deleuze and Guattari call the obscure "interkingdoms" of nature (*ATP*, 242). These molecular or transversal zones allow communication far beyond ordinary boundaries of sense and sensibility. In relation to Bergson's specification of a type of humanity at one with "naturing Nature," Deleuze and Guattari note that a sorcerer's becoming-animal (and ability to make intensive or "involuted" usage of animal consciousness) depends upon a power of fascination, a lure that draws consciousness beyond the fragile integrity of the conscious ego. Along carefully marked (because treacherous) paths, the sorcerer literally re-creates instinct, changing her body and mind into a supple and radiant center of many nodes and modes of communication. In many shamanic rites, initiation involves the symbolic act of removing and washing the organs, so as to create a subtle or astral body capable of shifting between liminal realms. As William Behun points out in a perspicacious article, this astral or light body, germane to so many forms of esoteric spirituality, has numerous connections with the "Body without Organs" Deleuze and Guattari conceive as subtending the living, dying, disorganization and reorganization of nature.[20]

To metamorphose, the sorcerer must exert discipline, and establish the requisite mental and ritual conditions. In Deleuzian terms, the outcome of the rite, the results of any activity, depends on a "line of flight" or continuity of imperceptible nodes that unite the sorcerer with the animal, the molecular, and the cosmic. Such exploits in symbiosis are carefully mapped through experience and tradition, forming a plane of composition resulting in new multiplicities: "A becoming, a population, a tale" (*ATP*, 241). These possibilities, though physical, are not "natural" in the ordinary sense: "These combinations are neither genetic nor structural; they are interkingdoms, unnatural participations. That is the only way Nature operates—against itself" (*ATP*, 242).

Deleuze and Guattari's conception of nature's operating "against itself" is no mere hyperbole. It is a phrase that captures the sense that there is a level of ontogenesis in nature that contains principles by which organisms may creatively diverge from the otherwise fixed limits of species and clearly demarcated phenotypes. Beneath "molar" or fully constituted structures of organization, there persists a molecular "plane of consistency," an immanence of speeds and slownesses, abstract lines of force in which all things develop and into which they devolve. At this level, affects, behaviors, morphologies, and other attributes belong to no one entity in particular, but are the effects of speeds, slownesses, and complex relations of disjunction. On this plan(e),

> Nothing develops, but things arrive late or early, and form this or that assemblage depending on their composition of speed. Nothing subjectifies, but haecceities form according to compositions of nonsubjectified

powers or affects. We call this plane, which knows only longitudes and latitudes, speeds and haecceities, the plane of consistency or composition (as opposed to the plan(e) of organization or development). It is necessarily a plane of immanence and univocality. We therefore call it the plane of Nature, although nature has nothing to do with it, since on this plane there is no distinction between the natural and the artificial. (*ATP*, 266)

Perhaps part of why Deleuze and Guattari can claim to have discerned a level at which there is no distinction between the artificial and the natural, is that certain types of activity, from the work of art to the work of the shaman, can only be described in terms of transformations that occur at this level of abstract composition, on a kind of transversal plane cutting across nature and culture. The ritual or thaumaturgical usage of materials (whether these be hair, mud, semen, alcohol, music, drawings, dances, even garbage) is a matter of activating transformative potentials that are uncannily suggestive to the initiate. In experiences of profound immersion, whether artistic, thaumaturgical, theatrical, erotic, or meditational, zones of exchange are opened between otherwise fixed boundaries between self and world, human and animal, terrestrial and cosmic zones, and there are particular lines, shapes, colors, and textures that emerge to facilitate communication. Deleuze describes the operation of such abstract lines of becoming in a late exchange with Claire Parnet.

> Man only becomes animal if the animal, for its part, becomes sound, color, or line. It is a bloc of becoming which is always asymmetrical. It is not that the two are exchanged, for they are not exchanged at all, but the one only becomes the other if the other becomes something yet other, and if the terms disappear. As Lewis Carroll says, it is when the smile is without a cat that man can effectively becomes cat as soon as he smiles. It is not man who sings or paints, it is man who becomes animal, but at exactly the same time as the animal becomes music, or pure color, or an astonishingly simple line: with Mozart's birds it is the man who becomes a bird, because the bird becomes music. Melville's mariner becomes albatross, becomes extraordinary whiteness, pure vibration of white (and Captain Ahab's whale-becoming forms a bloc with Moby Dick's white-becoming, pure white wall). (*D*, 72)

Experiments in becoming, whether artistic, scientific, philosophical, or traditionally hermetic, involve participation in the profound animations of the plane of composition, what Deleuze, in a moment of gleefully unrestrained writing, is not embarrassed to call "[H. P.] Lovecraft's Thing or Entity, the nameless intellectual beast, all the less intellectual for writing with its wooden clogs, with its dead eye, its antennae and mandibles, its absence of face, a whole mob inside you in pursuit of what, a witch's wind?" (*D*, 76).

From Deleuze's Bergsonian perspective, what is at stake here in the sorcerer is not simply the status of the outliner, but a reconception of the very center of human health and vitality. The potentials of becoming proper to sorcery, with the sorcerer's inhuman affiliation with animality and the insights available in microperceptual states, play the role in Deleuze's conception of thought played by mystical contemplation in Bergson. In both cases, what is at stake is not the affirmation of a minority or outcast community, but a radical reconception of the basic nature of life itself. For Deleuze, the potentials of sorcery do not constitute the exotica of the outlier, but the essential human prerogative, the imperatives of an intensified life of becoming. What would it mean to place a liminal or "outlier" subjectivity (whether it be of an artist, a mystic, or sorcerer) at the center of humanity, and to place thaumaturgy at the center of the image of thought? Part of what Deleuze and Guattari argue (in a sometimes oblique way) is that even if the *délire* of sorcery (and other "altered states") tends to manifest, in modern and secular culture, a kind of psychotic or schizoid self-destructiveness (or even more generally the infamous self-destructiveness of the artist), it may be that the disturbed nature in many an abnormal type is actually a reflection of social formations determined at any cost to maintain a mode of "normalcy" intent upon the suppression of the most vital and creative elements of humanity, elements sometimes trapped in the ghettos of the occult.

However, there is no a priori normative rule to be extracted here, since it will always be somewhat unclear what the elements of potential transformation might be, in advance of experimentation. What we seem to have to go on, ethically and politically, are informal legacies and dark legends. If at times Deleuze and Guattari seem to affirm deterritorialization at any cost, by any means necessary, encouraging us always to go further, a closer look at the character of the specific practices by which they exemplify the parameters of creative becoming tempers such a blanket affirmation, and suggests the need for immanent criteria. If there is a common thread to such criteria, it is clearly the resonance of a variety of aesthetic experiments with the directives and procedures of spiritual ordeals such as those found in many varieties of magical and ritual practice.

But this again is part of what is disconcerting in Deleuze's thought for contemporary life. Deleuze seems to return us to pre-Socratic avatars of thought—not only to some kind of precritical metaphysics, but also to an affinity of thought with the bastard, nomadic practices of ritual magic and sorcery. Even in the more familiar modern gesture of connecting thought to the work of art, Deleuze's work is inspired by artists and writers who experimented with unrespectable modes of travel, diet, drug use, sexuality, and nomadism as ways of ambulant, intensive thinking.

Deleuze's conviction that authentic thought is provoked by a kind of necessary contamination, a contagion of "primitive" forces, is part of why he has such a fraught relationship to Kantian philosophy. For Kant, our conception of nature never affects nature in itself (the noumenon) but only the organization of our experience at the phenomenal level.[21] Morality, for Kant, is likewise founded on the possibility of an isolation of reason and the will from contamination with passion, insofar as duty is taken to be apprehended on the basis of reason alone.[22] In this connection it is not accidental that, as Adorno and Horkheimer observed, the project of Enlightenment (with Kant its regnant champion) was to liberate the mind from magic.[23] As Marcel Mauss, Adorno's contemporary, argued in a monumental work on the subject, magic takes place through nonlocal (invisible) and nonuniversalizable (itinerant) powers. Mauss observed magic in many different cultures of belief and practice, and had attempted to encompass a multiplicity of belief and practice with his own famously ambiguous concept of *mana*.[24] Mauss argued that the key principle of all magical belief and practice (including many forms of traditional healing, divination, spell-binding, and sorcery) is that, at least under certain conditions, the mind has access to and can act in concert with deep-structural or "noumenal" reality, *mana*. The power that *mana* is, is nonlocal: it is simultaneously the magical will of the operator, the correct arrangement of materials, and the influence of the spirits upon the work undertaken.

The magician, shaman, or ritual healer could not be a more profoundly anti-Kantian figure, since her practice implies that she is able to do the impossible: to pierce the veil of phenomena and operate upon things in themselves. For Kant, the mind has no intuitive access to real cosmic forces, at least not as "cognition" or objective experience, and valid cognition is only of the phenomenal, as structured by transcendental categories. The empirical objectivity of judgments is measured, for Kant, by the extent to which our faculties of understanding and sensibility are functioning in accordance with certain a priori rules that govern possible experience in accordance with the limits of space, time, and causation. As José Gil puts it in his study of Ndembu healing rituals, *Metamorphoses of the Body*, magical and symbolic thought underwrite judgments that could be made only by what Kant called the hypothetical figure of the *intellectus archetypus*, a figure whose thought would be united to the generation of the reality it thinks.[25] Gil writes,

> Magical-symbolic thought and practice not only resolve the antinomies of the discourse of power, but also—and it is definitely the same thing—the antinomies of the power of discourse. Is this not to say that this way of thinking provides a solution to the problems posed by the transcendental dialectic of Kant? What was at stake there—in the question, What is it possible to know?—was the power of scientific discourse itself. For magical-symbolic thought there is no obstacle in getting to the noumena, and it is the same for the hypothetical Kantian figure of the *intellectus archetypus*, which knows the unconditioned: magical words are action, thought coincides with being, time and space do not impede the grasping of the thing in itself—because, on the contrary, they are organized in such a manner that they can be transformed by appropriate techniques (such as those at work in the therapeutic ritual) and at the same time remain linked to their normal perception—in order to create from it the conditions of possibility and the formal framework for knowledge of the absolute.[26]

Magical, symbolic thought implies knowledge not only of how nature operates, but of how nature can be directed. Such intuitive access is not given in ordinary perception, and is contingent upon the success of certain intensified actions or performances. This possibility may not seem felicitous to Kantianism, but as Kerslake has demonstrated, Kant himself seems to suggest in section seventy-seven of *Critique of Judgment* that if intellectual intuition were possible, it would have to be a comprehension of nature as a whole, the very presentation of which would *produce* that whole as a specific effect of intellectual activity.[27] As Kant puts it, "Such a whole would be an effect, a *product*, the *presentation* of which is regarded as the *cause* that makes the product possible. But the product of a cause that determines its effect merely on the basis of the presentation of that effect is called a purpose."[28] As Kerslake explains, in *Immanence and the Vertigo of Philosophy*, all of the post-Kantian thinkers of immanence, from Hegel and Schelling to Deleuze, take inspiration from the possibility that an archetypal intellect might precipitate the movement of the absolute.[29] However, unlike his idealist precursors, Deleuze does not proceed to determine an ultimate cause of the world under a historical or mythical form, but to diagram a multiplicity of a priori syntheses that link encosmic intensities to problematic ideas. With Guattari, Deleuze makes increasingly concrete what the immanent practice of such synthetic acts might amount to, at an extremely concrete level.

Writing the Body without Organs

For Deleuze it was Antonin Artaud who had envisioned—at least in gnomic outline—the contours of a body liberated from the restrictions of habit, memory, and societal expectations, a subtle or ethereal body that would be capable of perceptions and sensations beyond the limits of the organism as we know it. As Artaud put it in his 1947 radio play, "When you will have made him a body without organs / then you will have delivered him from all his automatic reactions / and restored him to his true freedom."[30] Although Deleuze makes passing reference to this concept in *The Logic of Sense*, it is in *Anti-Oedipus* and *A Thousand Plateaus* that, with Guattari, Deleuze make extensive use of Artaud's notion. For Deleuze and Guattari, the Body without Organs (or "BwO," as they refer to it) is a field or phase space of a body in which its energetic patterns are situated. If the body's habits and inclinations, typical gestures and modes of expression are revealed by its organs—by the particular actual organization those organs represent—the BwO represents a broader field of potential energy and activity against which such a body is formed. In a certain sense, the BwO is the "raw material" of the organs (*AO*, 326). The BwO is the totality of potential energy flows, but it is not exactly a synthetic or unifying whole into which a body can be integrated, and is not an aggregate of forms (not a restored or patched-together body of all bodies). The BwO is rather an unbounded field, a kind of subtle or astral body that exists alongside the actual body, through which a body exists. (Such bodies need not, however, be particular animal organisms, but also may be social bodies or geophysical formations, even organizations of sideral bodies spread over vast distances of space. Any system of interdependent parts that mobilizes a flow of energy toward discernible ends can be considered a body, in this view.)[31]

There are at least three characterizations of the BwO in Deleuze's and Guattari's thought: it can be empty, cancerous, or full. In *A Thousand Plateaus* the BwO is described as "full" if it is "healthy" in the sense of being a genuine source of creativity, difference, and intensity with which one can reach increasingly satisfying levels of vitality. It is cancerous if one's experiments are stuck in a repeating pattern, fixated on generating the same sensation or activity endlessly. In *Anti-Oedipus* the BwO appears as a principle of "antiproduction": it is an "empty" form at the limit of all forms of desire (*AO* 8–9). The problem, here, is how to approach this limit without becoming absorbed into it (which would be tantamount to catatonia). Here the body without organs is seen as an "immobile motor," like a limit of the various ways in which a song can be arranged and still be a song (*AO*, 327). The problem is how to experiment with the materials of life, the forms of possible "music" (i.e., meaning and sense) without being overwhelmed by the inherently unlimited nature of the field.

In *Anti-Oedipus*, the importance of the BwO for the articulation of an hermetic Deleuze lies in its connection to a primitive and magical usage of language. Here Deleuze and Guattari compare the sense-making mechanism of the modern artist to the primitive sign-making exploits of the sorcerer. They argue that art and sorcery function as experiments in modes of action and perception that would otherwise be utterly traumatic, leading to catatonia and madness. Part of what is at stake here is the strategic affirmation of schizophrenia as a kind of model, *ab negatio*, of what genuine health and vitality would look like.

One of the clinically determined aspects of schizophrenia is a magical (and terrifying) relationship to language, where the distinction between word and thing, concept and referent, constantly breaks down. For the schizophrenic, the word becomes the thing.[32] But for Deleuze and Guattari, schizophrenia has a positive aspect that could be activated differently than as psychotic breakdown, since the contours of a "schizoid" language usage are linked to real transformational potentials. The goal of the kind of ethics and aesthetics seen through the enigma of schizoid life would be to endure contact with the as yet unlivable, as yet unspeakable realities on the virtual continuum of cosmic dynamics from which schizophrenics seem to suffer direct, unmediated contact.

Although there are different strategies for composing on the BwO, its composition always begins with a decoding of dominant or "master" codes. The BwO reveals its contours in aberrant, nomadic regimes of signs, as opposed to the despotic chains linking representable forms. Nevertheless, the BwO is not merely irrational or simply arbitrary in its effects. As Deleuze and Guattari put it, "The molecular chain [on the BwO] is still signifying because it is composed of signs of desire; but these signs are no longer signifying, given the fact that they are under the order of the included disjunctions where *everything is possible*. These signs are points whose nature is a matter of indifference, abstract machinic figures that play freely on the body without organs and as yet form no structured configuration—or rather, they form one no longer" (*AO*, 328). At issue here is the relation between desire and language, between the names evoking desire and the nameless drives animating unconscious life. Is there a naming or a language proper to the unconscious, proper to flows on the BwO, or is the name always an imposition, a distortion of desire? Are there names that would be an indigenous or autochthonous code on the BwO, forming nodes or sigils through which profound transformation might take place? Much is at stake for Deleuze and Guattari in this question. In one of the key passages of *Anti-Oedipus*, they develop the view that, on the body without organs, names function not as representations of persons, but as designators of operations.

> [At the level of the unconscious] it is a question of . . . identifying races, cultures, and gods with fields of intensity on the body without organs,

identifying personages with states that fill these fields, and with effects that fulgurate within and traverse these fields. Whence the role of names, with a magic all their own: there is no ego that identifies with races, peoples, and persons in a theatre of representation, but proper names that identify races, peoples, and persons with regions, thresholds, or effects in a production of intensive quantities. The theory of proper names should not be conceived in terms of representation; it refers instead to the class of "effects": effects that are not a mere dependence upon causes, but the occupation of a domain, the operation of a system of signs. This can be clearly seen in physics, where proper names designate such effects within fields of potentials: the Joule effect, the Seebeck effect, the Devlin effect. History is like a physics: a Joan of arc effect, a heliogabulus effect—all the *names* of history, and not the name of the father. (AO, 86)

From the perspective of the BwO, proper names do not merely refer to, but in some sense *are*, the entities involved in a production of intensive quantities, in the sense that names like Volta, Watts, and Tesla are events in the history of electricity. On the BwO, naming is not a matter of representing but of occupying, "territorializing," even "operating," parallel to how a shaman operates through the names of spirits, plants, or ancestors in a healing or divinatory ritual. In therapeutic processes, names never reference static entities, but becomings. Names become operators, harbingers, and transformers across a profound complicity between mind and nature.

Working from anthropological studies of primitive ritual, Deleuze and Guattari articulate two kinds of what they call "vocal-graphic power." According to its magical and invocational powers, the voice retains a dominance proper to it, a power to tattoo or de-mark, but not to survey, totalize, or represent. Such an immanent magical power is opposed to, and uncannily doubled by, a transcendent despotic graphism that attempts at all costs to dominate the voice, and to gain power over the elusive grain in the voice connected to insubordinate potentials for affective transformation. Deleuze and Guattari write, "There is indeed a break which changes everything in the world of representation, between this [primitive] writing in the narrow sense and writing in the broad sense—that is, between two completely different orders of inscription: a graphism that leaves the voice dominant by being independent of the voice while connecting with it, and a graphism that dominates or supplants the voice by depending on it in various ways and by subordinating itself to the voice" (*AO*, 203). That is to say, in the case of "primitive" writing there is a dynamic, magical interplay between vocal and graphic powers, mediated by an eye or by a vision that sees the effect of the word on things, and mediates a disjunctive synthesis between word and thing. On the other hand there is a despotic reading of the effect of things-as-words (*AO*, 204).[33] Primitive graphism remains subordinate to a voice (although not necessarily a human voice, since it becomes an animal or divine voice in ritual practice). It does not represent or survey its referents so much as *present* them as potential talismans, vectors of still other forces with which the magic word intends to connect, other sense it would invoke.

Such incantatory speech, and the hieroglyphic form of marking it involves, is opposed to the despotic form of representation in which the eye no longer sees but reads the world (*AO*, 206). These are two very different forms of interaction with human, elemental, and cosmic others. With despotism there is an absorption of others as resources, as sources of energy, that is opposed to a positive, magical "adsorption," in which others are conjoined but not assimilated to the magical operator. According to Deleuze and Guattari, this difference is borne out in linguistic phenomena. In despotic signification, the voice is suppressed by writing, in a reduction of things to signs. This reduction makes writing present at the cost of making the voice absent. As Deleuze and Guattari put it, "in the first place, graphism aligns itself on the voice, falls back on the voice and becomes writing. At the same time it induces the voice no longer as the voice of alliance, but as that of a *new alliance*, that of *direct filiations* . . . Then there occurs a crushing of the magic triangle; the voice no longer sings but dictates, decrees; the graphy no longer dances, it ceases to animate bodies, but is set into writing on tablets, stones, and books, the eye sets itself to reading" (*AO*, 203). Despotic power is a fundamental perversion of magical power. That is to say, in despotic signification—in conceptual and representational language as we know it—writing buries the voice, even as the voice continues to haunt all writing (*AO*, 203).[34] Despotism in this view aims to consolidate power in the master in a way that makes meaning itself a consolidation of magic under representative power. The alliances of the magician with many elemental, animal, and ethereal spirits are converted into the direct filiation of the despot with the territory he dominates. Under despotic conditions, we do indeed write only to represent and be represented, to speak only as validated by that undead, immortal supplement Lacan called the "master signifier."

But because Deleuze and Guattari can distinguish between a variety of "regimes of signs," they need not reduce all graphism to what it is in the "signifying regime." Only in this (despotic) regime is every representation of desire a sign of the "lack in the big other," a relation to a fundamental and central social antagonism. For Deleuze and Guattari, desire only becomes the other's desire (and the unconscious only becomes Oedipal) under a despotic regime of signs. Here it is not the binary, oppositional nature of signification and representation that is inherently problematic in language, even if it is true that primitive societies work according to dualisms that are quite entrenched. As Lévi-Strauss demonstrated, in primitive societies binary oppositions remain supple, fluid, bricolage, and never constitute a closed totality (even if such a totality is presupposed).[35] That is to say, only in the modern state do societies form where organizations establish binary oppositions as ends in themselves and not as an open-ended search for coherence.

Deleuze and Guattari aver that it is true that the subtle and magical powers of primitive graphism are almost immediately betrayed, and that the shaman plants a tree between his legs, and thus draws power to himself as a center and centralizing force. But it also remains true that the circles of power emanating from him do not become rigidly concentric, as they do in modern bureaucratic societies. In state societies, "the segmentarity becomes rigid, to the extent that all centers resonate in, and all black holes fall on, a single point of accumulation that is like a point of intersection somewhere behind the eyes. The face of the father, teacher, colonel, boss, enter into redundancy, refer back to a center whose center is everywhere and whose circumference is nowhere. There are no longer n eyes in the sky, or in becomings-animal and -vegetable, but a central computing eye scanning all of the radii" (*ATP*, 211).[36]

The issue at stake here is the difference Deleuze and Guattari detect, not between a centralized and a segmented society, but between two different organizing principles, two different ways of orchestrating segments. What is important is not that primitive societies do not organize, but that such organizations inhibit easy translations of one form of power into another. At the level of magical belief and practice, power is not general but specific, singular, and as different as the things which concern it ("depending on the task and the situation")—even if magical power is centralized or organized in the shaman or priest-king (*ATP*, 209). Thus, as was true for Horkheimer and Adorno, magical power constitutes the primary "repressed" of civilization, against which its demythologizing forces are deliberately oriented.[37]

For Deleuze and Guattari, however, the kinds of occult communication mobilized by primitive, magical regimes of signs are not a lost historical possibility, but a present, if occulded dimension of our actuality. It is possible, they believe—however great the dangers, risks, and uncertainties involved—to create non-despotic regimes of signs and non-fascist modes of powerful communication. For such non-despotic regimes, segmentation occurs according to "another graphism, that of the "primitive territorial sign." This sign is nonsignifying—it is not a sign of signs, but a purely energetic connection of things among themselves. As Deleuze and Guattari describe it, "The primitive territorial sign is self-validating; it is a position of desire in a state of multiple connections. It is not a sign of desire nor a desire of a desire. It knows nothing of linear subordination and its reciprocity: neither pictogram nor ideogram, it is rhythm and not form, zigzag and not line, artifact and not idea, production and not expression" (*AO*, 203). In primitive territorial regimes, signs establish nexuses between peoples and milieus, even if societies become immediately set on forming networks of mobile signs, equivocal and analogical signs, that no longer require reenactment to have significance (*AO*, 204). But in the primitive territorial regime, what is at stake is perpetual and collective work, not the "expression" of a national consciousness that "reflects" its nature to itself. However, with the development of state power, all performance, all ritual, and all magic become transformed into mythically underwritten structures of "meaning" that offer not the things we desire but the master's desire for our desire, and the interminable paranoid dialectic of misrecognition by which we substitute one another for the desire of that gargantuan other.

There is a stridently utopian thought here. Deleuze and Guattari maintain that the potentials of a primitive territorial sign, and of magical, symbolic thought, are not lost in the past but germane to the present. José Gil's observations of Ndembu healing rites elaborate and help make more concrete Deleuze and Guattari's thought on this point. In his *Metamorphoses of the Body*, Gil asserts that "the relationship between signs and the forces that underpin them has not been sufficiently studied, and yet, whether it is a question of stories, rituals, art, or raptures, their signs appear to be shot through with particularly intense investments of affectivities, to the point where one is tempted to take their affectivities as their characteristic traits."[38] In Gil's study of the signs used in Ndembu healing rituals, he finds that force and signification cannot be opposed. Gil's study points to a third term between nature and culture that would nevertheless not be a simple "mediator" but an elusive and complex "operator." Gil asserts that understanding the meaning of signs in a healing ritual lies not in deciphering what signs refer to, or even discerning what coerces them (ideology), but that it is a matter of asking how signs direct and redirect the work of bodies. As Gil puts it,

> Now, what "work" does the operator do? It acts on a force and on its internal features and places it in communication with other forces. The first aspect refers to another characteristic of forces: their intensity has the property of being able to grow or diminish without changing in nature. This means it has the capacity to work with internal differentiations or rhythmic heterogeneities without losing its wholeness or even creating a division in its heart. The intensity of a force is not enough to give birth to meaning (force would not have this privilege of being able to produce meaning all by itself). For that to come about, some other limitation would have to apply to the intensity of forces. This limitation would be the result of its opposition to external force, and the "remainder" would add to the internal gap a double determination. It gives the force an orientation and, coming from the outside with an absolute limit, recalibrates the system of internal gaps around (while opening it up to) another system of references.
>
> As precipitate of the remainder, the sign thus refers both to another system of signs and to a relation of forces. It refers to a relation of forces because it is the result of whatever flies off from the struggle between two specific forces. It refers, by itself, to a body of signs because it is the result of a transformation of determinations which are internal to force. In starting up this transformation in this way the operator paradoxically

makes a force meaningful for a force of the same type, and at the same time makes it susceptible to the actions of other external operators. This is where the translatability of the sign comes from, why it is treated "fetishistically," giving it the power to mean all by itself (Thesis) and making it dependent on forces (Antithesis).[39]

What Gil is attempting to parse here is the fact that ritual practice not only transforms the meaning of ordinary signs (gestures, objects, words "take on" new meaning), but gives these signs themselves a power they would not otherwise have. How is this possible? Why is the ethnologist's attempt to reduce the forces of magic and sorcery to an external addition of force to a "normal" set of signs or representations or beliefs always frustrated? Gil supposes that the untranslatability of magical signs is due to the fact that certain forces are already meaningful: "Forces don't have to be signified; they signify."[40] His hypothesis is that "the discourses of the magician and the bewitched draw their powers and their effectiveness from a region where the surplus of meaning becomes mingled with a surplus of force."[41] That is to say, the signs of a ritual are meaningful only insofar as they mobilize the forces to which they refer, and insofar as those forces become present by transforming the meaning of signs.

While signs do not "originate with" the powers they invoke, such powers are not simply "added" to signs through coercive ideological pressure. A liminal or virtual region insists between and among signs, as much as within networks of forces. Such a complex milieu is precisely the space of ritual context and ritual purpose itself, a dynamic space and time that can be neither understood nor realized without activating relations of signs and force outside the parameters of ordinary practice.

This regional or territorial use of signs in ritual is markedly different from what Deleuze and Guattari call a despotical coding.[42] But both territorial and despotic forms of signification are immanent "planes of consistency"—the imperial despot as much as the territorial leader makes use of the energies of a connotative-magical power (*AO*, 205). However, territorial sign-making functions by pure connotation, by the establishment of multiple connections over nonlinear time and over a baroque, complex space. Despotic representationalism subordinates all connections to connection with or through the despot, the desire of the despot, a desire that, like the despot's anonymous voice itself, can no longer be experienced as belonging to anyone, and even more importantly cannot directly connect with things.

And yet it is to a multiplicity of singular belongings that the despot owes his power, a power that can be utilized otherwise than as state control. "At the level of pathos, these multiplicities are expressed by psychosis and especially schizophrenia. At the level of pragmatics, they are utilized by sorcery" (*ATP*, 506). Despotism does not produce multiplicities; it only regulates or restricts them. Although the fascist and the sorcerer are both magicians, they are worlds apart: one truly creates, while the other merely codes. The BwO consists in decoded flows and asignifying chains of signs, the passage into which is fraught with danger and even pain. But the point of *Anti-Oedipus* is not to make glamorous that violence or that suffering. Rather, the point is to show that there is a viable level of Dinoysian experience. And it is this viability that the hermetic tradition has all along sought to buttress and ramify, as it historically sought modes of power and signification beneath and beyond the pale of the organism and the state. The question remains as to whether such experiments can be continued, and under what auspices, in our times.

7

The Future of Belief

In one of his last works, a set of essays published under the title *Pure Immanence*, Deleuze laments how far contemporary thought remains from the vitality of immanence.

> Modes of life inspire ways of thinking; modes of thinking create ways of living. Life *activates* thought, and thought in turn *affirms* life. Of this pre-Socratic unity we no longer have even the slightest idea. We now have only instances where thought bridles and mutilates life, making it sensible, and where life takes revenge and drives thought mad, losing itself along the way. Now we only have the choice between mediocre lives and mad thinkers. Lives that are too docile for thinkers, thoughts too mad for the living: Immanuel Kant and Friedrich Hölderlin. But the fine unity in which madness would cease to be such is yet to be rediscovered—a unity that turns an anecdote of life into an aphorism of thought, and an evaluation of thought into a new perspective on life.
>
> In a way, this secret of the pre-Socratics was already lost from the start. *We must think of philosophy as a force.* (PI, 67)

This passage is remarkable for several reasons. First, it suggests that the original pre-Socratic impulse in philosophy was correct to align thought with an intensification of certain elemental powers: water for

Thales, fire for Empedocles, and so on. Second, Deleuze suggests that modern philosophy, split between Hölderlin's inspired madness and Kant's truculent docility, has not yet discovered a way to either affirm or activate the powers of thought as an immediate renewal of life. The passage also suggests, however, that philosophy could be allied to a kind of utopian project where a thought otherwise marked as a kind of madness would discover a viable synthesis, a form of life-thought that would render sane a vitality otherwise apprehensible only as autism or psychosis. This creatively emerging "fine unity," beyond any familiar delirium, would presumably have to do with that peculiar combination of passion and perception Bergson found in the mystic and to which Deleuze points, more darkly and obliquely, in the sorcerer. As we have seen, Deleuze's work suggests that the Nietzschean project of renewing philosophy as a "vital aphorism," as a law of forces, and as a machine for discriminating values, would not simply reflect but also somehow reinvent life by linking thought to sustained contact with imperceptible forces of desire.

What Deleuze also suggests, however, is that the contemporary dangers of being overwhelmed by the anorganic powers is a problem peculiar to a modern subject split between sober rationality and poetic *délire*. For this reason, Deleuze's exemplary characters, such as Tournier's Friday, Melville's Bartleby, and Dickens's Riderhood, should not be taken as icons, but only as indexes of a viably intensified existence. These characters index what happens to constituted subjects insofar as immanent forces are *not* sustained by "the people to come," by a utopian and collective body, and when individuals are ultimately abandoned to forces that, apart from eschatological collectivity, must remain the objects of a kind of deranged fascination. We might say that for Deleuze, sustained immanence is essentially a modern life that is missing, escaping even from those who heroically desire it. Be that as it may, it is arguable that the itinerary of Deleuze's heroes and heroines attempt to anticipate some kind of collective experience of the intensities of creation capable of sustaining its unleashed anorganic powers otherwise than as madness, self-destruction, and sheer death-drive.

Despite its preference for the radically new, Deleuze's hermetic vision could not be further from a pseudotransgressive sensationalism of solitary genius. In fact, Deleuze explicitly describes the "becoming-imperceptible" of the sorcerer as a version of Kierkegaard's knight of faith, who is indiscernible: "To look at him, one would notice nothing" (*PI*, 279). That is to say, the continuation of hermetic knowledge and practice is never a matter of self-aggrandizing exploits, but a subtle elaboration of potentials that delicately avoids total effacement and the absolute scrambling of elements. "The sobriety of the assemblages is what makes for the richness of the Machine's effects," Deleuze writes (*PI*, 344). The required operations in each case remain not only delicate, but also enigmatic, imprecise. We stammer over which images to work with, how much chaos to let in, how many spirits are required. If children and the mad sometimes indicate the direction we should go, they are not exemplary for the truly modern translator or transmuter: "The modern figure is not the child or the lunatic, still less the artist but the cosmic artisan. . . . To be an artisan and no longer an artist, creator, or founder, is the only way to become cosmic, to leave milieus and the earth behind. The invocation to the Cosmos does not at all operate as a metaphor; on the contrary, the operation is an effective one, from the moment an artist connects a material with forces of consistency or consolidation" (*ATP*, 345).

How closely does the itinerary of the cosmic artisan map onto that of traditional hermeticism? According to Antoine Faivre, the gnosis involved in Western esotericism is grounded in the "active imagination," a concept Faivre explicitly borrows from post-Kantian romantic and idealist traditions.[1] Faivre's borrowing is felicitous, since for esotericism in general (and for hermeticism in particular) "active imagination" indeed has the constructive relation with human freedom that the transcendental imagination had for romantics such as Friedrich von Schiller, Novalis, and Friedrich Schelling. Active imagination is a knowledge that liberates, a learning process that does not seek to fantasize the world but to participate in creation.

It is important to note that by "gnosis" Faivre is not referring to Gnosticism or to the Gnostic heresies. By "gnosis" Faivre means pursuits of knowledge, insight, and growth aimed at discerning the inner meaning of a range of religious revelations and scientific cosmologies. Gnosis is developed with the express purpose of seeing beyond clear divisions between orthodox and heretical religious positions, as well as between scientific and artistic perspectives. In terms of methods and techniques, the primary way esoteric gnosis is explored is through an exploration of the "inner sense" of traditional religious teachings, the sciences, and the arts, in order to deepen both cosmological speculation (developing a philosophy of nature) and personal transformation (manifested as an ethics). The goal of gnosis is to produce a knowledge of nature inseparable from ethical transformation viewed as theandric cocreativity.

Faivre characterizes gnosis as a mode of interpreting revelation in a way that outlines possibilities of cooperation between human and divine worlds. He favorably cites Raymond Abellio on this point, who calls gnosis "concrete and permanent participation in universal interdependence." By contrast with mysticism, gnosis does not seek that Eckhartian night in which the groundlessness of God intermingles with the soul's ecstatic unknowing. Gnosis is not opaque, but precise, and invokes the power of distinct mediators: archetypes, images, and symbols. "To esotericism thus understood," Faivre writes, "are attached procedures or rituals that aim at eliciting the concrete manifestation of particular entities. Such is theurgy."[2]

Faivre also declares it to be the explicit task of Western esotericism to reverse the trend of Enlightenment rationality, and to remythologize the cosmos. This project, Faivre avers, is undertaken in the context of a kind of double bind. On one side, risking heresy and persecution, gnosis attempts to reenchant the cosmos in the face of polemics against such enchantment by traditional views that insist upon the absolute transcendence of the divine and the clear externality of God to creation. On the other side, esoteric traditions also contend with the post-Cartesian view of mind and matter as inherently opposed, and with the binary contrasts of fact and fantasy, reality and myth, upon which post-Enlightenment culture has been established.

Faivre argues, however, that the traditions of gnosis are not reactionary, and that the esoteric remythologization of the cosmos unfolds not by way of new myths—whether of progress or capital or technoscientific utopia—but by hermeneutical enterprise, an activity that would, in Deleuze's sense, exceed the contrast between interpreting and transforming the world. Gnosis, Faivre contends, is a process of learning to read myths anew: "not adoring the ancient or recent idols but ceasing to idolize history or to succumb to philosophies of history as to any other form of idolatry." This relation to myth (as immanent revelation) involves a willingness to engage in an "anagogic hermeneutic of Nature, human activities, and texts," one intent on revealing "metalanguages or living structures of signs and correspondences. Reading in this way means seeking the depth of things in the right place, not in socio-economic infrastructures, nor in the latent contents of the unconscious, but beyond them, in Nature itself."[3]

There are strong connections between traditional Western esotericism, as Faivre understands it, and the philosophical program of Deleuze. We have seen Deleuze argue, for instance, that from an immanent perspective, nature and culture are crossed by a deeper "Unknown Nature" that connects the human to the animal, the social to the geophysical, the architectural to the cosmic, in a potentially unlimited multiplicity of ways. Deleuze and Guattari insist that from the perspective of a plane of immanence, boundaries between the animate and inanimate, human and animal, the living and the dead become imperceptible. In this view, there is thus a kind of "ecology of the virtual" deeper than the divide between the living and the nonliving, an ecology as much of the artificial as of the natural.[4] And through experimental exploits in art, science, and philosophy, this deep ecology can be activated.

It might seem, however, that Deleuze's emphasis on multiplicity and infinite divergence at the level of immanence would cut against the grain of a traditional quest for gnosis, insofar as such quests attempt to develop a set of finite perennial principles for navigating the inner contours of the cosmos. But Faivre insists that, dreams of a pure or perennial tradition aside, the quest for gnosis is in no way static, but inherently creative and experimental. Faivre argues that, contrary to any conception of a pristine Tradition (à la Guénon) that could be located in fixed, perennial archetypes and eternal forms of spirit, for the majority of esoteric practice, the development of symbolic systems is as much a matter of creative encounter as it is a deciphering of signs. Faivre writes, "In poeticizing the world by a multilayered reading of it, always both new and traditional, we risk forgetting that *poïein* means first of all 'to create.' Having occupied ourselves with their retrieval and having remained mere spectators, we may be tempted to euphemize the myths and their scenarios instead of returning, better actors each time, upon the stage where they are playing. Basically, the danger consists in giving in to the temptation of euphemizing that which in esotericism is necessarily dramatic."[5] Deleuze himself emphasizes repeatedly that the temptation to treat ideas as static concepts rather than ideal dramas must be resisted at all costs, if thought aspires to account for the full complexity of lived experience and its transformative potentials.

Faivre points out that, writ large, esoteric thought relies on three basic concepts: similitude, or the search for structural affinities; the participation of "entity-forces" in one another; and a view of nature as a composition of "concrete pluralities," rather than as self-identical individuals.[6] These principles can be translated almost directly into Deleuzian terms: hermeticism is a vision that can diagram "unnatural participations" and discover concrete syzygies (what Deleuze calls "sterile hybrids") on an immanent plane of composition. Deleuze's hermeticism is thus a vision of nature and culture as a set of complex assemblages composed of a plurality of relations, where entities are linked in what Faivre calls "concrete pluralisms" of sense. Faivre suggests that such a thought be called "nonidentific," since it seeks the true nature of individuals not in fixed properties but resonant conjunctions among many modes and relations.[7] Likewise, for Deleuze, the true essence of things, and their becoming, are located not in discrete individuals but in differential relations expressed across and transecting many ramifying series of sense and events.

According to Faivre, the esoteric or hermetic ontology is an energetics, a vision of being as unintelligible apart from series of fundamental "dualitudes" or coexistences of contraries between which life and mind take shape. In a line that could have been written by Deleuze himself, Faivre writes that the pursuit of gnosis intends "to substitute a metaphysics of Becoming for [any] opposition [between being and knowing]." In his own way, Faivre also seems to be explicitly calling for something like a Deleuzian ontology when he claims that the metaphysics of becoming cannot be achieved by "giving in to the dialectics of dualizing and reabsorbing, like the Neoplatonic schemas and German idealism or its materialist sequels, but [one must] think that everything, as Western esotericism has always known, takes place in an *ensemble of forces in living tension*."[8]

Deleuze's is no simple continuation of this tradition. In his somewhat dark relationship to hermeticism, Deleuze's thought effectively follows a pattern: his concepts function in relation to an unlimited or unbounded set of transformative potentials analogous to how traditional esoteric symbol systems relate to possibilities of gnosis and transformation. Rather than limit himself to a traditional cosmology, Deleuze designed his conceptual operations to exceed cognitive limits, evoking new figures, personae, and forms of life. Inspired in his adolescence by hermetic dreams of a *mathesis universalis*, and convinced by his own Spinozism and Bergsonism of a deep rapport of mind with nature, Deleuze developed a reading of symbolist and modern art as an oblique flowering of perennial hermetic aspirations. In the course of attempting to rethink philosophy in view of these alternate modes of thought, Deleuze developed a new image of thought, one ultimately linked to the intensities of spiritual ordeal. This ordeal is grounded in a certain nonidentical repetition of Platonism, a redirection of the sense of Platonic anamnesis toward an excavation of the interiors of nature's cave and the vertiginous realm of simulacra. This philosophy's peculiar mode of becoming is uncanny, humorous, and intense. It forges concepts linked to an abridgement of the intensive, and unfolds through the strategic evocation of enigmatic conceptual personae forming a plane of immanence: the creation of concepts. Deleuze finally attempted in *What Is Philosophy?* to clarify the different relations of art, science, and philosophy to a common plane of immanence, pointing to a new vision of immanent thought that might be sustained in the life of "a people to come."

Expressionism and its Discontents

Despite its centrality, Deleuze scholars have not until quite recently begun to take his hermeticism seriously.[9] In his 2005 work, *Out of This World: Deleuze and the Philosophy of Creation*, Peter Hallward argued for a greater complicity than many readers were perhaps prepared to recognize between Deleuze's philosophy and a theophanic vision of reality as absolute creation.[10] Hallward's claim is that, even without a transcendent God, Deleuze's philosophy valorizes a movement "out of this world," a movement of escape from the actual. Deleuze's vision is politically suspect, for Hallward, because it privileges attention to virtual processes at the expense of actual bodies, wills, and institutional structures. Hallward's argument is that the degree to which Deleuze's emphasis on the virtual nature of immanent being implies a vision of a reality that is beyond or flowing away from the actual (present, inside) toward the virtual (future, outside). He contends, moreover, that Deleuze does not account for the ultimate significance of actual configurations of power, personality, and material contradiction that energize and motivate ethical choice and determine political consequence. Deleuze's ontology thus constitutes, the argument goes, an inadequate ground for political projects of resistance and revolt.[11]

Hallward's reading has, at first glance, a certain seductive simplicity. There is admittedly a certain movement of transcendence at work in the intensification of immanence, but it is perhaps for this reason that astute readers have argued that Deleuze's philosophy trades on no simple opposition between immanence and transcendence.[12] There is arguably a kind of transcendence specific to immanence, but such transcendence is not marked by a desire to escape, but by intensified engagement with *this* world. I have argued that this engagement should be understood on the model of the intensive relations with matter exhibited in ritual, meditational, and magical practice.

There is a sense in which Deleuze himself partially obscures this point, by occasionally affirming deterritorialization as an end in itself. But if traced carefully, a line clearly runs from Deleuze's early interest in the dream of mathesis universalis to his attention to the cosmic dimension of art, to increasing attention, with Guattari, to the contours of specific forms of experimental practice. Deleuze and Guattari insist that such attention is informed first and last by the sufferings of humanity.

> This is, precisely, the task of all art and, from colors and sounds, both music and panting similarly extract new harmonies, new plastic or melodic landscapes, and new rhythmic characters that raise them to the height of the earth's song and the cry of humanity: that which constitutes tone, health, becoming, a visual and sonorous bloc. A monument does not commemorate or celebrate something that happened but confides to the ear of the future the persistent sensations that embody the event: the constantly renewed suffering of men and women, their re-created protestations, their constantly resumed struggle. (WIP, 176)

Deleuze's politics is only "virtual" in the sense that its monuments truly last: the "vibrations, clinches, and openings" revolution creates remain effective even after the revolution ossifies and dissolves into factions. Revolution is a "monument that is always in the process of becoming, like those tumuli to which each new traveler adds a stone" (*WIP*, 177). Against Hallward's perception, the virtual achieves sense and finality only in a transformation of social and individual life at the actual level.[13]

Anticipating Hallward's argument, Alain Badiou had already objected to Deleuze's philosophy precisely for its enthusiastic, ecstatic conception of nature. In *Deleuze: The Clamor of Being*, Badiou criticizes Deleuze's work for its fascination with a darkly or subliminally "enchanted" cosmos. "Yes, Deleuze will prove to have been our great physicist: he who contemplated the fire of the stars for us, who sounded the chaos, took the measure of inorganic life, and immersed our meager circuits in the immensity of the virtual. It may be said of him that he did not support the idea that 'the great Pan is dead.' "[14] Badiou's objection to a "great physics" such as Deleuze's is that it is simply a renewal of the Neoplatonic One, a subordination of multiplicity and difference to a single form of differentiation. It is beyond the scope of this book to enter into the complexities of Badiou's critique (and how it is bound up with his own metaphysics) but it is worth dwelling, at least momentarily, on Badiou's reading.[15]

Badiou correctly identifies Deleuze as a thinker for whom thought is generated only insofar as individuals are produced who exceed their own natures or powers: those who, as Badiou puts it, "go beyond their limits and endure the transfixion and disintegration of their actuality by infinite virtuality." Badiou also correctly notes that thought, for Deleuze, involves a "purification" and a "sobriety" that has been missed by those readers who search in Deleuze for a blanket affirmation of the "democracy of desire"—as if the representation of the intensity of one's own desires to oneself and others sufficed to count as thought.[16] What Badiou quite profoundly realizes is that the "powerful non-organic life" that is the subject of thought for Deleuze (and its ultimate content) is itself a power of death. What forces me to think is also what is killing me: forces too strong for my organism, my habits, or my society to integrate or ingest. We are forced to think of the forces that constitute us, but at the same time we are aware of such forces precisely to the extent that we cannot completely harness them.

However, this situation for Deleuze is supremely positive: it indicates the intransitive, impersonal nature of life and the possibility of (re)creation in connection with such an insight. Thus Badiou *overdetermines* Deleuzian ethics as simply a stoic preparation for dying.[17] What Badiou is missing here (but what Hallward somewhat more clearly sees) is that the ultimate backdrop is not preparation for death as a passive stoicism but as an active spiritual discipline. That is to say, in Deleuze there are many ways to die and many meanings of death, and many ways of communicating the senses of potential that flow through death into life. It is worth noting that when Badiou calls Deleuze a "prophet of Pan," he accurately notes the roots of immanent thought in those theological traditions accused of Pan-theism and heresy. However, Badiou in essence does not pursue his charge of a Deleuzian pantheism far enough. The concept of deep Nature does not simply renew the Neoplatonic One, but expands a hermetic conception of the potencies of lived creation, mathesis universalis, and regenerative gnosis.

What Hallward, for his part, does not see is that the spiritual experience to which Deleuze's work is indebted is not primarily mystical contemplation, but a tradition of gnosis as intense, initiatory, and transformative practice, an attempt to harness the forces of death-in-life through ritual and ascetic practice (as well as through ambulant and somnambulant experiment). Hallward's criticism of Deleuze's political vision is that a philosophy of absolute creation fails to attend adequately to the stakes of the present moment, and that because Deleuze sees revolutionary projects as carried out through incomplete "monuments" (i.e., through processes that relay their realization through the actual by way of the virtual), there is some way Deleuze's politics undercuts the demands of the present. Indeed, Deleuze's question is not how a political will can be formed or maintained in the face of opposition or oppression. For Deleuze there are no purely local struggles, and no purely particular hegemonies. From this perspective, it is a vast oversimplification to read history and politics as simply a history of local struggles.

For Deleuze it is the most immediate dimension of revolution that is virtual, nonlocal. Revolution consists in the "new bonds it installs between people," in the sense that the power of what is achieved in a political (as much as in an artistic) upsurge consists in that which cannot be reduced to the present, to the demands of the present moment. From Deleuze's perspective, any change demanded for oneself is immediately a demand for a change in others, and for the Other one also becomes on the basis of that claim. If the "here and now" of revolution were simply the satisfaction of the demands of the present, and not the transformation of those demands (and of what it is possible or conceivable to demand, to desire), then from a Deleuzian perspective politics would have foreclosed in advance on the meaning of revolution, restricting it to the satisfaction of present demand rather developing an operation in desire itself.

Secular Anxieties from Freud to Adorno

I evoke the critiques of Hallward and Badiou in order to use them to situate possible misgivings about Deleuze's hermeticism within a broader debate in modern and contemporary philosophy—misgivings, that is, about the validity of the visionary, prophetic, or "spiritual" dimension of thought. Although this might at first seem like a rather distant connection, I believe the reactions of Badiou and Hallward to Deleuzian spirituality can be traced back at least as far as Freud's discomfort with the "black mud tide of occultism" he saw animating Carl Jung's metapsychology.[18] Freud's discomfort with all things occult (despite his clinical encounter with paranormal phenomena) is symptomatic of the prejudices still dominating contemporary philosophy and critical theory.

In the fascination of nineteenth-century psychology and twentieth-century psychoanalysis with the occult (with paranormal modes of communication, telepathy, clairvoyance, and so on), there was something Freud wished could be dismissed by calling it an atavism, a return of an earlier phase of development, one that had been definitively surpassed by society but which the neurotic individual seems to refuse. For Freud, animistic thinking occurs when the mind fails to pass beyond the primary narcissistic phase. That is to say, animism represents a phase in human civilization that corresponds to the narcissistic phase in the development of the individual. According to Freud, animism is the belief in a world that is sensitive to and potentially commanded by our wishes, the "primitive" confidence that trees can be allies (or enemies), birds messengers, or the ocean a mother whose language we can speak.[19]

For Freud, neurotics and psychotics show that the animist phase is still with us, but only as an atavism. Freud himself was familiar with many of his patients' sensitivities to synchronicities, telepathic communication, clairvoyance, prescience, and action at a distance. In his essay on the uncanny, Freud argued that there is effectively "no cure" for such minds, and that all that can be done is to refuse to impute to these experiences any meaning or significance beyond that of failed attempts to deal with psychic trauma. The apparent reality of telepathic communication and synchronistic events must be put down to their true reality: traumatized narcissistic fantasy. The fact that such events occur is not in dispute—Freud acknowledges that the telepathic really can read a mind. But Freud insists that, through analysis, all psychic investment in such activities can and must be severed, just as one must lose one's attachment to infantile fantasy in order to mature.[20]

Of course, what is ironic here is that Freud cannot pretend to prove that there are no synchronicities, no clairvoyance, no telepathy, and so on. Freud himself confesses he has no explanation for why he "accidentally" returned three times to a red light district he did not know was there, in a city he was totally unfamiliar with.[21] In keeping with his own scientific, fully disenchanted perspective, Freud can only say that such phenomena are curiously coincidental—coincidence being a category of chance (recognized by science as a natural factor), and the curious being a category of merely human interest (excitement over the novel), neatly preserving the mind-matter split necessary to the "scientific" worldview to which Freud ascribed.

Anxiety about the epistemic, ontological, and moral status of occult connections between mind and matter, as evidenced in Freud's anxiety over the uncanny, is symptomatic of an anxiety expressed in the concerns of Hallward and Badiou about Deleuze's philosophy, and is related to the concerns of our great contemporary antiobscurantist and antioccultist, Slavoj Žižek, who never tires of taking up the Adornian mantle of bashing supernaturalism wherever it may be found in decadent late capitalist culture.[22] These concerns were perhaps best crystallized by Susan Sontag's penetrating essay introducing the collected works of Artaud. As Sontag laconically put it, "The project of creating in a secular culture an institution that can manifest a dark, hidden reality is a contradiction in terms."[23] Artaud, living through profound despair over the prospects of a purely secular reason, seemed to prophetically anticipate, in the disastrous course of his own life, the difficult prospects for cosmic reenchantment Susan Sontag predicted the countercultures of the 1960's would ignore at their peril.

That is to say, Artaud had already lived, in advance, the coming vogues for exotic spirituality, liberated eroticism, and the dream of a postcivilized mode of existence that would mark cultural revolutions after 1968 (and their eventual cooptation by global capitalism). Artaud's legacy was not the first (or last) that would be turned from a quest for an apocalyptic transformation of culture, an immanent eschaton, into a grim advancement of sinister market manipulation and soft-fascist class warfare. Artaud himself prophesied this doom in 1936, when he foresaw that the modalities of experience he had discovered in the Tarahumara would become "a collection of outwork imageries from which the Age, true to its own system, would at most derive ideas for advertisements and models for clothing designers."[24]

In an avowedly secular culture, twin reactions of skepticism and glib assimilation embody precisely the antinomy involved in presenting a dark, hidden reality to secular culture: that which is discovered through struggle, terror, and ecstasy can only appear, in a culture obsessed with control and certainty, as an illusion or a novel variation on the same—next year's fashion, as it were. In any case, insofar as a dark, hidden reality appears patently or publicly to satisfy deep hungers, the unknown betrays itself by failing to transform desire. However, from a hermetic perspective, Deleuze's philosophy might be seen as contributing to a thought (and future sociality) that subverts this antinomy and overcomes anxiety over the status of occult realities and esoteric prehensions of nature. In fact, during the final year of his life, Deleuze characterized his own thought as being situated at a kind of utopian and apocalyptic horizon, saying that *Difference and Repetition* should have been written as an "apocalypse" (*DR*, xxi). At least part of what I have been suggesting, throughout this book, is that Deleuze's philosophy has yet to be read as a perspective from which the anxieties of secular culture toward spirituality might be overcome.

Along these lines, Deleuze's thought can be brought into fruitful debate with that of Theodor Adorno, whose "negative dialectics" sought to discover a usage of reason that would subvert the consolidation of reason by the demands of capitalist "total administration" of desire and power. Elsewhere I have argued that despite its own profound melancholy, negative dialectics seeks to recover a lost rapport with the real, and its language often explicitly invokes an elusive, acentric form of magical action as a model of immanent thought.[25] In the essays of *Dialectic of Enlightenment*, Horkheimer and Adorno argued that Enlightenment culture—and by extension modernity—is founded on a decisive antagonism between reason and myth, disenchanted skepticism and magical animism.[26] The authors argued that enlightenment necessarily occludes any mode of mind whose concepts might subvert given, actual, recognized forms of power, and that rationality consummates its vocation in a supreme positivism that can affirm only the reality of a given social formation. Effectively, Enlightenment reason is opposed to the different, to which it subordinates the spiritual as irrational. In the same gesture, outliers, nomads, and spiritual entities become necessarily confused.

The result of the dialectic of Enlightenment is that the desire for something different from the administered world leads to a fascination with all things occult. Peculiarly sensitive to this problem, Adorno may have been modern occultism's most vehement philosophical critic. In his acerbic "Theses Against Occultism," Adorno identifies modern fascination with the paranormal—from the popularity of séances, to astrology, fortune-telling, necromancy, clairvoyance, and telepathy—with a despairing rationality that seeks to "rematerialize" and thus reenchant a lost world.[27] By contrast, for Adorno himself, the only possible avenue of reenchantment, within the administered world, lay in the mode in which certain works of art (paradigmatically those of Kafka and Beckett and serial music) internalize the abject conditions of their own creation.[28] Only a deflationary and tortured modernism has any chance, for Adorno, to reconnect us to the nature decimated by late capitalist orders. Any aesthetic, let alone "spiritual" refuge in the work of art, must simply be a declaration of what is present only in absentia, as unrecoverably lost. On this view, any aesthetic pleasure that knows itself as such is coopted in advance by the forces that render it available to public perception. Thus Adorno identifies the quest for occult knowledge (as well as the quest for pleasure in most popular art forms) with a disastrous abnegation of consciousness. In essence Adorno claims that occultism is simply another bogus spiritualization of the overwhelming powers of the industrial-entertainment complex. The only difference is that, instead of being managed by corporate overlords, the occult realm of submission is ruled by obscure foreign divinities. Occultism, like mass media, is simply an escape route for a mind no longer able to bear the terror of complete social control over nature.[29] To listen for the commands of the spirits, or even to take direction from a horoscope, is for Adorno simply to evade the horrors issuing from our own doomed exercise of freedom.

In other words, for Adorno, because the modern mind is unable to withstand the terror of its own power, occult consciousness stages a supplemental ritual of abjection, projecting its lack of power onto an inchoate matter conceived as dark or obscure gods, or lost ancestral voices. Such idolatry, Adorno argues, confuses the pure nothingness of self-consciousness with an inchoate plenitude of matter. It makes the vicissitudes of time, trapped in the prisons of bureaucratic administration, appear as "spirits" bearing an intractable message before which the mind can only lie prostrate. Perhaps more than any other phenomenon, the revival of occultism in the twentieth century portends, for Adorno, apocalyptic violence and the demise of civilization: "The veiled tendency of society towards disaster lulls its victims in false revelation, with a hallucinated phenomenon. In vain they hope to look their total doom in the eye and withstand it."[30]

The pronouncements of Slavoj Žižek are not needed to clearly see the ways the New Age movement's consumerist dabbling in spirituality has empowered a whole new generation of ruthless capitalists. But there is a profound possibility missed by Adorno's and Žižek's rejection of spiritualization and reenchantment as inherently complicit with capital. Their thesis is reversible. It may be that the persistence, even the flourishing of contemporary spirituality, derided as pseudognosis, is a direct result of the fact that, as Adorno himself put it, in capitalism "the exchange relationship substitutes for elemental power."[31] This alternative view would imply that capitalism should be seen as a perversion of animist elementalism, rather than the reverse.

On this view, the renunciation of devotion to occult powers is a necessity that follows only if one reads occultism in terms of ressentiment and a thwarted quest for control.[32] By contrast, a broader approach to the politics of spirituality, such as that found in the hermetic Deleuze, clarifies how the perennial desire is not for control but for the emergence of unexpected relations, uncanny mediations, and unforeseen creations.[33] But having addressed Adorno, we come to a slightly different and much more subtle objection to Deleuzian hermeticism, raised by one of his most sympathetic and insightful readers. Philip Goodchild, in *Gilles Deleuze and the Question of Philosophy*, pointed out there might be a subtle kind of abjection involved in Deleuze's avowal of immanence.[34] As Goodchild puts it, our encounter with the plane of immanence, according to Deleuze's materialism, involves a kind of submission to chaos, or at the very least a kind of humorous, even masochistic imploring. As Goodchild reads him, the strictly materialist Deleuze avers that everything we construct on this plane devolves immediately into a kind of false transcendence hovering momentarily between chaos and pure immanence.[35] The rule for the creation of concepts seems to be that one must renounce all content, abjuring everything but the form of construction that enables us to pass from immanence to chaos and back again. In other words, it seems that actual constructions (concrete syntheses) contain the inspiration of immanence only in a formal sense, the sense in which conceptual creation reconnects with the absolute abstraction of immanence. In this view, actual forms of content and matters of expression can only appear as temporary reifications of a more fundamental process, one that is profoundly indifferent, in its sublime motility, to its contingent realizations.

However, as I have tried to suggest, there are intimations in Deleuze's thought that particular diagrams and the figures emerge as more than mere effects of a ceaseless abstract shuttling between chaos and immanence. Some kind of mediation may play a genuinely constitutive role in his system, even if the redemptive function of such mediators is not something Deleuze explicitly theorizes.[36] Deleuze is often less than explicit about the specific ends toward which mediation is oriented, and for this reason Goodchild was compelled to suggest that what is needed for the completing of Deleuze's project is a renewed notion of transcendence, a transcendence of the "mental fetishes" or "outrageous characters" that exist and think.[37] I would argue that the *hermetic* Deleuze has just such a perspective. That is to say, if Deleuze's connection to esoteric traditions is made explicit, the rogues and outliers of the history of esoteric science, such as Malfatti (as much as any of the minor philosophical, artistic, and scientific figures affirmed by Deleuze) form *irreplaceable figures* on the plan(e) of immanence, and those who belong to this series of humorous avatars would index the contours of viable experimental life.

The future of immanent thought, and the future of belief, would then have to be a kind of typology of unforgettable characters. Such a transcendence of singular spirits rather than simply the forces of abstract materiality might better ground a perspective from which to evaluate experimentation. This conception of immanent spirit, oriented to the past and the present as much as to the future, would admittedly alter Deleuze's version of immanence, whose "absolute" realization occasionally seems wedded to a kind of pure transcendental futurity, ultimately indifferent to particular actualizations. But by highlighting Deleuze's connection to hermetic tradition, the case can be made that the philosophy of immanence is itself a product of a peculiar genealogy, one whose anorganic life depends as much on how it has been actualized in the past and is dynamized in the present, as how its future will have been actualized.

Animist Futures

By connecting it to hermetic tradition, we can read Deleuze's philosophy as something like a practical contemporary guide to experimental spirituality. By unfolding immanence to its hermetic core, we evoke an uncanny realm of spirit, a realm perhaps best invoked by Guattari himself, when he suggested in *Chaosmosis* that what is necessary for modernity is a revival of animism.[38] Such a suggestion in no way means to fetishize or reify the thoughts of nonmodern "others," but to recognize, in a postcolonial and global context, the need to discriminate, critically and clinically, the nature of our own spiritual culture, a culture beholden to an immanent organization of spiritual forces that tend to go more or less unrecognized. It is of course impossible to say exactly what such a revival would entail, but it would arguably be something like a nonidentical repetition of archaic animist insight into the role of a panoply of spirits that are indistinguishable from material vectors, mediators, and viable lines of flight. Here the conception of "spirit" would constitute a plan(e) of composition for symbolic interaction with the as yet unknown.

Such a project would entail a reconception of the boundaries of philosophical thought, and would connect philosophy to experimental forms of belief as well as to activities that might be characterized as extensions of ritual healing processes. Under this aegis, thought would be construed not simply as critical reflection but as a creative operation immanent to transformative signs. Such thought would develop a contemporary hermeticism beyond the opposition between exoteric, "open" rationality and the "closed" signs of those initiated into various local cosmologies. Overcoming this opposition would fulfill, in some sense, the ambitions the young Gilles Deleuze already articulated in connection with the mathesis of Malfatti.[39]

Contra Adorno, the invocation of the hermetic *Tabula Smaragdina*, "as above, so below," does not express the desire for ravishing by unaccountable spirits—such would truly be nothing but an abnegation of freedom. Rather, hermetic thought undertakes to comprehend what spirits may become of us, in a cosmos taken as a machine for the production of gods, leading to something like an itinerant, nomadic theandry. There are clear political stakes here. From the perspective of a hermetic Deleuze, hermetic thought within capitalism does not propose to fulfill impossible desires, but to unleash a cosmic dimension in desire that capitalism calls up only to restrict, survey, and control. Far from being the ultimate evidence of the triumph of that bourgeoisie positivism that identifies spirit with technological progress, it may be that hermeticism in our times (though always in danger of confusing "the emanations and the isotopes of uranium") can pose potentials for desire that will persist beyond the apocalypse of the planned society and the imminent demise of technological reason as we pass through the current ecological and economic holocaust.[40]

From the perspective of the hermetic Deleuze, contemporary life is locked into a situation in which it can only see its magicians as isolated hermits who withdraw into the cultivation of a superior ego, when in fact the visionary is nothing without the pack, tribe, or band—in a word, the collective he or she serves. The becomings-animal, -woman, and -molecular undertaken by the shaman are not self-serving, but ultimately for the purpose of the healing and transformation of a social body, and of the earth itself. Contact with what I would call the "shamanic virtual"—a plane of consistency populated by ancestors, totems, and spirits—is not primarily for the ecstatic enjoyment of the visionary. In fact, it is much more like a hallucinatory illness that the shaman sustains for the sake of the people. And the joy of the shaman's song comes directly from the pain of the people.[41] From this perspective, the "great health" Nietzsche writes about at the conclusion to *On the Genealogy of Morals* is not available in the first or even final analysis to a single individual. Belief in the world searches for that subtle or alchemical body that would be a collective yet to be realized, yet already uncannily present in our times.[42]

For Deleuze, the elements of this becoming arise in an ordeal that is as much spiritual as it is material.[43] What matters will be the immanent adequacy of our diagrams, and the directions those diagrams map—the configurations they produce, the vitality and variations they enable, the uncanny joy and transgression of limitations they involve. This strained hermetic passion provides Deleuze his most autochthonous paradigm of immanent thought. Hermetic science—the exploration of transhuman, microcosmic, and macrocosmic principles as the fundamental determinants of human subjectivity—is truly the most apt description of that essential nonphilosophy into which art, science, and philosophy delve, that "witch's flight" from which they return "with bloodshot eyes": the eyes of the mind.

Deleuze's texts prepare us for this unforeseen collectivity, uniting nature and culture, and for the problems of an uncannily animated cosmos. But these are problems both ancient Hermes and his Renaissance devotees prophesied we would one day have to face. From this perspective, Deleuze's thought offers not simply a pluralist pragmatics, but a spiritual metapragmatics, one that might outline a posthuman or transhuman future along archaic lines of spiritual ordeal. Such a thought traces a path toward the identification of immanence with an eschatological endgame of cosmic scale. If our times resonate with the global anxieties of late antique and Renaissance eras as much as with the late nineteenth century, with its gilded age of obese capital and stagnant politics but full of promising new material and spiritual technologies, perhaps it is may also be true that it is the twenty-first century and not the twentieth that will have been Deleuzian.[44]

Coda
Experimental Faith

What remains, then, is to explore how Deleuzian philosophy might directly connect to spiritual practices, forming immanent futures of belief. Deleuze and Guattari admit in *What Is Philosophy?* that "disturbing affinities appear on what seems to be a common plane of immanence" between philosophy and religion (*WIP*, 91). In accordance with the *I Ching*, "The Classic of Changes," Deleuze and Guattari acknowledge a properly diagrammatic moment in Taoism, a "to-ing and fro-ing" where "Chinese thought inscribes the diagrammatic movements of a nature-thought on the plane, yin and yang; and hexagrams are sections of the plane, intensive ordinates of these infinite movements, with their components in continuous and discontinuous features" (*WIP*, 91). Deleuze and Guattari also acknowledge that from the fifteenth century to the seventeenth, particularly in Spain and Italy, Catholic thinkers were experimenting with a radicalization of Christianity along similar lines. Here "Christianity made the *impresa* the envelope of a 'concetto,' but the concetto has not yet acquired consistency, and depends upon the way in which it is figured or even dissimulated" (*WIP*, 92). *Imprese* were combinations of symbolic images and pithy, witty conceits popular in the Renaissance and the baroque period. It was thought that an impresa could access levels of profundity not available to ordinary language.

Deleuze and Guattari praise the innovation of this kind of thinking, but ultimately view it as a "catholic compromise of concept and figure which had great aesthetic value but which masked philosophy, diverted it toward a rhetoric and prevented a full possession of the concept" (*WIP*, 103). In other words, the impresa approaches, but ultimately fails the immanent requirements of the concept: "The concept is not paradigmatic but *syntagmatic*, not projective but *connective*, not hierarchical but *linking*, not referential but *consistent*" (*WIP*, 91).[1]

However, Deleuze and Guattari acknowledge that a number of their contemporaries had begun to create genuine concepts using religious materials. Citing Levinas, Corbin, Jambet, and Lardreau, Deleuze and Guattari acknowledge a series of thinkers that, "by freeing themselves from Hegelian or Heideggerian stereotypes, . . . are taking up the specifically philosophical question [of immanence] on new foundations" (*WIP*, 223). They also suspect that there is a creative atheism peculiar to Christian culture, an atheism that Christianity "more than any other religion secretes," and that contains the germinal potencies of a radically immanent thought (*WIP*, 93). Deleuze and Guattari leave the details of such a development rather obscure, but I would suggest that the heretical christology of François Laruelle's nonphilosophy would here be exemplary.[2] In Laruelle's view, Christ's persecution, suffering, and ultimate rejection become a logic of absolute immanence, when Christ is taken not as the name of the unified God-Man but as a name of something universal that can only be revealed as persecuted, as what Laruelle calls the "in-man" or "humanity-in-the-last-instance."

For my part, I hope to have here simply taken the step to make more explicit Deleuze's own indebtedness to, and reliance upon, the continuing promise of extant and yet to be developed traditions of spiritual practice, the cultivation of visionary states, and the search for rapport between human and cosmic natures. The relation between hermeticism and the philosophy of immanence conceived of as experimental ordeal suggests that a spiritual dimension is the utopian parameter of immanence, some kind of eschatological limit at which life and thought, metaphilosophy and metapragmatics, would be intensively unified. This apocalyptic moment has dark precursors in the history of occultism, the prehistory of immanence in Neoplatonic expressionism, and in the history of philosophy insofar as certain periods such as the Renaissance, German idealism, and the certain strands of contemporary philosophy, psychology, mathematics, and aesthetics have anticipated the contours of an as yet unrealized synthesis of instinct and institution, affective and cognitive life. The project of a *mathesis universalis* remains genuinely unfinished.

The two most glaring inadequacies of my project might be (1) the lack of substantial treatment of the detailed history of particular hermetic or Western esoteric systems that might approximate Deleuze's (relying, as I have, upon general characterizations of practices and traditions Deleuze mentions) and (2) a lack of treatment of some of the more proximate eighteenth, nineteenth, and early twentieth-century thinkers (in particular Leibniz, Schelling, Wronski, and Warrain) whose explicit or implicit esotericisms inspired Deleuze. For this second inadequacy, I can say that at the earliest stages of my intuitions of a Deleuzian hermeticism, my interests in semiotics and aesthetics drew me to parallels between Deleuze and the Renaissance, rather than to the romantic retrieval of the Renaissance, and this connection formed the germinal core of this book. Fortunately we have the work of Christian Kerslake, whose two truly inspired projects, *Deleuze and the Unconscious*, and *Immanence and the Vertigo of Philosophy: From Kant to Deleuze*, should be read in tandem with this book for a fuller account of Deleuze's hermetic aspect, in connection with its idealist and romantic dimensions.

As for the first inadequacy, the lack of attention to the specific details of occult practices or esoteric "maps" in connection or conjunction with Deleuze's concepts, I can point readers to the work of the authors of a special issue of *SubStance*, "Spiritual Politics after Deleuze."[3] There the authors undertook to ground specific Deleuzian concepts as deeply as possible in their esoteric sources and in connection to their spiritual resources. Paul Harris, coeditor of the special issue, argues for a reading of Deleuze's cinematic "universe of light" as a cosmic plane of immanence.[4] Mark Bonta argues for correspondence between the system of *Difference and Repetition* and Jacob Boehme's theosophy.[5] William Behun excavates connections between the Body without Organs and the mystical Body of Light.[6] Rocco Gangle and Inna Semetsky indicate the power of Deleuzian thought to explicate divinatory and combinatory systems such as the *I Ching* and the tarot.[7]

Philip Goodchild was perhaps the first scholar of Deleuze to insist upon both the importance and problematic character of a distinctly Deleuzian spirituality. Goodchild's conception of piety as a radically immanent and transformative mode of attention, articulated in his two books expounding apocalyptic and utopian possibilities for the transformation of political economy, also finds expression in "Philosophy as a Way of Life: Deleuze on Thinking and Money."[8] Anthony Paul Smith and Daniel Colucciello Barber both argue for radically immanent modes by which to propagate a Deleuzian philosophy of religion (the latter through aesthetic, the former through radically ecological pragmatics).[9] Luke B. Higgins and Kristien Justaert indicate ways Deleuze's concepts might radically transform traditional theology itself, from liberation theology to mystical and apophatic discourses.[10] Finally, I want to acknowledge the work of Juan Ignacio Salzano and Matt Lee in *Nosotros, Los Brujos* and *Deleuze y la Brujería*, discovered too late to be integrated into this project, but obviously taking Deleuze's hermetic project far beyond the contours of what, in this book, must remain at the level of a kind of manifesto for precisely the kind of work they are already doing.[11]

The full history of how modern and contemporary philosophy has been inspired by esoteric traditions has yet to be written. In writing that history, it may become clear that the recent "return to religion" or "postsecular turn" in philosophy and the humanities may be but the latest iteration of a perennial investment of rational analysis in the valence of various spiritual practices. If this fact is fully countenanced, long-held cultural and philosophical prejudices pitting reason and the sciences against the arts of spirit may be seriously shaken. More modestly, it may become possible, from the perspective of the hermetic Deleuze, to conceptualize the power of thought along spiritually informed, rather than rigidly rationalistic, lines, since Deleuze offers a complex view of reality within which belief, desire, and the spiritual nature of imperceptible forces act in concert as effective, transforming, and mutually imbricated forces.

This book is a call for future research not simply because there is more work to be done on the relation between the *actualité* of Deleuzian thought and its pregnant pasts in hermetic theory and practice (on that score there is certainly more to do), but because I am convinced that philosophy, within and beyond Deleuze, has an eschatological dimension in that it calls for new concrete syntheses of thought and life, in the midst of a continuing crisis over the nature and future of secular, modern, and post-Enlightenment culture. I believe the development of future philosophical forms of exposition will rely in part upon a creative and nonidentical repetition of hermetic tradition, construed as the continuing exploration of that which is most vital in material, cultural, sideral, and spiritual time. What I hope to have shown here, at the very least, is how Deleuze's conception of philosophy as a spiritual ordeal has left an unparalleled set of directions for exploring a renewed relation to life that can ramify, in uncanny and unexpected ways, the ambitions of hermetic tradition.

Notes

Introduction

1. "I'll Have to Wander All Alone," Jacques Derrida, translated by David Kammerman, www.usc.edu/dept/comp-lit/tympanum/1/derrida1.html, accessed August 22, 2010.
2. Artaud, *Antonin Artaud*, 571.
3. Ibid.
4. Christian Kerslake has taken great pains to elucidate and struggle with the tensions between Deleuze's different conceptions of immanence in *Immanence and the Vertigo of Philosophy*.
5. In fact, Deleuze argues that thinkable being is *not* that which appears in representational form, but that which overloads or short-circuits the operations of understanding upon sensibility, the advance of concepts upon intuitions (*DR*, 189).
6. Deleuze and Guattari, *A Thousand Plateaus*, 149–66.
7. At some of his most intensely speculative moments, Deleuze enlists Artaud directly in order to demonstrate how such ideas alone can account for intensive properties of space and time, and how ideas in this way function not as static conceptual markers, but as nodal points of transformation. Deleuze writes, "When Artaud spoke of the theatre of cruelty, he defined it only in terms of an extreme 'determinism,' that of spatio-temporal determination insofar as it incarnates an Idea of mind or nature, like a 'restless space' or movement of turning and wounding gravitation capable of directly affecting the organism, a pure staging without author, without actors, and without subjects. Spaces

are hollowed out, time is accelerated or decelerated, only at the cost of strains and displacements which mobilize and compromise the whole body. Shining points pierce us, singularities turn us back upon ourselves: everywhere the tortoise's neck with its vertiginous sliding of proto-vertebrae. Even the sky suffers from its cardinal points and its constellations which, like 'actor-suns,' inscribe Ideas in its flesh. There are indeed actors and subjects, but these are larvae, since they alone are capable of sustaining the lines, the slippages, and the rotations. Afterwards it is too late" (*DR*, 219). What Deleuze is envisaging here is a "larval" subjectivity—preindividual and embryonic—that can be formed and reformed in ways that the fully developed organism, with its organs and metabolic functions firmly in place, no longer can. This nascent self is directly linked to an apprehension of ideas that are themselves the transcendental genetic condition of any self whatsoever. Ideas, in turn, are conceived as expressed in spatiotemporal singularities—spatial intensities incarnate in cardinal points in a sky, bodily intensities incarnate in the tortoiselike convolutions of a vertebrate neck. From this perspective, thought itself becomes an experience of acutely intense determination, as if each idea were a blow that indexes the genesis of the self to encounters with hollowed-out spaces, on extreme slownesses or speeds.

8. When Deleuze determines the profound nature of the singular intensities that bear witness to the incarnation of ideas, he writes that "difference without a concept, non-mediated difference . . . is both the *literal and spiritual* primary sense of repetition. The material sense results from this other, as if secreted by it like a shell" (*DR*, 25, emphasis added). But what could Deleuze mean, exactly, by a literal *and* spiritual sense of repetition? It would seem, if anything, that what is literal should be physical, or at least in some sense material; nothing seems, on the face of it, more brutally mechanical and reductively material than repetition. How can Deleuze claim that there is a spiritual sense of repetition? That is the enigma I intend to confront in what follows.

9. Alain Badiou's take on Deleuzian spirituality is entirely negative and polemical. Badiou finds in Deleuze's system a mystical affirmation of the human subject as subordinate to "the clamor of being," an affirmation of life as ineffable participation in the One-All that deserves reproach and refutation. More recently, Peter Hallward has taken this approach even further and has charged Deleuze's philosophy with political irrelevance on the basis of its "otherworldliness." A series of more positive approaches to this issue, to which this book hopes to contribute, can also be found in works as early as Philip Goodchild's *Gilles Deleuze and the Question of Philosophy*; *Deleuze and Religion*, edited by Mary Brydon; and a special issue of *SubStance*, "Spiritual Politics after Deleuze," edited by Joshua Delpech-Ramey and Paul A. Harris. Badiou, *Deleuze*. Hallward, *Out of This World*.

10. The preeminent academic interpreter of the hermetic tradition, Antoine Faivre, has pointed out that in scholarly usage, there is some confusion as to the referents of the terms "hermetic" and "hermeticism." *Access to Western Esotericism* (Albany: SUNY Press, 1996), 35. The terms can refer to the teachings and outlook of Hermes Trismegistus, as embodied in the Alexandrian Greek texts compiled in the *Corpus Hermeticum*, but can also refer more generally to alchemy and the gamut of esoteric traditions of the West that include Christian kabbalism, Paracelcism, Rosicrucianism, and theosophy. Faivre proposes that the term "hermetism" be used to refer specifically to Hermes Trismegistus and the *Corpus Hermeticum*. In using the terms "hermetic" and "hermeticism" throughout this text, and by conflating these terms in many instances with "esoteric," and "esotericism," I follow the general scholarly practice, rather than Faivre's suggestion. Faivre's distinction is useful for the purpose of clearly distinguishing the teachings of Hermes Trismegistus from the presence and influence of those teachings across esoteric traditions; my purpose here is to speak of Deleuze's work in terms of its relation to and continuation of that more general influence of "hermeticism," rather than specific teachings of the *Corpus Hermeticum* Faivre calls "hermetism."

11. Garth Fowden, *The Egyptian Hermes: A Historical Approach to the Late Pagan Mind* (Cambridge: Cambridge University Press, 1986).

12. Ibid., 34–35.

13. *Asclepius*, 25:1–26:2. All references to the Hermetica are to G. R. S. Mead's *Thrice Greatest Hermes*.

14. Notably Hegel and Schelling, but also the lesser-known post-Kantian esoteric thinkers Josef Hoëné-Wronski and Francis Warrain. See Magee, *Hegel and the Hermetic Tradition*, and Edward A. Beach, *The Potencies of God(s): Schelling's Philosophy of Mythology* (Albany: SUNY Press, 1994). See also Christian Kerslake's discussion of Wronski and Warrain in relation to Deleuze in *Immanence and the Vertigo of Philosophy*.

15. Carl Jung, *Memories, Dreams, Reflections*, translated by Richard and Clara Winston (New York: Vintage Books, 1989), 150.

16. Quite apart from academic and rationalistic prejudice, it may seem strange, even somewhat forced, to ally Deleuze's thought with spiritual traditions seeking perennial truths of nature, culture, and spirit. With its attempt to operate within distinct regimes of archetypal powers and principles, the hermetic tradition might seem to fail to make some putatively proper "Deleuzian" affirmation of difference, and thus fail to affirm with Deleuze that there are in principle an unlimited number of maps of human and cosmic transformative processes. By way of an initial response to this prima facie reservation, I will say from the outset that Deleuze's hermeticism affirms cosmologies that are itinerant rather than fixed, practices that are improvisatory, rather than

tradition-bound, symbolisms that are spontaneous, rather than archetypal, maps that are diagrammatic, rather than territorial, and patterns of initiation that are fraternal, rather than authoritarian. In this way, it is in Deleuze's creative variation on hermetic themes that his work takes on full significance as a sign of how it may yet be possible to think, both philosophically and in elaboration, of the hermetic tradition.

1. Modernity and Experimental Imperative

1. On Deleuze's indebtedness to the baroque and mannerism, see Gregg Lambert, *Return of the Baroque in Modern Culture* (London: Continuum, 2004).

2. "Seminar on Spinoza / Cours Vincennes 25/11/1980," Gilles Deleuze, www.webdeleuze.com, accessed June 22, 2010.

3. This is not to say that Kierkegaard and Pascal do not employ irony in their texts, but that the *worlds* in the face of which they think and speak, as people of faith, are not ultimately conditioned by tragic irony but by comic absurdity.

4. *Qu'est ce-que fonder?* was a series of lectures Deleuze gave as a *cours hypokhâgne*, (elite college preparatory course for aspiring humanities students) at the Lycée Louis le Grand in 1956–57. The text can be found at www.webdeleuze.com.

5. It should be noted of course that the fragmentation and dispersal of the ego in the ordeal leads not to total destruction, but to Dionysiac dismemberment. The self is not an illusion, but is that which is capable of affirming itself when it intuits participation in a cosmic form of differentiation and repetition sustained at an impersonal level of eternal return. This impassive level, the level of the body without organs, or God, functions in Deleuze's work as a Spinozistic *natura naturans*.

6. Put somewhat differently, if consciousness is general and continuous, for Deleuze, ideas are discontinuous and rare. Ideas do not so much occur within or "to" consciousness as provoke, disturb, and disrupt the patterns within which consciousness views itself as a principle of order and unity. Rather than as immanent to consciousness, thought, for Deleuze, consists in a transcendent exercise of the faculties. Thought is generated by, and remains immanent to, ideas that persist not as solutions but as problems. The mind is given in its problems, in a problematic element, and these problems form the genetic transcendental element—the immanence—of thinker and object of thought.

7. Kerslake shows how Deleuze's reading of Hume's project is more closely related to Kant's than is ordinarily supposed, because it already envisages something like an a priori synthesis. Deleuze believed that "before Kant, Hume already [showed] that the principles for ordering past experience [were] not derived from the given." Kerslake, *Immanence and the Vertigo of Philosophy*, 215.

8. I agree, however, with Kerslake's assessment that Spinoza is not the first modern but the last premodern philosopher, whose discovery of immanence shatters the mode of reflection proper to premodern concepts. In this sense, I would argue that the "cross" on which Spinoza is crucified is arguably the geometrical method itself, from which Deleuze argues thought is to be resurrected or reborn, not as reflection or even as knowledge, but as an altered mode of perception and a renewed possibility of action. Genuinely modern philosophy begins when the act of thought becomes a transcendental genesis, and when the question becomes the conditions (and typology) of various philosophical methods, such as the *more geometrico*, the Kantian critique, Hegelian dialectic, Husserlian *epoché*, and so on. Beginning at least with German Idealism, "diagrams of the absolute" are seen not as modes of reflection but as generative of the world itself. To conceptualize how this is possible, the problem of "transcendental genesis" emerges after Kant. Kerslake argues that Deleuze is attempting to resolve that problem in the wake of the efforts of Schelling and Wronski. "Deleuze's final 'resubjectification' of Life signals his arrival at the same point as Wronski and the later Schelling, who ended up positing the existence of subjectivity within a 'primordially living . . . actual being,' a 'being that is preceded by no other and is therefore the oldest of all beings.' Thus if immanence will remain the vertigo of philosophy for Deleuze, it will be in part due to the vertigo of this rediscovery of 'life,' and the reorientation it requires in order for a final kind of 'non-organic' vitalism to emerge." *Immanence and the Vertigo of Philosophy*, 213.

In what follows, I argue that Deleuze is "hermetic" in the sense that it is the hermetic tradition that already conceives the world as this interrelated, primordially living being, within which mind plays a regenerating and microcosmic role inseparable from the anorganic life of the all.

9. Perhaps even to the "ages of the world," according to Schelling, or to the history of being, in Heidegger.

10. For Deleuze, it was Sartre who restored the "rights of immanence" with his impersonal transcendental field (*WIP*, 47). See Jean-Paul Sartre, *The Transcendence of the Ego*, translated by Forrest Williams and Robert Kirkpatrick (New York: Noonday, 1957), 23.

11. In "Two Questions on Drugs," Deleuze writes that the problem with drug experimentation is that "*Microperceptions are covered in advance*, depending on the substance in question, by hallucinations, delirium, false perceptions, fantasies, waves of paranoia. Artaud, Michaux, Burroughs—who all knew what they were talking about—hated the 'mistaken perceptions' and 'bad feelings' which to them seemed both a betrayal and yet an inevitable result. That is also where all control is lost and the system of abject dependence begins, dependence on the product, the hit, the fantasy productions, dependence on a dealer,

etc. Two things must be distinguished, abstractly: the domain of vital experimentation, and the domain of deadly experimentation. Vital experimentation occurs when any trial grabs you, takes control of you, establishing more and more connections, and opens you to connections. This kind of experiment can entail a kind of self-destruction. It can take place with companion or starter produces, tobacco, alcohol, drugs. It is not suicidal as long as the destructive flow is not reduced to itself but serves to conjugate other flows, whatever the danger. The suicidal enterprise occurs when everything is reduced to this flow alone: 'my' hit, 'my' trip, 'my' glass. It is the contrary of connection; it is organized disconnection" (*TM*, 153–15).

12. Deleuze does not often emphasize the term "human" or "humanity." He is not a "humanist" in any ordinary sense. However, there is a certain humanism in Deleuze's work, a strange iteration of Renaissance humanism that envisages humanity as microcosmic and as a transformative operator and cocreator of nature. This vision is ultimately the fruit of the hermetic tradition in Western philosophy.

13. Miller's writings were testaments to travels and experiments that altered, endangered, and ultimately transformed his body and mind. Not only Miller, but a long series of writers and artists contribute to Deleuze's hermetic vision of thought as transformation, as spiritual ordeal. Reference to so many different writers and artists, throughout Deleuze's oeuvre, is due in part to the fact that for Deleuze the creation of concepts in philosophy is only one form of thought. The work of art (along with the scientific experiment) constitutes, on its own terms, as much of a fully formed thought as does any philosophical concept. The work of art, for Deleuze, does not constitute an object of spectatorial contemplation, but establishes an expressive function that produces new affects and percepts. Such a view entails that the artist is a kind of "cosmic artisan." Due to this view, Deleuze is particularly invested in a series of writers, painters, composers, and filmmakers who explicitly seek to discover vehicles of personal transformation and social metamorphosis, often within a more or less explicit quest for eschatological renewal of an exhausted humanity. To cite just a few examples, Leopold von Sacher-Masoch's attempt to evade patriarchal authoritarianism by contractually submitting himself to the powers of a dominant woman, Artaud's travels to Mexico in search of the desert gnosis of peyote, James Joyce's delivering over of narrative sense to the unconscious play of language, and Marcel Proust's submission of creation to an exploration of involuntary memory all form key models for a thought rooted in trials that initiate the self and reorder the world. To comprehend exactly the status of these exemplars in relation to philosophy, as Deleuze understands it, is what we undertake here by relating Deleuze's complex affirmation of artistic modernism to the complexities of occult (minor, nomadic, bastard) sciences.

14. Michaux, *Darkness Moves*.

15. For individuation as modeled by the egg, see *DR*, 251. On hermaphroditism, see "Mathesis, Science, and Philosophy." References to divination and sorcery abound in both *A Thousand Plateaus* and *What Is Philosophy?*

16. Kerslake, *Immanence and the Vertigo of Philosophy*, 212.

17. This would mean, as Philip Goodchild has already argued, that philosophical practice, the practice of the creation of concepts, would not only not exhaust the meaning of immanence, but that philosophy itself somehow would be incomplete without reference to a criteria transcendent to philosophy. Goodchild, *Deleuze and the Question of Philosophy*, 154–62.

18. Antoine Faivre, *Access to Western Esotericism* (Albany: SUNY Press, 1994), 3.

19. Tenny L. Davis, "The Emerald Tablet of Hermes Trismegistus: Three Latin Versions Which Were Current among Later Alchemists," *Journal of Chemical Education* 1.3, no. 8 (1926): 863–75.

20. *Asclepius* 22.

21. Brian Copenhaver, "Hermes Trismegistus, Proclus, and a Philosophy of Magic," in *Hermeticism and the Renaissance: Intellectual History and the Occult in Early Modern Europe*, edited by Ingrid Merkel and Allen G. Debus (Washington: Folger Shakespeare Library, 1988), 81.

22. Yates, *Giordano Bruno and the Hermetic Tradition*, 1–19.

23. As Hilary Gatti and others have demonstrated, Yates probably overstated her case for the importance of hermeticism during the Renaissance. As Brian Copenhaver notes, Ficino and the Renaissance draw, in their analysis of magic, much more upon the metaphysical and cosmological teachings of Neoplatonism itself than on the *Corpus Hermeticum*, whose references to magic and sorcery are at best oblique, encouraging its practice but leaving details vague. In general, the texts in the *Hermetica* are concerned with the practical nature of spirituality, including some teachings on alchemy and the fashioning of images suitable for calling forth spiritual allies. However, the sparseness of its teaching on magic does not mean that hermeticism was unimportant in the Renaissance or in the birth of the modern experimental spirit. The influence of hermetic notions is felt much more globally than simply as an incitement to take magic seriously. Due in large part to the resonance between hermetic cosmological teachings and the teachings of Judaism, Christianity, and Gnosticism, Ficino, Pico, and Bruno were inspired to develop complex syncretisms of Christian scholastic philosophy with more ancient systems—Pico especially dreamt of a unified system of all knowledge under the rubric of Christian incarnationalism. In the mind of the Renaissance, what the *Corpus Hermeticum* adds to Neoplatonic metaphysics is the possibility that occult activities such as alchemy, astrology, or kabbalah might belong within an encompassing, even "catholic,"

religious vision of syncretistic thought. Thus hermeticism is arguably, in a very broad sense, the inspiration, if not the source, for much of Renaissance and early modern thought.

24. Bergson, *The Two Sources of Morality and Religion*, 317.

25. In "Deleuze's Cinematic Universe of Light: A Cosmic Plane of Luminance," Paul Harris has suggested we conceive of a "plane of luminance" adjacent to the plane of immanence, on which the visions of the mystic become increasingly "adequate" to the expression of the universe. As Harris puts it, "As its 'dynamism' increases, so does the 'adequacy' of the mystical intuition's 'expression' of the universe, to the point that mystical intuition can peer into a void, an 'opening' of the Whole that would not be a spatial whole but an open Whole, a cusp of pure becoming." Delpech-Ramey and Harris, "Spiritual Politics after Deleuze," 121.

2. The Hermetic Tradition

1. Deleuze takes his own philosophical inspiration from Spinoza, who transformed expression into a radical monism in which the expressed (substance) was fully immanent to its expression (modes), without remainder, and without transcendence. However, in his own version of expressionism, Deleuze retains certain dimensions of the early Renaissance (Christian and Neoplatonic) conception of the world. Deleuze's conception of the world as imbricating series of difference and repetition owes much, for instance, to Nicholas of Cusa's notion of the world as a *complicatio* or contraction of the divine essence. Cusa conceived the universe as a maximal finite or "relative maximum" expression of the infinite God, the "absolute maximum." Cusa's thought (like Eriugena's and Dionysius's before him) clearly echoes the "as above, so below" principle of hermetic philosophy, according to which each element or dimension of the universe is implicated in every other. Deleuze has his own version of this principle in his notion of the immanence of every event in each event.

2. Augustine, *The Literal Meaning of Genesis*, trans. J. H. Taylor, Ancient Christian Writers, No. 41; New York: Newman Press, 1982. chap. 23, 175–76.

3. I.-P. Sheldon-Williams and J. J. O'Meara, trans. (1987). Eriugena, *Periphyseon (The Division of Nature)*. Montreal and Paris: Bellarmin, II.678c.

4. Ibid., III.681a.

5. Cusa, *On Learned Ignorance*, II.4.115.

6. Many have made this observation, but perhaps none more magisterially than Hans Blumenbert in *The Legitimacy of the Modern Age*.

7. Cusa writes, "The ancients did not attain unto the points already made, for they lacked learned ignorance. It has already become evident to us that the earth is indeed moved, even though we do not perceive this to be the case.

For we apprehend motion only through a certain comparison with something fixed. For example, if someone did not know that a body of water was flowing and did not see the shore while he was on a ship in the middle of the water, how would he recognize that the ship was being moved? And because of the fact that it would always seem to each person (whether he were on the earth, the sun, or another star) that he was at the 'immovable' center, so to speak, and that all other things were moved: assuredly, it would always be the case that if he were on the sun, he would fix a set of poles in relation to himself; if on the earth, another set; on the moon, another; on Mars, another; and so on. Hence, the world-machine will have its center everywhere and its circumference nowhere, so to speak; for God, who is everywhere and nowhere, is its circumference and center" (Cusa *On Learned Ignorance*, 2.12,162).

8. For a strong contemporary version of this perspective, one that draws deeply upon the analogical tradition, see John Milbank, *Being Reconciled: Ontology and Pardon* (London: Routledge, 2003).

9. Rocco Gangle has comprehended the radical implications of Spinoza's perspective for philosophical practice in an article that explicitly identifies immanence with an apocalyptic meaning of "theology." Gangle writes, "Because the *Ethics* demonstrates a transcendental dissolution of philosophical possibility, an 'impossible' dissolution of philosophy *as* transcendental prior to any and every effectivity or act, the concrete work of the *Ethics* must be understood as effecting a conversion in thinking more radical than any Platonic or religious *metanoia*. The term 'theology' is capable of bearing the signification of what thought becomes in the presence of such dissolution as the index of a new practice only because it has never named anything other than its own impossibility, its own performative contradiction—to speak *of* the Absolute Other, to say what strictly cannot be said. God, as Spinoza himself saw, is *the* singular term drawn from the Western tradition of thinking, the radical selfcontradictoriness and inconsistency of whose 'saying' lends it unique capacities to express immanence in the most powerful way." "Theology of the Chimera: Spinoza, Practice, Immanence," in *After the Postsecular and the Postmodern*, edited by Anthony Paul Smith and Daniel Whistler (Newcastle upon Tyne: Cambridge Scholars, 2010), 41.

10. For Deleuze, the limitation upon the theological tradition is not so much dogmatic as pragmatic: it perpetuates a system of *judgment* as the primary dimension of thought, rather than a system of *experimentation*. For traditional theology, the primary task of the creature is to discern with the heart and mind the beauty of the divine orders, rather than to recreate, intensively vary, or repeat differently those orders. Accordingly for traditional theological perspectives that introduce immanence only to subordinate it, it is not production but reflection that is adequate to being as expression.

11. This tradition in turn is passed onto Leibniz, German idealism, and Bergson in ways that Deleuze's thought recapitulates and radicalizes. In the context of reading Deleuze's major works I will explore this legacy, but my emphasis is on perennial hermetic themes that reappear in Deleuze's own terms. Christian Kerslake has done much to outline the contours of early modern, idealist, and nineteenth-century esoterica within Deleuze's corpus, in both *Deleuze and the Unconscious* and *Immanence and the Vertigo of Philosophy from Kant to Deleuze*.

12. Against certain skeptical and humanist trends that led, respectively, to the Cartesianism and fideism of the early modern period, certain Renaissance philosophers, such as Pico and Bruno, sought to maintain the centrality of metaphysics for both theology and science, and to articulate how the intellect might have a transformative role in reality. And from the Renaissance through such figures as Leibniz, Schelling, and Bergson, modern philosophers took quite seriously (though in a cautious and guarded way) the possibility that the knowledge that enabled such practices as alchemy, astrology, Kabbalah, and theurgy, might be rooted in a universal science of sciences, a mathesis universalis that would be an ecstatic and symbolic language unifying science and art, humanity and cosmos, heaven and earth. Furthermore, certain post-Kantian thinkers such as Hegel, Schelling, Novalis, and Josef Hoëné-Wronski were all strongly influenced by esoteric traditions. As Kerslake has now definitively shown, this post-Kantian esoteric line had a profound influence upon Deleuze. Kerslake reveals that the Kantian tradition produced a series of mystical and apocalyptic thinkers, including Wronski, whose "messianic" interpretations of the calculus as revealing fundamental cosmic patterns is an important source for Deleuze's *Difference and Repetition* and contains fundamental insights about what a fully realized immanence might be like as a form of vital thought. Kerslake, "Hoëne Wronski and Francis Warrain," in Graham Jones and Jon Roffe, ed., *Deleuze's Philosophical Lineage* (Edinburgh: Edinburgh University Press, 2009), 167–89.

One of the interesting implications of Deleuze's own appropriation of this minor tradition (or rather, minor aspect of the major modern tradition) is that his philosophy of immanence is not so much a recursion to the premodern as it is part of a kind of strange, "occult" modernity, one that is most prominent in German idealism, but still remains to be fully integrated into contemporary accounts of the subsequent history of philosophy. As Kerslake has suggested, Deleuze's thought is part of a certain esoteric modernity that extends continuously, if in subterranean fashion, from the Kantian discovery of transcendental subjectivity to an impersonal transcendental field in which the mind is no longer recognizably human, and the earth no longer in its place. Kerslake, *Immanence and the Vertigo of Philosophy: From Kant to Deleuze*, 227. Here thought becomes involved in genetic acts of repetition within an open whole of mobile cosmic forces, elemental powers encountered by thought in the form of spiritual ordeals. Deleuze's radicalization of the transcendental, a certain hermeticism, persists as a "practical philosophy of the absolute" in which the transcendental genesis of mind is identified with practices of intense creation and psychic transformation.

13. Plotinus, *Enneads* 6:4–5, translated by Stephen MacKenna (New York: Larson, 2004).

14. Ibid.

15. This seems, logically, to create a scenario in which actual being "hovers" between an imperceptible or "indiscernible" principle whose power is identified with the One's infinite potency and whose presence, by contrast, is some kind of arbitrary instance. Milbank argues that in Damascius and in Iamblichus there is an idea of a "one beyond the one" that would be shared by both the one and the many without hovering between them. "Sophiology and Theurgy: The New Theological Horizon," John Milbank, http://theologyphilosophycentre.co.uk/online-papers, accessed August 23, 2010. Milbank, for related reasons, thinks a problem of "hovering" between unity and multiplicity, concepts and intuitions, plagues Deleuze's ontology and makes difference, against Deleuze's intention, undecided as between equivocity and univocity; Badiou says much the same thing in *Deleuze: The Clamor of Being*, 51–52. See also John Milbank, *Theology and Social Theory: Beyond Secular Reason* (Oxford: Blackwell, 1990), 312–13.

16. Augustine, *De genesi ad litteram*, 5.7.20, in *Ancient Christian Writers: St. Augustine, The Literal Meaning of Genesis*, edited by John Hammond Taylor (Westminster, Md.: Newman Press, 1982).

17. Cusa, *On Learned Ignorance*, 3.1.188.

18. Iamblichus, *De mysteriis Aegiptiorum*, translated by Emma C. Clarke, John M. Dillon, and Jackston P. Hershbell (Leiden: Brill, 2004).

19. Porphyry, *Sententiae* 3:4, in *Porphyry's Launching-Points to the Realm of Mind: An Introduction to the Neoplatonic Philosophy of Plotinus*, translated by Kenneth Sylvan Guthrie (Grand Rapids, Mich.: Phanes, 1988).

20. On the complexities of these issues in relation to later developments in Christian theology, see "Sophiology and Theurgy," Milbank, 47.

21. Iamblichus, *De mysteriis Aegiptiorum* 5:232–33.

22. Catherine Pickstock has argued that Plato himself was led to this conclusion and the need for the consummation of philosophy in a rightly ordered or liturgical inhabitation of city and cosmos. See *After Writing: On the Liturgical Consummation of Philosophy*. (Oxford: Blackwell, 1998).

23. Shaw, *Theurgy and the Soul*.

24. Ibid., 50; Iamblichus, *De mysteriis Aegiptiorum* 3:142, 5–10.

25. For a contemporary reiteration of Iamblichus's line of thought in rela-

tion to both Platonism and Christian liturgical theory, see Catherine Pickstock, *After Writing: The Liturgical Consummation of Philosophy*.

26. O'Regan, *Gnostic Return in Modernity*.

27. With her *Face of the Deep: A Theology of Becoming*, Katherine Keller makes an affirmative and deeply Deleuzian gesture, drawing on biblical resources that support a feminist process theology. Her feminized or "invaginated" trinity explicitly embraces the logic of folds Deleuze also derived from Cusa and Bruno. She writes, "Chaos, as Tehom, the heterogeneous depth of divinity and of world, place of places, forms the first member of a tehomic trinity. Borrowing from Cusa and Bruno, Deleuze cannot resist its formula: 'the trinity *complicatio-explicatio-implicatio*.' This is a trinity of folds, *plis*, indicating a relationality of interweaving rather than cutting edges. *Complicatio*, 'folding together,' in Cusa folding of the world in God, signifies, 'the chaos which contains all.'" *The Face of the Deep* (London: Routledge, 2003), 231.

28. Cusa, *On Learned Ignorance*, 1:20.61.

29. Christology in this sense justifies (more than it is justified) by so-called Renaissance humanism, since the humanism of the homo-creator topos was clearly anchored in the paradigmatic status of the miraculous God-Man, Jesus Christ. In Cusa's language, the centrality of Christ is due to the fact that only a being that has achieved the maximum of the species can be said to be the maximum. Only a member of the human is potentially all beings, since humanity is alone at the center of the orders of nature. Thus, only a member of the human species can be the maximum species of all genera, and only a perfect human can be the maximum member of that species. For Cusa, incarnation has to do not so much with restoring a merit to humanity that it has lost through sin, but with the completion of creation. That is to say, for Cusa, as in the Renaissance generally (and here lies its affirmation of humanity more than in any nascent secularism), incarnation is not seen so much in terms of divine intervention as it is an expression of the original creative intent, an intent to deify humanity and thus complete the creation.

30. Cusa, *On Learned Ignorance*, 2.3.107.

31. Ibid., 1:13–17.

32. Ibid., 2:3.

33. Eugene Thacker astutely points out that Deleuze's naturalism is in an equivocal relation with pantheism, since Deleuze insists that the virtual "structure" of life is irreducible to the diversity of actual biological forms. Some kind of "God" perdures in Deleuze's own system, as a principle of expression that is irreducible to what is expressed, and whose ultimate nature is not comprehensible in terms of its manifestations. This "unthinkable" God may be, as Thacker suggests, a kind of "non-life" or *nihil* that would be Deleuze's atheological ver-

sion of Eriugena's and Cusa's inscrutable God. See Thacker, *AfterLife* (Chicago: University of Chicago Press, 2010), 222–28.

34. Ibid., 2.11.12.
35. Blumenberg, *The Legitimacy of the Modern Age*, 524.
36. Cusa, *On Learned Ignorance*, II.2.103.
37. Ibid.
38. Ibid., II.2.104.
39. Blumenberg, *The Legitimacy of the Modern Age*, 561.
40. Nicholas of Cusa, *On Learned Ignorance*, II.2.100–101.
41. *Corpus Hermeticum*, book 10, "Hermes to Tat."
42. See Stephen Greenblatt, *Renaissance Self-Fashioning: From More to Shakespeare* (Chicago: University of Chicago Press, 1980).
43. Farmer, *Syncretism in the West*, 497.
44. On this issue, many of Deleuze's most severe and insightful critics, particularly Alain Badiou and Jacques Rancière, have faulted Deleuze for trading on a kind of "incarnationalism" of the virtual, in which Deleuze presupposes the necessity of a betrayal of the intensive in extension such that his heroes are all doomed to madness, delirium, or isolation. For Badiou this macabre incarnationalism is due to Deleuze's inability to maintain his own "ascetic voluntarism" in refusing any model or mediating category, emblem, or type, in the relation between the univocity of virtual being as difference and the equivocity of actual being as sameness. In what follows I will argue for the centrality of a series of mediating types in Deleuze's thought, despite Deleuze's own reticence on this point. See Jacques Rancière, "Deleuze, Bartleby, and the Literary Formula," in *The Flesh of Words: The Politics of Writing*, translated by Charlotte Mandell (Stanford: Stanford University Press, 2004), 146–64. See also Badiou, *Deleuze*, 32–33.
45. Garth Fowden, *The Egyptian Hermes: A Historical Approach to the Late Pagan Mind* (Cambridge: Cambridge University Press, 1986).
46. Ficino's Catholicism was colored by syncretistic and humanist aspirations, and his most famous student, Pico della Mirandola, would claim that in addition to his miracles, nothing proved the divinity of Christ as much as Kabbalah—the Jewish mystical system must point, as must all true wisdom, to the centrality and divinity of Jesus. Pico's Latin phrase, from the text of the 900 *conclusiones*, or points of doctrine he planned to defend at Rome before the assembled doctors of the world's theologies (maybe the greatest event in Western intellectual history that never took place), is "nulla est scientia, que nos magis certificet de diuniatate Christi, quam Magia & Cabala." Farmer, *Syncretism in the West*, 497.
47. Copenhaver, *Hermetica*, xlviii.
48. While it is true, as Copenhaver and others have pointed out, that Cusa,

Ficino, Pico, and Bruno did not derive the new anthropology of homo creator and homo magus directly from hermetic texts, the hermetic notion that cosmological and metaphysical knowledge culminate in ecstatic apprehension and co-creative activity was a fundamental inspiration to Renaissance thought. Bruno, in an attempt to advocate for naturalism in the guise of hermeticism, even goes so far as to claim that Egypt's is the only true religion. Bruno, *The Expulsion of the Triumphant Beast*, 235–42. But for much of the modern era, the significance of hermeticism was neglected, due in part to Enlightenment dismissals of esoteric approaches to nature as superstitious irrationalism. A lack of serious interest in hermeticism was also part of a narrative (still persistent) that Renaissance magic was simply an adolescent precursor to mature scientific thought. But groundbreaking work of Frances Yates and D. P. Walker showed that, far from being merely a syncretistic attempt to integrate rational philosophy and Egyptian religion, Renaissance hermeticism was a serious continuation of Neoplatonic speculation, one that has to be evaluated on its own terms.

49. *Asclepius* 1:6.

50. Gary Tomlinson has shown how the music of Monteverdi was a practical (if unconscious) application of Ficino's principles of effective musical song, and that one can trace, from a kind of Foucauldian archeological perspective, the shift from a magical to a disenchanted world within the evolution of Monteverdi's madrigals. See Gary Tomlinson, *Music in Renaissance Magic: Toward a Historiography of Others* (Chicago: University of Chicago Press, 1993).

51. The most famous instance of this kind of thinking lies in Aquinas' so-called "Five Ways" of proving the existence of God based on the observation of nature, in *Summa Theologiae* Ia, q. 2, a. 3.

52. William B. Ashworth, "Natural History and the Emblematic World View," in *Reappraisals of the Scientific Revolution*, edited by David S. Lindberg and Robert S. Westman (Cambridge: Cambridge University Press, 1990), 303–32.

53. Foucault articulated the difference between the emergent classical episteme and that of the Renaissance in terms of a contrast between a world entirely written, and a world of knowledge constituted by a gap between the tables on which knowledge is represented, and represented knowledge itself. This rift, between representation and object, or concept and referent, was unknown to the Renaissance.

54. Foucault, *The Order of Things*, 39.

55. Ibid., 40.

56. Ibid., 41.

57. Ibid., 33.

58. For a fuller account, see Gershom Scholem, *Kabbalah* (New York: Meridian, 1974), 122–27.

59. Farmer, *Syncretism in the West*. Pico della Mirandola was the Florentine

intellectual whom Walter Pater's *The Renaissance: Studies in Art and Poetry* eulogized as a kind of proto-romantic genius.

60. Pico della Mirandola, "Theses According to His Own Opinion: Magical Conclusions," 9.9. Farmer, *Syncretism in the West*, 497.

61. Pico della Mirandola, *On the Dignity of Man and Other Works*, 4–5.

62. See Augustine, *On Free Choice of the Will*, translated by Thomas Williams (Indianapolis: Hackett, 1993).

63. Pico della Mirandola, *On the Dignity of Man and Other Works*, 28.

64. Ibid., 26–29.

65. Pico della Mirandola, *Heptaplus*, translated by Douglas Carmichael (Indianapolis: Hackett, 1998).

66. See "The Hymn of Man," in *A Sourcebook in Asian Philosophy*, edited by John M. Koller and Patricia Joyce Koller (Upper Saddle River, N.J.: Prentice Hall, 1991), 7–8.

67. Blumenberg, *The Legitimacy of the Modern Age*, 524–25.

68. Sheila Rabin, "Pico on Magic and Astrology," in *Pico della Mirandola: New Essays*, edited by M. V. Dougherty (Cambridge: Cambridge University Press, 2008), 152–78.

69. Ficino took a more reserved, aristocratic interest in *magia*, and Ficino had little interest in real operations of transformation, divination, or sorcery. In a sense, the more academic Ficino attempted to tame the magic of the hermetic *Asclepius* in his *Pymander* by making magical talismans correspond to the celestial hierarchies of the Pseudo-Dionysus. Ficino approved only of an Orphic magic in which the operator ascends through ranks of divine names or angelic hierarchies, for the express purpose of worshipping the Triune God.

70. Yates, *Giordano Bruno and the Hermetic Tradition*, 123.

71. Farmer, *Syncretism in the West*.

72. There is controversy in Bruno scholarship over the exact relation between his more speculative, hermetic, and metaphysical claims, and the natural philosophy such claims were thought to underwrite. Images, signs, and ideas are always approximations for Bruno. The critical question in Bruno's scholarship is whether the veracity of these approximations are anchored in hermetic or occult truths about the cosmos, as Yates argued, or whether they are grounded in a notion of experimental science that has not yet found its vocabulary, as Hilary Gatti contends in *Giordano Bruno and Renaissance Science*. Gatti contends that Bruno is *not* a hermeticist but a neo-Pythagorean who uses hermetic imagery in lieu of a sufficiently complex form of modeling to account for complexity in the natural world.

73. The natural theology that Bruno proposes is a moral vision opposed to the voluntaristic basis of "justification" that permeates both the late Middle Ages and the Reformation.

74. Bruno, *The Expulsion of the Triumphant Beast*, 255.

75. Ibid.

76. Ibid., 256.

77. Ibid., 255.

78. Ibid., 268–69.

79. Bruno calls himself *magis laboratae theologiae doctor* in a preface to some editions of his *Ars reminiscendi* (London, 1583), the text that contains the *Explicatio triginta sigillorum* [The interpretation of the thirty seals] and *Sigillus sigillorum* [The seal of seals]. The preface is called *Ad excellentissimum oxoniensis academiae procancellarium, clarrisimos doctores atque celeberrimos magistros* [To the excellent vice-chancellor of Oxford University, its most illustrious doctors and renowned teachers].

80. This kind of heresy resonates deeply with twentieth century heretics like Bataille, whose *Theory of Religion* claimed that the essence of all religion is a search for a lost intimacy. For Bataille, sacrificial religion attempts to do the impossible: to restore us to our animality by symbolically returning the animals or harvests that have become mere "things" to the immanence of the world in which they exist "like water in water." Bataille proposed that even the excessive expenditures of speculative capitalism and the brutalities of modern warfare are the continuation of this sacrificial desire by other means. For Bataille, the violent extremes of modern capitalism represent not so much the failure of Enlightenment liberalism to militate against capital's excess, but a particular expression of a more general failure of all forms of humanism to comprehend humanity's impossible desire for intimacy with its own unimaginable animality. As would Deleuze, Bataille attempts to continue the Nietzschean project of thinking without the human condition, beyond all humanism, without the presupposition of a self transcendent to its animality. Because the mania for sacrifice persists beyond every attempt to balance and order the self as a stable and enduring whole, the real problem of ethics for Bataille is not how to distinguish the human from the beast, but how to evaluate and creatively repeat the lure that our animality maintains. Georges Bataille, *Theory of Religion*, translated by Robert Hurley (New York: Zone Books, 1992), 28.

81. Giorgio Agamben, *The Open: Man and Animal*, translated by Kevin Attell (Stanford: Stanford University Press, 2004), 2.

82. Deleuze and Guattari, *A Thousand Plateaus*, 239–52.

83. Artaud, "To Have Done with the Judgment of God," in *Antonin Artaud*, 571.

84. See in this regard the important essays collected in *After the Postsecular and the Postmodern*, edited by Anthony Paul Smith and Daniel Whistler (Newcastle upon Tyne: Cambridge Scholars, 2010).

85. Bruno, *Cause, Principle, and Unity*, 61.

86. In one passage among many that seem to be an elaboration of a vision Bruno only partially realized, Deleuze writes that "qualities and extensities, forms and matters, species and parts are not primary; they are imprisoned in individuals as though in a crystal. Moreover, the entire world may be read, as though in a crystal ball, in the moving depths of individuating differences or differences in intensity" (*DR*, 247).

87. Bruno, *Cause, Principle, and Unity*, 61.

88. Deleuze writes, "Individuation emerges like the act of solving a problem, or—what amounts to the same thing—like the actualization of a potential and the establishing of communication between disparates. The act of individuation consists not in suppressing the problem, but in integrating the elements of the disparateness into a state of coupling which ensures its internal resonance. The individual thus finds itself attached to a pre-individual half which is not the impersonal within it so much as the reservoir of its singularities. In all these respects, we believe that individuation is essentially intensive, and that the pre-individual field is a virtual-ideal field, made up of differential relations" (*DR*, 246).

89. Aristotle, *Metaphysics* 7:1–4, 1028a10–30b13.

90. Aristotle, *Categories* 2a27–2b6.

91. Bruno, *Cause, Principle, and Unity*, 55.

92. Catana, *The Concept of Contraction in Giordano Bruno's Philosophy*, 35.

93. See Deleuze's conception, especially *Bergsonism* and *Cinema II: The Time-Image*.

94. Bruno, *Cause, Principle, and Unity*, 61; Bruno, *Expulsion of the Triumphant Beast*, introductory epistle.

95. Recently Graham Harman has argued that Bruno's refusal to attribute the title "substantial" to individuals that are perishable is part of a history of error in philosophy that includes figures such as Descartes, Spinoza, and Leibniz. Bruno's tendency to reduce the role of form to a temporary vicissitude of matter, Harman argues, means that only one form, that of the world soul, matters at all, and thus there is no place in Bruno's theory for a robust account of individual objects. Materialism reduces to monism. From this perspective, Deleuze arguably makes the same (putative) error with his location of essence on the side of the virtual. See Harman, "On the Undermining of Objects: Grant, Bruno, and Radical Philosophy" in *The Speculative Turn: Continental Materialism and Realism* (Melbourne: re:press, 2011), p. 33.

96. Bruno, *Cause, Principle, and* Unity, ii, 147.

97. Graham Harman, "On the Undermining of Objects: Grant, Bruno, and Radical Philosophy" in *The Speculative Turn: Continental Materialism and Realism* (Melbourne: Re:press, 2011).

98. Bruno, *The Heroic Frenzies*, 2:1, 193.

99. This activation of divine potencies in matter has its paradigm in theurgy, the ritual invocation of the gods praised by Iamblichus as the culmination of Platonic philosophy. A kind of theurgy occurs in the *Furori* through the construction of love sonnets in praise of the All. Iamblichus had anticipated heroic frenzy as an authentic Neoplatonic path when he justified the apparently random or irrational voicing of sounds and syllables in pagan rituals as a proper and even exclusively authentic means of invoking the gods. As Gregory Shaw puts it, for Iamblichus and the tradition he inspired, "following the rule that first principles contained and yet remained hidden in their pluralities, the theurgist reached the primordial silence of the One only by embracing the plurality of sounds. Just as the monad was present in multiplicity monadically, preexisting silence was present in the seven sounds silently, and the theurgist entered this silence by chanting/containing the sounds that proceed from it." Bruno's construction of images, signs, and ideas can be thought of as a kind of aesthetic theurgy. Despite the fact that Iamblichus considered the fashioning of images to be a debased theurgy, it is perhaps the acceptance of the infinity of the cosmos that finally elevates the status of the image to a genuine cipher of reality, indeed "overturning" Platonic bans on imitation long before Deleuze.

100. Rita Sturlese, "Per un'interpretazione del *De umbris idearum* di Giordano Bruno," in *Annali della Scuola Normale Superiore di Pisa*, third series, vol. 22 (1992): 943–68.

101. Catana, *The Concept of Contraction in Giordano Bruno's Philosophy*, 86.

102. Bruno, *The Heroic Frenzies*, 2:2, 225.

103. Plotinus, *Enneads* 2:4–5.

104. Bruno, *Cause, Principle, and Unity*, 173.

105. Plotinus, *Enneads* 2:4.

106. Bruno, *Cause, Principle, and* Unity, iii.

107. Ibid., 173. The rest of the passage is worth regarding, as well: "The love by which we love, and the tendency by which all things desire, are intermediaries between good and evil, between the ugly and the beautiful (not themselves being ugly or beautiful). And so they are good and beautiful because of a sort of sharing and participation, for the bond of love has a nature which is both active and possible. And by this, things act, or are acted upon, or both, as they desire to be ordered, joined, united and completed, insofar as it is within the nature of each nothing to be occupied with order, joining, union, and completion. Without this bond there is nothing, just as without nature there is nothing. Because of this, therefore, love is not a sign of imperfection when it is considered in matter and in the chaos before things were produced."

108. Hallyn, *The Poetic Structure of the World*, 155.

109. Ibid., 160.

Notes to Chapter Three 243

110. Bruno, *On the Composition of Images, Signs and Ideas*.

111. Christopher I. Lehrich, *The Occult Mind: Magic in Theory and Practice* (Ithaca: Cornell University Press, 2007), 43.

112. Cornelius Agrippa, *De occulta philosophia*, 1:38, in Yates, *Giordano Bruno and the Hermetic Tradition*, 53.

113. Gatti, *Giordano Bruno and Renaissance Science*, 141.

114. Cornelius Agrippa, *De occulta philosophia*, 1:50, in Yates, *Giordano Bruno and the Hermetic Tradition*, 230–31.

115. Ordine, *Seuil de l'ombre*, 310–11.

116. This is why in the critical literature Bruno is sometimes thought of as a proto-Kantian, since it seems that certain fundamental images of nature (derived by Bruno from magical talismans or "seals" of nature) function as transcendental schemata. Like Kant's line drawn in thought, Bruno's magical images seem to somehow express, even in their very incompletion, the limits and conditions of reality itself. The difference between Kant and Bruno (echoing that between Kant and Deleuze) is that the "rules" for constructing images do not, for Bruno, answer to finite categories governing the conditions under which objects can be apprehended.

117. Ordine, *Le Seuil de l'ombre*, 309, and following.

118. "Inadequate" should not be thought of as "incomplete" or "finite," and should be translated into Deleuzian terms. Each figure embodies a distance proper to difference in itself, a bounded yet unlimited intensive quantity proper to each multiplicity of sense.

119. Robert Klein, "Form and Meaning," in *Form and Meaning: Essays on the Renaissance and Modern Art*, translated by Madeleine Jay and Leon Wieseltier (New York: Viking, 1979), 60.

120. This text has striking parallels to Foucault's ontology of power in *The History of Sexuality, Volume 1: An Introduction*, translated by Robert Hurley (New York: Vintage, 1990), 94–95.

121. Klein, "Form and Meaning," 60.

122. Marsilio Ficino, *Commentary on Plato's Symposium on Love*, oratio 6, cap. 10.

123. Giordano Bruno, "A General Account of Bonding," in *Cause, Principle, and Unity*, 165.

124. *Asclepius* 7:1.

3. Deleuze and the Esoteric Sign

1. In *Immanence and the Vertigo of Philosophy from Kant to Deleuze*, Christian Kerslake has suggested that these options represent a kind of unresolved

tension in Deleuze's thought about immanence, an oscillation between immanence as a metaphilosophical axiom and immanence as *une vie*. One pole of immanence tends to make it seem something quite abstract, the other pole renders it extremely concrete. Kerslake suggests, provocatively, that there might be some kind of "practical" resolution to this tension, a kind of lived or "concrete" synthesis that would reconcile the metacritical and vitalist poles of immanence in a set of transcendental practices that would express, modify, and ramify intensive modes of personal and cosmic becoming. Such practices would be identified directly with modes of thought. Much of what follows in this book might be read as an attempt to elaborate Kerslake's suggestion to the furthest possible extreme. To read philosophy as spiritual ordeal is to attempt to discover the lineaments of a practical philosophy of immanence.

2. For a much fuller treatment of the problem of signification in Spinoza, see Rocco Gangle, "Spinoza in a Postmodern Context: Reading the Ethics with Peirce, Levinas and Deleuze" (Ph.D. diss., University of Virginia, 2006).

3. For Spinoza, there are three types of signs: indicative signs that allow us to infer something from the state of our bodies or the bodies of others; imperative signs that convey commands and allow us to "grasp laws as moral laws" (to "see" that laws are good for us); and finally revelatory (or prophetic) signs that, as Deleuze puts it, "lead us to obey them and which at the very most disclose to us certain '*propria*' of God" (*E*, 181). Each of these modes of signification, according to Deleuze, has a flaw that inhibits our apprehension of the univocity of being (and thus of the expression of immanent causes). Indicative signs appear in the midst of a "confused state of involvement": "hunger" could mean any number of things, from dehydration to nervousness, and so as a sign it does nothing to clarify the relation of my body to itself or to the world, and so "hunger" is "powerless to explain itself or its cause." Likewise, imperative signs are not expressive because of their "deontic" nature: in the form of commandments, the laws of nature do not seem to express the truth of being but appear as heteronomous, as impositions from outside. Finally, revelation or prophecy is obscure because it is a "cultivation of the inexpressible, a confused and relative knowledge through which we lend God determinations analogous to our own (Understanding, Will), only to rescue God's superiority through his eminence to all genera (the supereminent One, etc.)" (*E*, 182). By this Deleuze means, I think, that the content of revelatory signs (i.e., the hands or the anger of God) are taken to be only analogous to what they represent or indicate, as if all these signs accomplish is to gather or situate the inexpressible in an icon without specifying precisely how or why this icon "measures" what it presents.

4. For a fuller treatment of Malfatti's biography and writings, as well as further analysis of the possible influence of mathesis on Deleuze's thought, see "The Somnambulist and the Hermaphrodite: Deleuze and Johann de Monte-

reggio and Occultism," Christian Kerslake, www.culturemachine.net, accessed July 29, 2010.

5. See Mackay, ed., *Collapse III*, "Unknown Deleuze" (Falmouth: Urbanomic, 2008).

6. François Dosse, *Gilles Deleuze et Felix Guattari: Biographie Croisée* (Paris: La Découverte), 114–16.

7. Allison Coudert, *Leibniz and the Kabbalah* (Dordrecth: Klewer, 1995).

8. Kerslake, *Immanence and the Vertigo of Philosophy*, 262.

9. While the present work will deal only in passing with the mathematical aspect of Deleuze's esotericism, in *Immanence and the Vertigo of Philosophy*, Kerslake has painstakingly reconstructed the currents in pre-Kantian rationalism that make a post-Kantian version of mathesis plausible for Deleuze.

10. Deleuze's thoughts here anticipate in outline the intensive character of space he will more fully articulate in *Difference and Repetition*, where he writes that "a dynamic space must be defined from the point of view of an observer tied to that space, not from an external position. There are internal differences which dramatize an Idea before representing an object. Difference here is internal to an Idea, even though it be external to the concept which represents an object" (*DR*, 26).

11. Reproductions of Malfatti's Decade can be found in Mackay, ed., *Collapse III*, "Unknown Deleuze," 156–75.

12. Ideas are problematic and inhere not in concepts but in a series of simulacra: arresting or uncanny signs (*DR*, 181). The idea of swimming, for instance, is discovered not through the deciphering of signs, but through an experimental relation between a body and a wave. What Deleuze is seeking to theorize with the simulacra is how otherwise imperceptible and pure relations of force and movement can make an appearance.

13. As Antoine Faivre puts it, in a characterization that applies to the whole of the hermetic tradition, including the medicinal and symbolic mathesis of Malfatti, "Behind the complexity of the real, the theosopher seeks the hidden meanings in the ciphers and hieroglyphics of Nature . . . he tries to seek the becoming of the divine world . . . to understand the world at the same time and to possess thereby the intimate vision of the principle of the reality of the universe and its becoming." Antoine Faivre, *Access to Western Esotericism* (Binghamton: suny Press, 1994), 28.

14. In *Difference and Repetition* Deleuze will distinguish "nominal" concepts that have finite comprehension, from "natural" concepts that have an indefinite comprehension (*DR*, 13). Concepts with indefinite comprehension include, for Deleuze, the concept of space, which is defined by the fact that it "subsumes perfectly identical objects" (*DR*, 13). The concept of space remains indefinite or unlimited because it can only be fully mapped by tracing or indexing the

number and kind of objects it subsumes—the nature of space is discovered in the "intensive" differences in space that are revealed through the "differential" relations it expresses between objects.

15. As Kerslake explains, for Malfatti, "The purpose of *mathesis* was to articulate bodily forces numerically, identifying their points of threshold and transformation, and relating them back to macrocosmic patterns in the evolving universe. What Malfatti has to say about Indian mysticism is rooted in ideas from the Tantric tradition of Indian mysticism, the great sexo-cosmic system which took hold of Medieval India for several centuries before undergoing convulsion and dissolution at around the time of the flowering of the European Renaissance. Malfatti puts Schelling's emphasis on *Erzeugung* [procreation] right at the centre of his system, taking the concept at both sexual and metaphysical levels, attempting to find the pathways between the two. He continually focuses on the sexual and ecstatic aspects of Indian mysticism, laying out a vast sexualised ontology, culminating (as in Baader's system) in the 'hermaphroditic' consciousness of the human sexual act. In *Anarchy and Hierarchy* it is as if Schelling's final theosophy comes to completion in a hallucinatory Tantrism, in which the living body of God, in its most complete self-development, itself appears in hermaphroditic form in human sexuality, where the coming-to-divine-consciousness becomes identical to the psychosexual attainment, along Tantric lines, of spiritual 'bisexuality.' This 'system,' uncovered by Malfatti, is said to form the basis for all subsequent Eastern and Western esoteric thought, and now furnishes us with the long-lost key to the ultimate system of medicine" (Christian Kerslake, "The Somnambulist and the Hermaphrodite: Deleuze and Johann de Monteregio and Occultism").

16. The "extension" of natality, Deleuze notices, is sexuality. Sexuality as a resonance of discrete individuals producing other individuals (spiritual or physical offspring) is perhaps the paradigm of esoteric knowledge (*co-naissance*) of the All, where the integral unity of each one is discovered not within herself, but in relation to another. As Kerslake has explained, this is why Malfatti takes a special interest in the hermaphrodite as symbolic of the cosmic whole.

17. The vision of the divine here, however, is not of a pure relationality. Ecstatic union is not a dissolution of difference. The poles of an esoteric conjunction of opposites, a syzygy such as that of partners in ecstatic embrace, are nodes that remain distinct, despite the fact that the energetic work indeed seeks to unite the two into one hermaphroditic whole. Not only at the actual level, but even at the virtual level, the "poles" remain disjunct, paradoxically distinguished by the relation that brings them together. That is to say, differences become resonant because they coalesce as a singular assemblage of virtual disjunction (disjunct because a unity open to multiple other connections)

within an actual conjunction (the intensification event of a particular form of communion). Thanks to Rocco Gangle for helping to clarify this point in conversation.

18. In the lecture course *What Is Grounding?*, Deleuze expounds existentialist, and specifically Heideggerian themes of finitude: the singularity of destiny as indicated by the nonsubstitutable character of human nature, and the lack of common measure of one existence with another in the light of that singularity. But in both the preface to Malfatti and that early lecture course (1955–56), Deleuze links the self-differentiation of life to a profound complicity among subjects (one that Heidegger only briefly considers, at the end of *Being and Time*, in terms of shared historical destiny). However, the theme of destiny links the young Deleuze and Heidegger.

19. Erik Davis has explored the idea that profound solidarity can be discovered not in compromise but in something like the "apart playing" of polyrhythm. Here the collective groove is established partly by the ability of players to time their beats to an inner sense of the cadence that is not heard (or counted), and is in fact lost if one attempts to clearly identify one's place in the beats of others. In other words, in polyrhythmic music it is the greatest danger to find a representation of the whole or to tune oneself as a part within a whole that is heard. In polyrhythm, the whole, and the relation of the individual player to the whole, is at once virtual, real, and distributed, as well as "unrepresented." "Roots and Wires: Polyrhythmic Cyberspace and the Black Electronic," Erik Davis, www.techgnosis.com, accessed September 9, 2010.

20. In Lawrence's reading of the Apocalypse of St. John, he notices (as many readers have) that there seem to be two voices, and two responses to the crises of the late Roman Empire. One voice is enraged and demanding destruction. Another is ecstatic and announcing transformation, heaven's descent to earth. The enraged voice of *ressentiment* produces a discourse (the discourse that dominates the text) meant to "disconnect us from the world and from ourselves." The angry, nihilistic voice in the Apocalypse gives us the right to give up on our flows, to give up on life, in view of the finality of the last judgment. Yet there is another tone, still apocalyptic. Deleuze says there is an "apocalyptic" tone to *Difference and Repetition*. Is this the other voice in the Apocalypse of St. John? There is an eschatology that is proper to immanent thought, a consuming fire. D. H. Lawrence, *Apocalypse* (New York: Penguin, 1996).

21. Guattari says that there is a renewed animism entailed by his ethical-aesthetic paradigm. *Chaosmosis: An Ethico-Aesthetic Paradigm*, translated by Paul Bains and Julian Pefanis (Bloomington: Indiana University Press, 1995), 77.

22. D. H. Lawrence, *The Plumed Serpent* (New York: Vintage, 1992).

23. D. H. Lawrence, *Apocalypse* (New York: Penguin, 1996).

24. Ibid., 31.
25. Ibid., 27.
26. Ibid.
27. Ibid., 29.
28. Christian Kerslake, "The Somnambulist and the Hermaphrodite: Deleuze and Johann de Montereggio and Occultism."
29. For Pico, the essential human prerogative is to ascend, through moral discipline and mystical contemplation, to the superangelic realms. This teleological orientation towards transcendence and an eminent source foreign to Deleuze's perspective. Be that as it may, Pico's ontology represents a serious break with tradition.
30. In *Anti-Oedipus*, when Deleuze and Guattari take interest in ritual and symbolic practices as alternatives to the interpretive strategies of traditional psychoanalysis, they will repeatedly emphasize the functional and "machinic" role that symbols play in social activity, especially in ritual acts of healing, such as those found among the Ndembu as studied by Victor Turner (*AO*, 166–92).
31. It is through elaborating a "physics" of the symbol that Deleuze heads off typical reservations about the universal or "absolute" applicability of symbols. Are not symbols culturally relative phenomena, and thus only locally effective? Deleuze claims, on the contrary, that it is precisely the singularity of the symbol that gives it an absolute status as a crystalline formation, rather than a mode of opinion formation or ideology.
32. Henry Corbin, *Alone with the Alone* (Princeton: Princeton University Press, 1969), 179.
33. Novalis, *Notes for a Romantic Encyclopedia*, translated by David Wood (Albany: suny Press, 2007). Deleuze was searching to articulate the crystalline power of symbols as early as the *What Is Grounding?* lectures. On this score, Deleuze follows up on the work of Novalis, who had sought a philosophy, and not merely a psychology, of the imagination. In *What Is Grounding?*, Deleuze approvingly cites Novalis, who had written, "It is by the same movement that nature produces the grasses and flowers that I imagine them . . . the seashell conch has its own roots in the imagination, insofar as the movement through which it is produced in the imagination appeals to an identical spiral" (*WG*, 49–50). For Novalis, Deleuze asserts, "the images the poet has are just products of nature."

4. The Overturning of Platonism

1. There are multiple references to Castaneda in *A Thousand Plateaus*, and Deleuze and Guattari explicitly invoke the figure of the sorcerer as a model for

thought not only in that text but also in *The Logic of Sense*, where the thinker is described as a figure that would combine the traits of a Zen master with the playfulness and plasticity of Carroll's Alice (*LS*, 178).

2. See for example Youru Wang, *Linguistic Strategies in Daoist Zhuangzi and Chan Buddhism* (London: Taylor and Francis, 2007).

3. Aristotle criticized Plato for precisely this point: Plato's ideas do not enable the clear division of genus into species. In the *Sophist*, for instance, Socrates divides the arts into productive and acquisitive arts, and places fishing among the arts of acquisition. For Aristotle, this conceptual division should simply be the inverse of a generalization, the separation into species of what is collected in a genus. But Deleuze argues that Platonic division has no intention, or only an ironic intention, of establishing genus and species.

But no "reason" is given for this particular division between acquisition and production. No single concept both unites and clearly divides production and acquisition. In order for them to count as species of a genus, what makes acquisition an art and what makes production an art would have to be the same thing, just as what makes a brick house and a plaster house species of the genus house would "mediate" or make clear the difference between the species. But acquisition and production are not arts in the same sense. But "being an art" is not present in production and acquisition in the same way. Nor is "fishing" placed on the side of acquisitive arts because it is logically a member of that species.

4. Aristotle, *Prior Analytics* 1:31; *Posterior Analytics* 2:5, 13.

5. Plato, *Statesman* 303d–e.

6. Duchamps's readymades are good examples of simulacra, since, for example, his urinal presented in a gallery is neither a urinal (it cannot be used for micturition) nor a representation of a urinal (it *is* a urinal). As Arthur Danto would put it, the readymade is a real thing presented as a work of art. Readymades pose a particularly difficult problem for a Platonist, because these objects present neither a truth (a true resemblance or copy of some essential form) nor a falsity (a bad, incorrect, or incomplete resemblance to a model or ideal). Simulacra have the power to throw an entire regime of judgment and truth into suspense in favor of a multiplicity of possible sense, provoking thought, interpretation, and suggesting hitherto unexplored expanses of reality. Arthur Danto, "The Artworld," *Journal of Philosophy* 61, no. 19 (1964): 571–84.

7. For the later Plato, there is a distinct idea for each thing, even for mud or hair. But ideas differ from one another, according to the *Sophist*, not due to "material" contingency, but as an effect of the idea of the Other. The difference the form of the Other makes is, to say the least, occult, and perhaps even incoherent, exactly as Aristotle argued it was.

8. In Plato there is a kind of nonbeing or questionable being ("?-being," as Deleuze writes it in *Difference and Repetition*) which is a positively problematic determination (*DR*, 63). Plato confronts this problem when he confronts the nature of nonbeing in the *Sophist*. If the sophists speak falsity, they must speak of what is not, or of "nonbeing." But to speak of nonbeing is to speak of nothing. Yet we must admit the sophists speak not of nothing but of something which is not true. How can this be accounted for? Plato attempts to comprehend the sense of not-being on the basis of his theory of forms (*Sophist* 257b–259b). The supreme forms or great kinds—being, activity, inactivity, sameness, and difference—all "share" in both being and not-being, because they all absolutely are, yet are not each other. Activity "is," yet it is not being (or inactivity, or sameness). A paradoxical way to comprehend this relation, which Plato ultimately rejects, is to say that activity partakes of being by also partaking of not-being. Plato rejects this proposal because the "not-being" activity partakes of could not be a real contrast with being (if it were, such not-being would negate the being activity shares). According to Plato, *me on* (not-being) can only be difference (the form of the Other). Difference is the kind by which activity partakes of being but also prevents activity from being the same as being. Strictly speaking, for Plato there is no nonbeing, but only difference, and true discourse is the elucidation of true interrelations among the forms.

This position (that there is no nonbeing, only difference) resolves the sophism according to which to say what is false is to speak of what is not. According to the sophists, it is impossible to speak falsely, and thus there is neither truth nor falsity, and thus no truth. According to Plato, to speak falsely is to speak other than the truth, to speak differently from what is, and this amounts to having incorrectly divided or collected the forms (or the ultimate sense of the existent). Plato here reveals his Parmenidean commitment to the notion that there is no idea of nonbeing: we cannot think nonbeing, since, according to Parmenides, to think and to be are the same. Given this view, Plato works to suppress the possibility that the form of the Other is in fact nonbeing. One cannot speak falsely if one cannot say what is not, but one can speak falsely if one speaks what is other. There can be nothing inactive in activity itself, otherwise, as Plato says, discourse will fail—we will never be able to truly speak of anything (*Sophist* 259e).

9. For Deleuze, difference understood as differential force of individuation does not exist apart from that very play of appearances, but forms its virtual halo, much as every color is implicated or "perplicated" in white light even though light is always only manifest as a single color.

10. Plato, *Republic* 510.

11. Appearances (in the Platonic sense) on this view are no longer simple sensorial repetitions. Rather, identity is a surface consistency produced by inter-

connected series of simulacra: series of disjunctive inclusions. For instance, a body, for Deleuze, is a series of contractions—genetic, habitual, and psychic—none of which are reducible to the others, but whose networks temporarily converge to form a surface.

12. Nicholas of Cusa, *Of Learned Ignorance*, 2:6.

13. Kierkegaard showed that the intricacies of faith were too subtle for the generalities of the moral law, and that the leap of faith was a leap into the absurd. Only *if* Abraham does not know what the results of his willingness to sacrifice Isaac will be, and only *if* this action seems to transgress every known rule coordinating faithfulness to human flourishing will his action count as a genuine repetition of faith. Thus Kierkegaard called for a "theological suspension of the ethical" in the name of the singular demands of faith.

Likewise, Nietzsche's "geological" reduction of morality to will-to-power demonstrates that moral law is an invasion from below. Morality does not descend from the starry heavens, but emerges from the varieties of will in human nature, from a secret and unfathomable "interior of the earth" (*DR*, 6). The variety of these interiors, these lines of force, manifest as the singular perverse ends of wills-to-power.

14. The contrast here is with Hegelianism. If the *Phenomenology* is a reflection "on" the world's forces (history as the ruse of reason), it is not yet, for Deleuze, a repetition *of* the world, or of the infinitesimally small, subrepresentational ideas that are truly at work in the world. If what truly moves Spirit are secret, subterranean pressures that cannot be represented, but only repeated, then Hegel's "mediation," which occurs only through "large" contradictions (instead of small differences), is not truly that which "forces" thought. The *Phenomenology* remains an afterthought. For the forces of difference to come to mind, Deleuze argues, we had to await Kierkegaard and Nietzsche. They were the ones who introduced a truly radical theater of ideas into philosophy. "They do not reflect on theatre in the Hegelian manner," Deleuze writes in *Difference and Repetition*, "neither do they set up a philosophical theatre. They invent an incredible equivalent of the theatre in philosophy" (*DR*, 8).

In what does this theater consist? More even than being a theater "without representation," (although it is certainly that) it is a theater of immediate encounters between mind and the movements of material forces, like the theater of Antonin Artaud, which was meant to assault the sensibilities of his audience. Deleuze believed the theater of Kierkegaard and Nietzsche should be a model for how to create a theater not so much of but *in* philosophical texts. He writes, "It is a question of producing within the work a movement capable of affecting the mind outside of all representation; it is a substituting of direct signs for mediate representations; of inventing vibrations, rotations, whirlings, gravitations, dances, or leaps which directly touch the mind" (*DR*, 8).

The theater of Nietzsche and Kierkegaard introduce, through their disguises, pseudonyms, animals, masks, and dances, a response to and a re-creation of powerful signs of life, signs that force thought and that cannot be thought apart from repetition: disguise, displacement, diversion, divertissement. For Deleuze this is how we contact (if not communicate with) forces that go directly from *physis* to psyche, without mediation in concepts (*DR*, 8).

15. This is why Kant was right, Deleuze notes, to insist that we look in vain to the order of nature for that on which we might model the authentic repetition moral life seems to call for. Our sense that duty demands the enactment of the "same" moral will in every situation cannot be grounded in "natural" reactions to situations. Kant was right, Deleuze argues, to think that the moral law is noumenal, not grounded in particular desires to do good or in the contingent pleasure we might take in so doing. The moral, the good, demands something irreducible to virtuous habit or to disposition (*DR*, 4). The fulfillment of duty would, in fact, introduce something radically novel into each situation, since it imposes an idea upon a situation. The limitation of Kant's view, for Deleuze, is that because it so squarely rejects grounding morality in habit and disposition (character and desire) Kantian morality cannot conceive of the free exercise of duty as a form of repetition. The series of actions of the life of the Kantian man of duty consist in a vague generality. Even though the man of duty in each case legislates, deciding each time what is right to be done, he can only do this in situations that resemble one another or are connected through a law that would identify instances of duty as analogous to one another. Even though the instantiation of the moral law (and its categorical imperative) are supposed to be repetitions of a noumenal principle irreducible to phenomenal facts, the perfection of intention (the moral will) takes place as a subsumption of particulars to a general rule (such as the rule to always treat other rational beings as ends in themselves). Thus although the noumenal freedom expressed by Kantian pure practical reason seems to be a possible model for authentic repetition, Kant provides no model for thinking how the noumenal will iterates itself in the phenomenal without itself appearing as a general pattern (and in fact the model of duty is surreptitiously grounded in a particular empirical pattern). Thus, Deleuze argues, we cannot look to morality any more than to science for the rule of genuine repetition (*DR*, 5). Neither moral nor natural law captures the ipseity of repetition.

16. As most musicians are well aware, it takes a lifetime to master the playing of what appear to be very simple parts in traditional drum ensembles. Not only because of the difficulty of being able to maintain a part that is in dramatic rhythmic tension with other parts, but because the dance (and the presence of the spirits) depends essentially on a collective feel or rhythmic timbre that is irreducible, a singular performative effect.

17. See Nathan Widder's excellent explanation in "The Rights of Simulacra: Deleuze and the Univocity of Being."

18. Although, Deleuze admits, it may ultimately be possible to reconcile the univocity he wishes to attribute to being with a certain refined notion of analogy (see *DR*, 38).

19. Even Leibniz and Hegel, for Deleuze, succumbed to this temptation, since each attempted in his own way to restrict infinity to the contours of a representable whole. Both thinkers subordinate difference to representation by allowing a particular difference (the differential, in Leibniz' case, and the contradiction, in the case of Hegel) to stand in for difference in itself. These moves fail (although Deleuze will preserve something of Leibniz's intuitions), Deleuze thinks, because they fail to fully account for the complexity of microphysical and nonlocalizable aspects of individuation processes.

20. This is a paradox Deleuze confronts again and again in his work, posed as a question early in his career: "How can a subject transcending the given be constituted in the given?" (*ES*, 86).

21. This was arguably how Warhol perceived the advertised image, or how the French New Wave confronted the clichés of Hollywood. Warhol never rejects graphic design principles any more than Godard abandons the formulas of Hollywood. Warhol transforms them. (There does not seem to be much at stake, for Deleuze, in the contrast between modern and postmodern art.) For example, the achievement of Warhol, for Deleuze, was to extract singularities from habits of consumption (*DR*, 294). By repeating stereotyped images, Warhol's work forces the iconic image to bend toward intensive features visible only through the decentering (discoloration, repetition) of their pristine identities. Deleuze writes that an art like Warhol's "does not imitate, above all because it repeats; it repeats all the repetitions, by virtue of an internal power (an imitation is a copy, but art is simulation, it reverses copies into simulacra). Even the most mechanical, the most banal, the most habitual and the most stereotyped repetition finds a place in the work of art, it is always displaced in relation to other repetitions, and it is subject to the condition that a difference may be extracted from it for these other repetitions. For there is no other aesthetic problem than that of the insertion of art into everyday life. The more our daily life appears standardized, stereotyped, and subject to an accelerated reproduction of objects of consumption, the more art must be injected into it in order to extract from it that little difference which plays simultaneously between other levels of repetition, and even in order to make the two extremes resonate—namely the habitual series of consumption and the instinctual series of destruction and death . . . [art] aesthetically reproduces the illusions and mystifications which make up the real essence of this civilization" (*DR*, 293).

22. These works do not experiment merely with logical incompossibility, but

with real incompossibility: a smile without a cat is not only logically impossible, but really, empirically, incompossible. This world, the one we live, cannot contain a smile without one who smiles.

23. On Joyce's use of Bruno, see Gose, *The Transformation Process in Joyce's Ulysses*. See also Boldereef *Hermes to His Son Thoth*.

24. Manuel DeLanda makes this point clear in the glossary to his *Intensive Science and Virtual Philosophy*.

25. As Jacques Rancière has more recently described it, Plato's vendetta against the arts is rooted in the problem that artistic appearances confuse the proper distribution of what can and should be seen and said in common. According to Rancière, Plato was insistent about his delimitation of proper art to military songs and communal dances not because the Homeric tradition preached immorality (Plato professes profound, even erotic love for Homer), but because the public stage on which dramatic poetry was recited violated the "distribution of the sensible" that should hold in the ideal republic. Tragic festivals were Dionysian rituals involving feasts, sexual licentiousness, and the temporary anarchic abandonment of social roles. As Rancière puts it, theatrical and rhapsodic performance distorts "the distribution of the sensible," the proper arrangement of roles and emotions that should constitute the visible community. Jacques Rancière, *The Politics of Aesthetics*, translated by Gabriel Rockhill (London: Continuum, 2004), 17–19.

26. In his critique of dramatic poetry, these imperceptible forces are precisely the aspects of life Plato sought to keep at bay by censoring art that indulged the passions.

27. *Proust et les signes* first appeared in French in 1964, but was later expanded and republished. References are to the complete English edition translated by Richard Howard.

28. Interested primarily in Proustian *thought*, Deleuze makes very little reference to the texts themselves, and is not involved in literary criticism in any ordinary sense. For a work more closely attentive to Proust's textual apparatus (but inspired by Deleuze's approach), see Miguel de Beigstegui, *Jouissance de Proust* (Paris: Michalon, 2007).

29. See Mark Rölli, "Intensity Differentials and the Being of the Sensible," *Deleuze Studies* 3, no. 1 (2009) 26–53.

30. Marcel Proust, *À la recherche du temps perdu* (Bibliothèque de la Pléiade), 2:205.

31. Is this a subjective or an objective affair? In some sense it is both. It is as if those who are sensitive to the signs of a given world or territory or *patrie* come into existence with that world itself—it is as if the reality of a world were something paradoxically producing both an objectivity and subjectivity proper to it. The model here is the Leibnizian monad, but without any prearranged

harmony between monads guaranteed by God—only a resonance that yields "epiphanies" of forces beyond our ken. The "harmony" of perspectives is something external to every conceivable "whole," be it history, man, God, or *Geist*. It arises from a paradoxical element or "dark precursor" that belongs to no one series but *insists* in the resonance of any two discontinuous lines, or worlds, and is constantly displaced with relation to itself and constantly disguised in the series to which it gives rise.

32. Socrates, for Deleuze, is still fundamentally passive, lying in wait for the truth. For Socrates, truth is eternal, always already in place, even if absent, and it is up to the ascetic preparations of the vigilant mind to tune the soul to its subtle yet eternal music. That is why Socrates, for Deleuze, remains a reactive thinker, in Nietzsche's sense, even if he was the thinker, as Nietzsche admits, who took the reactionary stance to its highest possible level. Proust's superiority lies in the fact that he does not anticipate the strange encounters that provoke his work, but responds creatively to them. Socrates still imagines that his intelligence—and his *daimon*—somehow grasps the truth prior to experience, a truth that subsists prior to the encounter: "The Socratic demon, irony, consists in anticipating the encounters" (*PS*, 101). The point here is that when Socrates says "no" to an answer, this is because he has already organized the situation (the question) in an intellectual way—the responses to the "what is x" questions that Socrates asks himself and others are already rendered ironic by the impossibility of answering that specific question in that specific way. Deleuze's view of Socrates is a product of the scholarship of his time. Gregory Vlastos and others have argued that Socrates's irony may be more complex than Deleuze realizes: Socrates may know in advance that the views of others are incorrect, but he may not yet know if his own views are sound, healthy, etc., and may be truly "encountering" himself, if not others. See Vlastos, "Socratic Irony," in *Essays on the Philosophy of Socrates*, edited by Hugh H. Benson (New York: Oxford University Press), 66–85.

33. Heidegger had a way of criticizing the history of metaphysics that is similar to the approach used by Deleuze. For Heidegger the prejudices of modern scientism and those of Platonism are at one. For Deleuze also, because of the energy Plato exerts to eliminate not difference but certain kinds of difference or a certain image of difference from the field of thought. The sophist is auto-disqualified by being a dissembler, by willfully attempting to be what he or she is not. So also the false statesman. What the philosopher sees or knows is not so much the brilliance of the ideas per se but the differential lineage or heritage that can properly manifest itself—she or he knows which copies of the idea are idols and which are icons. The dialectic can only bring us to the point at which Socrates and the sophist appear identical in all respects except the one the philosopher can recognize.

Deleuze argues that Socrates is only partly endowed for signs. He only partly gives himself over to the obscure intensity of the sign. The logos is kept in readiness, and truth is protected under the aegis of recognizability. For Socrates, "the intelligence always comes after; it is good when it comes after; it is good only when it comes after" (*PS*, 101). For Deleuze, as for Nietzsche, the cannon of recognition poisons the intelligence. What is needed is a cannon of creativity, the kind of selection of intensities that artists are peculiarly capable of. Socrates is right to say, listen not to me but to something else, something that is not reducible to communication. His error is to say that we should listen to a tale of metaphysical homecoming, of immutable and immemorial recapitulation. If truth lies in those encounters that interrupt the functioning of recognition, in encounter with the different, Proust's recollection of lost time is a recollection without recognition. Proust is thus a Socrates who can rightly say, "I am Love more than the friend, I am the lover; I am art more than philosophy; I am constraint and violence, rather than goodwill" (*PS*, 101).

5. Becoming Cosmic

1. See Christian Kerslake's important work on Deleuze's fascination with Toynbee's conception of a universal history that works through an unfolding of civilizational time according to repetitions of key archetypal patterns. Christian Kerslake, "Becoming against History: Deleuze, Toynbee, and Vitalist Historiography," *Parrhesia* No. 4 2008, 17–48.

2. For an extensive use of the concept of plasticity, see Catherine Malabou, *What Should We Do With Our Brain?*, translated by Sebastian Rand (New York: Fordham, 2008).

3. Filmmakers like Alain Resnais, Welles, Godard, and Fellini enable us to pose a new question of "meaning," in the old existentialist sense. Existentialism asked us to seek in the affirmations of human volition what was lost in the rejection of divine benevolence, but for Deleuze (as for Foucault and Nietzsche) this only substituted for the lost God a man who limited life and expression as much as the old divine being. To think in terms of this "man" is still the attempt to discern or receive a meaning that is given apart from its production—whether this meaning is discerned beyond man's betrayal of the gods or beyond the gods apparent indifference to humanity makes no difference. In both cases we turn away from the real game, what Nietzsche called the "ideal game," the game of inventing sense played out by events that engender meaning below God and above man, on a surface of preindividual singularities and radically impersonal events.

4. Paradoxically this strength to create is not an active or even a voluntary strength. It is not so much a penetrating, initiating force, as it is a receptive,

even nurturing power to endure: a capacity that is initiated rather than initiating. Thus, following both Leibniz and Nietzsche, Deleuze defines force not as the power to act but the power to feel and to perceive (*WIP*, 130).

Strictly speaking, an artist's ability to undergo the ordeal of creation at the level of material intensity is a kind of masochism, in the highly precise way Deleuze creatively interpreted the writings of Leopold von Sacher-Masoch. For Deleuze, the essence of masochism is not simply the desire to identify with the wounded mother (as opposed to the sadistic desire to identify with the wounding father), but is a specific, highly coded and contractual activity in which the subject ultimately seeks not blind submission to mastery but the reinvention of life outside the parameters of domination and submission altogether. This occurs when the suffering experienced at the hands of the animal-woman (it is crucial that Venus is in furs, since this opens a line of flight from human to nonhuman sexuality and desire) effectively reorganizes the zones of pleasure and pain on the body, such that the ego is forced to reinvent itself. A feminine ferality is contracted to destroy or transform the cruelty and desire for revenge lurking at the heart of the dispossessed ego, replacing this ego with a profound capacity to be affected, a capacity not so much to feel for the other, but to feel otherwise as oneself. The connection of immanence to masochism makes sense of Deleuze's profound sympathy for certain male writers who deliberately "unman" themselves (Woolf is an interesting exception in this series). These are generally English or American writers who evade civilization or deliberately exile themselves from it (although Deleuze mentions them far less frequently, Rimbaud, Artaud, and Henri Michaux should be included here, as well). See Deleuze, *Masochism*, 99–101.

5. The "involuntary" character of the Proustian work is exemplary here. Proust cannot simply describe Combray as it was in the past, but must produce a new Combray, a transfigured Combray, on the basis of a visionary palette that does not write or paint using memories, but remembers with paints or sounds or characters themselves. Art proceeds through composition, which is the creation of combinations—vibrations, embraces, cinches, withdrawals, diversions, distensions (*WIP*, 168). Yet this is not the cultivation of a subjectivity, or a subjective point of view. Melville and other writers do not so much give us a view on things but give us things or landscapes or characters as points of view into which the eye or mind of the artist has been fully absorbed.

6. See Freud, *The Uncanny*.

7. But Deleuze argues that what art captures is not so much this intimate or tender point of "ideal coincidence" between body and world, but something that becomes within the flesh or at the site of the flesh both a deeper interior and a framing exterior. Blocs of sensation, affect, and percept, are not revealed "in" the flesh but pass through it and distend it, stretching or compressing the

flesh. Francis Bacon's paintings are of course exemplary in this regard, for Deleuze. On the one hand, the flesh is drawn into a zone where it is indiscernible from the affective states of the plant or animal, where it "wells up like a flayed beast or peeled fruit beneath the bonds of pink in the most graceful, delicate nude, Venus in the mirror" or "suddenly emerges in the fusion, firing, or casing of broken tones, like the zone of indiscernibility of beast and man" (*WIP*, 179). On the other hand, the flesh is pulled or pushed from the outside by the planes that frame it (in musical terms melody and rhythm push sound towards its pulsing vitality, an intensity indistinguishable from animal and plant life; harmony represents the planes that intersect and frame sound in a cosmos, a universe of vectors and dimensions). This paradox is resolved once one accepts that artistic experimentation is the creation of blocs that correspond to the being of sensation. In painting, the flesh is "sectioned" by the houses or arbors or immediate environs. These "sides" of the blocs of sensation give frames to color. It is the construction of these planes or frames upon which the construction of blocs of sensation depend, as much as on the combining of colors. Panting renders life not simply by rendering flesh but by joining planes—not only the planes of a house or interior, but of the cosmos, and that saturated monochrome which for Deleuze is the "universe-cosmos." Flesh is not life, because life is a force of life, a line of force or life connecting mineral-animal-architecture-cosmos.

8. Composers such as Stockhausen, Steve Reich, Philip Glass, and Arvo Pärt have all been called mystics because of the incantational and invocational aspect of their "minimalist" styles. Pärt is profoundly religious and links the purity of the tone structure to its spiritual power. Kerslake argues that we should prefer Deleuze's appellation of "cosmic artisan" to that of "religious genius," but on the line I have been tracing here, there is ultimately less of a difference between these two roles than might at first appear. The problem becomes how to think of a religious "immanence" that resists or subverts the directives of religious authority.

9. It seems to me that Bruno Latour's work can be seen as following up on that of Deleuze on this point. See especially Latour's recent *On the Modern Cult of the Factish Gods*.

10. Whereas traditional anthropology tends to define the cultural status of the smith in terms of a difference from or contrast with either the sedentary farming culture or migratory people groups (essentially how the smith is evaluated by an "other"), Deleuze and Guattari insist (following the work of anthropologists like Marcel Griaule and V. Gordon Childe) that this middle or "mixed" personage of the smith, existing between the "smooth" or "deterritorialized" flow of ore and the "striated" or territorialized food supplies of an empire, should not be understood as a bastardized or impure amalgam of Others,

but as something Husserl might have called an "anexact essence" (without Husserl's stipulation that the anexact is only a precursor to ideal exactness through further phenomenological intuition).

11. However, holey space is not a utopian space: there are no smiths without imperial prospectors who have gone before and imperial merchants who come after the work (*ATP*, 415).

12. The farmer, the herdsman, and the merchant seem in their own ways to follow the ebb and flow of a peculiar material assemblage (crops, herds, money). But whereas the farmer follows the seasons, changes crops in rotation, etc., this is always to bring the labor back to a certain fixed point from which the process can begin again. What is expected from the land is wholly determined by what it has produced in the past in accordance with the form imposed upon it, with preconceived goals. The farmer is not truly itinerant—nor is the merchant, who is bound to a flow of goods that must depart from and return to the same fixed points. These other, blankly repetitive "transhumants" do not so much follow a flow as continually draw a closed circuit (*ATP*, 409, 410). The smith or artisan, on the other hand, is the true itinerant, the true ambulator.

13. The artisan more closely doubles nature's "never quite true" spoken of by Benjamin Paul Blood and quoted by Deleuze in *Difference and Repetition*. "Nature is contingent, excessive and mystical essentially.... We have realized the highest divine thought of itself, and there is in it as much of wonder as of certainty.... Not unfortunately the universe is wild—game flavored as a hawk's wing. Nature is miracle all. She knows no laws; the same returns not, save to bring the different. The slow round of the engraver's lathe gains but the breadth of a hair, but the difference is distributed back over the whole curve, never an instant true—ever not quite." Whereas the migrant moves in a completely smooth space and the farmer and the merchant bind flows to rotation, the artisan is bound most intimately to the liminal space of the machinic phylum itself, the turning of nature's lathe.

14. This life is not organic, and not exactly an "autopoiesis" that would rigorously distinguish the living and the nonliving. Eliot Ross Albert has exhaustively covered the topic of the great distance between Deleuze's vitalism and any form of "autopoetic" thinking in his dissertation, "Towards a Schizogenealogy of Heretical Materialism: Between Bruno and Spinoza, Nietzsche, Deleuze and Other Philosophical Recluses" (Ph.D. diss., University of Warwick, 1999), chapter 2.

15. Deleuze's view of matter cuts against the grain of the hylomorphic assumptions underpinning much traditional philosophy. In hylomorphism, change must have measurable thresholds determining when potencies are or can become matters that can be considered as potencies to be actualized, or

used as form—that is, there must be something like a sufficient reason, due to form, why some sounds and not others can be composed to make a symphony. All this would be well and good except that hylomorphism misses the passages proper to the materials themselves, passages that are vague or anexact. It determines as attributable to "form" all that is recognizable or knowable in materiality. There may be an acknowledgement, as Husserl seems to have made, that there are intermediate forms, but these are always constricted to being "intermediaries" or "passages" that have intelligibility only in terms of what is becoming finalized, which is still an ideal object, the form of a mathematical intuition.

On the Husserlian view the essence of a circle emerges from vague roundness into sensible, clear roundness, achieving an *eidos*. But Deleuze argues for an autonomy to roundness (or to music), a "threshold affect" (neither flat nor pointed, neither silence nor noise) or a "limit process" (becoming rounded, becoming music). Whereas the traditional or "statist" impulse is to account for variation as simply "variables in content" or "distortions in expression," for Deleuze anexact essences are differences in themselves distinct both from the things that incarnate them (wheels, glasses, songs, nations) and ideal, fixed essences (of circularity, music, or justice).

Even though Husserl acknowledged the presence of intermediate essences, essences anexact yet rigorous ("essentially and not accidentally inexact"), he always considered them stopping points on the way to complete eidetic substance (*ATP*, 367). For Deleuze, anexact essences are essential as differences in themselves, as differential "passages to the limit" or "thresholds" in material flows that cannot appear via "reflection upon the object," even under conditions of the phenomenological bracketing of all "objectivity" (in the *epochê*). The singularity of a material flow, for Deleuze, becomes evident only when mind ambulates along with matter in a state that is not reflective but active in a mantic sense, a rhythmic sense that redoubles the intense states of artisanal proximity to materials in transition. Such anexact essences are the subject of a minor or nomad science, proper not to the state but to minor science and a "war machine" that is always caught up in flows, caught up in the delirious flow of materials.

16. Minor science, as the nomadic, does all it can to keep moving with matter, to remain in apprenticeship, in a doing-with-matter. Minor science builds up not arborescent or organized hierarchies of knowledge, but rhizomic surfaces of connection between extraordinary points, between singular traits that are not so much "given in nature" as perceptible under certain intense physical conditions, conditions such as artistic experimentation or theurgic ordeal. There is thus a peculiarly affective dimension to minor science. The artisan belongs to the stone, the smith wanders with the ore, the composer is led by

the music, the painter feels her way along the canvas, just as a shaman's body becomes the body of the entire tribe.

17. But the movement Deleuze traces in minor science and nomad art is not what flows through the soul of the composer whose heart is tuned to the soul of the world. It is not a reverie, but a forced movement that carries the composer away on a line of flight. Deleuze's theory of music is not simply an aesthetics of form à la Eduard Hanslick, who argued that "all musical elements have mysterious bonds and affinities among themselves, determined by natural laws." For Deleuze, music's power lies not in its formal purity but in its mixed or impure affect, its "suggestiveness" or becoming-other. What matters for Deleuze is the function music plays in forming an assemblage, a linking of sound forms to animal form or child form or cosmic form. In this way Deleuze is closer to someone like Susan Langer (*Feeling and Form*) than to Hanslick. Eduard Hanslick, *On the Musically Beautiful* (Indianapolis: Hackett, 1986), 28–44.

18. For an extremely prescient take on music from the perspective of affect, see Steve Goodman, *Sonic Warfare: Sound, Affect, and the Ecology of Fear* (Cambridge: MIT Press, 2010).

19. Then a second thing that distinguishes an animal is that it also has a territory (Deleuze indicates that with Guattari, he developed a nearly philosophical concept about territory). Constituting a territory is nearly the birth of art: in making a territory, it is not merely a matter of defecatory and urinary markings, but also a series of postures (standing or sitting, for an animal), a series of colors (that an animal takes on), a song. These are the three determinants of art: colors, lines, song, says Deleuze, in art in its pure state. Gilles Deleuze, "L'Abécédaire de Gilles Deleuze," interview by Claire Parnet, translated by Charles J. Stivale, 1988, www.langlab.wayne.edu. Television presentation by Deleuze, 1988–89. Produced by Pierre-André Boutang.

20. Kodwo Eshun, Erik Davis, and Steve Goodman have all gone to great lengths to articulate the dimensions of black Atlantic afrofuturism in contemporary dance music. See Eshun, *More Brilliant Than the Sun: Adventures in Sonic Fiction* (London: Quartet Books, 1999); Davis, "Roots and Wires: Polyrhythmic Cyberspace and the Black Electronic," www.techgnosis.com; Goodman, *Sonic Warfare*.

21. See Bogue, "Natura Musicans: Territory and the Refrain," in *Deleuze on Music, Painting, and the Arts*.

22. The rule of artful becoming is to be always present, accompanying, ambulating rather than identifying, imitating, or representing. How is this possible? By forcing what we can perceive and experience to speed up, slow down, be cut up, compacted, put alongside things it doesn't belong next to. Not only Artaud's theater of cruelty but also the theater of Jacques Lecoq, which Artaud inspired. In the Lecoq method, character is built from the outside in,

from gesture, and above all from the "neutral mask": an impersonal, indiscernible, nearly imperceptible double of a face that is put on and must be animated by the body of the actor. Seeing an actor in a neutral mask forces us to wait much longer than normal for the revelation of psychological states (fear, joy, etc.) because the entire body must work through it or distill it in a time much longer than the actual "consciousness" of the emotion. At the same time what the actor is doing (running, jumping, hitting, pointing) happens much faster than it would if we could slow it down through the face-machine, through reference to the "personality" from which we could imagine the action derived. Lecoq's methods make linguistic self-consciousness subordinate to massive or microphysical affects that continually provoke and interrupt the superficial continuity of intentional activity—hence his emphasis on clowning and its almost unbearable witness to the real. See Lecoq's *Lettre à mes élèves* (Paris: Ecole Jacques Lecoq, 1995).

23. Psychoanalysis reduced artistic becoming-everything and -everybody to a narcissism gone wild. But it has missed the boat, missed the true plane, the true surface. "They see the animal as a representative of drives, or a representation of the parents. They do not see the reality of a becoming-animal, that it is affect in itself, the drive in person, and represents nothing. There exist no other drives than the assemblages themselves" (*ATP*, 259). In Peter Schaffer's *Equus*, the young man, Allen, who has put out the eyes of five horses, is cured by a psychoanalyst of the religious mania that drove him to worship horses and to fear their witness to his "infidelity" to them when he nearly succumbs to the seduction of his girlfriend in their stable. In a deeply moving speech at the play's end, the analyst effectively condemns the value of his own ability to cure or work through the trauma with the boy, because now that it has been narrated and reduced to meaning, or interpreted, the passion—the line of flight—connecting the boy's body to Equus (his god-horse) is effectively destroyed. He reenters normalcy at the cost of his desire, his passion.

24. In the spirit of Deleuze's and Guattari's enterprise, working rigorously with a variety of mathematical and formal-logical possibilities, Rocco Gangle and Gianluca Caterina have embarked on an extraordinary line of experimental research using diagrammatic reasoning in application to a number of fields, at the Center for Diagrammatic and Computational Philosophy at Endicott College. Some of their already published results can be found at www.cdcp.org.

25. In *A Thousand Plateaus* Deleuze and Guattari (and Deleuze alone in a later essay on Melville's "Bartleby, the Scrivener: A Story of Wall Street") present "stammering" as diagrammatic in the sense that it makes one a "foreigner in one's own tongue." Such a becoming-foreign is not a matter of creating a minor language, an alternative dialect or *patois*, but of creatively varying the mother tongue from within, so as to contact unrealized potentials.

26. Deleuze locates Bacon's gesture at the third position in his four-part schema of sign-creation. As Deleuze analyzes it in *A Thousand Plateaus*, signs pass through at least four moments (which are not necessarily distinct): generative, transformational, diagrammatic, and machinic.

27. Part of the difficulty and the scandal of addressing the inherence of concepts in conceptual personae is that the work of public, academic, or what Deleuze calls "state" philosophy is not undertaken by private thinkers like Sartre (or novelists like Dostoyevsky) but by citizens who occupy roles of teachers, judges, or public servants. The duty of such types is ultimately to establish reasonable doctrines—even doctrines about renegade or subversive intellectuals like Deleuze. What would it really mean to follow through on the notion of thought as a form of becoming? To confess or profess that thought itself must pass through this bizarre mediumship or a kind of channeling of forces, an intensification of life in thought? And yet is it not that all thinkers, even the most renowned or public, all live their thought through such personae: Kant through a transformation of the judge, Lacan through that of the Zen master, Žižek through a preadolescent boy staring in horror at the sexual act?

6. The Politics of Sorcery

1. Antoine Faivre, *Access to Western Esotericism* (Binghamton: SUNY Press, 1994), 45.

2. Ibid., 47.

3. Ibid., 46.

4. As Philip Goodchild has demonstrated, Deleuze's systematic thought remains wedded to a certain "materialist" logic of space as pure continuum and time as empty form. Deleuze conceives of the plane of immanence as a kind of absolute, differential possibility of novelty based on abstract, sterile processes of anorganic differentiation. Goodchild, *Gilles Deleuze and the Question of Philosophy*, 156–57.

5. Mauss, *A General Theory of Magic*.

6. Williams, *Gilles Deleuze's Logic of Sense*, 142. Especially pertinent for a reading of Deleuze as hermetic is Williams's emphasis on the importance of divination for ethics—that is to say, for a prophetic anticipation of how future possible relations will play out as indicated, paradoxically, by the singularity of events.

7. For Deleuze, amor fati is an ethics of humor, not of irony. Humor always involves active selection, as opposed to passive reflection. Deleuze calls this selection a studied "perversion" of the real, as opposed to the Platonic conversion or pre-Socratic subversion of reality (*LS*, 133). Humor is the becoming-Herculean of philosophy at the surface, as opposed to its becoming-Apollo

above or becoming-Dionysus below. As Deleuze puts it, "[Hercules] always descends or ascends to the surface in every conceivable manner. He brings back the hell-hound and the celestial hound, the serpent of hell and the serpent of the heavens. It is no longer a question of Dionysius down below or Apollo up above, but of Hercules on the surface, in his dual battle against both depth and height: reorientation of the entire thought and a new geography" (*LS*, 132).

8. Proust's literature, to which Deleuze returns constantly in his work, forms a paradigmatic exemplar of the effort to "make pre-individual and nonpersonal singularities speak." Proust's works constitute, for Deleuze, a veritable esotericism of the sign, and a spiritualism of essence, one that models that amor fati in which an ethics of sense would culminate.

9. These radicals include not only authors and artists themselves, but fictional characters such as Dickens's Riderhood, Michel Tournier's Friday, and D. H. Lawrence's Kate in *The Plumed Serpent*.

10. On this point, see Jacques Rancière, "Deleuze, Bartleby, and the Literary Formula," in *The Flesh of Words: The Politics of Writing*, translated by Charlotte Mandell (Stanford: Stanford University Press, 2004), 146–64.

11. A reference to a group of Anglo and American writers, from Thomas Hardy and D. H. Lawrence to Henry Miller, Alan Ginsberg, and Jack Kerouac, in *Anti-Oedipus*, 132.

12. Despite the subtlety of his position, many critics have conflated Deleuze's affirmation of thought as proximity to intensive or germinal life with a direct affirmation of different or "extreme" individuals, isolated or marginal personalities, populations of countercultural movements. This position is ultimately incorrect, but it is fair to say that Deleuze, as a philosopher of minor or nomadic figures, had an affinity with groups who creatively broke with the strictures of constituted group formations and standardized identities. Furthermore, Deleuze, along with Guattari, was supportive (at least initially) of the cultural politics of France after 1968, and of the demands of the students and workers for greater autonomy and self-determination. However, Deleuze's affirmation of "divergent becomings" is no simple statement of support for countercultures or splinter groups, and thought for Deleuze is never simply the sheer affirmation of difference.

13. Girard, "Delirium as System." Rancière, "Deleuze, Bartleby, and the Literary Formula."

14. For this perspective, see especially Harold Bloom's view of Blake, Emerson, and Shakespeare as outlined in *Omens of the Millennium: The Gnosis of Angels, Dreams, and Resurrection* (New York: Riverhead Books, 1997).

15. Kerslake, *Deleuze and the Unconscious*, 166.

16. Bergson's argument for this claim is, in part, a result of his demonstra-

tion in *Matter and Memory*, against the positivist psychology of his time, that memory is not strictly physical and cannot be located in the brain. This argument is worth recapitulating briefly because of its influence on Deleuze. Bergson argues that since at least some memories are tied to unrepeated events (rather than recurrent or habitual events), memory represents a power of consciousness that is truly spiritual: freely selective and liberated from physical determinants. At the same time, Bergson argues that the present moment, in all of its concrete, material immediacy, is not a separate substance from spirit or consciousness. Consciousness, as spiritual, is simply the past of the present moment, whose present actuality is physical. Perduring in time, matter is not brittle but plastic and malleable, and should not be considered an inherent resistance to spirit but a contingent realization of it.

17. Pico della Mirandola, *On the Dignity of Man*.
18. Bergson, *The Two Sources of Morality and Religion*, 317.
19. Yates, *Giordano Bruno and the Hermetic Tradition*.
20. See William Behun, "The Body without Organs and the Body of Light," in *SubStance* 39, no. 2 (2009): 125–40.
21. Kerslake has done much to complexify our understanding of Deleuze's relation to Kant, with his *Immanence and the Vertigo of Philosophy*.
22. Immanuel Kant, *Groundwork of the Metaphysics of Morals*, translated by Mary J. Gregor (Cambridge: Cambridge University Press, 1997).
23. Max Horkheimer and Theodor W. Adorno, *Dialectic of Enlightenment: Philosophical Fragments*, translated by Edmund Jephcott (Stanford: Stanford University Press, 2002).
24. Mauss, *A General Theory of Magic*.
25. Immanuel Kant, *Critique of Judgment*, 292.
26. Gil, *Metamorphoses of the Body*, 84.
27. Kerslake, *Immanence and the Vertigo of Philosophy*, 225.
28. Kant, *Critique of Judgment*, 292.
29. Kerslake, *Immanence and the Vertigo of Philosophy*, 225.
30. Sontag, ed., Antonin Artaud, *Selected Writings*, 571.
31. See *ATP*, 40, for an account of the earth itself as a BwO.
32. Deleuze and Guattari wonder if this is terrifying for the schizophrenic only because the schizophrenic is already institutionalized, already judged (*AO*, 88).
33. See *ATP*, 237, on the sorcerer and becomings as super-mythic—tales or legends not reducible to mythical formulas with their "territorial" agendas.
34. In *ATP*, "1933: Micropolitics and Segmentarity," Deleuze and Guattari argue that despite the fact that binary oppositions are very strong in primitive societies, these binaries are produced from multiple centers of power and

not from a single despotic center whose effects are everywhere the same. Only in modern societies, they argue, are such dualisms as man-woman and ruler-ruled elevated to the level of a self-sufficient organization (*ATP*, 210).

Whereas for Jacques Derrida the necessity of writing perennially repeats the loss of the magic triangle, and this loss constitutes history as the history of a metaphysics that would pretend to reassure us against the absence at the heart of signs, for Deleuze and Guattari, despotic graphism is not the structure of historicity as such, but a contingent effect of certain forms of power. Jacques Derrida, *Of Grammatology*, translated by Gayatri Chakravorty Spivak (Baltimore: Johns Hopkins University Press, 1998).

35. Lévi-Strauss, *The Savage Mind*.

36. This is another account of the "panopticism" Foucault identified with modern state formations, which tends to force all the circles of power to resonate with each other. See Michel Foucault, *Discipline and Punish* (New York: Vintage Books, 1995), 202–3.

37. Horkheimer and Adorno, *Dialectic of Enlightenment*.

38. Gil, *Metamorphoses of the Body*, 88.

39. Ibid., 12.

40. Ibid.

41. Ibid., 18.

42. This is why, in the last analysis, Deleuze and Guattari reject the idea of a deep grammar or universal grammar that all regimes of signs would conform to (à la Chomsky). The ultimate elements, even the "transcendental" elements of a regime of signs—the conditions of intelligibility that are effectuated in each regime—belong not to the order of the statement but to the enunciation, to the act of utterance. There are types of acts of utterance or enunciation that belong to each regime specifically, and mark them out from one another. In the presignifying regime, this is the act of "segmentarization" that marks out local territories and maintains local disputes and resolutions in order to ward off the state (including potlatch, cannibalism, tattoo, and totemism). In the signifying regime, this is "significance and interpretation": the metonymic and metaphorical ramification of the signifier, the absence of the transcendental signified, the establishment of circles of meaning or spheres of influence radiating from the occult center of meaning, the sovereign and imperial throne. In the countersignifying regime this is the act of "numeration," the nomadic action of counting, the organization of peoples into tens, hundreds, thousands, the direct militarization of everyday life for the purpose of subverting the state, for maintaining a nomadic war machine that can evade and attack the state by refusing all interpretation and significance. In the postsignifying regime the enunciative act is subjectification, the act through which the individual cogito or passional couple internalizes the state and the imperial power, converting

paranoia into hysteria and delusion. Finally, the act of absolute deterritorializing or diagrammaticizing would correspond to the line of flight leading out of all signifying regimes. "Regimes of signs are thus defined by variables that are internal to enunciation but remain external to the constants of language and irreducible to linguistic categories" (*ATP*, 140). In this sense, every regime of signs is "less than a language."

7. The Future of Belief

1. Antoine Faivre, *Access to Western Esotericism* (Binghamton: SUNY Press, 1994), 21.
2. Ibid., 22, 23.
3. Ibid, 43.
4. As Kerslake has suggested, without reference to any notion of a pregiven totality or closed whole (but rather with regard to an open whole or One-All), Deleuze proffers a new microcosm-macrocosm synergy. This conjunction of individuation and multiplicity is based on the contractions of a continuum of rhythm or periodicity that defines matter, and that is varied in intensity along a scale running from inorganic to organic life. In *Immanence and the Vertigo of Philosophy*, Kerslake explains that here Deleuze follows the Polish messianist philosopher Josef Hoëné-Wronski and his twentieth-century disciple Francis Warrain. For Wronski, transcendental philosophy realizes not merely the identity of the conditions of knowledge with the conditions of objects of knowledge, but the genetic or creative capacity of the mind to assert reason as freedom, as unconditioned creation (236). For Wronski's disciple Warrain, Kant's archetypal intellect—an intellect that would think from the perspective of the noumenon—would be rooted in an apprehension of the "virtuality of creation." This apprehension would be a kind of messianic knowledge, a knowledge identical with the human ability to re-create the conditions of existence based on correct apprehension of the vital rhythms and pulsations of matter itself (238). Deleuze's inspiration for the theory of ideas in *Difference and Repetition*, is derived in part from Wronski, who Deleuze calls a "profound mathematician who developed a positivistic, messianic, and mystical system which implied a Kantian interpretation of the calculus" (*DR*, 170).
5. Faivre, *Access to Western Esotericism*, 45–46.
6. Ibid., 43.
7. Ibid., 45.
8. Ibid., 44, 45.
9. This trend seems to have shifted, lately, at least in part in response to Hallward's work in *Out of This World*. Christian Kerslake's pioneering *Deleuze and the Unconscious* was followed by Volume III of *Collapse*, "Unknown Deleuze,"

which saw several authors follow up on Kerslake's suggestions of the occultist roots of Deleuze's thought. More recently a series of thinkers such as Ray Brassier, Reza Nagarestani, Eugene Thacker, and Nicola Masciandro have developed positions that in fact attempt to go explicitly *beyond* Deleuze's own esotericism into darker, more nihilist versions of gnosis informed less by the optimism of the hermetic tradition than by a kind of Valentinian pessimism focusing on the melancholic, chaotic, and destructive aspects of nature.

10. Hallward, *Out of This World*. For an excellent review and criticism of Hallward, see Anthony Paul Smith, "Review," *Angelaki* 12, no. 1 (2007): 151–56.

11. Hallward, *Out of This World*, 6, 162–63.

12. Exemplary in this regard is Philip Goodchild's *Gilles Deleuze and the Question of Philosophy*.

13. Perhaps if Hallward had paid closer attention to the actual relations between esotericism and politics, he might have discovered that, in general, mystical and esoteric traditions have maintained quite radical and subversive political programs. Correctly connecting Deleuze to his Renaissance and Neoplatonic forbears makes clear how ill-informed this critique actually is. It is no accident that historically the philosophers most serious about magic were also utopian visionaries with ambitious projects of political and religious reform. From Cornelius Agrippa's astonishing feminism to Pico della Mirandola's kabbalistic christology, from Giordano Bruno's lifelong struggle against academic complacency and religious hypocrisy to Campanella's utopian experiment, hermetic passion is aligned with revolutionary zeal.

14. Badiou, *Deleuze*, 141.

15. Ibid., 73. For Badiou, speculative empiricism is a nonstarter for thought. This is because in Badiou's conception, "being" (or we might say, nature), as a subject of empirical investigation, is nothing but a random set of potential "situations" in which events might take place. Events, for Badiou, are the only object of "truths." But truths are the subject, then, of a profound subtraction from being, nature, and intracosmic dynamics. For Badiou, if thought truly thinks, and does not merely reflect the vicissitudes of languages and bodies, it thinks of truths that open "generic" or site-specific interventions, lineages of "fidelity" to truth-events.

Badiou argues that Plato already conducted the trial against the "physicists" (and so against Deleuze as a "speculative empiricist"), and gave thought a truly philosophical basis (a basis, that is, that transcends the ordeal of the sensible and is immanent only to itself as a thought of the event). For Badiou, with the logos of forms (which becomes, in Badiou's hands, axiomatic logic), Plato gave thought a way to reflect on itself, on its own presuppositions, without an intuition of the virtual or contemplation of the universe. Badiou, *Deleuze*, 101.

16. Ibid., 12, 11.

17. Dorothea Olkowski has gone far in attempting to develop an ontology in the spirit of Deleuze's attention to both mathematical and affective intensities that nevertheless more clearly departs from any vestige of stoic resolutions, and situates ethics as much as ontology in the development of vulnerable and incommensurable localities. *The Universal in the Realm of the Sensible: Beyond Continental Philosophy* (New York: Columbia University Press, 2007).

18. See Freud's letter to Jung published in appendix 1 of *Memories, Dreams, Reflections*, translated by Richard Winston and Carla Winston(New York: Vintage, 1989).

19. Freud, *The Uncanny*, 147.

20. Ibid., 159.

21. Ibid., 144.

22. See especially Žižek's recent *Living in the End Times* (London: Verso, 2010).

23. Artaud, *Antonin Artaud*, xlv.

24. Are we in a different phase, now some forty-plus years from 1969? What has changed? Ecological and economic crises continue to motivate new views of nature and the self-in-nature, beyond the utilitarian calculus warranted by secular liberal ideologies. But the rise of fundamentalisms and the threat of global instability have created a simultaneous hostility to the "return of religion." It is a curious mix. On the one hand, websites like Reality Sandwich, www.realitysandwich.com, demonstrate a growing body of ever more sophisticated approaches to spiritual technologies and an attempt to seriously integrate cultural revolution and new economic theory with the latest in scientific research. At the same time, demographically the United States and Europe are seeing their moderate, liberal-minded religious dwindle in numbers, and seeing the rise of radical Pentecostal or otherwise charismatic styles of belief, largely due to immigrant populations. What kind of secularism can negotiate a postliberal political terrain? For a Deleuzian perspective on this issue, see especially Connolly, *Why I Am Not a Secularist*.

25. See Joshua Delpech-Ramey, "Lost Magic: The Hidden Radiance of *Negative Dialectics*," in "Art, Praxis, and Social Transformation: Radical Dreams and Visions," edited by Anne F. Pomeroy and Richard A. Jones, special issue, *Radical Philosophy Review* 12, nos. 1–2 (2009): 315–37. On Deleuze and Adorno, see also Daniel Colucciello Barber, "The Production of Immanence: Deleuze, Yoder, and Adorno" (Ph.D. diss., Duke University, 2008).

26. Max Horkheimer and Theodor Adorno, *Dialectic of Enlightenment: Philosophical Fragments*, translated by Edmund Jephcott (Stanford: Stanford University Press, 2002), 2.

27. Theodor Adorno, "Theses Against Occultism" in *Minima Moralia: Reflections on a Damaged Life* translated by E. F. N. Jephcott (London: Verso, 2005), 238–44.

28. However, it is arguable that Adorno's profound longing for the genuine beauties of childhood, dreams, and natural landscapes were truly magical thoughts. I owe this insight to Lucio Angelo Privitello's "Three Difficult Adornian Lessons," an unpublished paper delivered at the Radical Philosophy Association bi-annual conference, San Francisco State University, 2008.

29. Adorno, *Minima Moralia*, 238–44.

30. Adorno claims that it is not "historical" animism, the primitive devotion to the spirits, that spells our collective late capitalist demise. Rather, it is the decadence of a half-hearted "return" to spiritualism that spells our doom, and a retreat from the deadlocks of hyperrationalized industrial society that truly endangers thought. Adorno, *Minima Moralia*, 239.

31. Ibid.

32. Adorno opposes occultism with conceptual labor, where the labor of thought is defined as enduring or "bearing" the vicissitudes of contingency (the banal violence of the mundane), while conceiving an "unconditional" whose only virtue is its absolute difference from the contingent, its mantra that being and meaning, object and subject, matter and mind, are united only in negatively dialectical acts of false assimilation. But arguably, dialectical materialism, by tracing the failure of ideology to capture the real, does no better and no worse than the artificer of a séance who asks us to hear the spirit through the "tiny door" that the ritual procedure leaves open onto the beyond. In some ways the occult practitioners Adorno so despised are simply more honest than the mandarin dialectician: the fact that the message from the spirits is often comically mundane should confirm that it too, as much as negative dialectics, wishes simply to put the machine back in the ghost.

33. The masochistic fantasy of occultists, Adorno seems to think, is that the technoscientific authority to destroy ourselves can be viably transferred into some "complicity with anonymous materials" (to borrow Reza Nagarestani's title). Nagarestani has written a kind of Islamic theosophical apocalypse that is undeniably an exercise in hermetic materialism, after Deleuze. *Cyclonopedia: Complicity with Anonymous Materials* (Victoria: Re.press, 2008).

34. Goodchild, *Gilles Deleuze and the Question of Philosophy*, 150–69.

35. Ibid.

36. However, in *Negotiations*, Deleuze explicitly connects the possibility of philosophy to complex forms of mediation. "Mediators are fundamental. Creation's all about mediators. Without them nothing happens. They can be people—for a philosopher, artists or scientists; for a scientist, philosophers or artists—but things too, even plants or animals, as in Casteneda." *Negotia-*

tions, 1972–1990, translated by Martin Joughin (New York: Columbia University Press, 1995), 125.

37. Ibid., 166.

38. Félix Guattari, *Chaosmosis: An Ethico-Aesthetic Paradigm*, translated by Paul Bains, and Julian Pefanis (Bloomington: Indiana University Press, 1995), 77.

39. Mauss, *A General Theory of Magic*; Lévi-Strauss, *The Savage Mind*.

40. Adorno, *Minima Moralia*, 241. From this perspective, it is worth observing intellectual historians such as Christopher I. Lehrich perform the necessary work of decomposing the static opposition between rationality and magic. In a critique of how Western anthropology dismissed the possibility of scientifically defining magic, Lehrich makes a remark that can be turned against Adorno's own dismissal of the occult, and toward an elaboration of the hermetic Deleuze. Lehrich writes, "Ultimately, to eliminate 'magic' from second-order scholarly discourse would require that native, first order term to refer to nothing at all—nothing anyway that cannot be designated otherwise. Their 'magic' is *really* something else. But this entails that magic *really is* something—or that it is a sign of a vast chain of deferral whose ultimate end we (alone) can identify as nonexistent. That in turn requires us to know the difference between terms or concepts that ultimately end in fixed meaning and those, like magic, that merely walk in circles. Yet one cannot have it both ways: either *all* signification depends on endless circularity and deferral whose end one only determines pragmatically; or one must have recourse to a transcendental signified (God, Being, and so forth). From no position can one legitimately pick out a term from another discourse as *simply meaningless*, such that the word itself need not even exist, because the selection and delineation itself reifies the object, or better identifies it as an already meaningful sign—albeit an endlessly receding one, like Levi-Strauss's *mana*. Thus the very ease with which it seems 'magic' can be discarded demonstrates that there is an 'it' to *be* discarded." This profound argument has deep implications for all of modern thought, but in particular for positions such as Freud's on the uncanny and Adorno's on the occult. Adorno would reserve for negative dialectics the prerogative of magic: to be a science of difference-in-itself. But to succeed, at the level of methodology Adorno is forced *ab negatio* to attribute to the occult the positivity of a "nothing but" of which he alone is master, in this case, the determination that the occult is nothing but a fantasy of discouraged and alienated capitalist bourgeoisie. The true eschatological hope with which desire for contact with occult sympathies, relations, and actions is charged might arguably be precisely that which Adorno reserves for dialectical negativity: the right to pronounce upon the end of things, to constellate the real beyond the contradictions of a fully administered society. What is ungrounded here is the manner in which Adorno above all reserves the position of enunciation the melancholy judge (as much

as does Freud for the disenchanted analyst) over against the improvisatory sagacity of any set or subset of hermetic collectivities. Christopher I. Lehrich, *The Occult Mind: Magic in Theory and Practice* (Ithaca: Cornell University Press, 2007), 170.

41. Joan Halifax, *Shamanic Voices: A Survey of Visionary Narratives* (New York: Penguin Compass, 1979), 29–34.

42. This would have some resonances with Agamben's "coming community" if it were not for the way the revelation of such a community is discovered in melancholy and not in joy, as it is for Deleuze. See Giorgio Agamben, *The Coming Community*, translated by Michael Hart (Minneapolis: University of Minnesota Press, 1993).

43. Even in the case of an orthodox esotericism such as the sophiology of Sergei Bulgakov, there is a profound sense in which the absolute nature of spirit is expressed paradigmatically not in any incorporeal or paracorporeal agency, such as an archon, daimon, angel, etc., but in and as a body. "We know that Scriptures frequently speak of God's body, or at least of its separate parts or organic head, ears, eyes, hands, feet, for example. It is usual to interpret this only in the sense of an allegory or an inevitable anthropomorphism. But would it not be more exact to understand it ontologically, in the sense that the organs of the human body, being instruments for revealing the spirit, must themselves have a spiritual prototype in the fullness of the divine life? In other words, the bodily form of the human being corresponds to the formal aspect of that divine glory, which is itself the fullness of the life of God . . . The very expression 'spiritual body' [I Cor. X15.ww] far from being a contradiction in terms or a paradox, corresponds to the prime exemplar of the body, which has its prototype in the Wisdom and Glory of God." Sergei Bulgakov, *Sophia: The Wisdom of God* (Hudson, N.Y.: Lindisfarne, 1993).

44. Clearly evidenced in the fascinating exchange between Žižek and Milbank in *The Monstrosity of Christ: Paradox or Dialectics?* John Milbank, Creston Davis, and Slavoj Žižek, *The Monstrosity of Christ: Paradox or Dialectics?* (Cambridge: MIT Press, 2010).

Coda

1. To whom exactly these remarks are directed remains obscure, but perhaps they are thinking in particular of Ignatius of Loyola with his *Spiritual Exercises* that laid out certain "imaginal" planes of composition designed to intensify contemplative prayer.

2. François Laruelle, *Future Christ*, translated by Anthony Paul Smith (London: Continuum, 2011).

3. See Delpech-Ramey and Harris, "Spiritual Politics after Deleuze."

4. Ibid., 115–24.
5. Ibid., 62–75.
6. Ibid., 125–40.
7. Ibid., 76–102.
8. Goodchild, *Theology of Money*; Goodchild, *Capitalism and Religion*, 24–37.
9. Ibid., 38–48, 103–14.
10. Ibid., 154–64, 141–53.
11. *Nosotros, Los Brujos: Apuntes de Arte, Poesía y Brujería*, edited by Juan Salzano (Buenos Aires: Santiago Arcos, 2008); Matt Lee and Marc Fisher, *Deleuze y la Brujería*, selection, translation, and prologue by Juan Salzano (Buenos Aires: Las Cuarenta, 2009).

Bibliography

Agamben, Giorgio. *Homo Sacer: Sovereign Power and Bare Life*. Translated by Daniel Heller-Roazen. Stanford: Stanford University Press, 1998.

Artaud, Antonin. *Antonin Artaud: Selected Writings*. Edited by Susan Sontag. Translated by Helen Weaver. New York: Farrar, Straus and Giroux, 1976.

———. *The Theatre and Its Double*. Translated by Mary Caroline Richards. New York: Grove, 1958.

Badiou, Alain. *Being and Event*. Translated by Oliver Feltham. London: Continuum, 2005.

———. *Deleuze: The Clamor of Being*. Translated by Louise Burchill. Minneapolis: University of Minnesota Press, 2000.

———. "Kant's Subtractive Ontology." In *Alain Badiou: Theoretical Writings*. Edited and translated by Ray Brassier and Alberto Toscano. London: Continuum, 2004.

———. "Language, Thought, Poetry." In *Alain Badiou: Theoretical Writings*. Edited and translated by Ray Brassier and Alberto Toscano. London: Continuum, 2004.

———. *Le Siecle*. Paris: Editions du Seuil, 2005.

———. *Logiques des mondes: L'être et l'evenement 2*. Paris: Editions du Seuil, 2006.

———. "Truth: Forcing and the Unnamable." In *Alain Badiou: Theoretical Writings*. Edited and translated Ray Brassier and Alberto Toscano. London: Continuum, 2004.

Baugh, Bruce. "Deleuze and Empiricism." *Journal of the British Society for Phenomenology* 24, no. 1 (1993): 31.

Bergson, Henri. *Matter and Memory*. Translated by N. M. Paul and W. S. Palmer. New York: Zone Books, 1991.

———. *The Two Sources of Morality and Religion*. Translated by R. Ashely Audra and Cloudesley Brereton. Notre Dame: University of Notre Dame Press, 1977.

Blumenberg, Hans. *The Legitimacy of the Modern Age*. Translated by Robert M. Wallace. Cambridge: MIT Press, 1983.

Bogue, Ronald. *Deleuze on Music, Painting, and the Arts*. London: Rutledge, 2003.

———. "Word, Image and Sound: The Non-Representational Semiotics of Gilles Deleuze." *Mimesis in Contemporary Theory: An Interdisciplinary Approach*. Volume 2: *Mimesis, Semiosis, and Power*. Edited by Ronald Bogue, 77–97. Philadelphia: John Benjamins, 1991.

Boldereef, Frances M. *Hermes to His Son Thoth: Being Joyce's Use of Giordano Bruno in Finnegan's Wake*. Woodward: Classic Non-Fiction Library, 1968.

Brassier, Ray, and Alberto Toscano, eds. and trans. *Alain Badiou: Theoretical Writings*. London: Continuum, 2004.

Bruno, Giordano. *The Ash Wednesday Supper*. Edited and translated by Edward A. Gosselin and Lawrence S. Lerner.

———. *The Cabala of Pegasus*. Translated by Sidney L. Sondergard and Madison U. Sowell. New Haven: Yale University Press, 2002.

———. *Cause, Principle, and Unity*. Edited by Richard J. Blackwell and Robert de Lucca. Cambridge: Cambridge University Press, 1998.

———. *The Expulsion of the Triumphant Beast*. Translated by Arthur D. Imerti. New Brunswick: Rutgers University Press, 1964.

———. *The Heroic Frenzies*. Translated by Eugene Memmo Jr. Chapel Hill: University of North Carolina Press, 1964.

———. *On the Composition of Images, Signs and Ideas*. Translated by Charles Doria. New York: Willis, Locker, and Owens, 1991.

Buchanan, Ian. "Deleuze and Cultural Studies." *South Atlantic Quarterly* 96, no. 3 (1997): 483–97.

Buchanan, Ian, and Nicholas Thoburn. *Deleuze and Politics*. Edinburgh: Edinburgh University Press, 2008.

Bryden, Mary, ed. *Deleuze and Religion*. London: Routledge, 2001.

Carroll, Lewis. *The Annotated Alice*. New York: Norton, 2000.

Castaneda, Carlos. *The Teachings of Don Juan*. Berkeley: University of California Press, 1971.

Catana, Leo. *The Concept of Contraction in Giordano Bruno's Philosophy*. Burlington, Vt.: Ashgate, 2005.

Copenhaver, Brian P., ed. *Hermetica: The Greek Corpus Hermeticum and the Latin Asclepius in a New English Translation, with Notes and Introduction*. Cambridge: Cambridge University Press, 1995.

Connolly, William E. *Capitalism and Christianity, American Style*. Durham: Duke University Press, 2008.

———. *Why I Am Not a Secularist*. Minneapolis: University of Minnesota Press, 2000.

DeLanda, Manuel. *Intensive Science and Virtual Philosophy*. London: Continuum, 2002.

Deleuze, Gilles. *Cinema I: The Movement-Image*. Translated by Hugh Tomlinson and Barbara Habberjam. Minneapolis: University of Minnesota Press, 1996.

———. *Cinema II: The Time-Image*. Translated by Hugh Tomlinson and Robert Galeta. Minneapolis: University of Minnesota Press, 1997.

———. *Desert Islands and Other Texts (1953–1974)*. Edited by David Lapoujade. Translated by Michael Taormina. Los Angeles: Semiotext(e), 2004.

———. *Difference and Repetition*. Translated by Paul Patton. New York: Columbia University Press, 1994.

———. *Empiricism and Subjectivity: An Essay on Hume's Theory of Human Nature*. Translated by Constantin Boundas. New York: Columbia University Press, 1991.

———. *Essays Critical and Clinical*. Translated by Daniel W. Smith and Michael A. Greco. Minneapolis: University of Minnesota Press, 1997.

———. *Expressionism in Philosophy: Spinoza*. Translated by Martin Joughin. New York: Zone Books, 1990.

———. *Francis Bacon: The Logic of Sensation*. Translated by Dan Smith. Minneapolis: University of Minnesota Press, 2003.

———. *The Fold: Leibniz and the Baroque*. Translated by Tom Conley. Minneapolis: University of Minnesota Press, 1993.

———. *Foucault*. Translated by Sean Hand. Minneapolis: University of Minnesota Press, 1988.

———. *Kant's Critical Philosophy*. Translated by Hugh Tomlinson and Barbara Habberjam. Minneapolis: University of Minnesota Press, 1984.

———. *The Logic of Sense*. Translated by Mark Lester and Charles Stivale. New York: Columbia University Press, 1990.

———. *Masochism: Coldness and Cruelty*. Translated by Jean McNeil. New York: Zone Books, 1989.

———. *Nietzsche and Philosophy*. Translated by Hugh Tomlinson. New York: Columbia University Press, 1983.

———. *Proust and Signs*. Translated by Richard Howard. Minneapolis: University of Minnesota Press, 2000.

———. *Pure Immanence: Essays on a Life*. Translated by Anne Boyman. New York: Zone Books, 2001.

———. *Two Regimes of Madness: Texts and Interviews 1975–1995*. Edited by

David Lapoujade. Translated by Ames Hodges and Mike Taormina. Los Angeles: Semiotext(e), 2006.

Deleuze, Gilles, and Félix Guattari. *Anti-Oedipus*. Translated by Robert Hurley, Mark Seem, and Helen R. Lane. Minneapolis: University of Minnesota Press, 1983.

———. *What Is Philosophy?* Translated by Hugh Tomlinson and Graham Burchell. New York: Columbia University Press, 1994.

———. *A Thousand Plateaus*. Translated by Brian Massumi. Minneapolis: University of Minnesota Press, 1987.

Deleuze, Gilles, and Claire Parnet. *Dialogues*. Translated by Hugh Tomlinson and Barbara Habberjam. New York: Columbia University Press, 1987.

———. *Dialogues II*. Translated by Hugh Tomlinson and Barbara Habberjam. New York: Columbia University Press, 2002.

Delpech-Ramey, Joshua, and Paul A. Harris. "Spiritual Politics after Deleuze." Special issue, *SubStance* 39, no. 121 (2010).

Derrida, Jacques. *Writing and Difference*. Translated by Alan Bass. Chicago: University of Chicago Press, 1978.

Ebeling, Florian. *The Secret History of Hermes Trismegistus*: *Hermeticism from Ancient to Modern Times*. Ithaca: Cornell University Press, 2007.

Eco, Umberto. *The Aesthetics of Chaosmos: The Middle Ages of James Joyce*. Translated by Ellen Esrock. Cambridge: Harvard University Press, 1989.

Farmer, S. A. *Syncretism in the West: Pico's 900 Theses (1486): The Evolution of Traditional Religious and Philosophical Systems*. Tempe, Ariz.: Medieval and Renaissance Texts and Studies, 1998.

Faubion, James D., ed. *Foucault: Aesthetics, Method, and Epistemology*. New York: New Press, 1998.

Foucault, Michel. "The Prose of Acteon." In *Foucault: Aesthetics, Method, and Epistemology*. Edited by James D. Faubion. New York: New Press, 1998.

———. "Nietzsche, Genealogy, History." In *Foucault: Aesthetics, Method, and Epistemology*. Edited by James D. Faubion. New York: New Press, 1998.

———. *The Order of Things: An Archaeology of the Human Sciences*. New York: Random House, 1970.

Freud, Sigmund. *The Freud Reader*. Edited by Peter Gay. New York: W. W. Norton, 1989.

———. *The Uncanny*. Translated by David Mclintock. London: Penguin, 2003.

Gatti, Hilary. *Giordano Bruno and Renaissance Science*. Ithaca: Cornell University Press, 1999.

Gil, José. *Metamorphoses of the Body*. Translated by Stephen Muecke. Minneapolis: University of Minnesota Press, 1998.

Girard, René. "Delirium as System." In *"To Double Business Bound": Essays on*

Literature, Mimesis, and Anthropology. Baltimore: Johns Hopkins University Press, 1978, 84–120.

Goodchild, Philip. *Capitalism and Religion: The Price of Piety*. London: Routledge, 2002.

———. *Gilles Deleuze and the Question of Philosophy*. Cranbury, N.J.: Associated University Presses, 1996.

———. *Theology of Money*. Durham: Duke University Press, 2008.

Gose, Elliot B., Jr., *The Transformation Process in Joyce's Ulysses*. Toronto: University of Toronto Press, 1980.

Guattari, Félix. *The Anti-Oedipus Papers*. Translated by Kalina Gottman. New York: Semiotext(e), 2006.

Hallward, Peter. *Out of This World: Deleuze and the Philosophy of Creation*. London: Verso Books, 2006.

Hallyn, Fernand. *The Poetic Structure of the World: Copernicus and Kepler*. Translated by Donald M. Leslie. New York: Zone Books, 1990.

Hegel, G. W. F. *Phenomenology of Spirit*. Translated by A. V. Miller. Oxford: Clarendon, 1980.

Horkheimer, Max, and Theodor Adorno. *Dialectic of Enlightenment*. Translated by Edmund Jephcott. Stanford: Stanford University Press, 2002.

Iamblichus. *De mysteriis Aegiptiorum*. Translated by Emman C. Clarke, John M. Dillon, and Jackston P. Hershbell. Leiden: Brill, 2004.

Jarry, Alfred. *Selected Works of Alfred Jarry*. Edited by Roger Shattuck and Simon Watson Taylor. New York: Grove, 1965.

Kant, Immanuel. *Critique of Judgment*. Translated by Werner S. Pluhar. Indianapolis: Hackett, 1987.

———. *Critique of Pure Reason*. Translated by Norman Kemp Smith. London: Macmillan, 1978.

Kerslake, Christian. *Deleuze and the Unconscious*. London: Continuum, 2007.

———. *Immanence and the Vertigo of Philosophy: From Kant to Deleuze*. Edinburgh: Edinburgh University Press, 2009.

———. "The Somnambulist and the Hermaphrodite: Deleuze and Johann de Montgreggio and Occultism." Culture Machine, Interzone website.

Kierkegaard, Søren. *Fear and Trembling and Repetition*. Translated and edited by H. V. Hong and E. H. Hong. Princeton: Princeton University Press, 1983.

Klossowski, Pierre. *The Baphomet*. Translated by Sophie Hawkes and Stephen Sartarelli. New York: Marsillio, 1988.

———. *Nietzsche and the Vicious Circle*. Translated by Dan Smith. Chicago: University of Chicago Press, 1997.

Lacan, Jacques. *Le seminaire, livre XVII: L'envers de la psychanalyse*. Paris: Seuil, 1991.

Latour, Bruno. *We Have Never Been Modern*. Translated by Catherine Porter. Cambridge: Harvard University Press, 1993.

———. *On the Modern Cult of the Factish Gods*. Translated by Catherine Porter and Heather MacLean. Durham: Duke University Press, 2010.

Lecoq, Jacques. *Lettre à mes élèves: 1956–1996*. Paris: Ecole Jacques Lecoq, 1996.

Leibniz, G. W. *Philosophical Writings*. Edited by G. H. R. Parkinson. London: Dent, 1973.

Lévi-Strauss, Claude. *The Savage Mind*. Chicago: University of Chicago Press, 1966.

Magee, Glenn. *Hegel and the Hermetic Tradition*. Ithaca: Cornell University Press, 2008.

Majercik, Ruth. *The Chaldaean Oracles: Text, Translation, and Commentary*. Volume 5. Leiden: E. J. Brill, 1989.

Mauss, Marcel. *A General Theory of Magic*. Translated by Robert Brain. London: Routledge, 1972.

Mead, G. R. S. *Thrice Greatest Hermes: Compete in One Volume: Being a Translation of the Extant Sermons and Fragments of the Trismegistic Literature with Prolegomena Commentaries and Notes*. London: Watkins, 1964.

Merkel, Ingrid, and Debus, Allen G. *Hermeticism and the Renaissance: Intellectual History in Early Modern Europe*. Washington: Folger Books, 1988.

Michaux, Henri. *Darkness Moves: An Henri Michaux Anthology, 1927–1984*. Translated by David Ball. Berkeley: University of California, 1994.

———. *La vie dans le plis: Poèmes*. Paris: Gallimard, 1949.

———. *The Major Ordeals of the Mind and Countless Minor Ones*. Translated by Richard Howard. New York: Harcourt Brace Jovanovich, 1974.

Middleton, John, ed. *Myth and Cosmos: Readings in Mythology and Symbolism*. Garden City, N.Y.: Natural History, 1967.

Nicholas of Cusa. *Of Learned Ignorance*. Translated by Germain Heron. London: Routledge Kegan Paul, 1954.

Nietzsche, Friedrich. *Basic Writings*. Translated by Walter Kaufmann. New York: Modern Library, 2000.

———. *The Portable Nietzsche*. Edited and translated by Walter Kaufmann. New York: Penguin, 1982.

Ordine, Nuccio. *Giordano Bruno and the Philosophy of the Ass*. Translated by Henryk Baranski and Arielle Saiber. New Haven: Yale University Press, 1996.

———. *Le seuil de l'ombre: Literature, philosophie et peinture chez Giordano Bruno*. Translated by Luc Hersant. Paris: Les Belles Lettres, 2003.

O'Regan, Cyril. *Gnostic Return in Modernity*. Albany: SUNY Press, 2001.

Patton, Paul, and John Protevi, eds. *Deleuze and Derrida*. New York: Continuum, 2003.

Pearson, Keith Ansell. *Germinal Life: The Difference and Repetition of Deleuze.* London: Routledge, 1999.

Peirce, Charles. "How to Make Our Ideas Clear." In *Philosophical Writings of Peirce.* Edited by Justus Buchler, 23–41. New York: Dover, 1955.

Pico della Mirandola, Giovanni. *On the Dignity of Man and Other Works.* Edited by Charles Glen Wallis. New York: Bobbs-Merrill, 1965.

Plato. *Complete Works.* Edited by John M. Cooper. Indianapolis: Hackett, 1997.

Rajchman, John. *The Deleuze Connections.* Cambridge: MIT Press, 2000.

———. *Michel Foucault: The Freedom of Philosophy.* New York: Columbia University Press, 1985.

Reggio, David. "Jean Malfatti de Montereggio: A Brief Introduction." Working Papers on Cultural History and Contemporary Thought. Department of History, Goldsmiths, University of London.

Scott. Walter, ed. and trans. *Corpus Hermetica: The Ancient Greek and Latin Writings Which Contain Religious or Philosophic Teachings Ascribed to Hermes Trismegistus.* Volumes 1–4. London: Dawsons of Pall Mall, 1968.

Shaw, Gregory. *Theurgy and the Soul: The Neoplatonism of Iamblichus.* University Park: Pennsylvania State University Press, 1995.

Spinoza, Benedict de. *The Ethics and Other Works.* Edited and Translated by Edwin Curley. Princeton: Princeton University Press, 1994.

———. *Theologico-Political Treatise.* Translated by Samuel Shirley. Indianapolis: Hackett, 1998.

Spruit, Leen. "Giordano Bruno and Astrology." In *Giordano Bruno, Philosopher of the Renaissance.* Edited by Hilary Gatti, 229–50. Hants: Ashgate, 2002.

Tournier, Michel. *Friday.* Translated by Norman Denny. New York: Doubleday, 1969.

Turner, Victor. *The Forest of Symbols: Aspects of Ndembu Ritual.* Ithaca: Cornell University Press, 1967.

———. *Revelation and Divination in Ndembu Ritual.* Ithaca: Cornell University Press, 1975.

Vico, Giambattista. *The New Science.* Translated by David Marsh. New York: Penguin, 2001.

Walker, D. P. *Spiritual and Demonic Magic from Ficino to Campanella.* London: Warburg Institute, 1958.

Widder, Nathan. "The Rights of Simulacra: Deleuze and the Univocity of Being." *Continental Philosophy Review* 34 (2001): 437–53.

Williams, James. "Deleuze on J. M. W. Turner: Catastrophism in Philosophy?" In *Deleuze and Philosophy: The Difference Engineer.* Edited by Keith Ansell Pearson, 233–46. London: Routledge, 1997.

———. *Gilles Deleuze's Logic of Sense: A Critical Introduction and Guide.* Edinburgh: Edinburgh University Press, 2008.

Yates, Frances A. *Giordano Bruno and the Hermetic Tradition*. Chicago: University of Chicago Press, 1965.

———. *The Occult Philosophy in the Elizabethan Age*. London: Routledge, 1979.

Žižek, Slavoj. *Organs without Bodies: On Deleuze and Consequences*. London: Rutledge, 2004.

———. *Tarrying with the Negative: Kant, Hegel, and the Critique of Ideology*. Durham: Duke University Press, 1993.

Žižek, Slavoj, Creston Davis, and John Milbank. *The Monstrosity of Christ: Paradox or Dialectics?* Cambridge: MIT, 2010.

Index

Absolute, logic of, 47
Absolute deterritorialization, 24
Access to Western Esotericism (Faivre), 27
Active imagination, 202
Adorno, Theodor, 212–14
Affirmations of intensity, 180–81
Alchemy, 29–30, 129
Alice's Adventures in Wonderland (Carroll), 135, 173–74, 186
Allegory, 105–7
Analogical thinking, 133–34
Animals, animality, 130–31, 186
Animism, 210; modernity's revival of, 216
Anorganic vision of life, 95
Anti-Oedipus (Deleuze and Guattari), 180, 192, 199
Apocalypse, 104
Apology (Socrates), 119
Apprenticeship, 138, 141. *See also* Learning
Archetypes, 137
Aristotle: Aristotelian cosmology and, 51; identity and difference in, 132–33; Plato vs., 116–17
Ars magna, 90
Art, artists, 7, 152; belief in world and, 149–50; color and, 125, 153; as cosmic artisans, 148; embryonic aspects of, 141, 153; experimental, 23–26, 153–54; hermetic traditions and, 149, 152; immanence and, 25–26, 103; knowledge and, 147; mannerism in, 11–12; as medicine, 179, 181; nomadic organizing principle in, 134; philosophy and, 145–46, 165–66; repetition and, 132; secret pressures of, 138; spiritual ordeals and, 22–23; as symptomologist and, 135; as transcendental empiricism, 136. *See also* Cinema; Writers
Artaud, Antoine, 1–2, 22, 129, 211–12; immanence and, 25; mathesis and, 104; peyote dance of, 23. *See also* Theater of Cruelty
Astrology, 54–55

Atheism, creative, 220
Authentic thought, 188

Bacon, Francis, 134–35
Badiou, Alain, 208–9
Becomings, 106, 124, 128–29, 205–6; names as in therapy, 193
Becomings-animal, 181, 184
Behun, William, 185
Belief, 55; change in, from seventeenth to eighteenth century thought, 13; justification of, 18–19; nonhuman mode of existence and, 21–22; religious faith as nonparadigm of, 13; renewal of, as modern project, 26
Belief in the world: cinema and, 150–51; Proust and, 150
Bergson, Henri, 30, 182–84, 187
Betrayal, 126–27
Blumenberg, Hans, 47–49
Body without organs, 1–2, 95, 105, 180, 190, 199
"Brain people," 103
Bruno, Giordano, 43–44, 61–80, 136, 145, 152; burning of, at stake, 90, 184; Renaissance hermeticism and, 51–52

Capitalism and Schizophrenia (Deleuze), 97
Capitalist sorcery, 8
Carroll, Lewis, 135, 173–74, 186
Castenada, Carlos, 178
Chaos, 20
Chaosmosis (Guattari), 216
Characters, 132, 158–59, 161, 165–66, 178
Christianity, 39, 42–43, 219–20, 231; Renaissance revival of hermeticism as groundwork for, 29
"Christ the Word," 44, 84. *See also* Nicholas de Cusa

Cinema, 149; avant-garde, 151–52; restoration of belief in world and, 151
Cinema II: The Time Image (Deleuze), 13, 149
Circles, 99, 101
Cliché, 112
Cogitatio natura universalis (natural universal reason), 113
Coincidentia oppositorum, 128
Color, 28, 125, 153. *See also* Art, artists
Common sense, 138
Complicatio, 39, 44–47, 49, 136, 145
Complicity, 97–98, 100–101, 140, 150
Conceptual personae, 165–69
Concrete pluralisms of sense, 205
Corbin, Henry, 108–9
Corpus Hermeticum, 3–5, 27, 52–53, 231
Cosmic artisans, 148, 169, 202
Cosmic repetition, 127
Cosmos, cosmology, 26–30, 53; Aristotelian, 51; chain of being in, 106; esoteric remythologization of, 203; hermaphroditic account of, 99–100; individuation and, 29
Creation, 39–40; in medieval philosophy, 19; Nicholas de Cusa and, 44; singularity of, 145
Creative emotion, 30
Crystallization, 109
Cubes, 93

Davy, Marie-Madeleine, 89–90
Death, universality of, 98
Death of God, 43
Deleuze: The Clamor of Being (Badiou), 208
Deleuze and the Unconscious (Kerslake), 182, 221
Derrida, Jacques, 1, 25
Descartes, Henri, 113

Index 285

Desert Islands and Other Texts (Deleuze), 112
Desire, 100, 191–92, 195–96
Despotic signs and power in rituals, 193–95, 198–99
Deterritorialization, 24, 187, 207; of spirit and organic matter in hermeticism, 21–22, 29–30
Diagrams, 162–65; symbols as immanence, 110; in Taoism, 219
Dickens, Charles, 178–79, 201
Difference, 110, 120, 124–28; art and, 135; intensive difference, 125; multiplicity and, 133–34; Plato and, 116–18, 127–28; Plato vs. Aristotle, 133; true opinion and, 122–23
Difference and Repetition (Deleuze), 14, 16, 29, 39, 137, 145; good will in philosophy and, 113; image of thought in, 17, 114; Mathesis Universalis in, 91; in modern art, 136; nature and, 130; thought as Theater of Cruelty in, 22
Dostoyevsky, Fyodor, 165–66

Eckhart, Meister, 34
"Ecology of the virtual," 204
Egyptian spirituality, 4
Ellipses, 101
Emanation, 38–40
Emerald Tablet, The, 27. See also *Corpus Hermeticum*
Empiricism, 136; empiricist conversion and, 21; superior, 137; transcendental, 136
Eriguena, 33, 39, 43
Eschatological immanence, 24–25
Essays Critical and Clinical (Deleuze), 105
Essence, 128, 133–34, 144–45, 147
Eternal return, 127
Ethics: *amor fati* and, 176; time and, 172–75

Éventail (poem, Mallarmé), 94
Existentialism, 97–99
Experimental modern thought and spirituality, 6, 16, 36, 216; aesthetics in, 188; *Amor fati* as, 176; art and, 25–26; in becoming, 187; belief in world and, 26; drugs and, 23; experimental limits, 179, 181; modern art as, 135; nature and, 7; occultism and, 24; "Pragmatics of the intense" and, 30; religious faith and belief and, 13; transformation of human life and, 21–22; witches flight and, 17–18
Expressionism, 33, 37, 39–40, 43, 83
Expressionism and Philosophy: Spinoza (Deleuze), 33, 35

Faith. *See* Belief
Faivre, Antoine, 27, 202–5
Fantasy, 108, 110
Federation, 100–101
Ficino, Marsilio, 28, 43, 52–53
Finite mind, 19
Finnegans Wake (Joyce), 135–36
Foucault, Michel, 53–55; Deleuze on, 21
Founding, 26–27
Freud, Sigmund, 7, 210–11

Gambler, 14, 18
Gil, José, 189, 197
Gilles Deleuze and the Question of Philosophy (Goodchild), 215–16
Gnosis, 149, 204–5; active imagination and, 202; Deleuze's version of, 30; esoteric, 26; gnostic return and, 43; myth and, 203; optimist, 28; Western hermeticism as search for, 27. *See also* Hermeticism, Deleuze and; Western esoteric and hermetic thought

God, 11–14, 142; as circle, 101; death of, 43; Deleuze's lecture on, 11; in medieval philosophy, 19; in moon, 34. *See also* Atheism, creative; Belief
Goodchild, Philip, 215–16, 221–22
Good will, 113
Grounding, 21–22; of belief in modern and premodern thought, 18–19
Guattari, Félix, 23, 231

Hallward, Peter, 206
Healing, 90, 102, 149; art as medicine and, 179, 181; mind and, 147; signs in, 197
Heracliteanism, 123
Hermaphroditic cosmos, 99–100
Hermes Trismegistus, 3–4, 26–28, 52; Neoplatonists and, 28
Hermeticism, Deleuze and, 3, 6–8, 31, 51–52, 128, 181, 199, 205, 215–18; artists and art and, 149–50, 152, 206; Badiou's critique of, 208–9; "deterritorializing" of spirit and organic matter in, 21–22, 29–30; lack of detailed history of specific practices relating to, 221; lack of discussion of earlier philosophers influencing, 221; microcosmic mind and, 22; need for future research on, 222–23; overturning of Platonism and, 115; political critique on virtualness of, 206–20; Proust and, 138, 141–42, 145; spiritual ordeal as, 30; unknown nature in, 204. *See also* Bruno, Giordano; Immanence; Nicholas de Cusa; Pico della Mirandola; Spiritual ordeals; Western esoteric and hermetic thought
Hieroglyphics, 126–27, 141, 143; in Proust, 144

Hindu iconography, 92–94
Hoëné-Wronski, Josef, 91
Hölderlin, Friedrich, 200–201
Humanity: eschatological vision of, 56; parataxic position of, 106
Hume, David, 11, 18–19; God as illusion in, 12

Iamblichus of Chalcis, 40–42
I Ching, 37, 219
Ideas, 18, 124; theory of, in Deleuze, 119–20, 121–22, 125
Identity, 126; in Aristotle, 132–33
Idiot, 165–66
"I'll Have to Wander All Alone," (eulogy, Derrida), 1
Imagination, 108–10
Immanence, 2, 6, 42–43, 51–52, 83–89, 216; Artaud and, 1, 25; as chaos, 21; eschatological immanence, 25, 220; experimental thought and, 30–31; extremes in thought and, 23; God and, 19–20; grounding and, 26–27; infinite divergence and, 204; interlinked meanings of, 2; irreplaceable historical figures of, 215; learning and, 139; Mannerist painting and, 29; mantra of, 23–24; mathesis and, 102–3; medieval philosophy and, 19; mind as microcosmic and, 19, 22; in modern philosophy, 19–20; non-philosophical apprehension of, 25–26, 103, 220; people to come and, 206; planes of, 16–17, 23, 102, 204; reason and representation's break from, 12; recharging of by Kierkegaard and Pascal, 14; in religious ideas, 37; reterritorializing of, 30; roots of in expressionism, 37; Spinoza and, 19–20, 84; symbolic force of, 110;

transcendence and, 207; utopian aspects of, 103; vitalist notion of, 180, 200
Immanence and the Vertigo of Philosophy: From Kant to Deleuze (Kerslake), 190, 221
Imprese, 219–20
Infinite, 11–12, 14
Intellectus archetypus, magical-symbolical thought vs., 189
Intensity, 2, 124–25; affirmations of intensity, 180–81; artistic vision and, 136; exemplary fictional characters and, 201; of spiritual ordeals, 206; symbolic, 107
Intensive naturalism, 16
"Interiorization of the universal," 100
Intuition, 95–96, 188–90

Jesus, 44
Joyce, James, 134–35, 136

Kabbalism, 54–55; Leibniz and, 91
Kant, Immanuel, 7, 18–19, 188, 190, 189, 200–201; God as limit idea in, 12; spiritual practices and, 189; unanswerable questions of, 142
Kerslake, Christian, 182, 221
Kierkegaard, Søren, 14, 19, 129–30, 179, 201
Knowledge: art and, 146; therapeutic approach to, 102

Language, 54; names and, 192–93; in Renaissance, 53, 55, 82
Laruelle, François, 220
Lawrence, D. H., 104–7, 178
Learning, 17–18, 121, 137, 139; swimming and, 140, 142. *See also* Apprenticeship
Legitimacy of the Modern Age, The (Blumenberg), 47

Leibniz, Gottfried, 11; Mathesis Universalis and, 91
Life: as "open whole," 98; as paradox, 97; thought as affirming of, 200–201; unity of, 110
Logic of Sense (Deleuze), 96
Logos, defined, 146
Lull, Raymond, 90

Magia naturalis, 51, 55
Magical idealism, 108–9; knowledge and, 152. *See also* Sorcery, sorcerers
Malfatti de Montereggio, Johann, 89–95, 98, 101–2, 215; sexuality and, 99
Mallarmé, Stéphane, 94
Mana, 188
Mannerist painters and painting, 11–14; immanence and, 29
Mantra of immanence, 23–24
"Mathesis, Science, and Philosophy" (Deleuze), 89, 91–92, 96–97
Mathesis Universalis, 89–98, 104, 110, 206; Bruno and, 90; in *Difference and Repetition*, 91; immanence and, 102–3; as knowledge of life, 101–2; Leibniz and, 91; patterns revealed in, 97, 101
Matter, 69–70, 73, 207; engagement with, in ritual, 67
Mauss, Marcel, 188
Medicine, art as, 179, 181
Medieval philosophy and theology, 34, 38, 53; chain of being in, 106; immanence in, 19. *See also* Nicholas de Cusa
Melville, Herman, 159, 165, 201
Meno's slave, 118–19, 129
Metamorphoses of the Body (Gil), 189, 197
Michaux, Henri, 22–23

Microcosmic, 19, 53, 100; humanity as in Renaissance, 106; mind and, 22

Miller, Henry, 22, 135, 148, 154, 178

Mind, altered states of, 17, 84, 187–88; Kantian philosophy vs., 188–90; nature and, 206; *nous* as, 27, 40–41; yet to be realized states of, 2

Modern experimental and spiritual thought, 220

Modernism and modern art: in *Difference and Repetition*, 136; singularity and cliché and, 134–35

Modern philosophy, 220, 222; discomfort of, with spiritual thought, 210–14; energy in painting and, 11–12; thought and life in, 200–201. *See also* Philosophy, philosophers

Moon, 34, 105

Moses, 14

Multiplicity, 121–22, 128, 143, 149, 204; difference and, 133–34; in modern art, 135; schizophrenia and psychosis and, 199; in swimming, 142

Music, 186, 191, 207, 213

Mysticism, 181–84, 187, 201; imaginal mode of, 108

Myth, 203

Mythical grounding, 14–15

Names, 192–93

Nature: common notions of, 33–36; as concrete plurality, 205; mind and, 206; plane of consistency in, 185–86; repetition and, 130–31; unknown, 204

Ndembu healing rites, 197

Negotiations (Deleuze), 108–9

Neoplatonism, 6, 33–34, 40–42, 83–84, 208–9; expressionism in, 39; Hermes Trismegistus and, 28; optimist gnosis and, 28

Nicholas de Cusa, 33–35, 37, 39–40, 43–47, 128, 145; Blumenberg on, 47–49; Creation and, 44; Idiot of, 165–66; Renaissance hermeticism and, 49–51, 53

Nietzsche, Friedrich, 19, 106–7, 129–30, 217; vitalist aphorism and, 201

Nietzsche and Philosophy (Deleuze), 123

"Nietzsche and St. Paul, Lawrence and John of Patmos" (essay, Deleuze), 104

Nomadism, 188

Nominalism, 34

Nonphilosophical, 23–25, 103, 220

Nous, 27, 40–41

Novalis, 108–9

Numerology, 93–94

Occultism, 7–8, 24, 211, 215–16, 231; Freud's discomfort with, 210–11; modern art as occult communication, 135; Renaissance philosophers and, 28

Oedipus, 14–15

Of Learned Ignorance (de Cusa), 44

One, 38–39, 41–42

On the Mysteries of the Egyptians (Iamblichus), 40

"Open whole," 98; art as, 144–45

Oracles: Delphic, 119; symbols as, 107, 110

Order of Things, The (Foucault), 53

Out of This World: Deleuze and the Philosophy of Creation (Hallward), 206

Paganism, 104

Paradox: life as, 97; spiritual ordeal as, 114

Parmenides (Plato), 38

Partial objects, 146
Participation, 118
Pascal, Blaise, 14, 19
Peacocks, 54
Periphysion (Eriugena), 33
Peyote, 23
Philosophy, philosophers, 165–66, 222; as apprenticeship, 119; art and artists vs., 145–46; connection of, to art and science, 111; defined by Deleuze, 181; lack of discussion on influences on Deleuze' hermeticism and, 221; as legislator, 107. See also Modern philosophy
"Philosophy as a Way of Life: Deleuze on Thinking and Money" (Smith and Barber), 222
Pico della Mirandola, 43, 51–53, 56–61, 106
Plato, 119–21, 124–25; Aristotle vs., 116–17; difference and, 116–17, 133; Heracliteanism and, 123; spiritual ordeals and, 113; truth and, 138, 143
Platonism, 6–7, 124, 126–27, 206; dialectics and, 115; difference in itself and, 116; leaving cave of, 128–29, 206; problem of participation and, 38–39; Proust and, 143–44; qualitative contrariety and, 124–25; simulcra and, 137; thinking and, 113; thought images in, 114
Plotinus, 38–39
Plumed Serpent, The (Lawrence), 104
Politics of sorcery, 170, 181
Porphyry, 40
"Pragmatics of the intense," 30
Primitive: contagion in thought of, 188; territorial signs of, 191, 196; vocal-graphic power and, 193–95
Prisca theologia, 28, 52

Problematic structures, 142
Proclus, 38
Protagoras, 123
Proust, Marcel, 126; belief in world and, 150; learning in, 137, 142–43; Platonism and, 144–45; signs in, 141–45; truth and good will and, 138
Proust and Signs (Deleuze), 83–84, 128, 137, 145
Psychosis, 200–201
Pure Immanence (Deleuze), 200

Qu'est-ce que fonder? (What is grounding?, Deleuze), 14

Reason, 7–8, 11
Redon, Odelon, 153
Religion: faith as non-paradigm of modern belief in, 13; in *What Is Philosophy?*, 36–37
Remaking of world, 150–51
Renaissance hermeticism, 28–29, 47–61; cosmology and, 53; Giordano Bruno and, 51–52; as groundwork for Science, 28–29; Nicholas de Cusa and, 49–51, 53; Pico della Mirandola and, 51–52
Repetition, repetitions, 110, 125, 128, 129; cosmic, 127; as hiding and, 130–31; in Proust, 144; rhythm and, 131–32
Revenge, ethical refusal of, 176
Revolution, 99, 169, 207, 209–10
Rhythm, 131–32
Rituals, 7, 102, 186, 198, 203; vocal-graphic vs. despotic power in, 193–95
Rocks and minerals, 21–22, 29, 128

Salons, Deleuze and, 89–90
Science, Renaissance hermeticism as groundwork for, 28–29
Search for Lost Time, The (Proust), 144

Secret pressures of art, 138
Secular culture, 211–12
Sense in the unsensed, 137
Sexuality, 99–100
Shamanism, 194
Signs and symbols, 43–44, 92–94, 96, 103, 198; allegory vs. force of, 105; as creative endeavor, 204; cubes and, 93; D. H. Lawrence and, 105; ellipses, 101; force of action and decision, 107; grasping of dynamics of, 96; in healing, 197; immanence and, 110; immediacy of, 106–7; intensity and, 125–26; as oracles, 107, 110; physics of, 108; in Plato, 121–22; power of, 6; in Proust, 137–39, 142–45; during Renaissance, 82–83; response to, 94–95; simulacrum and, 126–27; Sphinx's riddle as, 105–6; truth and transformation and, 137–38. See also Hieroglyphics; Malfatti de Montereggio, Johann; Mathelis Univeralis; Numerology
Simulacrum, 126–29, 137, 206
Singularity, 21, 40, 42, 96, 100, 134; truth and, 138
Socrates, 113, 116, 118–19, 122, 129; execution of, 120; ironic stance of, 14
Solidarity, 101
Solitude, 97–98
Sommeil (self-involuting process), 106–7
Sontag, Susan, 211
Sorcery, sorcerers, 184–85, 187–88, 198–99, 201; healing rituals and, 7; politics of, 170, 181; "Sorcerers drawings," 102
Soul, 40
Sphinx's riddle, 14–15, 105–6
Spinoza, Baruch, 11, 22, 33, 36, 82, 84; God as nature in, 12; immanence and, 19–20; vision of reality and, 34–35
Spinoza: Practical Philosophy (Deleuze), 22
Spirituality, 2, 9, 222; ambivalence among philosophers and, 3, 210–14; eclectic nomadic bastard, 5, 7, 134, 153, 188; esotericism and, 5–6; modern thought's deviation from, 11; objections to, in Deleuze and Guattari, 7; spiritual automaton and, 151; of thought, 8, 11. See also Egyptian spirituality
Spiritual ordeals, 2–3, 6, 26–27, 103, 181–82, 188, 206, 220; art and, 22; Artaud and, 25; dialectics and, 115; heretics and, 30; mythical grounding and, 14–16; need for research on, 222–23; paradox and, 114; Plato and, 113; Proust and, 138; as renewal, 181; of writers, 23–24
"Spiritual Politics after Deleuze," 221
St. Augustine, 39
Statesman (Socrates), 117–18
Stengers, Isabelle, 8
SubStance (journal), 221
Sum ergo genero, 103
Superior empiricism, 137
Swimming, 18, 139–40; learning and, 142; multiplicity in, 142
Symbiosis, 97
Symptomologist, artist as, 135
Synchronicities, 210–11
Syzygy, 99

Tantra, 99, 105
Taoism, 219
Telepathy, 210–11
Theaetetus, 122
Theater of Cruelty, 2; thought as, 22
Theater of Repetition, 129

Theater of Representation, 130
Theophany, 33–34
Theosis, 28, 30
Therapy: knowledge and, 102; names as becomings in, 193
Theurgy, 40, 203; rites of, 41
Thought, 2; art and, in *Difference and Repetition*, 134; cliché and habitual, 112, 149; difference and, 123; ideas and, 18, 124; life as activating of, 200–201; morality and, in Plato, 113; nonrepresentational, 56, 95–96; primitive contagion in, 188; rotative, 107–8; as theater of cruelty, 22. *See also* Experimental modern thought and spirituality
Thought images, 113–14, 138
Thousand Plateaus, A (Deleuze and Guattari), 24, 97; art and esoteric spiritual practices in, 153–54; sorcerers in, 184
Time, ethics of Deleuze and, 172–75
"Time-images," 109, 151
"To Have Done with Judgment" (Deleuze), 104
Transcendence, 19–20; outrageous characters and, 215
Transformation, 102, 149, 186, 209; remaking of world as, 150–51; states of mind and, 147; thought and, 29. *See also* Spiritual ordeals
Transversal ontology, 154–62
Transversal planes, 186
Truth, 143; in Plato, 138, 143; in Proust, 138
Two Sources of Morality and Religion, The (Bergson), 182

Ulysses, 14–15
Uncanniness, 2, 16, 129, 141, 143, 223; in art, 153–54

Unity, 91, 110; division and, 97–98
Univocal, 134
Unknown nature, 204

Virtual, 110; ecology of, 204; ideas, 140–41; learning, 142; political critique of Deleuze's, 206–20
Vocal-graphic power, 193–95

Western esoteric and hermetic thought, 3, 26, 28–29, 204, 215, 220; dualitudes in, 205; interchangeable terms in, 27; need for future research on, 222–23; remythologization of cosmos and, 203; Renaissance hermeticism and, 47–61; similitude, entity forces, and nature in, 205. *See also* Bruno, Giordano; Hermeticism, Deleuze and; Nicholas de Cusa; Pico della Mirandola
What Is Grounding? (lecture series, Deleuze), 105–6, 181–82
What Is Philosophy? (Deleuze and Guattari), 13–14, 206; art and esoteric spiritual practices in, 153; eschatological immanence in, 24–25; nonphilosophical immanence in, 103; outlying realms of thought and experience and, 17; religious thought in, 36–37
Witchcraft, 17, 23
Writers, 135–36, 154, 165–66, 178, 201; spiritual ordeals of, 23–24. *See also* Characters; *and under names of individual writers*

Yates, Frances, 28
Yellow, intensity of Van Gogh's, 125
Yoga, 27

Žižek, Slavoj, 211

JOSHUA RAMEY IS A VISITING ASSISTANT PROFESSOR OF
PHILOSOPHY AT HAVERFORD COLLEGE.

Library of Congress Cataloging-in-Publication Data
Ramey, Joshua Alan
The hermetic Deleuze : philosophy and spiritual ordeal / Joshua Ramey.
p. cm. — (New slant : religion, politics, and ontology)
Includes bibliographical references and index.
ISBN 978-0-8223-5215-0 (cloth : alk. paper)
ISBN 978-0-8223-5229-7 (pbk. : alk. paper)
1. Deleuze, Gilles, 1925–1995.
2. Hermetism. I. Title. II. Series: New slant.
B2430.D454R36 2012
194—dc23
2011053338